David Dale

A LIFE

David J. McLaren

Stenlake Publishing Ltd.

Publication of this book has been financially supported in part
by the Friends of New Lanark and New Lanark Trust.

ISBN 9781840336801 (Paperback Edition)
ISBN 9781840337204 (Hardback Edition)

**The publishers regret that they cannot supply
copies of any pictures featured in this book.**

Acknowledgements

I am indebted to a great many people for their help and support during the writing of this book. It simply could not have been undertaken or sustained without the support, encouragement and advice from those involved in New Lanark Conservation Trust and the Friends of New Lanark – in many cases, people I have known for a very long time. My sincere thanks to Lorna, Ian, Graham, Ann, Annie, Claudine, Jane, Jim and all the team past and present in New Lanark. Sadly, Harry Smith is no longer with us but I should like to record my thanks for his unwavering support over a long number of years. Thanks also to Kenny Kerr for his early detective work on Dale's family, to David Blackie and the Blackie family for allowing me to use the portrait of Carolina and William Dale and to Pat & John Brandwood of the Robert Owen Museum in Newtown.

I am also grateful for the considerable help provided by R.B.S. Archivist, Ruth Reed, and by R.C.A.H.M.S. Many individuals offered help and I am delighted to acknowledge at least some of them here: Lady Etain Hagart-Alexander, Professor Donald Christie, Tony Cooke, Molly Cumming, Jane Dobie, Jess Duncan, John Hume, Alan Laurie, Ian MacDonald, Dr. Stuart Nisbet, Professor Edward Royle, Richard Stenlake, Frances Stewart, Bob Teevan and Nicholas Young. Thanks also to library and archive staff in Strathclyde, Glasgow, Edinburgh, Oxford and Toronto Universities; the Mitchell Library, Glasgow; the British Library and the Friends Library, London; Shropshire County Council and the National Trust for Scotland. Finally, my thanks to Alistair Tough of Greater Glasgow Health Board; Jacqueline Mackenzie of the WISE Group; Thomas Davidson, Lanark & District Archaeological Society; Ian Wallace of Lanarkshire Family History Society and to office-bearers of Masonic Lodge 21, Old St. Johns Lanark. Colleagues at Strathclyde University have also been very supportive and will now be hopeful that I can find something else to talk about at work. Thanks also to Strathclyde University School of Education for funding the purchase of some of the pictures. Finally, my thanks to Richard and Callum at Stenlake Publishing for all their efforts.

Finally, I am particularly grateful to Lorna Davidson, Director of New Lanark Conservation Trust and to Ian Donnachie, Professor Emeritus at the Open University, Scotland and Chair of the Friends of New Lanark. Their advice, guidance and support have been invaluable. Thanks also to Iwona and Kirsty who have had to listen to me talking about David Dale, Robert Owen and New Lanark for a very long time. The book is dedicated to my family and to the memory of my late parents.

CONTENTS

PART 7: The End of the Beginning

Appendices

Foreword

For much of my professional life I was involved with the village and mills of New Lanark, and at a fairly early stage reached the provisional conclusion that David Dale's role in their creation had been undervalued. I remember meeting David McLaren when he was completing his first book on Dale, and being delighted that he, too, felt that there was much more to Dale than historians generally had concluded. This first volume was, I felt, an important contribution to Scottish history. Now we have the conclusions Dr. McLaren has reached on the basis of another thirty years of research and reflection, embodied in this splendid new publication. This is a work of first-class scholarship, tracing David Dale's life from a list of disparate sources. What emerges from this penetrating and thoughtful study is a man of great humanity and humility, of exceptional creativity, a man who deserves a full measure of respect, admiration and, indeed, love. The more I have learned about David Dale, the more I have seen him as a role model, a person doing what came to hand with all his energy, a man for whom loving God and loving neighbour was at the core of his being. And this is richly endorsed by David McLaren's masterly study. I feel greatly honoured to have been asked to write this preface and I wish both author and publisher every success in bringing this important work to the public.

Professor John R. Hume,
Chairman, Royal Commission on the Ancient and Historical Monuments of Scotland

March, 2015

Introduction

'Here if ever, a tribute of respect and admiration is due to departed worth.'

These words appeared in Dale's obituary notice in *The Glasgow Courier* on 20th March, 1806.[1] Robert Dale Owen, remembering the day of his grandfather's funeral, talks of the streets being lined with mourners. All the shops were shut as a mark of respect and he notes that Dale's death was seen in Glasgow as 'a public calamity'.[2]

Whoever and whatever this man was, the Glasgow public clearly knew of him and considered him worthy of recognition. In many ways, this new biography of Dale accords him similar 'respect and admiration', although I have taken great care not to produce an uncritical, hagiographic account.

I was struck by how little we actually knew about the man who founded arguably the most famous cotton-spinning community in the world. Like many people, I had come to know about Dale only through an interest in Robert Owen's New Lanark and, in particular, Owen's visionary attempts to forge a 'new view' of society, based on his famous social and educational experiments in the village. Quite properly, there were and there still are countless books, articles and journals about Robert Owen. However, most of these include Dale as a rather minor figure in the history of New Lanark. This is not entirely surprising, given Owen's fame and his international connections. It is also important to remember that, although the mills were internationally renowned during Dale's ownership, Dale was very much an 18th-century Scottish figure while Owen played on a wider, international, 19th-century stage.

Nevertheless, Scottish historical figures are worthy of study in their own right. Dale is no exception to this, even more so when research confirms that Dale was indeed a significant figure in Scotland's history. One of the parish ministers who made a return for the *Statistical Account* of 1798 (from the Perthshire parish of Doune in which Deanston Mill was situated) clearly saw him as a figure whose importance and influence extended beyond the Lanarkshire area, referring to Dale as a 'bright luminary to Scotland'.[3] Robert Owen's achievements in New Lanark and beyond were enormous, but the mills at New Lanark had been operating for almost fourteen years and had been attracting visitors from across the world before Owen and his partners bought the business and before Owen himself began to work his own form of magic on the community.

It was therefore obvious, even when I first put pen to paper over 30 years ago, that Dale was a figure worthy of closer study. Information at that time was extraordinarily difficult to unearth and what there was tended to be rather one-sided, often anecdotal and, to use a Scottish expression, somewhat 'couthy' or comfortable. There were lots of anecdotes about the portly, benevolent patron of the marvellous cotton works in New Lanark. This rather contrasted with Owen's fairly uncomplimentary description of New Lanark in *A New View of Society*.[4] The implication, despite Owen's protestations to the contrary, was clearly that Dale was responsible for this situation. On the other hand, given that Owen was prone to exaggeration and immodesty it was quite possible that he had exaggerated the negative side of village and factory life under Dale in order to magnify his own (undoubtedly considerable) achievements in the community after Dale's death. I set about looking for a "Life of Dale" to clarify the situation. Apart from one or two potted histories which were rather brief and apocryphal, such a "Life" did not exist and so I wrote *David Dale of New Lanark*, published originally in 1983. However, after 30 years in which Scottish history has blossomed, it became clear that a completely new book was required – one which looked in depth at Dale's life and which put him fully in context.

In recent years, the history of New Lanark, and indeed Scottish history as a whole, has been particularly well served. By that I mean that we are fortunate to be living in a period when arguably some of our best historians are or have been hard at work. John Butt (sadly no longer with us), John Hume and Ian Donnachie – all at one point associated with Strathclyde University – have written extensively on Robert Owen and New Lanark. Ian Donnachie continues to publish in this field. The Strathclyde University connection continues in a wider context with Tom Devine (now in Edinburgh), Allan Macinnes, Hamish Fraser and Richard Finlay. Robert Davis and Frank O'Hagan from Glasgow University have recently completed a major biography of Owen. Furth of Strathclyde (and in some cases, furth of Scotland), other names come easily to mind – Gregory Claeys, Robert Anderson, Christopher Smout, Michael Lynch, R.A. Houston, Christopher Whatley and the late Donald Withrington – to name but a few. Some of them have focused a well-trained eye on New Lanark while others have provided a different or wider historical context in which to understand what was happening in Scotland.

As a result, we are much better informed nowadays, not only about New Lanark but also about some of our abiding myths, e.g. the lad o'pairts, the democratic intellect, the parish school, literacy levels, emigration patterns and urbanisation. We also see Dale as a figure in his own right and not merely as Owen's father-in-law. Because of the work which has been done in the last 30 years in relation to New Lanark and Scottish history generally, coupled with the invention of the Internet, a re-evaluation of Dale is eminently more feasible that it might otherwise have been. It is also worth noting in passing that one of the many spin-offs from the Internet has been the increase in genealogical research and a significant rise in the number of family history societies. An increasing number of people are tracing their New Lanark roots and I have had a number of letters from far-flung places which express interest in (and knowledge of) Dale and Owen. Overall, therefore, the time is right for a new, modern, fully researched biography of Dale.

The book looks in some detail at Dale's many and varied interests in an attempt to get a clear picture of this man. He was more than a 'founder' of a cotton mill, more than a 'merchant' or 'preacher' or 'philanthropist', laudable as these are in themselves. He was all of those things and more, but in many ways he represented the times in which he lived. He typified the Glasgow merchant class in terms of his lifestyle and varied business interests and yet was atypical in his public support for the abolition of the slave trade. He represented the fortunes (literally and metaphorically) of the cotton (and to a lesser extent the linen) trades in Scotland at that time. Similarly, the schools at New Lanark mirrored many of the traits of the Parish schools and some of the elements of the Burgh schools, yet all within a completely new setting in Scotland – the factory community. His evangelism and religious affiliation was representative of the Presbyterian Church in Scotland at that time, riven as it was with dissenting sects over the question of patronage and other religious issues.

Even his early experiences in Stewarton and his move to Cambuslang and Glasgow were representative of much wider social and economic issues of the day – e.g. the 'Improving' climate of the 18th-century landlords and farmers and the changing fortunes of farm workers, spinners and handloom weavers as the towns expanded. Dale was an important figure in his own right, but his life was also a microcosm of major events in Scottish history during the crucial period 1760–1800. As such, he was much more of an Enlightenment figure than he has been given credit for. His commitment to progress in the commercial world, allied to innovation in his adaptation of the factory community and his commitment to a progressive education system, decent living conditions and a common humanity all have a part in this. Similarly, his active, public support for the abolition of the slave trade and his strenuous efforts to alleviate poverty and stem the flow of emigrants from Scotland are examples of Enlightenment ideas in action.

In this biography, Parts 1 and 7 take a generally chronological approach (although Part 1 includes some family details which extend outwith the early years period). The family tree in this book has been compiled from the most reliable sources I could find, i.e. the original birth, baptism and death certificates. These do not always match the various versions of the family tree sent to me over the years by interested parties but they are based on the best evidence available at the time of writing. The pivotal years of 1783–1785 are crucial to the story as they mark the beginning of Dale's entrepreneurial career. Parts 2–6 illustrate the main issues in Dale's life and provide a full picture of the man – his many business interests but also his educational provision, his philanthropy, his public works and his religious beliefs.

New Lanark was his single greatest achievement, combining as it did significant commercial success and an enlightened approach to employment, social conditions and education – particularly for the pauper apprentices. Part 2 of the book is therefore focused on events in the village. 'Dale's New Lanark' merits consideration in its own right, not merely as a precursor to Robert Owen's New Lanark'. Owen inherited an extremely successful business from his father-in-law. Equally important, he inherited a business with an established record and reputation for taking care of its employees, young and old. Part 2 deals in some detail with the operation of the business – the use of indentures, child labour and the fundamental importance of education and welfare in the community.

Dale was an entrepreneur and although New Lanark represented the hub of his business empire, any biography needs to consider the other commercial enterprises with which he was involved. Part 3 looks not only at his partnerships in other mills and his property portfolio but also at his highly significant role as joint agent of the Royal Bank of Scotland.

Part 4 discusses some new information I was able to unearth about Dale's hitherto unknown role as Chair of the Glasgow Society for the Abolition of the Slave Trade. Slavery, slave cotton and New Lanark's role in the slave trade has never been fully addressed. Given that this is the case and that Dale's involvement with the Abolition movement has only come to light relatively recently, this topic has been dealt with separately, rather than as part of the 'Philanthropy, Benevolence and Public Office' chapters in Part 5, which look in some detail at Dale's extensive and lifelong commitment to charitable ventures, large and small and his commitment to civic duties. All of this, it is argued in Part 6, was founded on Dale's strong Christian beliefs and his commitment to spreading the Word. In Part 7, the original intention was to conclude by looking at the events surrounding Dale's illness, the sale of New Lanark and his demise in 1806. However, it soon became clear that more was required here on Dale's 'legacy'. Owen's comments about New Lanark under Dale and the problems associated with the Dale estate meant that any assessment of Dale had to include a consideration of some of the evidence which continued to appear in the public domain for many years after Dale's death.

In each chapter I have included new information from primary and secondary sources. Many of these I have tracked down myself, but some have come from colleagues and friends who are involved in the life and history of New Lanark and I am grateful for their contributions. I have also found it necessary to say a little more in this book on the historical context. For example, the discussion of Dale's school and the pauper apprentices requires a consideration of some of the wider educational and social contexts of the time. Similarly, it is necessary to say something about the Abolition movement and about the rise of the merchant classes in the city of Glasgow if we are to understand the significance of a figure like David Dale. The result is, I hope, a balanced view of Dale which credits him with more than founding New Lanark, significant as that was.

I noted earlier that much had changed in the last 30 years, not least the physical condition of the village. With the passage of time and an immeasurable amount of work by the community itself has come increased recognition of its importance and its designation as a World Heritage Site. Vast improvements have taken place under the auspices of New Lanark Conservation Trust and there is a life and energy in the community which simply was not there when I first began to write about Dale and which I have found inspirational. Indeed, in the early 1970s, few beyond the village and Burgh knew much about David Dale. But New Lanark lives again and thrives through the efforts of the Trust members and many others who live and work there or who have an interest in its future. To that extent, the story of Dale continues to be told where it might otherwise have disappeared. It seems entirely appropriate that New Lanark with its new status, its new building projects and its new energy should breathe new life into the story of Dale, given that he was the person who gave it life in the first place.

References: Introduction

1   The same sentence appeared in *The Scots Magazine*, March, 1806.

2   Owen, R.D. (1874) *Threading My Way: Twenty Seven Years of Autobiography.* New York: Carleton & Co., p.39.

3   Sinclair, J. (ed) (1791–99) *The Statistical Account of Scotland, 1791–1799*, 21 vols. [Referred to hereafter as *The Statistical Account*] Vol. XX. Parish of Kilmadock or Doune., p.89.

4   Owen, R. (1813–16) 'A New View of Society; or Essays on the Principle of the Formation of Human Character and the Application of the Principle to Practice', Second Essay, in G. Claeys (ed) (1991) *Robert Owen: A New View of Society and Other Writings.* London: Penguin.

Part 1

Weaver to Entrepreneur

Chapter 1: The Early Years

In contrast with his later wealth and success, David Dale's background was fairly inauspicious. He was born in January 1739 in Stewarton, Ayrshire, son of William Dale, a grocer and general dealer in the village.[1] Dale's date of birth is normally given as 6th January but the parish records do not appear to confirm that date, or indeed any other date, as there is no officially recorded date of birth.[2] Parish registers in the 18th century are not always accurate and are often a fairly rough guide to dates.[3] However, as far as Dale is concerned, the records are a little clearer regarding the date of baptism. He was baptised in the parish church on 14th January 1739 and the event is recorded in language redolent of the previous century: '*David, lawfull son, procreat Dale, betwixt William Dale and Anne Blackwood, his spouse*'.[4]

David's father, William, born in 1708, was a Stewarton man, like his father (Hugh) before him. Hugh Dale, David's grandfather, either owned or worked on Stacklawhill ('Staklyhill') farm in the local area, although William did not follow him into the farming business. Exactly when William married local girl Anne Blackwood is uncertain but we do know that he was 31 years old and Anne was 29 when their first child, David, was born. Appendix 1 contains a version of the Dale family tree.[5] David's brother Hugh was born two years later. Their mother died in March 1750 when David was eleven years old and Hugh not yet nine. Their father remarried within two years, this time to Martha Dunlop and their first child, James, half-brother to David and Hugh, was born in August 1753. James was later to play a significant role in the management of New Lanark and four of James Dale's eight children were born in the village. He subsequently left New Lanark and established himself as an agent and cotton broker in Glasgow.[6] In similar vein, Hugh Dale's son David (i.e. David Dale's nephew) was also involved with the village. Later, however, his uncle '*put him into business in Glasgow*'.[7]

The conditions in Ayrshire during Dale's early years were yet to experience the 'improving' climate of the 18th century. The Chancellor of the Burgh of Prestwick, Colonel Fullarton, noted that there was '*scarcely a practicable road*' and that:

> The farmhouses were mere hovels, moated with clay and having an open fireplace in the midst of the floor ... the manure heap at the door – the cattle starving and the people wretched.[8]

Although Fullarton was referring to Ayrshire around 1760, very little would have changed since Dale's childhood in the 1740s. Prior to the introduction of new farming techniques such as the enclosure system, 'run-rigs' were still in operation and the land is reported as being full of weeds and thistles – the 'scanty' soil gathered on top of the ridge and the furrows 'drowned' with water. There was, according to this rather grim picture, '*hardly a potato or any other esculent root; no garden vegetables except a few Scotch kail which, with milk and oatmeal, formed the principal diet of the people*'.[9] The tenant farmers generally paid their rent in kind. Any surplus crops from the thin soil and overworked plots of land were for their own use, but they were entirely at the mercy of the seasons. Famine was not uncommon here and elsewhere in Scotland – a fact which Dale recognised in later life and, as a wealthy businessman, made every effort to alleviate.

As a young 'herd laddie', it would have been Dale's job to look after a small herd of cattle, usually in the summer months only, when the beasts were out of doors. Even here, Fullarton's description talks of starved beasts, seldom much use for market:

> '... indeed, very little butcher meat was used, excepting the 'Mart', which was generally the most unsaleable of the flock, and which farmers generally salted at Martinmas, to serve for food through the winter. A small portion of this, with groats or home-made barley and kail, was the usual dinner, and with porridge, oatmeal cakes and milk, and on rare occasions, the luxury of butter or a bit of cheese, formed the only food of the people. So small was the consumption of butcher meat at this time, that not more than fifty head of cattle were killed annually in the county town of Ayr, although it contained a population of from four to five thousand.'[10]

There were no 'manufactures' (factories) or major industries in the area, with two significant exceptions – bonnet-making in Dale's home town of Stewarton and an expanding business in carpet-making in the town of Kilmarnock. Given that there were harbours at Ayr, Irvine and Saltcoats (something which many coastal towns elsewhere in Scotland were to lack until the British Fisheries Society came into existence some years later) it might be expected that there would be some significant trade in these towns, both in terms of fish and other exports and imports. However, even here, trade seems to have been 'very trifling'.[11]

Fullarton's picture of starving tenant farmers living in desperate conditions contrasts with Burns' view of the situation in *The Cotter's Saturday Night* which presents a sentimental, idealised version of poverty, albeit some 25 years later. Both are extreme representations of reality, particularly in relation to Dale's early life. While it is absolutely the case that tenant farmers often endured grinding poverty, Dale's family, although hardly wealthy, was not in that position. Extreme poverty was not something he experienced directly. He was not, after all, from a farming background, subsistence or otherwise. However, as a 'herd laddie', he would certainly have come into contact with tenant farmers and cannot fail to have been aware of the drastic issues facing them.

Nevertheless, his father was a shopkeeper/merchant in the bonnet-making town of Stewarton and, as such, various options were open to him. The most obvious of these would have been to encourage his son to follow in his father's footsteps and help run the business in Stewarton after finishing his schooling in the parish school. Such schooling would have been that 'which was usually given at the period' i.e. basic reading, arithmetic and, in Dale's case, writing, (not all families were willing to pay for writing), alongside the other pupils in the parish school.[12] While there is much exaggeration in Scottish history about the 'lad o' pairts', i.e. the poor boy who makes good, thanks to the efforts of the 'dominie' (teacher) in the local school, there is certainly a great deal of evidence that, inspired by John Knox's *First Book of Discipline*, Scotland had established a strong parish school system and that literacy rates were amongst the highest in western Europe. It has been argued that Dale did not enjoy '*the advantage of a polished or liberal education*' but he was certainly well served by the parish system.[13] He was literate and numerate well beyond the merely functional and it is interesting to compare Dale's letters during the New Lanark years, for example, with those of the great business tycoon, Sir Richard Arkwright, who had been schooled in a quite different tradition and who was possessed of only the most rudimentary writing skills.

However, rather than work with his father, it was decided that David Dale should be apprenticed to the weaving trade, '*by which, in course of time, he might be enabled to earn his twelve or fourteen shillings weekly ... nay, he might even aspire to the ultimate dignity, responsibility and emoluments of a 'bowl cork' or dealer in yarns*'.[14]

Dale was sent off to Paisley to serve this weaving apprenticeship (i.e. hand weaving, which involved passing the wooden shuttle from hand to hand). At this early period in his life, dates are difficult to ascertain. It is known that he arrived in Glasgow some years later at the age of 24, but from his childhood up until his arrival in Glasgow, dates are very unclear. In the 1750s, silk gauze manufacture was booming in Paisley and, later in the decade, Paisley was competing in the prestigious fashion market with the French. A combination of circumstances seems to have made Paisley the centre of a particularly lucrative market at this time. According to Murray, cheap labour and 'local skills' (presumably a tradition of domestic weaving which continued in Paisley until the late 1830s) attracted the manufacturers.[15] Added to this must be the proximity of water and the damp climate. By 1784, 10,000 people were employed in the silk gauze line, half of whom were weavers. The market in silk declined as the cotton and linen markets expanded, but given the above conditions, it seems that the weavers could adapt and transfer their skills to cotton. Assuming, then, that Dale arrived in Paisley some time during the 1750s, he almost certainly followed the pattern of apprenticeship of the time, i.e. of hand-loom weaving done at home, or at most in a shed where local weavers would gather to work.[16]

These sheds were a precursor of the factory, except that in these early factories there were no set hours of work or standards of work to be achieved. The orders and raw materials came from an agent who would have someone deliver them. Terms were agreed on each order. The weaver(s) then got to work and the finished product was uplifted. If it was a big order, many weavers would be involved and in the early days this meant a lot of foot-slogging on the part of the agent or his assistant, as the weavers were still very much home-based. It also meant different standards of work from different weavers and also, on occasions, different rates for the job.

Dale's apprenticeship appears to have been with these home-based weavers. It is unclear at what point he left Paisley but, according to one source, he moved to Hamilton because he '*disliked the sedentary occupation*' in Paisley.[17] It would seem that he was in pursuit of a more active lifestyle, which suggests that the various accounts of Dale tramping the countryside delivering material and picking up completed merchandise apply to the period after his Paisley apprenticeship, i.e. during his time as a journeyman in Hamilton and Cambuslang.[18]

Very little seems to be known of this period in Hamilton and Cambuslang, except that he was probably employed as a packman, giving out flax to be spun and then collecting the yarn to be woven into cloth. It is possible, however, that the Cambuslang period may have seen him employed in some more senior position, which would explain his subsequent move to Glasgow as a clerk. It is difficult to find any hard evidence for this and even the date of his removal to Glasgow is unclear. One account talks of Dale tramping the country, buying '*from farmers' wives and others in the neighbouring counties their home spun linen yarns*' which he then sold in Glasgow.[19] It was claimed that the object of every packman's ambition was to become '*a settled shopkeeper or merchant in some commercial town*' and thus it was for David Dale. By 1763 he had left Hamilton and Cambuslang behind and had moved to Glasgow. Perhaps his experiences as a packman stood him in good stead. It is reported that in later life, many of his friends were surprised at his intimate knowledge of the '*country places ... in the neighbourhood of Glasgow, not being aware that in early life he had again and again tramped the spots to purchase home-made yarns*'.[20]

Glasgow

In Glasgow, he worked as a clerk to a silk merchant for a while. Presumably his apprenticeship with the hand-loom silk weavers in Paisley and his experience in Hamilton and Cambuslang helped to elevate him to this position of clerk. He began to attend the Blackfriars or College Church and it is highly likely that friendships made there were influential in his appointment with the silk merchant.

After some time as a clerk in Glasgow, it is reported that '*With the assistance of friends he commenced business on his own account in the linen yarn trade*', which suggests that Dale, quite naturally, used the experience he had gained in the trade and through his connections with the Church to raise capital for this new venture.[21] Nevertheless, this might well be '*estimated a bold step on the part of a comparatively penniless lad, namely, to try his fortune, sink or swim, in the great whirlpool of Glasgow commerce*'.[22] Again, this period in Dale's life is not well documented. Robert Reid, who later worked with Dale, (and who wrote under the pseudonym of 'Senex') noted that he had never seen any written account of this period in Dale's business career but he quotes a local newspaper advertisement '*from one Gavin Millar*' which showed '*the nature of the trade which first enticed Mr. Dale to commence yarn merchant*':

> *Gavin Millar, at his house in Gallowgate ... sells all kinds of Dutch lints, drest and undrest; yarn bought and sold, and lint given out to spin. Any person well recommended and willing to engage to take out lint and gather in yarn, will meet with good encouragement by applying as above; also manufactures and sells all sorts of green and white Holland cloth at the lowest price.*[23]

In 1763, Archibald Paterson, one of Dale's church friends and a well known 'tallow chandler' (candle maker) with premises at No. 130, Southside, Gallowgate, became Dale's partner in a one-room shop in Hopkirk's Land on the east side of the High Street.[24] The shop was five doors from Glasgow Cross in the heart of commercial Glasgow.[25] It seems that Paterson was a sleeping partner who provided the money but took no share in the management of the company which soon extended its transactions by importing linen yarns from Flanders and Holland to be woven into lawns and cambrics. Paterson would appear to have been a man of some wealth, since he was able to finance the erection of a meeting house a year or so later when a number of dissatisfied members of the College Church (including Dale and Paterson) seceded and formed their own breakaway group.

Prior to the cotton 'revolution', the linen yarn business in Glasgow, and, in particular, the manufacture of *'figured and plain lawns'* was well-established and could be highly lucrative. Reid described the trade as *'the great staple of our city'*, particularly when the cloth was woven from the fine yarns available from France and Holland, rather than the coarse and uneven local ones which were *'quite unfit for these delicate and showy fabrics'*.[26] In the Anderston district of the city, James Monteith (whose family were to become famous as cotton spinners) had been successfully weaving linen for some time and would certainly have been known to Dale. It is possible that Dale sold some yarn to Monteith in the early years but Monteith decided to cut out the 'middle man' and began to import the yarn direct from France and Holland. One of Monteith's suppliers, an M. Mortier in Cambrai (hence the word 'cambric'), later recalled hearing Dale's name mentioned as a significant dealer at this time, which gives some indication of Dale's success even at this early stage in his business career.[27] There was a great deal of money to be made in these fine continental yarns and Glasgow was the place to make it.

He could have chosen Glasgow or Edinburgh as a base. They were both great cities with opportunities for a young man willing to work hard but they were quite different cities. Glasgow, later infamous for its slum conditions in the 19th century, was described by Daniel Defoe as *'the cleanest and beautifullest, and best built city in Britain, London excepted'*.[28] His description was still valid in the 1770s and well into the 1780s and 90s. The population was growing but not yet at an alarming or uncontrollable rate (from 13,000 in 1707 to 40,000 in 1780).[29] The city had a long established history of mercantile success in tobacco, rum, sugar and textiles and the new merchant classes were building mansions both in the city centre and also in the new suburbs such as Blythswood and Laurieston. It was a city of commerce and trade. The Trades House and the various Incorporations controlled a very large workforce which depended on the success of the new merchant class, and vice versa and the social conditions were far removed from the horrendous scenes which followed the explosion in population in later years (from 40,000 in 1780 to 200,000 in 1830).[30] For most of Dale's time in the city, Glasgow was very much a city of the industrial middle classes. Interestingly, Edinburgh attracted five times as many noblemen and gentry and twice as many 'professional men' as Glasgow. Glasgow's 'gentry' were merchant adventurers and successful artisans. Highly significant here is Smout's analysis of the street directories for Edinburgh & Glasgow (for 1773 and 1783 respectively). He notes that the word 'manufacturer' is used repeatedly in the *Glasgow Directory* but is not used at all in the Edinburgh one – indicative of the stark contrast between the two cities.[31] Further, *'the greatness of Glasgow was built upon the entrepreneurial skills of her businessmen, whether merchants of manufacturers'*.[32] It is hardly surprising, then, that Dale chose to base himself in Glasgow.

It is important at this point to stress the fundamental change in the lifestyle of David Dale at this stage in his career. Clearly it cannot be argued that at the age of 24 he suddenly found himself a rich man and lived the rest of his life in luxury. Dale did enjoy great prosperity and comfortable surroundings, but this was only a gradual process. The point here is that by 1763, Dale's status had changed from weaver and itinerant journeyman to merchant or trader with a base and capital (albeit limited at this stage) from which to work. Simply put, he became a businessman.

Even at the age of 24, he was astute enough to realise that a great deal of money could be made in buying and selling yarn and in manufacturing cloth. Silk and linen yarns and cloth had been traded for years and there were established markets for both. Although linen would continue to be important, cotton would soon sweep the world and revolutionise production methods. Merchants like David Dale were very well placed to take full advantage of this and to transfer their skills to the world of cotton. As one historian has noted, Dale was the most prominent of the linen merchants who made this transition.[33] Dale always thought ahead and was prepared to venture into various business partnerships. This, combined with a Calvinistic attitude towards work and a genuine talent for making money, ensured Dale's success as an entrepreneur.

All empires have to have a beginning and in Dale's case, it was in Glasgow's High Street. The Hopkirk's Land property, formed over a number of floors, had originally been the tenement townhouse of Thomas Hopkirk, a wealthy merchant who had made his money in tobacco and who had diversified into mining, brewing and banking (including a partnership with others in the Glasgow Arms Bank). Dale rented the shop premises on the ground floor and, although the Hopkirk family owned an estate in Dalbeth and a very grand house on the corner of Argyle Street and Dunlop Street, they continued to use the High Street accommodation on occasion.

The shop was, by any standards, a modest affair. The room had an annual rent of £5, yet, small as it was, Dale sub-let half of it to a watchmaker to ease the payment of rent, and in fact continued to be associated with it after 1783 when it became the first Glasgow branch of the Royal Bank of Scotland.

In his essay on Dale in *The Curiosities of Glasgow Citizenship*, Stewart paints a quaint, couthy picture of Dale at work in the shared space:

> *We like to picture the round-faced, thick-set, brisk lad, bustling among his dusty yarn bundles, or haggling over their price, in one corner of the little low-roofed ware-room, and on the other side a solemn gentleman peering into one of those strange-looking turnip-shaped watches, while ranks of old-fashioned eight-day clocks, with their sober faces, are swinging their pendulums hither and thither along the walls.*[34]

Doubtless, this is a sentimentalised view of events, although there may be an element of truth in it. Later sketches of Dale sometimes pick up on his pawky humour, rotund shape and very extensive charitable work. The charitable work is certainly true and there is more than a glimmer of truth about his good humour and his corpulent frame in later years, as the illustration below (c.1793) indicates, but these views of him need to be balanced against the picture of a very dedicated (and sometimes ruthless) businessman.

It is possible that the shop traded under the name of David Dale & Co. but it was probably Paterson's name which was used for trading in the first few years because Dale's name does not appear until 18th October 1769 as a Burgess and Member of the Guild Brethren.[35]

Although, strictly speaking, this Burgess ticket gave Dale the title of 'merchant', the fee which he paid really only gave him the right to function as a trader in the city, and all who were in business had to do likewise. Those who sought membership could pay for the privilege (as in Dale's case) or could become members by right of marriage to or kinship with family members past and present. Dale's brother, Hugh, for example, became a Burgess and member of the Guild Brethren in August 1787 by virtue of his marriage to Margaret Wilson, whose father had been a Burgess. Consequently, Hugh's son, David Dale Junior became a Burgess in July 1790 as a result of Hugh's membership.[36] All new members were required (until 1793) to be Protestants and to swear '*an oath for the faithful discharge of duty*' (which included a commitment to '*the true religion, presently professed within this realm and authorized by the laws thereof*'.[37] This oath was later to figure prominently in the Secession movement and the establishment of a large number of dissenting religious groups in the city.

A further annual fee was required by the Merchants' House before any merchant could have any voting rights or be eligible for election to office within the house. It was a further eighteen years before Dale became a fully matriculated member of the Merchants' House, by which time he had become well-known in the city. Nevertheless, it is important to note that after six years in the Hopkirk's Land shop he was able to use his own name to trade in Glasgow. He had completed the transition from weaver to entrepreneur.

Dale from "*The Morning Walk*".

It is important to emphasise firstly, that Dale operated from the High Street for some twenty years and, secondly, how successful this business was. Liddell is quite correct to note that Dale was importing *large quantities of French yarn from Flanders, which brought him large profits and laid the foundation of his fortune*.[38] This twenty-year period is not well documented but there can be no doubt that Dale accumulated considerable capital (and reputation) in Glasgow. According to one source, *Mr. Dale's speculations throve wondrously* and he became one of the most extensive importers of French and Flemish yarns in the city, *and year by year increased in riches and honours*.[39] It is not clear where Dale lived in the city during this period, although it is at least conceivable that he rented a living space above the shop from the Hopkirk family. In any event, by 1783 he was wealthy enough to have his own mansion built in Charlotte Street, to be one of the directors of the first Chamber of Commerce in Britain and to consider a business partnership with Richard Arkwright. Dale's early success was all the more noteworthy when we consider that *the winning prizes of trade, as well as of social and civil standing, were in the hands of a distinguished caste, who had guardedly surrounded themselves by a distinctive circle* from which small tradesmen and shopkeepers were rigorously excluded.[40] In the same vein, his appointment that year as the first Glasgow agent of the Royal Bank reflected his increasing importance in the commercial and financial life of the city. His marriage in 1777 to Ann Caroline Campbell (or Carolina as she was known), daughter of the Royal Bank of Scotland's Chief Cashier, and Dale's appointment a few years later in 1783 as the bank's first agent in Glasgow are the crucial links between the High Street period and the national fame and fortune which was to come with his association with New Lanark.

Marriage and Children

We simply do not know how Dale and Carolina met or how their courtship developed into marriage. Even the precise date of their September 1777 marriage is uncertain. One source cites the 17th of the month but there is no evidence for this.[41] There are two entries in the parish records of the time. *David Dale, Esq., merchant, Glasgow* is recorded in the parish register of Edinburgh City as marrying *Ann Carolina Campbell, daughter of the late John Campbell Esq. of the Royal Bank of Scotland* on 7th September 1777 and this is most likely to be the date nearest to the actual wedding ceremony itself.[42] Five days later, the marriage was further recorded in parish records of the City of Glasgow, presumably when the couple returned to the city.[43]

Although Dale was making money and establishing himself as a successful merchant in Glasgow, he was from humble origins and it would have been surprising if the Campbells had consented to Carolina's marriage without some kind of formal contract or agreement. Her father was dead but Carolina was not short of support and protection. Principal among her supporters was her brother John, a Writer to the Signet (lawyer) in Edinburgh and it is quite likely that he was behind the formal 'Contract of Marriage' signed by both parties on 18th September 1777.[44]

The contents of the marriage contract make it clear that, although the date of signing was after the marriage ceremony, it had been drawn up prior to that date, noting that the parties *accept each other as lawful spouses and promise to solemnize their marriage with all convenient speed*.[45] This lengthy document spells out Dale's obligations to Carolina and to any children of the marriage and in places it reads more like a last will and testament than a pre-nuptial agreement but clearly the Campbells were taking no chances. The document was drawn up in John Campbell's Edinburgh office by William Macfarlane, who was Campbell's own clerk. The five witnesses included Macfarlane, John Campbell and Colin Campbell (Carolina's other brother). The Campbell family were similarly over-represented in the list of Executors. Of the six individuals named as Executors, four (including witnesses John and Colin) were directly related to Carolina and the remaining two were part of the Edinburgh legal establishment.[46] The contract is clear about Dale's financial commitment to Carolina and any children of the union. Dale promised Carolina, *his promised spouse*, that he would provide £1,500 *in conjunct with her* – apparently some kind of minimum maintenance allowance for both of them. She would also receive £70 per year *from and after his decease*. She stood to inherit all their *plate and china* and she had *the right and free disposal of all her paraphernalia*.[47] Dale reserved the right to make any decisions about how money might be divided up amongst any children. If he died, the £1,500 would be divided equally amongst the children but he reserved the right to award differing amounts to different children. If there were to be only one daughter and no sons, the daughter would receive £1,000.[48] Any children would be entitled to an equal share of *any lands … sums of money or other funds whatsoever that he shall conquest or acquire during his marriage*, over and above the £1,500 already referred to. Interestingly, any such sums could be divided up equally *with the children of any other marriage*.[49] Finally, there was an agreement that, even if the marriage dissolved *within a year and day*, the whole contract (assuming no issue) would still apply.[50]

In return, Carolina's dowry was straightforward enough. She agreed to sign over the sum of £500 from her father's estate. Even here there was additional protection for her. The £500 would be paid back to her in the event of Dale's death and there being no children (although the liferent of £70 would consequently be reduced to £45 per annum). It seems that the Campbell family ensured that Carolina could not be disadvantaged in any way by her marriage to Dale, but there was no need to invoke the contract because Carolina pre-deceased her husband by some fifteen years.

There is no record of where the newlyweds lived. It was certainly in Glasgow, although not yet in Dale's famous Charlotte Street house. Their first child, named after her mother, was born in the August following the wedding. There has been considerable uncertainty over the years regarding the number of children of the marriage. When Andrew Liddell wrote his *Memoir of David Dale* in 1854, (intended for publication the following year in Chambers' *Biographical Dictionary of Eminent Scotsmen*), he noted that Carolina was '*the mother of six children whom she trained up in the fear of the Lord*'. According to Liddell, Dale had '*one son named William, who died in 1789 when in his seventh year, and five daughters, all of whom survived him*'.[51]

However, when the 1854 *Memoir* was published as an entry in the *Biographical Dictionary* a year later, the numbers had changed. Mrs. Dale was reported to have given birth to seven children during her marriage. This is further confused later in the same entry when a total of six children is once again referred to.[52] In fact, a careful search of the parish registers of the period indicates that Carolina gave birth to nine children during the course of her marriage.[53] She was 25 years old when Anne Caroline (the future Mrs. Robert Owen) was born in 1778. In the following six years, she gave birth to four children (Arabella, Christian, Katherine and William) - all of whom died in infancy or early childhood. After the death of William, she had another four children (Jean Maxwell, Mary, Margaret and Julia Johnson), all of whom survived their parents.

Large families and a high infant mortality rate were not uncommon in the late 18th century but the loss of four children, one after the other, must have been a heavy blow to the family. With the death of Arabella in 1780, Dale was faced with the necessity of purchasing a family burial plot or lair. He purchased a small plot in the Ramshorn churchyard, near the top of the High Street in what is now Ingram Street. This explains why Dale's tombstone on the east wall is inscribed with the date 1780. Sadly, Arabella was not the last of Dale's family to rest there.

Some parish records note the cause of death and in some cases, these are predictable, while in others, less so. For example, Arabella's cause of death is listed as '*teething*' and Christian's simply as '*fever*', although whether these are accurate terms for the illnesses concerned is another matter altogether.[54] Katherine died at seven months of '*chincough*' (whooping cough) which killed many children at the time.[55] William, the only male child, was six when he died and was laid to rest in '*David Dale's lair, south* [side]'. William died of smallpox - a notorious disease then and for many years thereafter.[56] Inoculation was still in its infancy and was met with some resistance by many - even those who could afford it. A few years later, Dale wrote a letter to Claud Alexander, his business partner in Catrine, expressing the hope that that Alexander's son would fare well after having been inoculated.[57]

It is possible that Dale had his own family inoculated but there is no concrete evidence of this. Certainly, it would seem that the rest of his children either avoided smallpox or recovered from it. In 1791, Dale refers to the health of his children in a letter to Alexander Campbell of Barcaldine:

> I came from Lanark on Tuesday morning & left Mrs & Miss Campbell ... & my children well. I was happy to learn that your children have got happily through the smallpox ...[58]

In 1790, a few months before William's death, Dale commissioned a portrait of Carolina by artist William Stavely, described variously as '*an eminent portrait painter*' who appears to have worked on occasion in London and exhibited at the Royal Academy between 1785 and 1805. There is some debate as to whether the figure of William was added to the painting at a later date, after the young boy's death in June of that year.[59]

As the family tree makes clear, from the age of 25 until her death in 1791 at the age of 38, Carolina gave birth to nine children – a large number in a short space of time, even by 18th century standards. What this did to her general health can only be guessed at. Perhaps the couple were keen to have a male child after William's death. This certainly seems plausible. Whatever the case, it now seems almost certain that the business of pregnancy and childbirth eventually led to her early death.

The parish records indicate that Carolina died on 28th January, 1791, very soon after her 38th birthday. The cause of death is given as 'childbed', an umbrella term covering a number of symptoms, all of which relate directly to pregnancy or childbirth.[60] Given that, and given that there was no child born to the couple at that time, it would appear that Carolina and her unborn child died at some point during her tenth pregnancy. They were laid to rest alongside the other children in Dale's family lair in the Ramshorn Kirkyard.[61]

All of this, however, lay years ahead of the young and prosperous couple who, in the early 1780s were in the process of establishing themselves in Glasgow and who, after some five years of marriage, decided to make a very public statement about their success and prosperity by having their own mansion built in the newly-created Charlotte Street.

Portrait: *Mrs David Dale, nee Campbell and her only son, William.* W. Stavely, 1790.
Private collection. Courtesy of David and Sebastian Blackie.

References: Chapter 1

1   Liddell, A. (1854a) *Memoir of David Dale*, Glasgow: Blackie. A slightly revised version of this (1854b) appeared a year later as an entry in R. Chambers (ed), (1855) *A Biographical Dictionary of Eminent Scotsmen*, Glasgow: Blackie.

2   National Records of Scotland (NRS) confirm that there are no dates recorded for Dale's birth. In such a situation, the NRS electronic system defaults to a date of birth of 1st January in the year concerned. Therefore Dale's birth appears as 1st January 1739. See also Registers of Scotland GROS 616/00 0010 0145.

3   Parish registers are often inconsistent and sometime contradictory. For example, dates of birth are sometimes recorded as dates of baptism; dates of registration/entry into the Register (births and deaths) may be recorded instead of the actual date of birth/death; some parishes recorded age at death while others did not; some recorded the place of burial and others not and sometimes the given age of the deceased does not square with the date of birth recorded separately.

4   I am grateful to Ian MacDonald and the Stewarton & District Historical Society for much of the information on Dale's early family life in Stewarton.

5   The family tree comprises information from various sources – mainly the NRS, online at: http://www.scotlandspeople.gov.uk but also from Stewarton & District Historical Society; Mr. David Blackie and from innumerable books, newspapers and journals and letters to the author.

6   Donnachie, I. (2000) *Robert Owen of New Lanark and New Harmony*. East Linton: Tuckwell Press, p.78.

7   Liddell (1854b) *Memoir*. p.174. Dale's nephew caused him some consternation (bearing in mind the concerns about events in France under the banner of liberty etc.) by joining a group of 'democrats' or 'Friends of the People' and attending their meetings in Glasgow. What particularly annoyed Dale were reports in the papers that 'David Dale' had been present at such meetings.

8   Stewart, G. (1881) *Curiosities of Glasgow Citizenship*. Glasgow: Maclehose. p.45. Vide supra, Chapter 14.

9   Ibid., p.58.

10 Ibid., p.47.

11 Ibid., p.47.

12 Liddell, *Memoir*, p.162.

13 Stewart, *Curiosities*, p.62.

14 Ibid., p.48.

15 Murray, N. (1978) *Scottish Handloom Weavers 1790–1850: A Social History*, Edinburgh: J. Donald, p.13.

16 This is difficult to verify but the *Dictionary of Eminent Scotsmen* notes that at that time, weaving was "*the most lucrative trade in the country*", which suggests that the period referred to is around 1750-60, since this was the beginning of the 'boom' time in weaving. See also Stewart's *Curiosities* p.422.

17 Liddell (1854b) *Memoir*, p.162.

18 Stewart, *Curiosities*, pp.45–7.

19 Reid, R. (Senex) (1884) *Glasgow Past and Present*, 3 vols. Glasgow: David Robertson & Co. Vol. III, p.171.

20 Ibid., p.372.

21 Liddell (1854b) *Memoir*, p.162.

22 Stewart, *Curiosities*, p.49.

23 *The Glasgow Journal*, 25th December, 1766, in Reid, R. *Glasgow*, Vol. III, p371.

24 *Tait's Directory for the City of Glasgow*. Glasgow, 1784. See also *Jones's Directory or Useful Pocket Companion* (1787) Glasgow: J. Mennons.

25 Reid, R. *Glasgow*, Vol. III, p.372.

26 Reid, R. *Glasgow*, Vol. II, p.70.

27 Ibid., p.71.

28 From Daniel Defoe's *Tour through the whole island of Great Britain*, Cole, G.D.H. (ed) (1927), 2 vols. Vol. II, pp.748ff in Smout, T.C. (1998) *A History of the Scottish People, 1560–1830*. London: Fontana, p.356.

29 Smout, T.C. (1998) *A History of the Scottish People, 1560–1830*. London: Fontana, p.356.

30 Ibid.

31 Ibid., p.357.

32 Ibid., p.358.

33 Cooke, A. (2010) *The Rise and Fall of the Scottish Cotton Industry, 1778–1914: The Secret Spring*. Manchester: M.U.P., p.3.

34 Stewart, *Curiosities*, p.50.

35 Cullen, A. (1910) *Adventures in Socialism*. Glasgow: John Smith, p.3. Also Anderson, J.R. (ed) (1935) *The Burgesses and Guild Brethren of Glasgow, 1757–1846*. Edinburgh: J. Skinner & Co., p.67.

36 Anderson (1935) *Burgesses*, pp.169, 182.

37 Cleland, J. (1816) *Annals of Glasgow, Comprising an Account of the Public Buildings, Charities and the Rise and Progress of the City*, 2 vols. Glasgow: James Hedderwick. Vol. II, p.304.

38 Liddell (1854b) *Memoir*, p.162.

39 Stewart, *Curiosities*, p.50.

40 Ibid., p.49.

41 Johnston, W.T. (2000) 'An Essay on David Dale' in W.T. Johnston (ed), *David Dale & Robert Owen Studies*. Livingston: Officina Educational Publications.

42 NRS, Old Parish Records (O.P.R.), Marriages 685/01 0510 0082, Edinburgh.

43 NRS, O.P.R., Marriages 644/01 0260 0205.

44 *Contract of Marriage between Mr. David Dale, Merchant in Glasgow and Miss Anne Carolina Campbell, second daughter of the deceased John Campbell, Esq, First Cashier of the Royal Bank of Scotland*. Royal Bank of Scotland Archives. R.B.S. 1480/17.

45 Ibid., p.1.

46 Ibid., pp.6–7. The Hon. James Erskine was a Senator of the College of Justice in Edinburgh and Robert Watt was an Edinburgh lawyer.

47 Ibid., p.1.

48 Ibid., pp.2–3.

49 Ibid., pp.3–5.

50 Ibid., p.6.

51 Liddell (1854a) *Memoir*, in W.T. Johnston (ed), (2000) *David Dale & Robert Owen Studies*. Livingston: Officina Educational Publications.

52 Liddell (1854b) *Memoir*, pp.164, 174.

53 I am indebted to Mr. K. Kerr for providing me with dates for Arabella & Christian. While checking these, I discovered the existence of Katherine Dale.

54 Arabella: NRS: O.P.R. Deaths 644/01 0590 0066 Glasgow. Christian: O.P.R. Deaths 644/01 0590 0256 Glasgow.

55 NRS: O.P.R. Deaths 644/01 0590 0125 Glasgow.

56 NRS: O.P.R. Deaths 644/01 0600 0061 Glasgow.

57 Dale to Alexander, 26th Aug 1789. *Dale–Alexander Correspondence, 1787–1797*. Glasgow City Archives: MS 63/7.

58 Dale to Alexander Campbell, 18th Aug 1791. Nat. Archives of Scotland. GD 170/1743/13, in W.T. Johnston (ed), (2000) *David Dale & Robert Owen Studies*.

59 *The Monthly Magazine* (1811), Vol. 32, London, p.397. See also *Scottish Studies*, (1989) Vol. 5. *Literature & Literati*. London: Lang, p.194. I am greatly indebted to David & Sebastian Blackie, direct descendants of David Dale, for contacting me about this portrait and for giving me permission to reproduce it here. The painting is a Blackie family heirloom. The reverse of the frame has the following inscription: *Mrs. David Dale nee Campbell and her only son William. W. Stavely 1790*. Sebastian Blackie is of the view that the painting was originally of Carolina and that William was added posthumously. He argues that there are visual clues to substantiate this, viz., the position of Carolina's right arm and the ghost of the seat showing through; the quality of the representation of William's face.

60 NRS: O.P.R. Deaths 644/01 0600 0076 Glasgow.

61 Ibid.

Chapter 2:
Home and Business: Glasgow, Charlotte Street and
The Chamber of Commerce.

The two-year period 1783-1785 was a major turning point for Dale. Having moved from herd laddie to apprentice and journeyman, Dale had now become a merchant in the city of Glasgow, dealing in foreign yarns and making a considerable amount of money in the process. He had married into a very respectable and influential family and a successful future seemed assured. However, 1783-1785 marked the beginning of a career for Dale which was to take off in several directions. Most notable was his involvement with Richard Arkwright (1732-1792) when the latter visited the city in 1784 and the subsequent development of New Lanark which led in turn to Dale's involvement in many other business partnerships across the country. The educational and social conditions he provided for his workers in New Lanark were the first of their kind in the U.K. and became the focus of much attention. His twenty-year involvement with the Royal Bank of Scotland began in 1783, as did his involvement with the nascent Glasgow Chamber of Commerce, his extensive charity work in the city and in the Highlands, and his evangelical work across the city. He became a very well known figure in and around the bustling merchant city, not least in the newly-extended Tontine Rooms. So extensive did his business and charitable affairs become after 1785, that it is necessary to disentangle the web of partnerships and projects thematically rather than chronologically. The period 1783-1785, however, is the tipping point, marking the end of a period of prosperity as successful linen merchant in the city and the beginning of a career as a nationally recognised cotton spinner and dyer, mill owner, philanthropist, banker, educationalist and evangelist.

Dale was nothing if not ambitious and the first stage in this pivotal change was to move his wife and family into a very expensive new house in the newly-created Charlotte Street – a house which was to become almost as much a symbol of his success as the mills at New Lanark. Archibald Paterson, Dale's friend and sleeping partner in the High Street shop, played an important role once again.

Charlotte Street

The house was built on the Merkdailly lands, next to Gallowgate Green. The area had always been close to the centre of Glasgow life, as indicated in an early map of 1760 (opposite).[1] Merkdailly (the spelling varies – often *Merkdaily*) originally referred to a piece of land or *daill* where an annual feu duty of one *merk* (13s. 4d.) would be payable. It was bounded on the north side by Merkdaily Street and a strip of land known as 'Ghostyard' which already had established properties, and on the east and west sides by orchards.

The southern part of the land bordered on to the Low Green. The bulk of the land was virgin territory and prime building land in the expanding city. By 1778 Glasgow had grown considerably and extensive building work had taken place on the northern part of Merkdaily, as McArthur's Map of 1778 illustrates.[2] The remaining 'Merkdaily Yard' had been advertised originally in 1777:

> To be sold, in lots, for house steadings, the ground lying on the south side of the Gallowgate, known by the name of Merkdaily. As this ground fronts the Green, and lyes so near the Cross of Glasgow, it is a most convenient as well as pleasant situation for houses.[3]

However, after passing through several hands, it was readvertised in *The Glasgow Mercury* on 17th February 1780:

> Ground for building to be sold. That, upon Wednesday 1st of March 1780, there is to be sold, by public roup, within the house of Mr. Buchanan, vintner, Saracen's Head, Glasgow, that piece of ground in Merkdailly, in the Gallowgate of Glasgow... . The progress of Writs and conditions of sale will be seen in the hand of Thomas Buchanan of Boquhan, Writer in Glasgow.[4]

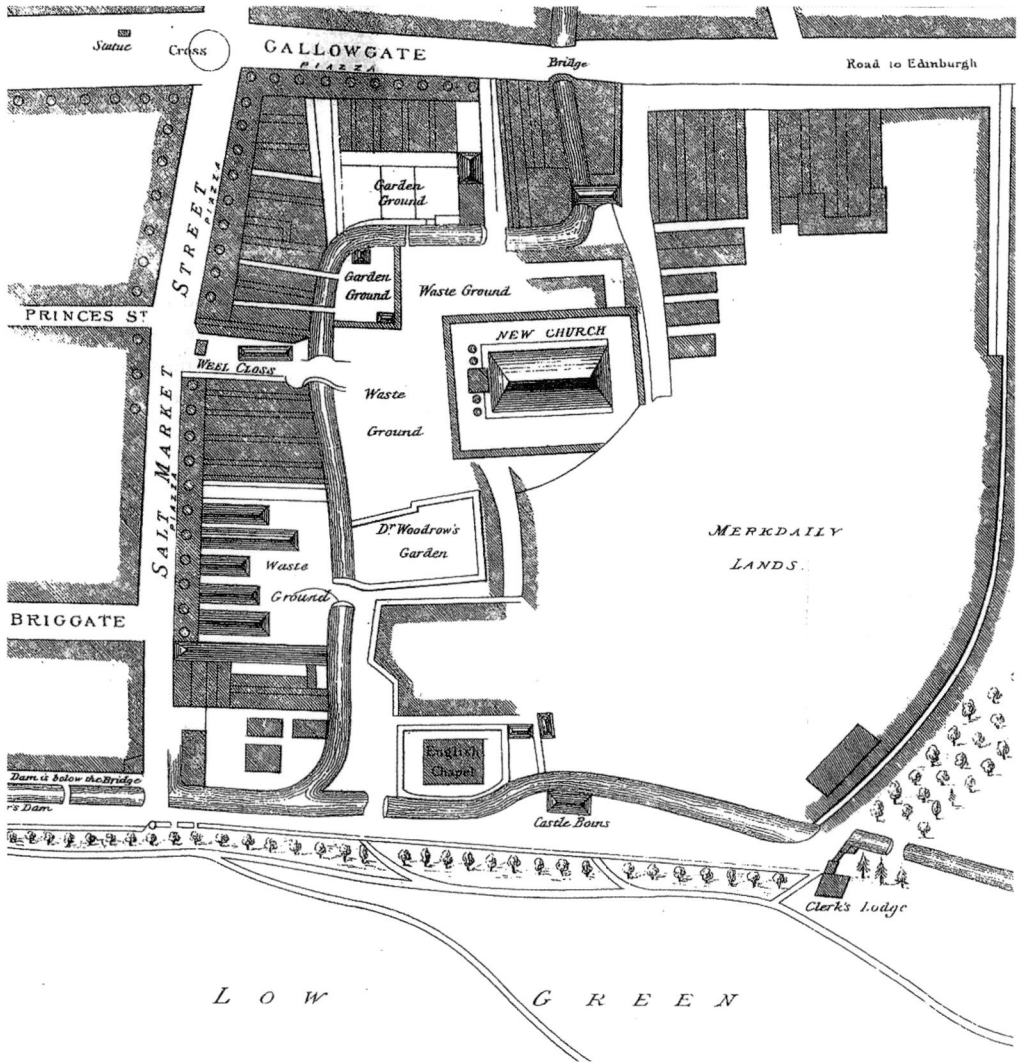

Merkdaily Lands. *Plan of the Low Green of Glasgow and its Environs, 1760.*

Paterson bought the land and ensured that the purchase included properties in the northern section (Merkdaily Street and Ghostyard) running up to the Gallowgate. He wanted to connect the Gallowgate with the Low Green, by way of a new street running parallel to Mungo's Lane. Paterson was clear from the beginning what he planned to do with the land, namely to lay off the majority of the grounds for the purposes of a regular street to be named Charlotte Street in honour of the Queen. The proposed street would run from north to south with plots or steadings for building and garden ground on each side. He lost no time in setting about the task, firstly by entering into negotiations with the proprietors of the existing routes into the Gallowgate, i.e. Merkdaily Street (later referred to – although not officially – as 'North Charlotte Street') and Ghostyard and secondly by selling off plots of land in Merkdaily Yard itself to fund the creation of the new Charlotte Street which he intended to build through the middle of the land. In so doing, he would create a number of desirable plots of land on either side of the new street. The new street was to have only self-contained houses *'of superior description for the residence of people of some note'*.[5] A narrow lane separated *'aristocratic South Charlotte Street'* from the northern section where there were plans for *'flats ... of less pretension'*.[6]

David Dale was one of the first to buy a plot or steading and on 23rd June, 1780, he paid Paterson £233. 16s. for a plot on the western side of the proposed street – plot number eight in the ground plan. This was at the south western corner, bounded

McArthur's Map of Glasgow, 1778.

by the common road along the green dyke and the burn to the south.[7] Fleming's Map of Glasgow shows the new street and indicates the extent of Dale's land in the south west corner.[8] There were strict terms and conditions written into the Disposition. Paterson was very precise about building regulation and went into great detail about what was and what was not allowed. The width of the street was prescribed, as was the type of stone to be used, the number of windows, paving stones to be used in the street, boundary walls and so on. All the owners were to share the cost of erecting and maintaining street lighting, a well and pump and a palisade and gate at the south end of the street. They were also prohibited from engaging in '*any business of brewing, distilling, tanning leather, making soap or candle, casting or founding metal, glass work or any other business which may be nauseous or disagreeable to the other inhabitants of the street*'.[9]

Even the ornamentation to be used on cornices and walls was specified and it has been suggested that Paterson was using Glasgow's prestigious Miller Street as his model.[10] All the houses had extensive gardens – many with fruit trees from the Merkdailly orchard. Paterson could have made a great deal of money if he had opted to build more houses and fewer gardens but this seems to have been of little concern to this modest and unassuming man whose purpose was '*an earnest desire to improve the eastern district of Glasgow, which so greatly required amelioration*'.[11]

Houses had to be built within a period of three years and so building work began soon after Dale's purchase of the land in 1780. Six properties were built on each side of the street and, once again, Paterson seems to have had more than an advisory role in all of this. According to one reliable source, Paterson was a man who '*cared little for the financial return of his project compared with it being carried out in the most worthy and complete manner*'.[12] Accordingly, '*there can be no doubt*' that all the buildings in Charlotte Street are the work of one man, namely Robert Adam, one of the most famous architects of the 18th century.[13] Paterson was a wealthy man and could certainly afford to engage Adam for his project. All the evidence from the external and internal features of Dale's house certainly support the view that Robert Adam was the designer responsible. Quality, however, then as now, did not come cheap and Paterson had to recoup at least some of the costs. Building work was finished in late 1782 and in 1783, Dale, Carolina and their two children moved in to their exclusive new home. Dale was faced with a bill of £6,000 – an enormous sum, '*which greatly exceeded his calculations*', according to Liddell.[14] However, it seems unlikely that Dale would have been too shocked if the following is accurate:

> Mr. Paterson consulted his then partner, Mr. David Dale, *regarding the purchase and laying out of the Merkdailly lands and had the approval of that gentleman to all the measures which he adopted on the occasion in question.*[15]

This was certainly a mansion of some note. As a point of comparison, William Cunninghame, one of Glasgow's wealthiest Virginia merchants, owned a house in Queen Street which had been built in 1780 at a cost of £10,000. This was one of the most splendid urban mansions in Scotland and later became Stirling's Library. The mansions in Charlotte Street were smaller but were clearly intended for the new merchant class and other important people. This is reflected in the ownership of the buildings. According to Robert Reid, Dale's neighbours in 1783 were mostly merchants. John Craig, like Dale was a merchant and yarn dealer and David Black was a tobacco merchant. Other neighbours included James Mackenzie, William McNeil, Robert Blair, James Jackson, James Mckenzie and William Urquhart, who had businesses in the city and at least one minister (John Lockhart) of the Established Church.[16] It is not entirely clear whether Paterson himself owned one of the new houses. Reid lists James Paterson (a relative of Archibald's) as a resident but elsewhere notes that Archibald was the owner of a house next door to David Dale's.[17]

Tait's Directory of 1783–1784 (despite the fact that it lists only Dale's business address in the High Street) is an additional source of information on the residents of Charlotte Street, although these names are not always the same as those on Reid's list. Tait includes famous merchant names such as William Wardlaw, Archibald Coats, Thomas Whytelaw, John Burnside, Walter Ewing and William Ingram, among others – many of whom were, along with Dale, signatories to the first charter of the new Chamber of Commerce established in the city in 1783.[18] Throughout Dale's lifetime, Charlotte Street continued to attract Glasgow's wealthy merchants. Fleming's Map (overleaf), published shortly after Dale's death, includes the names of his neighbours in 1806–1807 and, if Reid's list is correct, the map indicates that the majority of Dale's neighbours in 1783 were still there twenty years later.[19]

Despite the enormous cost of the new house, it would appear that money was not a particular problem for Dale. He had access to capital of his own but it is equally likely that Carolina's connection with the Royal Bank (a potential source of credit) played a part here. Dale's appointment as Glasgow agent of the Royal Bank at precisely the same time as the move to Charlotte Street might be described as fortuitous at the very least. Not only was Dale able to find the money to pay Paterson in 1783, he was also able to buy two adjacent plots of land – one in February 1784 and one in December of the same year. His land now stretched some distance westwards along what is now Greendyke Street, almost to the corner of what would shortly become St. Andrew's Square (later the site of the R.B.S. Glasgow office) and also *along the back of all the gardens of his neighbours to the head of the street in an oblong enclosure*.[20] This additional L-shaped enclosure can be seen in Fleming's Map and goes some way to explaining a reference in one source to *David Dale's stables*.[21] The house itself was grand affair, as the architectural drawings illustrate.[22]

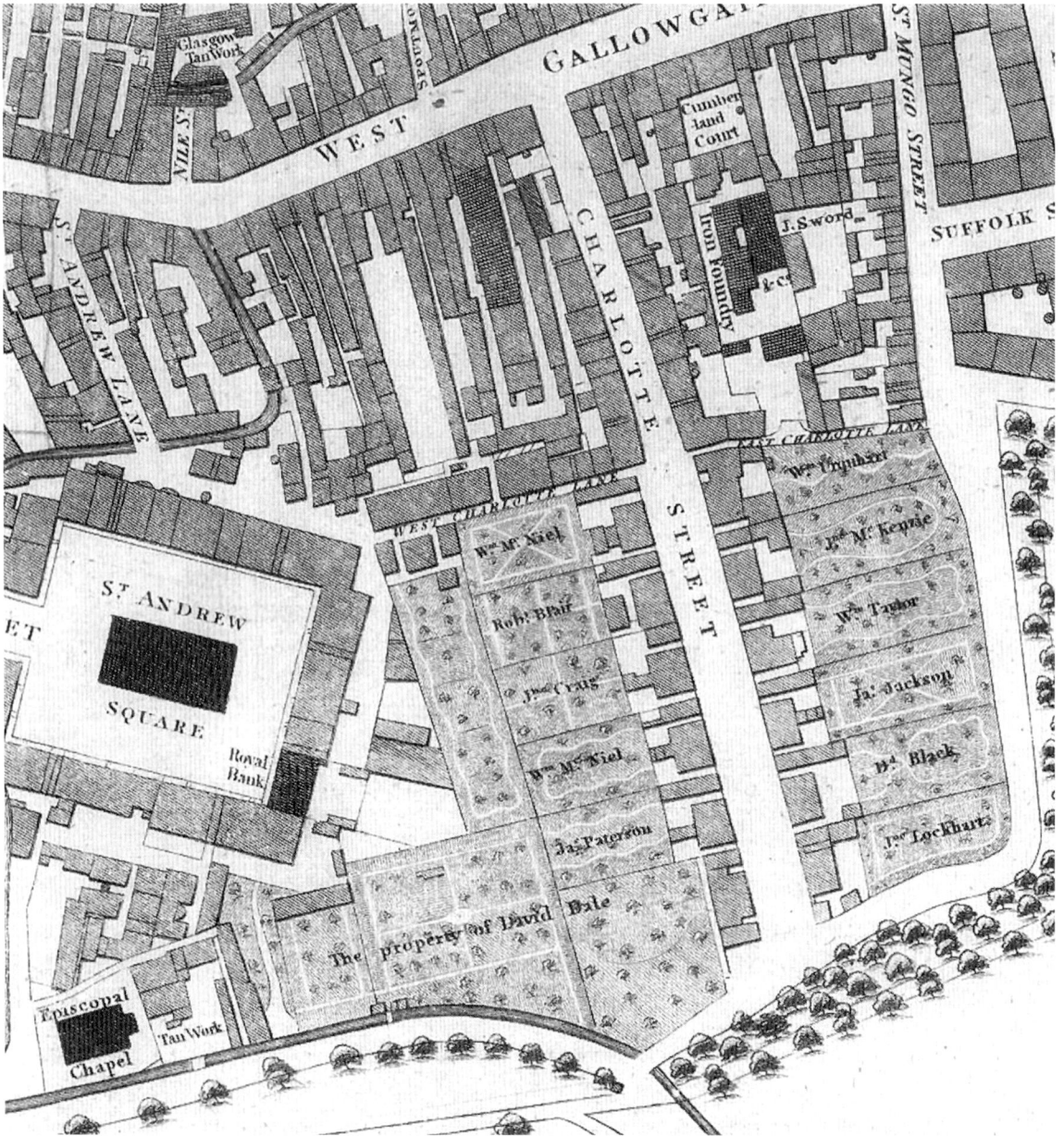

Fleming's Map of Glasgow, 1807. By permission of University of Glasgow Special Collections.

DAVID DALE'S HOUSE IN CHARLOTTE ST. GLASGOW.

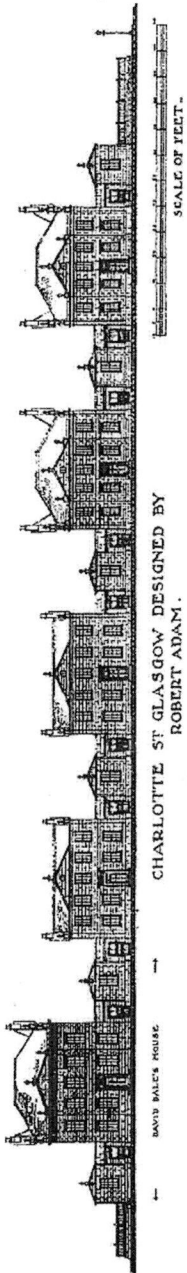

NOTE
DAVID DALE'S HOUSE, WAS DESIGNED BY ROBERT ADAM AND BUILT IN 1783 AT A COST OF £6,000.

NAMING OF ROOMS CONJECTURAL.

CHARLOTTE ST GLASGOW DESIGNED BY ROBERT ADAM.

SCALE OF FEET.

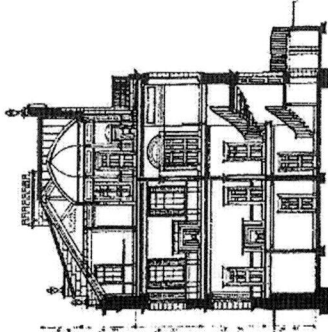

CROSS SECTION A.A.

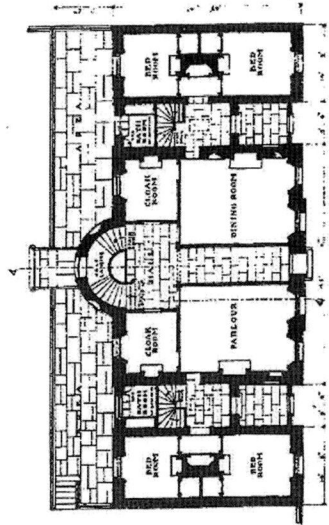

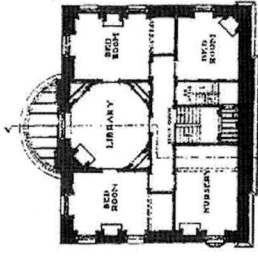

PLAN OF SECOND FLOOR.

MEASURED AND DRAWN BY J. GORDON SMITH.

LIBRARY

BED ROOM

NURSERY

BED ROOM

NURSERY

MATERIALS
WOOD FINISHINGS, MAHOGANY, PAINTED IN WHITE AND GOLD. ROOF EDGES RED PINE. FLOOR JOISTS RED PINE. SASH FRAMES AND FINISHINGS OF DOME, WINDOWS, ETC.

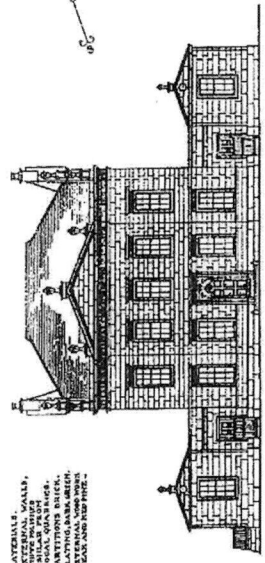

FRONT ELEVATION" TO CHARLOTTE ST.

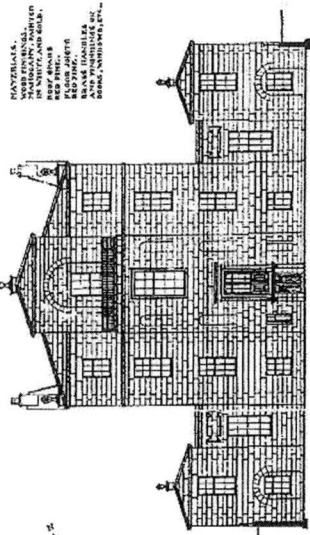

BACK ELEVATION" TO GARDEN.

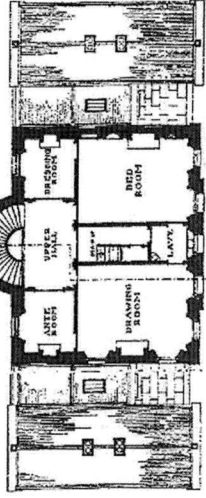

PLAN OF FIRST FLOOR.

FEET.

BED ROOM DRESSING ROOM

UPPER HALL

BED ROOM

LAVY.

ANTE ROOM

DRAWING ROOM

DAVID DALE'S HOUSE.

MATERIALS
EXTERNAL WALLS, WHITE POLISH ASHLAR FROM LOCAL QUARRIES. PARTITIONS BRICK. SLATING, SARK LINING EXTERNAL WOOD WORK, TEAK AND RED PINE.

N
W   E
S

BED ROOM

BED ROOM

CLOAK ROOM

DINING ROOM

CLOAK ROOM

PARLOUR

BED ROOM

BED ROOM

PLAN OF GROUND FLOOR.

NOTE: AS THE EXISTING HALF LANDING HAS NO ACCESS TO THE ROOMS, THEY HAVE BEEN PLANNED FROM AN OLD DRAWING.

SCALE OF

House Plan & Elevations – New Lanark Trust.

25

There were two storeys at the front and four at the back, incuding a kitchen and basement and an attic at the top of the house. On the two main floors were four large rooms (each about 24 feet x 16 feet) facing the street; these served principally as a dining-room, library and two drawing-rooms. The octagonal room on the second floor was Dale's own personal study, although, as the illustration from W.G. Black shows, the actual designation for each room is not entirely clear, and would, in any event be subject to change over a period of time.[23]

The house had dark green slates on the roof with external walls of white polished ashlar. External woodwork was mahogany or red pine. On each side of the main building were one storey 'wings' – bedroom areas joined to but separated from the main building and which appear to have had their own front entrances onto the street.[24]

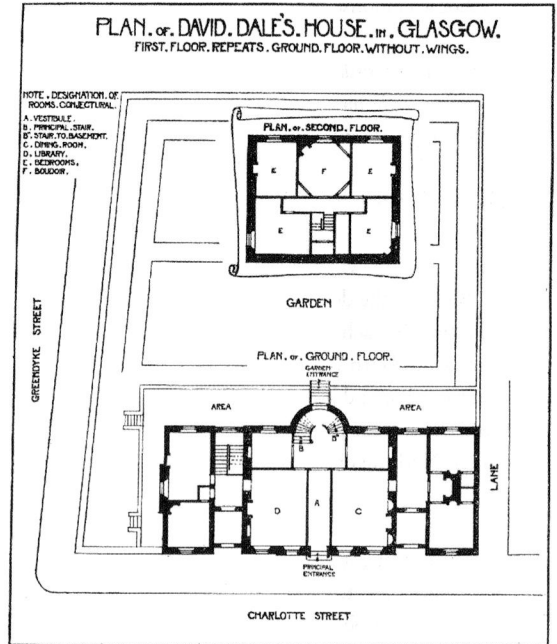

PLAN . of . DAVID . DALE'S . HOUSE . in . GLASGOW.
FIRST . FLOOR . REPEATS . GROUND . FLOOR . WITHOUT . WINGS.

NOTE . DESIGNATION . OF ROOMS . CONJECTURAL.

A . VESTIBULE .
B . PRINCIPAL . STAIR .
B¹ . STAIR . TO . BASEMENT.
C . DINING . ROOM.
D . LIBRARY.
E . BEDROOMS.
F . BOUDOIR.

PLAN . of . SECOND . FLOOR.

GREENDYKE STREET

GARDEN

PLAN . of . GROUND . FLOOR.

GARDEN ENTRANCE

AREA   AREA

LANE

PRINCIPAL ENTRANCE

CHARLOTTE STREET

David Dale's house in Charlotte Street in the 1950s. (New Lanark Trust)

Internally, the house demonstrated the elegance always associated with Robert Adam:

> A special characteristic of Adam's work was the care he bestowed upon, and the grace with which he invested the internal finishings of his work – the chimney pieces, wainscoting, plaster ceilings and even the door handles and shutter knobs ...[25]

As a result, internal woodwork was mahogany, sometimes painted in white and gold and all door and window handles and finishings were made of brass.[26] There was a fireplace in each room, including the wine cellar, because there was no such thing as damp-coursing in those days. Some of the decorative work can be seen in the detail of these fireplaces.[27] Even with coal fires in each room, the house would still have been damp, made worse when the Camlachie Burn overflowed, which it did frequently and it was a common occurrence for the cellar and kitchen to be flooded to a depth of several feet. On one such occasion, there was a great panic because Dale had invited some directors of the Royal Bank for dinner. Nothing daunted, he sent out servants to ask whether his neighbours would object to his staff using their kitchens to prepare the food, and the situation was saved. That is, except for the wine. Rather than stretch his neighbours' kindness too far (and in doing so deprive his guests of the fruits of his famous wine cellar) 'a seafaring man' was brought in to wade through the cellar and Dale's eldest daughter, Anne Caroline had to climb on top of this gentleman's shoulders to reach some of the bottles.[28] Some years later in 1799, Caroline and Robert Owen were married in the house by the Rev. Robert Balfour, minister of the Outer High Church and one of Dale's neighbours in Charlotte Street.

From the plans, it would appear that Dale's house was one of the largest in the street. Not shown on the map of 1807 but mentioned in Paterson's Disposition is the large metal gate at the south end which was used to keep the street private. Robert Reid also noted that the street was kept private 'by means of a large and handsome iron gate at the south end, flanked by posterns'.[29] A version of this was still in existence in 1845 and can be seen in the watercolour painting of that date.[30] Although Dale had a house in New Lanark and, towards the end of his life, a country house ('Rosebank') in Cambuslang, the Charlotte Street house was his principal residence, one where he was to host numerous parties and social events and where five of his nine children were born.

Corner of Fireplace in Dale's House

Charlotte Street, c.1845.

Business and the Glasgow Chamber of Commerce.

With his status as merchant in the city confirmed by the purchase of a grand house, the new beginning continued for Dale in a number of ways. The Royal Bank involvement which was subsequently to make Dale an extremely influential figure in the city began in 1783, just as the family took possession of the new house. His marriage to Carolina was undoubtedly a major factor in his appointment as joint Glasgow agent for the bank. Carolina's father had been the Chief Cashier during the upheavals of the Jacobite Rebellion and beyond, and had been a leading force in the bank's development until his death in 1783, only a few months before the Dales moved into Charlotte Street. Her brother, John, had been appointed to the board of the bank in 1781. It could have been no great surprise that Carolina's successful and entrepreneurial husband would join the 'family business' at some stage – a connection from which Dale could not fail to benefit personally and professionally:

> There is reason to suppose her father's connection with the Royal Bank of Scotland as Director led to Mr. Dale's appointment as agent of that establishment in Glasgow and this increased his commercial credit and command of capital.[31]

There is also every 'reason to suppose' that Dale knew about this appointment a few months before it was made public. He may even have met his future Royal Bank partner, Scott Moncrieff. It would certainly explain why the following advertisement appeared in the *Glasgow Journal* in May 1782:

> The partnership between Archibald Paterson and David Dale, carried on under the name of David Dale & Co., is dissolved. Those who have claims upon the company may have them settled when they please, by applying to David Dale; and all who are indebted to the company, either by bill or open account, to pay the same to him. David Dale continues to carry on the same business on his own account.[32]

The impending Royal Bank appointment had created a new situation which had to be dealt with, and one which Dale was to face very frequently from that point on, namely the matter of business partnerships and professional behaviour. The business in the High Street was technically a joint venture with Paterson. The agreement with the watchmaker was no more than a convenience which allowed Dale to cut his operating costs but Paterson was his principal business partner and continued to be so. Not only had Paterson contributed a great deal financially to the business (helping to make Dale a wealthy man), he had supported Dale since the latter's arrival in Glasgow in the 1760s. They were partners but also friends through their strong, shared religious beliefs and through their involvement in the Charlotte Street venture. This was Dale's first business partnership – one of very many he would make from 1783 onwards. For the first time, he was forced to deal with a partnership 'issue'. The impending Royal Bank appointment meant that an agency office would need to be set up in the city and Dale's premises in the High Street would be suitable. Space could be found by dispensing with the watchmaker's services.

However, the decision to convert half the space into a bank could not be achieved without Paterson's agreement. It seems highly likely, given Paterson's support for Dale and his relaxed attitude to business, that Paterson would have agreed but any profits arising would have to be discussed and possibly shared between them. Dale was wealthy and, although banking was still a risky business, the Royal Bank connection offered great potential in terms of profit and influence. Dale is often portrayed in the literature as a kindly, corpulent, benevolent, good humoured man. While that is almost certainly true, he appears for the first time in 1783 in a more hard-headed professional, role – one which he was to enact more than once in his life. The fact was that the High Street business had done very well and Dale no longer required a sleeping partner. On a purely commercial basis, it made good sense to end the partnership.

Whether it was right to dispense with the services of a friend and supporter is a different matter but in commercial terms it seems that Dale had no hesitation. A few years later he was to make similarly clinical business decisions when he refused to return young James Monteith's money for the Blantyre Mill.

Unsurprisingly, perhaps, the dissolution of the partnership came as something of a shock to Paterson, who thought it *'rather sharp'* on the part of Dale to dissolve it at the height of its success. Paterson, however, was a man not overly concerned with profit and loss. He remained involved with Dale in the Charlotte Street development and:

> ...through life he continued on the most friendly terms with Mr. Dale, which were greatly strengthened by a unison of sentiment in their religious views.[33]

The way was now clear for Dale to establish a new partnership with Scott Moncrieff in a venture not directly related to textiles, while at the same time building his existing business on his own. In fact, business was becoming a less solitary career for the merchants involved. There had always been the Merchants and Trade Houses but now, with the need to seek out new business in the post-tobacco era, an opportunity presented itself for like-minded businessmen in the city to group together and pursue common business aims with a united voice. This was particularly important in the development of multiple partnerships which became increasingly necessary, given the fluctuating fortunes of businesses related to the textile industry. At this pivotal point in his life, Dale was not going to pass up such an opportunity to widen his professional and personal interests (particularly if the other new businesses required credit from banks such as the Royal) and to engage in what might be referred to today as 'networking'.

This opportunity presented itself in the form of the Glasgow Chamber of Commerce, the first of its kind in Britain. The main protagonist here was not Dale but the wealthy and influential Patrick Colquhoun (1745–1820), who was elected Lord Provost in February 1782. Originally from Luss, he had made his fortune in Virginia and lived in style in his Kelvingrove mansion. During the 1780s, although he supported a number of commercial ventures, he developed a particular interest in the cotton industry and became a well-known figure throughout Great Britain. The Glasgow Chamber later appointed him to represent their interests in London, where he established a number of agencies for that purpose and became an adviser to the Government of the day.

By 1782, following the decline in trade with America, Colquhoun had come to recognise the need for *'a parliament of businessmen concerned with the commercial and industrial interests of Glasgow and the west of Scotland'* and his election as Provost gave him the civic platform he needed.[34] It is important to emphasise that this new era required the input of the new commercial and industrial entrepreneurs. The days of the old tobacco lords dominating the commercial landscape were gone. They either required to retire to their mansions or to diversify into other areas and, in so doing, rub shoulders with the new merchant classes. This mixing of classes, albeit limited, is fundamental to the development of the concept of a Chamber of Commerce. A considerable number of the 200+ signatories of the Glasgow Chamber were, like Dale, merchants or manufacturers *'who had raised themselves by their talents from the plebeian ranks'*.[35]

Colquhoun lost no time in setting about his task. He drafted a Constitution which outlined some of the purposes of such an association. For example, the Chamber would seek to:

- protect and improve trade and manufacture
- support members negotiating business with the Board of Trustees or Parliament
- consider all matters relating to the Corn Laws
- oppose Parliamentary actions injurious to Scottish trade
- point out new courses of prosperity
- liaise with Royal Burghs and the Board of Fisheries & Manufactures [36]

The following notice appeared in *The Scots Magazine* in December 1782:

> A plan for establishing a Chamber of Commerce and Manufactures in Glasgow, comprehending the towns of Paisley, Greenock, Port Glasgow and places adjacent has been submitted by the Lord Provost, to the consideration of the merchant traders and manufacturers of these towns; and many respectable gentlemen of all ranks are already become members ... The management is to be committed to the care of thirty Directors to be chosen from the most intelligent class of merchants and manufacturers.[37]

The Chamber was formally established on 1st January 1783, although it was not given its Royal Charter until July that year. There were some 216 members and the membership was heavily weighted in favour of Glasgow merchants.[38]

According to Stewart in his *Curiosities of Glasgow Citizenship*, there were two main 'lists' of subscribers, the most substantial of which was '*Campbell & Ingram's List*' with 189 names and '*David Dale's list*', which had sixteen names. There are ten additional names on a separate list and some names appear twice, so the figure of 216 is not entirely accurate. Campbell & Ingram were a firm of merchants with interests in the West Indies sugar trade and they were also insurance brokers. Some famous Glasgow names appear on their list e.g. the Finlays, the Buchanans, James Bogle, James Oswald, James Dennistoun.[39] Dale's list, '*mostly of manufacturers, doubtless David's customers for yarn*', according to Stewart, included William Wardlaw, sometime neighbour of Dale in Charlotte Street and Messrs. Young, Lang & Auchincloss who were partners in a warehouse in the Gallowgate.[40] According to Robert Reid, members paid an initial membership of five guineas and one guinea each year thereafter.[41]

II. DAVID DALE'S LIST.

Glasgow Chamber of Commerce. David Dale's "List".

While these lists, fees etc. may well have existed, the actual minutes of the Chamber do not mention Campbell & Ingram or Dale in this respect. Members are simply listed as 'Merchants' or 'Manufacturers'. Dale's name appears under the former category, along with some of the city's most distinguished merchants – established and emerging. Stewart is correct to identify Buchanan, Bogle, Oswald and Dennistoun in this category (and he might have added John Glassford, Wm. Dunmore, Robert & John Dunlop, Robert Houston and George Macintosh, Dale's future partner in Dalmarnock and Spinningdale, among many others) but figures such as William Wardlaw, James Auchincloss, William Findlay, John Tennant, Thomas Buchanan, James Monteith Senior and others are listed as 'Manufacturers', not 'Merchants'.[42] Similarly, Reid is only partly correct in relation to the membership fees. Some members (including Patrick Colquhoun, William French & William Stirling), subscribed twenty guineas each, as form of life membership; some (including James Finlay & David Todd) paid ten guineas for membership with an annual subscription of one guinea thereafter, while most paid five guineas with an annual subscription of one guinea thereafter.[43] By the time of the presentation of the Royal Charter in July 1783, attended by Dale, the minutes record that twelve members had paid twenty guineas each, six had paid ten guineas each with an annual subscription and the majority (some

199 members) were paying five guineas each with an annual subscription. Dale is not specifically mentioned in the first two categories so it is reasonable to assume that he was one of the 199 members in the last membership category.[44]

According to one source, Dale was the '*most notable of all the merchants*' involved with Colquhoun and '*was in many ways a pupil of Colquhoun's although his senior by six years or more*'.[45] Given the names already mentioned above, this claim seems somewhat exaggerated at this point in Dale's life, although Dale was certainly a wealthy man and was becoming well known in the city. He was elected as one of the first members of the board of directors, alongside major city figures such as Colquhoun, John Glassford, Wiliam Cunninghame and James Bogle.[46] There were 30 such directors, with six of their number demitting office on an annual basis, '*according to the rate of seniority*' and they elected a Chairman, Deputy Chairman and Secretary.[47] These senior posts were tenable for a maximum of two years.[48] In a *Glasgow Herald* article written in 1886, J.O. Mitchell claimed that Dale was Chairman in the early years but that is not the case.[49] Pat Colquhoun was Chairman from 1783–86.

Nevertheless, Dale's initial commitment in 1783 was clearly substantial. He became Deputy Chairman in 1786 and again in 1787 and the Chamber became one of his most enduring projects because he served as a member or director for more than twenty years – '*one of its most honoured and trusted Directors*'.[50] His last recorded attendance was on 22nd January, 1805 – fifteen months before he died.[51]

During the period of Dale's involvement, the Chamber went from strength to strength, campaigning against the East India Company's monopoly on trade; meeting regularly in the new Tontine Rooms; sometimes joining with Lancashire cotton merchants to protect mutual interests; petitioning Parliament and lobbying M.P.s on matters of trade – and David Dale was a member of a great many of these committees. His membership (or leadership) of some twenty committees over the years is listed in Appendix 2 and is a testament to his increasingly important role in the commercial life of the city. His committees dealt with matters which he might have been expected to have some knowledge of, e.g. the Thread Bill; the regulations about the length and quality of yarns; new developments in bleaching and dyeing; weaving machines and export duties and tariffs on cotton and linen. However, he was also involved in other committees looking at more diverse but equally crucial issues such as the stamping of paper; disbursement of Government funds; Fisheries and Manufactures; a new road to link Lanarkshire (and therefore Scotland) and England; the Crinan Canal and the slave trade.

The Chamber campaigned against legislation which might adversely affect cotton and linen goods. For example, one of the issues was that manufacturers used different sizes of reels for cotton twist and that the twist itself varied in quality and quantity. The Chamber appointed a committee in December 1783 to look into this and when it reported, they appointed Dale and William Carlisle 'to wait on the Hon. Board of Trustees at Edinburgh' and ask for their support '*in order to procure an act of Parliament for regulating the count and likewise the weights of ounce thread*'.[52] This 'Thread Bill' became a long-running saga but the Trustees did support the measure and the Bill was passed in 1787. The Chamber lobbied influential politicians as part of this process and one such politician, George Dempster (1732–1818) was enrolled as an Honorary Member of the Glasgow Chamber in April 1784.[53] In the same month, the Chamber appointed Ilay Campbell, the recently-elected M.P. for the Glasgow Burghs (and Lord Advocate) as an Honorary Member.[54]

Other chambers of commerce were forming all over the U.K. and although Glasgow was keen to establish connections with like-minded organisations, it was hesitant about any suggestion of merger, amalgamation or 'junction' with colleagues in London. Dale was asked by the Glasgow Chamber in early 1786 to join seven other members on a committee looking at the possibility of '*a junction*' with London (at the latter's request). Just one month later, the committee reported that it could not '*with propriety*' form a junction with London '*on any permanent basis*'.[55]

Nevertheless, the Glasgow Chamber was keen to work with emerging chambers of commerce. Principal among these was Manchester. An important link was established between the two cities in 1784 when Manchester Chamber sent Glasgow a copy of a letter written by four Lancashire doctors to their local Justices of the Peace on the best ways to combat contagious fevers which had been affecting some cotton mill workers in Radcliffe.[56] There are two points of significance here for the New Lanark story. Firstly, the doctors stressed the need for adequate ventilation and fumigation and suggested that child employees '*should not be debarred from all opportunities of instruction*' – issues which Dale was to address directly in New Lanark.[57] Secondly, two of the Manchester Chamber were to re-appear twelve years later when Thomas Percival, one of the four doctors and Thomas Bayley, one of the local J.P.s became founder members of the Manchester Board of Health and sent Dale a questionnaire regarding the health and welfare of his child employees. The questions and Dale's response are discussed in Chapter 6.

Not only was the formation of the Glasgow Chamber in 1783 an important element in Dale's life and career, it was crucial to the commercial success of the city itself – a city which had to come to terms with the consequences of the U.S. Declaration of Independence in July that year. One source recalls the city's reaction to the events of 4th July. The citizens were '*melancholy and dejected*' because of the '*loss*' of America:

> There were no rejoicings here at this peace, no illuminations, no bonfires, no squibs or crackers, no firing of guns or ringing of bells – all was silence and sorrow.[58]

This kind of reaction is understandable, given the loss of trade with a colony which had long been considered '*the grand outlet for the manufacturers of Glasgow*' and the main source of its wealth and prosperity.[59] Nevertheless, businessmen in the city could not afford the luxury of gloomy introspection. Families such as the Campbells, Dunmores, Houstons, McDowalls and Raes had strong connections with the sugar trade. There had always been a very lucrative trade in sugar and rum (and, to a lesser extent, raw cotton) from the West Indies and this would continue to expand. Linen was still a profitable business but it was becoming clear that the next great boom would be in the cotton industry in all its manifestations – spinning, weaving, dyeing, bleaching and printing. Indeed, with the exception of tobacco, most of the city businesses continued to flourish and the city's population of 44,000 in 1783 was rising rapidly. The city boundary was also expanding and the centre of the town now included the lands of Ramshorn and Meadowflat, recently acquired from Hutchesons' Hospital. Colquhoun, Dale and the other directors could see that the age of the tobacco lord was over. A new, merchant middle class was on the rise, driven in the first instance by the manufacture of cotton.

> ...the energy of her citizens soon carved out new channels to wealth for Glasgow and this year [1783] may be called the cradle in which our cotton lords were laid in their swaddling clothes, and the dawning of the glorious days of our late West Indian princes.[60]

The Chamber existed to promote the interests of these new merchant classes and to decrease the gap between merchants and tradesmen – in so doing to spread the profits among a much wider group of people. Before long, more ornate, elegant buildings appeared in the city, as did new, wider, streets with pavements and lighting. There were great changes in '*dress, housing, furniture*' – everything now seemed '*more showy and elegant than before*'.[61]

The city's Tontine Buildings next to Glasgow Cross embodied much of this new spirit. Colquhoun was determined that the Chamber of Commerce should meet in suitable premises; buildings which would become the focus for the new merchants as they tried to expand their businesses. Immediately on his election to the office of Lord Provost, he took charge of the money (£5,000) which had been raised by the Tontine Society for such a purpose and ensured that the first phase of the building work was completed on schedule in late 1782, at which point the Coffee Rooms began to do some business. By 1783 the first part of the Tontine Hotel was open for business. Prior to this period there were no hotels in the city, although there were plenty of inns and taverns. It seems that '*the common people were amazed at the novelty and always pronounced the name the Tontine Hottle*'.[62] In addition to accommodation, there were offices and sample rooms for brokers. Shortly thereafter, a Mr. Smart took up the lease and started a daily '*ordinary*' (lunch) at one shilling, every day at 3.15pm. Such a thing was unheard of at the time.[63] Meeting or Assembly Rooms and Reading Rooms were opened over the course of the following 24 months. When the Hotel and new Coffee Rooms were formally opened in the spring of 1784, they hosted the most splendid ball ever seen in Glasgow.[64] Not long after that, the Chamber of Commerce meetings moved from their previous venue, the Town Hall, to the Tontine. Dale met his colleagues and chaired many committee meeting in these rooms over the next twenty years of his life.

Tolbooth (centre) and the Tontine Buildings (left), c.1812.

It is certainly true that 1783 ushered in a new period, characterised by greater co-operation and harmony between merchants and tradesmen. Robert Reid claimed that '*all classes met upon a state of perfect equality*' particularly in the Reading Room, where they conversed with each other as they exchanged newspapers.[65] However, although there was undoubtedly a much greater mixing of the classes from 1783, these claims seem somewhat exaggerated and, if true at all, are likely to refer to the situation pertaining some years later. In 1783, remnants of the 'old guard' were still around. When young Henry Monteith (a friend of Dale's) presumed to attend an Assembly in the Tontine, a notice appeared the next day on one of the pillars, indicating that if the young gentleman who attended the Assembly on the previous night appeared at another of these gatherings, he would go out quicker than he came in.[66]

The reality was perhaps that the new Tontine and the new Chamber of Commerce were not as classless as they appeared. However, both marked the beginning of a very significant change in thinking about who could make money and who could not. Despite this initial snub, Monteith went on to make a fortune in business, build his own mansion, become Lord Provost and eventually a Member of Parliament. For David Dale too, the Chamber and the Tontine were significant factors in his subsequent success.

According to Stewart, by 1783, Dale had become:

'...*the prosperous Glasgow merchant, who, by virtue of pure force of character and intelligence, had fairly broken down that wall of distinction which once separated him from the great tobacco and sugar lords and could now wear his cocked hat jauntily, display his silver knee buckles showily and take the place of honour on the crown of the causeway with the proudest of them all*'.[67]

Similarly, Liddell notes that Dale:

> was now sole proprietor of, or connected as a managing partner with, several of the most extensive mercantile, manufacturing, and banking concerns of the country.[68]

While it is true that Dale was becoming a major figure in the city, Liddell's estimation of the situation in 1783 is a little overdone. The Royal Bank partnership had only just begun and Dale was still actively engaged with fellow entrepreneurs across the city and beyond. There was one final partnership in the following year which was to lead to the establishment of one of the world's most famous cotton communities and which opened up a whole new series of opportunities for Dale. From that point onwards, Dale's career took off in a number of different but related directions. He became more than a wealthy Glasgow merchant. He became an entrepreneur on a national level, a factory owner, cotton spinner, broker and trader, a major employer, a financier, a philanthropist, an educator and an evangelist, both in terms of his Christian beliefs and his entrepreneurial spirit. It is no exaggeration to say that most of his fame and fortune in the new industrial era stemmed directly from a meeting between Dale and the famous Richard (later Sir Richard) Arkwright during the latter's visit to Glasgow in 1784.

References: Chapter 2

1   Reid, R. (Senex) (1884) *Glasgow Past and Present*, 3 vols. Glasgow: David Robertson & Co. *Plan of the Low Green of Glasgow, 1760*. Vol. III, Frontispiece.

2   Reid, R. *Glasgow*, Vol. 1, Appendix.

3   *The Glasgow Journal*, 14th August 1777 in Black, W.G. (1912) 'David Dale's House in Charlotte Street': Regality Club (1889–1912). *Transactions of the Regality Club* (1889–1912), 4 vols. Vol. 4 (1912): 93–121. Glasgow: James Maclehose & Sons. p.98.

4   Reid, R. *Glasgow*, Vol. II, p.465. See also W.G. Black, *David Dale's House*, p.98.

5   Ibid., p.466.

6   Ibid., p.467.

7   See Black, W.G. (1912) *David Dale's House*, pp.93–121 for more detail.

8   Fleming's Map of Glasgow, 1807. University of Glasgow Library. Special Collections MU 24-Y-21.

9   W.G. Black, *David Dale's House*, p.109.

10 Reid, R., *Glasgow*, Vol. II, p.466.

11 Ibid., Vol. III. p.180.

12 Black, W.G. (1912) *David Dale's House*, pp.110–111.

13 Ibid., p.111.

14 Liddell, A. (1854b) 'Memoir of David Dale', in R. Chambers (ed), (1855) *A Biographical Dictionary of Eminent Scotsmen*. Glasgow: Blackie, p.167.

15 Reid. R. *Glasgow*, Vol. III, p180.

16 Reid, R. *Glasgow*, Vol. II, p.467 and Vol. III, p.180.

17 Ibid.

18 Tait, J. (1784) *Directory for the City of Glasgow from 15 May 1783 to 15 May 1784*. It is possible that Reid simply used the 1807 names and assumed that they had all been present in 1783. See Reid, R. *Glasgow*, Vol. II, p.467 and Vol. III, p.180. The situation is further complicated by the fact that there were properties in 'North Charlotte Street' where superior lodgings were available for cabinet makers, saddlers and architects.

19 See Annan, T. (1871) *Old Maps of Glasgow*. Glasgow: Maclehose.

20 W.G. Black, *David Dale's House*, pp.109–110.

21 Reid, R., *Glasgow*, Vol. 1, pp.137–8.

22 New Lanark Trust. See also SCRAN Ref No. 000-000-183-853-C.

23 W.G. Black, *David Dale's House*, p.119.

24 Ibid., p.96. Photograph courtesy of New Lanark Trust. SCRAN Ref. No. 000-000-183-854-C.

25 Ibid., p.111.

26 Ibid., p.112.

27 Ibid., p.111.

28 Ibid., p.113.

29 Reid, R. *Glasgow*, Vol. II, p.467.

30 I am indebted to Simon Leslie Carter, 52 Charlotte Street for this information and for a photocopy of the painting.

31 Liddell, A. (1854b) *Memoir*, p.164.

32 *Glasgow Journal*, 24th May, 1782.

33 Reid, R. *Glasgow*, Vol. II ,p.372.

34 Eyre-Todd, G. (1934) *A History of Glasgow*, 3 vols. Glasgow: Jackson, Wylie & Co., Vol. III, p.320.

35 Reid, R. *Glasgow*, Vol. III, p.346.

36 Eyre-Todd, G. *History*, pp.321–2. For a full list see Stewart, G. (1881) *Curiosities*, pp.170–71.

37 *The Scots Magazine*, Vol. 44, December 1782, p.712. N.B. this was published in 1783, by which time a *post script* had been added, intimating the establishment of the Chamber in January 1783.

38 Cooke, A.J. (2009) 'The Scottish Cotton Masters', *Textile History*, 40(1): 29–50, p.35. There were 38 Glasgow manufacturers; 23 Paisley merchants & manufacturers; sixteen Greenock merchants & manufacturers; seven Port Glasgow merchants & manufacturers; two Kilbarchan manufacturers.

39 Stewart, G. (1881) *Curiosities*, pp.155ff.

40 Ibid., p.246.

41 Reid, R. *Glasgow*, Vol. III, pp.346.

42 Glasgow Chamber of Commerce Minutes. TD 1670/1/1, 1st Jan 1783.

43 Ibid.

44 Ibid., 1st January 1783: 1st July 1783.

45 'The Merchant Princes of England', in *London Society*, 8:47 (1865: November). p.467.

46 *Scots Magazine*, Vol. 44, December 1782, p. 712.

47 'Abridgement of the Charter erecting the Society of the Chamber of Commerce & Manufactures in the City of Glasgow into a body politic, in 1783', in Cleland, J. (1816) *Annals of Glasgow, Comprising an Account of the Public Buildings, Charities and the Rise and Progress of the City*, 2 vols. Glasgow: James Hedderwick. Vol. 2, p.381.

48 Ibid., p.381.

49 Mitchell, J.O. (1886) 'David Dale. An old Glasgow Worthy', in *The Glasgow Herald*, 27th August.

50 Stewart, G. *Curiosities*, p.51.

51 Glasgow Chamber of Commerce Minutes. TD 1670/1/3. It is possible, if unlikely because of illness, that he attended after that date. There are some earlier occasions where his attendance is not recorded but where he was almost certainly present, most notably 9th January 1787 where he was re-elected as Deputy Chairman and 25th April 1787 when he was asked to join yet another committee. See GCC Minutes, TD 1670/1/1).

52 Glasgow Chamber of Commerce Minutes, TD 1670/1/1, 17th Dec, 1783; 7th Mar 1786. See also Brown, A. (1795-7) *History of Glasgow and of Paisley, Greenock, and Port-Glasgow, comprehending the ecclesiastical and civil history of these places, from the earliest accounts to the present time: and including an account of their population, commerce, manufactures, arts, and agriculture*, 2 vols. (1795, 1797) Glasgow: W. Paton. Vol. 2, p.279.

53 Glasgow Chamber of Commerce Minutes, TD 1670/1/1, 13th April 1784.

54 Ibid.

55 Ibid., 10th January & 14th February, 1786.

56 Donnachie, I. and Hewitt, G. (1993) *Historic New Lanark*. Edinburgh: E.U.P., p.42.

57 Ibid.

58 Reid, R. *Glasgow*, Vol. II, p.46.

59 Ibid.

60 Ibid., p.48.

61 Ibid.

62 Reid, R., *Glasgow*, Vol. III, p.350.

63 Ibid, p.349.

64 Eyre-Todd, G. (1934) *History of Glasgow*, Vol. III, p.329.

65 Reid, R., *Glasgow*, Vol. III, p.346.

66 Minute Book of the Board of the Green Cloth, p.116 – in Eyre-Todd, G. *Glasgow*, Vol. III, pp.313–4.

67 Stewart, G. *Curiosities*, p.50.

68 Liddell, A. (1854b) *Memoir*, p.163.

Chapter 3:
Merchant Adventurers:
Dale, Arkwright and Dempster

At this critical stage in his career, Dale was associated with Richard Arkwright, the leading pioneer of the British cotton industry. Arkwright's contribution to spinning industry and to the early Industrial Revolution is inestimable. Brown refers to him as *'our father of the art'* and Robert Dale Owen was very clear about Arkwright's contribution:

> *It had not entered into the heart of man to conceive the physical results that were to follow a contrivance simple almost to commonplace: consisting, substantially, in the substitution of rollers, driven by machinery, for the human hand. That invention determined the fate of nations.*[1]

Arkwright, a colourful and controversial figure, six years older than Dale, was born in Preston, youngest son in a large and poor family. Interestingly, poverty and the lack of formal education were significant factors in Arkwright's life and motivated him to seek (and achieve) great wealth and fame, almost by way of compensation. Even in later life, at the age of 50, he was acutely conscious of his lack of formal grammar and writing skills and began to spend two hours a day working on these.[2] However, what he lacked in writing skills, he more than compensated for in entrepreneurial skills and he was one of the richest men in England when he died in 1792.

Printed by Jos.ᵖʰ Wright, R.A.   Engraved by J. Jenkins.

SIR RICHARD ARKWRIGHT.

His business career began inauspiciously enough as a Bolton barber and wig-maker, then a publican but he *'always seemed to have something better in view'*.[3] He had always had a fascination for machines and how things worked and *'his genius for mechanics was observed*'.[4] At the age of 36 he gave up his business to pursue his interest in a roller spinning machine, known a year or two later as a '*water frame*'.

Financed by John Smalley, a local merchant, Arkwright moved from Lancashire to Nottingham with his new assistant, John Kay, a clockmaker, and patented his version of the roller-spinning machine in 1769 – just as Hargreaves' 'spinning jenny' was attracting unwanted attention from workers who felt threatened by such mechanisation.[5] Arkwright's idea of a rolling machine, however, was not entirely new. Lewis Paul had taken out a patent for a similar machine 31 years earlier. Also, it is argued that John Kay, when he constructed the machine from wood, was using a design stolen from his original employer, Thomas Highs of Leigh. In any case, it is now widely accepted that even if Arkwright did use Highs' designs (and Highs never patented them) he improved them to such an extent that they hardly resembled the models of Highs, and Arkwright, unlike Highs, actually produced a working machine.

Arkwright's machine of 1769 is illustrated below. The principle is that cardings of cotton are drawn out by a number of pairs of rollers placed horizontally and Arkwright was later to claim that he had also patented the carding process. The carding is fed between the first pair of rollers to compress it and draw it out and then it is fed through another pair of rollers which are revolving faster than the first pair. This draws out the sliver even further and makes it finer. The next pair of rollers are revolving even faster, and so the cotton becomes longer and firmer as it passes through each pair. Finally, the sliver is twisted and wound on to a bobbin, the whole process being water-powered or horse-powered.[6] Cotton warps of considerable strength were made and women and children could attend the machines, since no physical force was required in the production process.

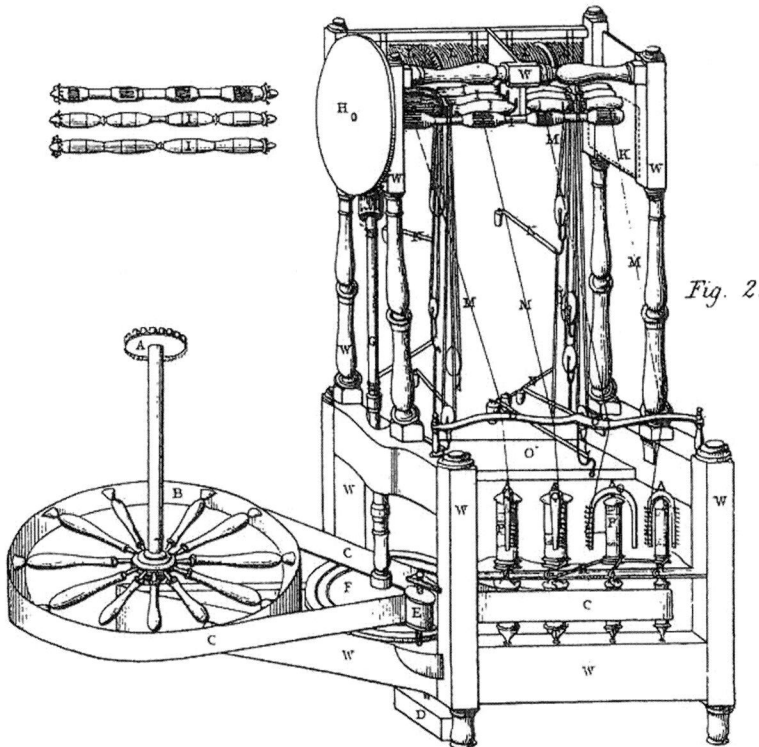

Sir Richard Arkwright's Spinning Machine.
Patent 1769.

Fig. 2.

Financed by Samuel Need, Arkwright entered into partnership with Jedediah Strutt (1726-1797) of Derby in Strutt's stocking factory in Nottingham and shortly thereafter in another partnership with Strutt in the Cromford Mill in Derbyshire, where an enlarged version of the machine which came to be known as the "water frame" was put into service. Within six years another mill had been built at Cromford and one at Belper. This partnership lasted for a number of years until Strutt continued on his own at Belper and Arkwright retained the hugely profitable Cromford mills, although they remained partners in Birkacre Mill in Chorley, Lancashire. By this time, Hargreaves had improved his original version of his "spinning jenny" (illustrated below).

THE SPINNING JENNY.

Engraved by T.E.Nicholson.

Hargreaves' Spinning Jenny

Here, the spindles are in a vertical position and the cardings are clasped between two horizontal bars of wood while the cotton is drawn out, lengthened and spun into yarn. Hargreaves' machine made weft and Arkwright's made warp, so the machines were not in conflict with each other. However, Hargreaves' machine multiplied the spinner's production by eight then later sixteen, twenty and 30 times, even from relatively small machines which could be gathered together in to jenny factories, known in Scotland as 'jeanie sheds'. Unsurprisingly, these machines were felt by many workers to be a threat to jobs and there were riots, particularly in Lancashire, during this period and Crompton's 'mule' jenny, invented in 1779, which was a combination of water frame and Spinning Jenny with wheeled carriages, only added to the workers' fears.

Arkwright, already a wealthy man, was by this time a particular target for the rioters. Despite troops being called in, Birkacre Mill was attacked and destroyed and Arkwright made preparations for the defence of Cromford. In the event, Cromford was not attacked but Arkwright's relentless pursuit of profit from his patents prolonged the tension and further alienated him from his fellow cotton spinners. Arkwright wished to claim ownership of the entire means of production by patenting everything as his own invention and his own property. Anyone who wished to spin cotton would be required to do so under licence, the price of which would be determined by Arkwright. It has even been suggested that he was so driven by profit that he contrived a '*vast and daring scheme*' to buy up all the world's cotton and monopolise the entire market.[7] It was certainly a lucrative business. It was claimed a few years later that Arkwright:

'...owned or had part interest in eleven different 'Engines', some consisting of 4,000 spindles, some working for 23 hours a day ... sales were described as being not less than £12,000 to £15,000 per month and his annual profits were said to exceed £40,000 in some years. Some bought the privilege of using his patent at £7 per spindle, others contended it 'and foiled him at law'.[8]

It is possible that Arkwright might have planned to expand into Scotland at some stage in any event but what brought matters to a head and persuaded him to look north as a possible base for expansion were his legal battles with English factory owners who believed (with some justification) that they were being exploited by a ruthless parvenu and who were preparing to mount a huge campaign against him.

This situation had been brought about largely because of two Arkwright patents in 1775. The first of these was his carding patent where cotton was carded by a series of comb-like instruments. Arkwright laid claim to this process but it may be that Hargreaves was the original inventor of this machine. (Lewis Paul had also invented a machine for carding cotton using rollers.) Arkwright's second patent of that year was for a series of machines – carding, drawing and roving (twisting). He claimed to be the sole inventor of the entire spinning process. (There may be some justification for this, given that he was the first to combine the various ideas into a commercially viable process.) Interestingly, this patent was never registered in Scotland – an 'oversight' on his part which would assist those who wished to steal his designs – another reason why Arkwright may have wished to keep a close eye on cotton spinning in Scotland.[9]

If Arkwright could legally enforce all three of his patents, he would virtually 'own' the whole cotton spinning process. Naturally, the other cotton spinners stood to lose by this, and took action against him. In a court action in 1775, the Lancashire spinners won their case against Arkwright, on the basis that he may have copied his inventions from Thomas Highs.[10] Undaunted, Arkwright asked Parliament in 1781 to support his combined patents but failed again and was equally unsuccessful in a subsequent court battle. Arkwright was furious. Matthew Bolton is reported as saying to Watt of Arkwright:

...He swears he will take the cotton spinning abroad and that he will ruin those Manchester rascals he has been the making of...[11]

In 1783, he approached Parliament again but he underestimated the influence of the Manchester merchants in the House and met with little success. Things finally came to a head in 1785, when the stakes were at their highest. For more than four years the situation had been in the balance, during which period some £150,000 had been spent building cotton mills 'for the better supply of the manufactures'.[12] This had enabled the manufacturers to expand their businesses considerably. Were they to lose their case, disaster would surely follow.

A few days later, The Evening Post carried the story of a momentous victory:

...when after a full hearing of nine hours, in which gentlemen of the first mechanical knowledge in this kingdom were examined and the whole process of Mr. Arkwright's very ingenious and useful invention was fully explained, the jury, without going out of court, brought in a verdict for Mr. Arkwright.[13]

Success, however, was short-lived. The Lancashire merchants, particularly the Manchester merchants, mobilised quickly and their appeal, 'a cause of the utmost importance to the town of Manchester' was heard in June that year:

It was objected to as not being a new invention; as not being his invention; as not being accompanied by a sufficient specification; and if a new invention, and if his own invention, as being inconvenient and injurious to his Majesty's subjects, and therefore contrary to the true nature of a patent.[14]

To Arkwright's fury, the court found against him and the patent was declared void.[15] Arkwright intended to appeal to the House of Lords but his application for a new trial was thrown out and he was finally forced to admit defeat.[16] The protracted process had finally come to an end but he had been far from idle or isolated during those years. The business at Cromford had continued to expand and Arkwright, '*being of an irritable temperament*', became increasingly resentful of the treatment he was subjected to by the English manufacturers during these battles '*and exerted himself to raise up a successful rivalry to Lancashire*'.[17]

He therefore '*favoured the Scottish spinners as much as possible*' and was certainly receptive to the idea that Scotland might become an important source of income, particularly if the patent battles were ultimately to be lost in England.[18] In any event, Scottish spinners had not been slow to pick up on Arkwright's technology and his influence on the Scottish cotton spinning industry was well-established from the beginning. Scotland's first cotton mill in Penicuik had been built under the direction of John Hacket, a former employee of Arkwright's and an acquaintance of James Hargreaves.[19] Rothesay, another early cotton mill '*soon came to rely on Arkwright's workmen versed in machine-making*'.[20] In Renfrewshire in 1782, '*the art of cotton spinning according to Sir Richard Arkwright's method*' was introduced into a new cotton mill in Johnstone, near Paisley.[21] Indeed, most of the new mills in Renfrewshire in the 1780s (Busby, Dovecotehall, Gateside, Crofthead, Bridge of Weir) were what Nisbet refers to as '*Arkwright mills*'.[22] Further, Nisbet argues that the Renfrewshire mill industry formed a large and varied sector, which in terms of its size and composition was far more important than New Lanark, Catrine, Stanley and Deanston.[23]

The Buchanan brothers, three of whom were intimate acquaintances of Arkwright, had been involved in the cotton industry since 1776 and acted as agents for the sale of Arkwright's yarn in Glasgow – a fact certainly not unknown to David Dale. Dale would also have known the Buchanans as 'English Merchants' – a term given to yarn dealers in the city who dealt with merchants from south of the Border. The Buchanan family were important for Arkwright and he was later to take Archibald Buchanan, the youngest of the brothers, under his wing and provide full training for him in Cromford, even allowing him to stay in his family home. Workers and managers from Arkwright's mills were in great demand and it was quite common for Scottish mill owners (such as James Kenyon in Rothesay) to 'poach' staff from Arkwright's English mills.[24] Such staff were in demand because they brought a skill set (and some of the trade secrets) with them from the most successful mills in Britain. Arkwright was certainly aware of the poaching problem and attempted (unsuccessfully) to have both Penicuik and Rothesay mills closed for infringing his patent.[25] He was therefore forced into accepting that the only way to deal with the poaching issue was to offer official training on payment of a licence fee. This fee, however, was subsequently abandoned as his involvement in the Scottish cotton industry increased.

The conditions were right for Arkwright to take a more sustained and focused involvement in the Scottish cotton industry. He was having major difficulties in England; the patent situation was still unresolved; his workers and his techniques were already in use in Scotland and the country offered great potential, not only to make money but in doing so to hit back at what he saw as his tormentors in Manchester.

In Glasgow, David Dale would have been well aware of Arkwright's reputation as a successful businessman and his difficulties in England. The papers were full of Arkwright's battles in the courts and Dale, as a wealthy yarn dealer in the city, was well connected to other brokers and dealers, including the Buchanans and Monteiths – all of whom were keeping a close eye on developments. If Arkwright could be encouraged to establish mills in Scotland, with Scottish partners, then the prospects were potentially excellent. Even if the patent issue were to be resolved in Arkwright's favour, having him as a business partner offered the possibility of much reduced (or non-existent) licence fees.

What was needed was a catalyst to bring Arkwright to Scotland as a potential partner in the spinning industry and to facilitate the establishment of such partnerships – from which profits could be made, jobs could be created, and from which all could benefit. If more mills could be established in rural areas, it could also provide an income source for a population under pressure and one where poverty and mass emigration were becoming major causes for concern.

George Dempster (1732–1818) was such a catalyst. Dempster, a lawyer and Member of Parliament for Perth Burghs 1761–1790, is an interesting and important, if relatively neglected, figure in Scottish history.[26]

Born in Dundee, educated at St. Andrews University, owner of the Dunnichen estate in Angus and, later, of the Skibo and Polrossie estates in Sutherland (where he was to become involved with Dale in the Spinningdale mill); friend of Henry Dundas, James Boswell, Thomas Telford and Adam Fergusson, Dempster was a huge supporter of the cotton industry. Similarly, he supported the creation of planned villages (including his own project at Letham on his Dunnichen estate), cotton mill communities, fishery communities and the building of roads, lighthouses and harbours in northern Scotland.

In the 1780s, Dempster was a leading member of the newly-formed British Fisheries Society, alongside notable figures such as the Duke of Argyll, Lord Breadalbane, Sir Adam Fergusson, Lord Gower, Francis Mackenzie (later Earl of Seaforth) and various sheriffs and army captains. In time, the efforts of 'improving lairds' and nobleman in ventures such as the Fisheries Society were supplemented by those of less noble birth, e.g. factors, surveyors and engineers who were able to improve the infrastructure in building turnpike roads and planning and building mills on the estates. The early members of the Fisheries Society were joined in their efforts by representatives of the new merchant class such as David Dale, George Macintosh and George Dempster.

George Dempster of Dunnichen & Skibo (1732–1818). Dundee City Council (Dundee's Art Galleries & Museums).

Dempster was one of the most influential members of the Society and by 1786 was exploring the possibility of building a harbour at the mouth of the Dornoch Firth.[27] Three years later, the directors were discussing the possibility of five new towns in addition to Stornoway and Fort William.[28] Later, new communities were established in Tobermory, Ullapool and Pultneytown (near Wick). Although Dempster's direct involvement waned after his retirement from Parliament in 1790, he devoted the remainder of his life to improving the lot of his workers and tenants on his own estates in Angus and Sutherland.

Dempster talked of '*cultivating the Highlands and multiplying its valuable inhabitants*', not just by establishing new ports with harbours and lighthouses and new towns on the coast but also by building new roads, bridges and canals.[29] Thomas Telford, writing in 1808, noted that Dempster's plans for the north of Scotland, which included spinning mills, crop cultivation, sheep pastures and '*industrious fishermen*', were not what he called '*romantic schemes*', but '*the natural progress of improvement for which the country is now prepared*'.[30] These projects required only '*the fostering hand of a wise and humane legislature and the sincere coordination of the landowners in the county*'.[31] In addition, there is clear evidence of Dempster's attempts to eradicate the feudal nature of land ownership on his own estates and to put land under the administration of commissioners to direct labour.[32] The tenants in his experimental village of Letham had security of tenure and managed their own affairs through a '*Constitution*' and an elected community. Dempster drew up laws '*for the happy government of this village*' and there was a brief attempt at something similar in Spinningdale.[33] Planned villages, jobs, good roads and well-managed estates were all designed to improve conditions in the Highlands and, in particular, to stem the tide of emigration – a cause which he (like Dale) espoused throughout this life:

> I am persuaded planning a town at each place and lotting it out for building purposes will induce the inhabitants to remain at home and become settlers in our new towns.[34]

Dempster was known as '*the Patriot of the North*' and *The Caledonian Mercury* often referred to him in glowing terms as a man who '*set a noble example, well worthy of imitation*' by giving every encouragement to his estate tenants, '*assisting them in improving and cultivating the ground and introducing trade and manufactures*'.[35] On a journey home from Parliament in 1783, Dempster and his wife broke their journey in Matlock and, impressed by the scenery, decided to stay for a few days:

> In the course of a forenoon's ride, I discovered, in a romantic valley, a palace of a most enormous size, having, at least, a score of windows of a row, and five or six stories in height. This was Sir Richard Arkwright's (then Mr. Arkwright) cotton-mills. One of our mess-mates being known to the owner, obtained his permission to see this stupendous work. After admiring everything I saw, I rode up to Mr. Arkwright's house – knocked at the door. He answered it himself, and told me who he was. I said my curiosity could not be fully gratified, without seeing the head from whence the mill had sprung. Some business brought him soon after to London. He conceived I had been useful to him; and offered to assist me in establishing a cotton-mill in Scotland, by holding a share of one, and instructing the people. Private business carried him the following summer to Scotland...[36]

It is highly unlikely that Dempster stopped off in Matlock and met Arkwright by chance. It is equally unlikely that Arkwright agreed to come to Scotland merely at the suggestion of Dempster. Both had much to gain. Dempster clearly had plans to involve Arkwright in as many business ventures as he could (including a spinning concern in Stanley, Perthshire) and Arkwright was keen to expand his business. From Arkwright's point of view, Dempster was clearly a man of substance, well-connected in the towns and burghs of Scotland and a potential supporter in Parliament. It is also likely that Dempster would make it known to Arkwright that any visit would involve great celebrations and tributes, including the freedom of various cities and burghs – all of which would certainly appeal to Arkwright.

Thus it was that on 29th September, 1784, Arkwright visited Paisley on the first part of a Scottish 'tour' which had been arranged by Dempster who, at the time of the Paisley visit, was '*on an excursion through North Britain to procure further information relative to the manufactures, fisheries, canals etc. of Scotland, which have, by means of this patriotic gentleman, become the object of parliamentary attention*'.[37] Arkwright was '*made and created a 'Free Burgess by the Magistrates and the Town Council' ... for his good deeds done and to be done for the well and the utility of the Burgh*'.[38] A few days later, Arkwright was in Glasgow (with Dempster), where they were entertained by Pat Colquhoun, the Lord Provost, and Magistrates in the Town Hall and Arkwright was given the freedom of the city – '*Mr. Dempster having received that honour on a former visit*'.[39] This was followed by a dinner:

> They were invited to dine with the Lord Provost at Kelvin Grove on Saturday. The manufacturers of Anderston, through which they had to pass, in order to testify their gratitude to Mr. Dempster, the patron of manufacturers in Scotland, and their esteem for Mr. Arkwright, assembled their workmen to receive them. On their arrival, the populace wanted to unyoke the horses from Mr. Dempster's carriage, in order to draw him to Kelvin Grove. This honour he declined, as it has been his uniform wish and practice to lead his countrymen to freedom, rather than put them under the yoke. Mr. Arkwright however was forced to comply with their offer, and the cavalcade proceeded, in a triumphant manner, to the Lord Provost's country seat.[40]

Great celebrations ensued and there was a grand dinner, followed by speeches. As a city magistrate, a friend and colleague of Colquhoun's, as a leading member of the Chamber of Commerce and as a businessman in his own right, Dale would certainly have been present. After the dinner:

> The inhabitants of Anderston, to testify their joy still further, lighted up bonfires, and prepared flambeaux to accompany them with in the evening upon their return to this city ... The procession entered about half past eight, which consisted of five carriages; in the first the Lord Provost, who was followed by Mr. Dempster in the second; his carriage was preceeded [sic] by a large transparent gauze-lanthorn, raised upon the top of a pole, inscribed with these words, on the front and back, 'The Patriot of his Country'. On the sides, 'The Guardians of our Manufactures'. The other carriages were taken up by the Lord Advocate, Member of Parliament for this city, &c. Mr. Arkwright, Colonel Campbell of the 9th Regiment, &c. In this manner they proceeded to the Saracen's Head, where they alighted, amidst the acclamations of many hundreds of the inhabitants.[41]

Arkwright remained in Glasgow for the weekend following the dinner in Kelvingrove and was also given 'an elegant entertainment in the Tontine by the Chamber of Commerce and Manufacturers of the City' where he must have met Dale once more and where he was also introduced to a number of other prominent yarn merchants in Glasgow – including James Monteith, William Gillespie, the McIlquhan brothers and 'a long list of wee Anderston corks' (linen dealers).[42] Also, when in Glasgow, Arkwright is reported to have made his famous gibe about finding 'a razor in Scotland to shave Manchester'.[43]

The reception in Glasgow was typical of the welcome Arkwright was to receive throughout his trip and it is important to emphasise how different this welcome was from anything he might have expected in England at the time. On a personal level, Dempster was reported to have been 'quite in raptures' with Arkwright, considering him to be a man whose great ingenuity had brought the country to 'rapid perfection in the cotton manufactory'.[44] Dempster anticipated the rapid expansion of 'that great invention' in Scotland, 'under the vast benefits from which millions yet unborn are to participate'.[45]

Dempster's 'rapture' seems to have been echoed by workers and manufacturers across the country and it is clear that he was considered to be something of a heroic figure who offered work and prosperity to all. The Scottish cotton industry could at last begin to compete with Manchester:

> This gentleman is justly intitled (sic) to be honoured as the parent of our muslin manufactory in this country which is now making rapid progress and hopes, in a short time, we shall carry this branch to high perfection, and vie with the town of Manchester in the cotton manufactories.[46]

Similarly, he was 'justly intitled' to the 'highest marks of respect this country can show him' and any honours or tributes which might be awarded by a grateful populace were almost insufficient for such a great man. Hence the Freedom of the Burgh of Glasgow was conferred as 'a small tribute to his great merit', marking the 'strongest marks of gratitude of the people'.[47]

The tour continued in this vein. On Monday 4th October, Arkwright visited the Royal Burgh of Lanark and received the honour of a Burgess ticket from the authorities there. Crucially, Dale must have been present because both men travelled from the town down the steep hill to the river below and inspected the site of what was to become New Lanark. Again, this was not mere chance. Dale was exploring the possibility of a partnership with Arkwright, who in turn was keen to develop his interests in Scotland. It is very likely that Dempster was also present as one of the 'principal people' who had requested the visit to the site because he too was to become involved in the early partnership arrangements of New Lanark. Arkwright is reported to have been:

> ...astonished at the advantages desirable from the Falls of Clyde and exultingly said that Lanark would probably in time become the Manchester of Scotland; as no place he had ever seen afforded better situations or more ample streams of water for cotton machinery.[48]

For the moment, however, the project had to wait. Arkwright had other people to see across Scotland. He travelled from Lanark to Donside Mills in Woodside, near Aberdeen and met Alex Milne, a partner in Barron & Co., linen bleachers. There was talk of a spinning mill on the River Don and Arkwright offered training in Cromford for work people '*in the erection and management of machinery and the manufacture of cotton*'.[49]

From there, Arkwright travelled south to Perth where he was given the freedom of the city on 27th October. He was already involved in a plan to build cotton mills at Stanley, seven miles north of the city. Two months prior to Arkwright's Scottish trip, Dempster had persuaded him to sign a deal with the Duke of Atholl, some Perth merchants and Dempster himself, to feu seven acres of land at Stanley to build a mill.[50] Shortly thereafter, 40-50 '*North Britons*' arrived in Cromford for training, including Andrew Keay, Stanley's first manager.[51] The contract was formalised a year later and Dale was one of the witnesses, by which time building work was almost completed on the first mill at New Lanark which was to become the single biggest and most influential cotton spinning community in Great Britain.

However, even before the Scottish tour was concluded, the news about a possible cotton spinning venture in New Lanark was beginning to spread far and wide. One newspaper confidently (if not entirely accurately) reported that the site surpassed anything that Arkwright had ever seen and that he had been offered the estate '*upon which the situation is, value £10,000, provided he will settle upon it and erect machinery for 10,000 spindles*'.[52]

There was a rather more reliable piece in *The Gazeteer & New Daily Advertiser* of 19th October:

> *We are informed that a most extensive cotton manufactory is to be erected in the immediate neighbourhood of Lanark, in Scotland. The partners in this Company are said to be George Dempster, Esq; Richard Arkwright, Esq; of Cromford in Derbyshire, who is just now on a tour through Scotland with Mr. Dempster and an eminent merchant in Glasgow.*[53]

The '*eminent merchant*' was, of course, David Dale.

References: Chapter 3

1   Owen, R.D. (1874) *Threading My Way: Twenty Seven Years of Autobiography*. New York: Carleton & Co., p.31.
2   Fitton, R.S. (1989) *The Arkwrights: Spinners of Fortune*. Manchester: M.U.P., p.210.
3   Letter from Thos. Ridgeway to Richard Arkwright Jnr., 1799. See Fitton, R.S. and Wadsworth, A.P. (1958) *The Strutts and the Arkwrights 1758–1830. A Study of the Early Factory System*. Manchester: M.U.P., p.62.
4   Ibid.
5   The patent was registered in England in 1769 but not until 1771 in Scotland. See Nisbet, S.M. (2008) *The Rise of the Cotton Factory in Eighteenth-Century Renfrewshire*. British Archaeology Report, Series 464. Oxford: Alden Press, p.60.
6   See Baines, E. (1835) *History of the Cotton Manufacture in Great Britain*. London: Fisher., pp.120–198 for a full description of the process.
7   Baines, E. *History*, p.196., quoted in Fitton, R.S., *The Arkwrights*, p. 213.
8   Cooke, A.J. (ed) (1979) 'Richard Arkwright and the Scottish Cotton Industry', *Textile History*, X: 196–202., p.192, referring to Atholl MS Box 25, Panel IX, 'Considerations on the Cotton Manufacture'. Undated.
9   Nisbet, S.M. *The Rise of the Cotton Factory*, p.60.
10 Donnachie, I. (2000) *Robert Owen of New Lanark and New Harmony*. East Linton: Tuckwell Press, p.41.
11 Fitton, R.S. and Wadsworth, A.P. (1958) *The Strutts and the Arkwrights 1758–1830. A Study of the Early Factory System*. Manchester: M.U.P., p.84.
12 *The General Evening Post*, London, 12th–14th February 1785.
13 Ibid., 19th–22nd February.
14 *Whitehall Evening Post*, London. 25th–28th June 1785.
15 Ibid.
16 *The British Evening Post*, London. 7th–9th July 1785 and *The London Chronicle*, 10th–12th November 1785. Arkwright dreamed up a similar scheme to monopolise the wool spinning industry at half the normal cost, the remaining half of the profits being split between himself and 'the person whom he instructs in the business' but this also came to nothing. See Fitton & Wadsworth, *The Strutts and the Arkwrights*, pp.88–9.

17   Baines, *History*, p.193n.

18   Ibid.

19   Fitton, R.S. (1989) *The Arkwrights*, p.89.

20   Ibid., p.71.

21   Signet Library Paper 264/2 in Fitton, R.S. (1989) *The Arkwrights*, p.71.

22   Nisbet, S.M. *The Rise of Cotton Factory*, pp.63–4.

23   Ibid., p.65.

24   Cooke, A. (2010) *The Rise and Fall of the Scottish Cotton Industry, 1778–1914: The Secret Spring*. Manchester: M.U.P., p.30.

25   Ibid., pp.29–30. The Lord Advocate ruled as early as 1778 that Arkwright's patents did not apply in Scotland. This was relevant to his first 1769/71 patent but as already noted, his 1775 patents had not been registered in Scotland.

26   *The Glasgow Mercury*, 7th October 1784.

27   J. Gallie to George Dempster, December 1786. Dempster, G.S. *The Papers of George Soper Dempster*, 19 vols. MS Coll. 126. Thos. Fisher Rare Book Library, University of Toronto MSS. Also catalogued as *The Dempster Papers. A Collection of Letters & papers relating to George Dempster of Dunnichen*. 19 Vols. MS Coll. 126. Vol. 5. Accession No. 35462.

28   Dempster to Mackenzie of Seaforth, 25th May 1789. *Dempster Papers*. Vol. 2. Accession No. 35451.

29   Notes, 24th July 1808. *Dempster Papers*, Vol. 10. Accession No. 35458.

30   Thomas Telford to George Dempster's grand nephew, William Soper Dempster, 19th November 1805. *Dempster Papers*, Vol. 8. Accession No. 35456.

31   Ibid.

32   Notes, 24th July 1808. *Dempster Papers*, Vol. 10. Accession No. 35458. See also Cooke, A.J. (1995) 'Cotton and the Scottish Highland Clearances – Spinningdale, 1791–1806', *Textile History*, XXVI: 89–94, pp.89–90.

33   Fergusson, J. (ed) (1934) *Letters of George Dempster to Sir Adam Fergusson, 1756–1813*. MacMillan: London, p.203.

34   George Dempster to Sir Adam Fergusson, 8th April 1788 in Fergusson, J. (ed) (1934) *Letters of George Dempster*, p.188.

35   Brown, A. (1795–7) *History of Glasgow and of Paisley, Greenock, and Port-Glagow, comprehending the ecclesiastical and civil history of these places, from the earliest accounts to the present time: and including an account of their population, commerce, manufactures, arts, and agriculture*, 2 vols. (1795, 1797) Glasgow: W. Paton. Vol. 2, p.225 and *The Caledonian Mercury*, 20th October 1791.

36   Sinclair, J. (1831) *The Correspondence of the Rt Hon Sir John Sinclair, Bart.*, 2 vols. London: Colburn & Bentley. Vol. 1. pp.361–2. Dempster is writing many years later and mistakenly recalls these as events from 1796. However, 1783 is the correct date.

37   *The General Evening Post*, 12th–14th October 1784. This 'letter' appears in various forms in newspapers across the country.

38   Arkwright family MSS in Fitton, R.S. (1989) *The Arkwrights*, p.72.

39   *The Glasgow Mercury*, 7th October 1784.

40   Ibid.

41   Ibid.

42   *St. James' Chronicle or British Evening Post*, London, 12th–14th October 1784. See also Reid, R., *Glasgow*, Vol. III, p.302. It is worth noting that all of these men were already or were to become mill owners, e.g. Gillespie in Glasgow; the McIlwhams at Crosslee. Monteith later owned Pollokshaws, Woodside and Blantyre mills. See Nisbet, S.M. *The Rise of the Cotton Factory*, p.90.

43   Baines, *History*, p.193n.

44   *St. James Chronicle or British Evening Post*, 12th–14th October 1784.

45   Ibid.

46   *The Public Advertiser*. London, 12th–14th October 1784.

47   *St. James Chronicle or British Evening Post*, 12th–14th October 1784; *The General Evening Post*, London, 12th–14th October 1784.

48   Sinclair, J. (ed) (1791–99) *The Statistical Account of Scotland, 1791–99*, 21 vols. Vol. XV, p.46.

49   Morgan, P. (1886) Annals of Woodside & Newhills, Historical & Genealogical. Aberdeen. Cited in Fitton, R.S. (1989) *The Arkwrights*, p.75.

50   Cooke, A.J. (ed) (1979) 'Richard Arkwright and the Scottish Cotton Industry', *Textile History*, X: 196–202. pp.197–8.

51   *The Derby Mercury*, 12th May 1785. Vide infra, Chapter 4.

52   *St. James Chronicle or Brit Evening Post*, London, 12th–14th October 1784.

53   *The Gazeteer & New Daily Advertiser*. London, 19th October 1784.

Part 2
New Lanark

Chapter 4:
The Business of New Lanark

After Dale and Arkwright's visit to New Lanark, the latter, according to George Stewart, was '*so satisfied that he voluntary offered to become a principal partner in the speculation*'.[1] According to Stewart, land was cleared and building immediately begun, but owing to the difficulty in excavating a rocky hill that interfered with the necessary water supply, spinning did not commence until March 1786.[2]

In fact, however, the process was rather more complex and protracted. The land around the Burgh of Lanark (known as Lanark Moor), had been a potential but under-exploited source of revenue for the local council for some years and they were keen to sell as much of it as possible. Part of the Bankhead land to the south of the Burgh had been sold in 1779 to Robert McQueen, Lord Braxfield, the Lord Justice Clerk. He was subsequently better known, perhaps, by the soubriquet '*the hanging judge*' because of his ferocious treatment of anyone remotely suspected of 'sedition' and he played a central role in the trial of Thomas Muir. He was highly regarded by the Council in Lanark and was a close ally of Henry Dundas (later Lord Melville), who was variously the Lord Advocate, the Home Secretary, the Minister for War and the Keeper of the Privy Seal of Scotland. Braxfield was the Government's '*chief agent in extirpating rebellious thoughts & actions throughout the country*'.[3]

In 1784 Dale feued the land at the Well of Spaw (the site of New Lanark) from Lord Braxfield, '*who influenced alone by the good of his country, very frankly feued the site to the benevolent Mr. David Dale at a very moderate feu duty*', although it is not clear whether this happened before or after Arkwright's October visit.[4] As Hume has pointed out, Braxfield did well out of the deal as the land had little or no agricultural value and the annual income of £32. 10s. was a valuable addition to his income. In addition, Dale paid a feu duty of £17. 7s. 8d. to the Incorporation of Shoemakers of Lanark who owned the part of the land on which village houses were to be built.[5] Dale was also '*high in favour with the Council, who refused him nothing*' and had little difficulty two years later persuading Provost Bannatyne that the Council should sell him the remaining Bankhead land and part of the Crosslaw land to the east of New Lanark.[6]

Liddell points out, however, that some of the other landed proprietors in the area had reservations about their privacy being invaded by a '*multitude of workpeople ... and more especially that fresh burdens would be entailed upon them for the support of the poor*'.[7]

The scene appeared to be set. Dempster and Arkwright had found a suitable partner in David Dale (and vice-versa) and the site in the Lanark valley presented a great opportunity, although it posed some difficulties as far as building work was concerned. William Lockhart's return for the *Statistical Account* refers to 'the romantic rocks and woods of Braxfield' but later in the same account he describes it thus:

> This spot of ground was at that period almost a mere morass, situated in a hollow den, and of difficult access. Its only recommendation was the very powerful command of water that the Clyde could be made to afford it; in other respects, the distance from Glasgow and the badness of the roads were rather unfavourable.[8]

In similar vein, he notes that there were some '*obstacles to manufactures*', including the undeveloped state of the local countryside and, in particular, '*the distance that raw materials are to be carried and the badness of the roads*'.[9] This was especially true of the Lanark–Glasgow road but he was sure that the situation would be improved '*by a new road now forming*' which was due to open in spring of 1794 which would '*form one of the most beautiful and romantic roads in Scotland*'.[10]

In reality, all of this was true. The spot was possessed of natural beauty but considerable feats of engineering would be required to build a working cotton mill there. Expansion could potentially be limited by the steep hills of the valley. The principal attraction was certainly the water power but the main Falls of Clyde were some distance from the proposed mill site and, in any event, the force of the water in the Falls was excessive and was ultimately not utilised to anything like its full capacity, given that Dale used the water from the much smaller rapids (Dundaff Linn) nearby. It has been argued that this was a missed opportunity and that, if Dale had used a flatter site and managed his water power better, the original ambition of New Lanark becoming the Manchester of Scotland may well have succeeded.[11]

However, the mills did become enormously successful, perhaps indicating that the management of the water power was entirely sufficient for purpose and much of New Lanark's eventual success was due to 'the genius and spirited industry' of William Kelly, Dale's talented manager and something of an engineer in his own right.[12] His trade was given as clockmaker and, as Donnachie & Hewitt point out, clockmakers were highly skilled craftsmen regularly employed in the cotton industry to build and repair complex machinery. Arkwright, for example, was quick to employ clockmaker John Kay in Cromford to develop the concept of the water-frame.[13] In similar vein, the Statistical Account reported a few years later in 1793 that Kelly had already invented and patented 'a new method of erecting the great gear or large machinery ... so as to require one fourth of less water than commonly needed.'[14]

Lanark itself, as a prosperous merchant Burgh, had a reasonable supply of skilled labour such as weavers, spinners, stocking makers, stonemasons, clockmakers and the like.[15] While Arkwright was involved in bitter and personal feuds with merchants and tradesmen all over the north of England, there were few such problems in the Lanark area. Dale was not in dispute with anyone and looked to the town for workers, although it is unlikely at this stage that he took into full consideration the fact that the labour force were not used to factory-style production methods and the fact that a small town could never hope to supply the large number of workers which would ultimately be needed for four substantial spinning mills.[16]

News of the partnership was spreading fast. Arkwright's tour with Dempster had generated a great deal of public interest and news of the proposed ventures in Lanark and Perth was not long in reaching England. In February 1785, the Manchester Mercury reported 'very great preparations making in Scotland by Mr. Arkwright, joined by several of the most conspicuous in the landed & commercial interests of that kingdom'.[17] In the same month, the following appeared in The Nottingham Journal:

> We hear that a very large cotton works are going to be erected at Glasgow, Perth and Lanark under the patronage of Messrs Dempster and Arkwright and some capital merchants and manufacturers of that kingdom and that every effort to complete the same will be made this Spring.[18]

According to the Statistical Account, work on the first mill building in New Lanark began in April 1785. The construction process was far from easy, given the marshy ground. 'Piles were driven in for a resting place to the stones and it was a considerable time before the workmen could find sure footing'.[19] A lade was also required and, after agreeing to pay local landowner Sir John Lockhart Ross £5 annual rent, 'a subteraneous (sic) passage of near 100 yards in length was formed through a rocky hill for the purpose of an aqueduct to it.'[20]

The construction of the aqueduct was considered at the time to be 'bordering on something superhuman'.[21] Local stone was used for construction and an embankment erected to provide a level site. Although there is no extant information on the first mill building, it is known that it was built at the northern end of the site, 'athwart the lade, with the tailrace discharging directly into the river'.[22] Hume suggests that it was a wooden-floored building (possibly with wooden supporting columns), probably four or five storeys high, with the waterwheel(s) situated at the centre of the building, 'either over-shot or high breast'.[23]

Arkwright, perhaps buoyed by his (short-lived) success in the English courts in February of that year, returned to New Lanark to discuss progress with Dale. It is likely that he also wished to see Dempster about the Stanley venture and to arrange the initial training of workers who had already been hired. Thus it was that a group of eleven men and fifteen boys were sent from New Lanark 'in complete dresses of brown cloth with red collars to their coats' to be trained in Arkwright's Cromford mills.[24] Appendix 3 lists the names of those involved. When the mills in New Lanark were ready, the boys were brought home.[25] At the same time (May 1785), a larger group was sent from Stanley for the same purpose. This group may also have included trainees from Deanston, where Arkwright's 'intimate acquaintances', the Buchanans, were setting up their cotton mills.[26] The local paper records the scene in Cromford:

... between 40 and 50 North Britons, with Bagpipes and other Music playing, arrived at Cromford ... from Perth, in Scotland. These industrious fellows left the Place on account of the Scarcity of Work, were taken into the Service of Richard Arkwright Esq; in his Cotton Mills and other extensive Works, entered into Present Pay, and provided with good Quarters. They appeared highly pleased with the Reception they met with, and had a Dance in the Evening to congratulate each other on the Performance of so long a journey.[27]

There may also have been a third reason for Arkwright's visit. His court victory in February (subsequently reversed in July) meant that English manufacturers had only two escape routes if they wished to avoid paying Arkwright vast sums in fees. One was to set up in Scotland, where Arkwright's patents did not yet apply (or where the application was limited or in dispute). Arkwright, however, was evidently intent on expanding north of the Border. He was now in a very commanding position in relation to a future cotton spinning industry in Scotland, thwarting any attempts by English merchants to establish there. The other opportunity open to the English was to set up in Ireland, where there were no restrictions.[28] It would seem that Arkwright had plans to get there first, if newspaper gossip was to be believed:

We understand that Messrs Arkwright, Dempster & Co. mean, in consequence of the late decision in favour of their machines ... to commence an extensive cotton manufactory in Ireland. One of the partners in the house is actually set off for that kingdom.[29]

In fact, Dempster was the only New Lanark partner to visit Ireland at this time and his reasons were more personal than commercial – namely *'to solicit the restoration of his brother's ship, The Ganges'*.[30] Spinning began in New Lanark in March 1786 and the following month, Dale took out an insurance policy with the Sun fire insurance company for £4,800.[31]

However, that year also saw Arkwright's sudden decision to leave the New Lanark partnership and the beginning of his withdrawal from direct involvement in Scottish spinning. He withdrew from the Stanley venture in February 1787, only fourteen months after Dale had witnessed his signature as a partner – and just as it was beginning to show a profit.[32] The reasons for this change of heart are not entirely clear. As far as New Lanark is concerned, there is an oft-quoted apocryphal account of an argument between Dale and Arkwright over the siting of the bell tower in the village. According to the story passed down to Robert Dale Owen via his father and John Wright, Robert Owen's *'confidential clerk'*, Arkwright took exception to the position of the wooden cupola which contained the factory bell.

At least three buildings and possibly five had been built by 1785-76. There were two houses, one thatched and the other slated (and valued by the Sun Insurance Co. at £100 and £200 respectively).[33] It is not clear whether these were the same two buildings as the two fine (although small) houses which were built – one for the managers and one as a summer residence for the Dale family.

In addition, it is alleged that it was the construction of Mill No. 1 which caused the argument between Arkwright and Dale. Much to Arkwright's irritation, apparently, Dale had sited the cupola and bell at the end of the building. Arkwright argued that it should have been sited over the middle of the building, although no reason is given for this opinion.[34] (In fact, the reverse is more likely. The belfries in Arkwright's other mills in Cromford and Stanley were sited on the end gable and we already know that Dale was attracted to the architectural symmetry of Robert and James Adam.) A brief but ill-tempered quarrel broke out, the result of which was that the partnership was allegedly dissolved that very evening.[35] The tale is described by Robert Dale Owen as an anecdote but it is one which has survived for a very long time. At first sight, it seems highly unlikely. And yet:

If such an issue in so important a matter seem strange, it was yet natural enough in the case of men born and circumstanced as these men had been. Successful strugglers both, through difficulty and opposition up to great success, accustomed as both had been, from their youth to take their own way and to find that way the fortunate one, they had become unused to contradiction. Men of strong, untrained energy, they had grown to be self-willed, even in petty things.[36]

It is entirely possible that the two men quarrelled about something, although perhaps not the bellcote. Arkwright was certainly known to be impetuous and frequently aggressive and ill-mannered.[37] His parsimony was legendary and he fell out with tax people, architects and even his first wife, '*from whom he separated because of her opposition to his schemes*'.[38] David Dale, universally known for his kindness and philanthropy and described in hindsight by Robert Owen as '*one of the most liberal, conscientious, benevolent and kind-hearted men*' he had ever met, could occasionally take a very strong line with partners and could be stubborn at times.[39] Owen found Dale at first to be cold and distant, with very strongly held views.[40] Much later, when family members tried to have Dale sign a letter regarding legacies for his sisters-in-law, he '*was very firm and decided not to sign it*', believing it to be unnecessary. In fact, '*the more Mr. Dale was solicited, the more unwilling he became to accede*'.[41]

John Winning's 1818 watercolour shows the offending cupola squarely in the middle of the building.
New Lanark, *c*.1818. (J.R. Hume/New Lanark Trust)

While an argument between Arkwright and Dale is entirely possible, it is probable that there were other reasons for the dissolution of the partnership at this early stage. The vexed question of patents and licences was finally resolved in summer 1786 when the English courts finally found against Arkwright. Dale therefore no longer needed Arkwright as an insurance policy (if he ever really did, given that Arkwright's patents were not fully enforceable in Scotland). According to one source, Dale had saved money to buy exclusive rights to use Arkwright's machines in Scotland and releasing Arkwright freed up his money.[42] It is quite possible that Dale was happy to dispense with Arkwright's services as a partner in the same way that he had been happy to dispense with Archibald Paterson's services a few years earlier, i.e. because they were no longer required. Nevertheless, one did not simply dismiss Richard Arkwright and, in any event, a complete fall out would have been inadvisable, given that Arkwright was a vastly experienced entrepreneur, apparently willing to provide training, advice and even machinery. Fortunately for Dale, relations between them remained relatively cordial for some time after the official partnership ended.

It is interesting to speculate why Arkwright wanted to detach himself (or allowed himself to be detached) from direct involvement in the Scottish cotton business after his initial enthusiasm. The bell tower notwithstanding, there may well have been a dispute of some sort between the parties but it would appear that Arkwright simply changed his mind about spinning partnerships in Scotland (although, as Dempster notes below, he did briefly offer to retain a share in New Lanark). He would have known about his impending Knighthood in December 1786 and perhaps even of his appointment as High Sheriff a few months later. If he were to survive as a businessman in England and to fulfill his various roles as Knight of the realm, High

Sheriff of Nottingham, estate owner, landed gentleman and provider of credit to Georgiana Duchess of Devonshire, his presence would clearly be required in England.

David Dale's house in New Lanark prior to restoration. (New Lanark Trust)

George Dempster was once again pivotal in the Dale/Arkwright relationship and, in an attempt to resolve matters, he was able to arrange a meeting of all concerned in December 1786, with quite dramatic results:

> Some misunderstanding happening between him and Mr. Dale which they submitted to me, I met them both at Sir Richard's house at Cromford in December 1786. Each gentleman offering to take the whole concern and to take my share also, I awarded the whole to Mr. Dale as being most convenient for him to manage. Mr. Dale thinking I had made him a valuable gift of my share offered me £1,000 by way of equivalent for it. But I was too glad to be rid of so extensive a concern to accept any compensation for it.[43]

Quite what happened to Arkwright's shares is less clear but we do know that Arkwright finally left the partnership at that point. Dempster's decision to gift the shares to Dale may have been the last straw for Arkwright. It seems, however, that Dale and Arkwright managed to maintain at least a working relationship after the dispute. For example, it seems very likely that Dale bought machinery from Arkwright's son (also Richard) between 1784-1786.[44] Arkwright Senior appeared to be happy to maintain his own relationship with New Lanark and contacted Dale in 1788 regarding machinery, including the mill wheels, for the Catrine mill.[45] Also, Arkwright continued to instruct 'Mr. Dale's artists and young children gratis, as he did those sent from Stanley'.[46] At the end of the day, it may be the case that Arkwright was simply unclear as to what he hoped to get from his Scottish projects and that he came to realise this by the end of 1786.[47]

This was an enormously advantageous situation for Dale. The business at New Lanark was now his. Dempster's refusal of Dale's offer of £1,000 for his shares was either an act of enormous generosity or of complete folly which simply lined Dale's pockets – depending on one's point of view. Throughout his life, Dempster was far less concerned with money than with improving social and economic conditions. When he was later faced with what he referred to as 'a Major Loss of £8,000 by Stanley Mills', he noted that this had left him 'as poor as a church mouse and as contented as any Pauper in the land', given that he had done his best and that he still had enough money to supply his 'few wants for a few years'.[48]

New buildings, prior to restoration, 1961. (New Lanark Trust)

With Dale now in full control, spinning in Mill No. 1 began in earnest. At this point work was begun on the weir which was built out some 95 feet into the river.[49] Eighteen months later, in October 1788, a second mill was in the process of construction when Mill No. 1 'was totally consumed by accidental fire'.[50] Fire was always a problem in the early mills owing to the dust and the use of candles for lighting but in this case, the fire may have been cause by boys lighting a fire to keep themselves warm:

> ...the boys in the morning feeling themselves cold, they got some old baskets and kindled them in the chimney; the sparks went up, and some of them fell into a chimney in a garret where waste cotton was kept, and the fire was not discovered until it burst out at the roof...[51]

Fortunately, no-one was injured and some of the machinery was saved. The Sun insurance policy paid out – £2,000 for the mill building, £2,500 for the machinery and utensils and £300 for two houses.[52]

Dale kept his workforce fed and clothed and paid their wages while Mill No. 2 was completed and No. 1 was rebuilt the following year, followed by two new mills.[53] The new Mill No.1 had a projecting stair bay and three waterwheels.[54] Rather than having the rather bleak appearance of a workhouse, the Mill included Palladian windows in the stair bay, a feature which was also to be found in Arkwright's Masson Mill in Cromford and again in Woodside, Catrine and Spinningdale mills, perhaps once again illustrating the influence of Arkwright on almost everything to do with the spinning industry at that time.[55]

When Mill No. 2 was completed, Dale wanted to extend the weir to the opposite bank of the river and to build a bridge which would connect both banks. Unsurprisingly, perhaps, these plans were opposed by the Edmonstone sisters who owned the estate of Corehouse opposite the mills, although they did eventually agree to the building of the weir. However, at low water, 'boys and idlers', crossed to the Corehouse side along the top of the weir and Dale, because of the complaints of his neighbours, made a break in it to stop this.[56]

By March 1791, 981 persons were employed in the four mills. This increased to 1,334 by November 1793, when Lockhart provided his return to the Statistical Account. Very little is known about the construction of housing in the village at this time, although research indicates that most of the housing provided for workers (with the exception of Nursery Buildings) was built during Dale's association with the village. New Buildings, Caithness Row, Braxfield Row, Double (or Broad) Row and Long Row were all erected in this period to accommodate the large workforce.[57]

For the benefit of tourists and others interested in visiting the Fall of Stonebyres, a 'gravel walk' was 'formed at the expense of Mr. Dale' – from Stonebyres wood down a steep hill:

> ...to the summit of a monstrous crag, overhanging the Clyde; where, surrounded with trees and coppice wood, and secured by a wooden palisade, that gentleman has placed a garden chair, from which you can with ease, with safety and without anxiety or perturbation, contemplate the wonders of this sublime scene.[58]

At that point, Mill No. 1 was operating 4,500 spindles, considerably fewer than the 6,000 spindles in operation in No. 2 Mill. In Mill 3 'a considerable number of patent jennies' were in operation '...going by water' (thanks to William Kelly's new patent which meant that an employee could operate twice as many spindles as before) alongside 55 'common' jennies. Mill 4 was apparently destined to be 'filled in the same way' but was at that time being used as a store room for cotton wool, as workshops for the different tradesmen employed and as 'a boarding house for 275 children who have no parents here and who get their maintenance, education and cloathing (sic) for their work'.[59] These children were the famous 'pauper apprentices'. An early view of the entire village appeared in The Edinburgh Magazine in 1793 and is shown overleaf.[60]

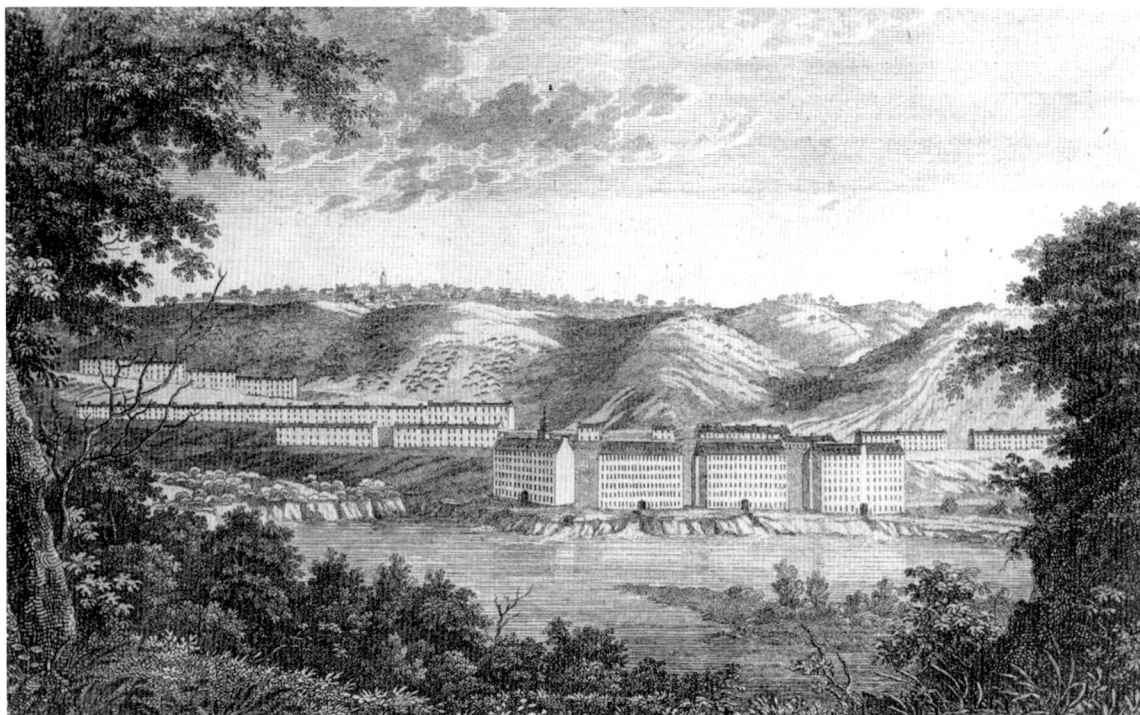

View of New Lanark, 1793. (*The Edinburgh Magazine*)

Table 1 below indicates the value of the enterprise according to the various Sun Fire Insurance policies in force in 1795.[61]

	Table 1		New Lanark Mills, 1795	
	Length (feet)	Width (feet)	Height (feet)	Insurance value
Mill 1	154	27	60	£2,200
Mill 2	154	27	60	£2,200
Mill 3	130	30	60	£2,200
Mill 4	156	33	70	£1,200

However, the insurance figures above do not include the valuations for other materials and machinery. For example, Hume's research shows that there was an undistributed sum of £5,900 insured with the Phoenix Insurance Company (whose representative, Morehead Loudon of the Glasgow office visited New Lanark on August 14th of that year) and that wheels and transmission shafts were valued at £600 in each of the 'working' mills, i.e. Mills 1, 2 and 3. In addition, spinning and carding machinery and various utensils were valued at £3,100 each for Mills 1 & 2 and £3,200 for No. 3 Mill. No. 4, as a warehouse, workshop and lodging house contained household goods valued at £500, wearing apparel at £100, stock at £3,500 and joiners' and millwrights' tools and utensils at £1,200.[62] The three-storey building at the far end of the site which became the mechanics' shed and the neighbouring single-storey foundry building were not built (or not included) at the time of the *Statistical Account* (nor were the three storage sheds on the riverbank behind the mills) and their date of construction is unknown. However a rough estimate can be made as to the value of the whole enterprise. Although there were slight fluctuations in valuations, in general the mills were insured for approximately £30,000 at least until 1801.[63] The mill buildings are in the centre/left of the picture (which includes buildings later built under Robert Owen's management).

As Table 2 indicates, the four buildings built for the purposes of spinning were of a considerable size and produced an average of 6,000lbs of 'cotton wool' (i.e. yarn) per week, the vast majority of which was sold on directly, although there was a small side industry of 324 persons 'and others in the proprietor's employ' working from home in the parish and neighbourhood who wove the yarn into cloth to be sold in Glasgow.[64]

The four mills in New Lanark provided work for a very large number of people. Table 2 is compiled from the return to the *Statistical Account* written in November 1793 and shows the numbers in employment. A breakdown of the entire population is provided in Appendix 4.

Table 2: Number Employed November 1793

			Number
Employed in erecting buildings for seven years past.	Masons, carpenters, labourers		90
Mechanics employed in making & repairing machinery.	Smiths (20), Clockmakers (12) Mill-wrights (9) Hammermen & Hangmen etc. (15)	Turners (10) Founders (2) Joiners (19)	87
Employed in carrying on the manufactory (cleaning cotton, carding, drawing, roving, winding, spinning, reeling etc.	Men (145) Women (217)	Boys (376) Girls (419)	1,157
	Total		1,134

Large numbers of women and children were employed in the mills. This had always been the case in the textile industry but by the 1790s, Kelly's new water-powered jennies had increased the demand for women and children, at the expense of adult male employees. His invention had reduced 'very considerably' the number of men 'that formerly were necessary in working the common jennies'. Such being the case, 'widows with large families' were in great demand in the village, 'as children can manage the patent jennies with great ease, while their mothers are employed in the other branches'.[65] The *Statistical Account* noted that:

> Families from any quarter possessed of a good moral character and having three children fit for work, above nine years of age, are received, supplied with a house at a moderate rent and the women and children provided with work.[66]

Many of the villagers were Highlanders (from Argyllshire as far north as Inverness and Caithness – hence 'Caithness Row' in the village) who had found themselves stranded and destitute in Greenock after their ship had been forced by bad weather to seek shelter in late summer or early autumn of 1791.[67] They were not the first Highland workers to find themselves in New Lanark. The minister of Reay in Caithness observed that 'some poor people and one or two reduced families' had gone from the parish to the cotton mills in Lanark and Stanley in 1788 – the latter fact confirmed by Dempster who noted that year that 80 Highland families had arrived in Stanley 'which have all proved sober, virtuous and industrious', although he went on to note that, because of their arrival, the company were able to lower their wages 'to the current price of cotton yarn and suffer less by its fall than most other cotton spinners'.[68]

In 1791, the *Fortune*, a brig of some 203 tons, built only six years earlier and carrying 400 passengers bound for North Carolina, was one of the many on its way to America (in this case from Skye) loaded with emigrants from across Highland Scotland. These families could no longer endure the difficult conditions in the north (amongst which were unemployment, crop failures, enclosures and increasing rents) and, rather than seeking seasonal work in agriculture, bleachfields and linen mills south of the Highland line (or even looking to settle permanently in the south, as some did) had opted to leave the country altogether in the hope of a new life across the Atlantic.[69] As Devine has pointed out, the Highlanders were still part of a peasant society, with what he refers to as a *'tenacious attachment'* to the land – a characteristic of such societies. They would rather emigrate across the world to work on the land *'and to cling to minute crofts rather than move in large numbers to an alien life in the towns of the south'*.[70]

Many had *'given their little all – some twenty pounds, some thirty pounds'* for the passage of their families to America.[71] *The Caledonian Mercury*, in a lengthy tirade against emigration, believed that such emigrants were deluded in thinking that life would be better across the seas.[72] As it turned out, many never reached America to find out. Conditions on board the overcrowded ship were desperate. Passengers slept on three tiers of bunks, fore and aft, (two tiers midships), only 18 inches broad, with a height of only 2 feet between the bunks. Passengers under 16 were not 'full' passengers (i.e. had not paid a full fare) and were not entitled to a bunk of their own. Food was scarce and had to be strictly rationed because there were only two 24-pint cooking pots for 400 people.[73] After twelve days at sea, the ship lost a mast and put in at Greenock, where *'many of the passengers, especially children, died from the effects of the voyage'*.[74] *The Caledonian Mercury* noted:

> The ship was driven into the Clyde and information was no sooner brought to that public spirited Citizen, and Honourable Magistrate, David Dale, Esq; than his benevolent heart suggested what his unbounded activity immediately executed.[75]

Dale *'sent a friend to ... invite the poor Highlanders'* to New Lanark *'to assure them of employment of man, woman and child and offering a supply for their present necessities'*,[76] promising also to educate their children and *'furnish them with school books gratis, and give the children clothes and wages as other children at his works'*. *The Statistical Account* notes that *'the greater bulk of them accepted'*.[77] The Royal Highland Society took a similar view of Dale's offer;

> These unfortunate people were completely cured of their passion for America and happily found an asylum in the benevolence of Mr. David Dale who employed them in his extensive cotton manufactory in the vicinity of Glasgow.[78]

Actual numbers are unclear but seem to be *'above a hundred'*, and probably nearer two hundred.[79] It is important to note, however, that Dale's offer could only be accepted by passengers who had already paid the fare in full and who had no outstanding debt to the shipping company. It would seem that Dale was not the only mill owner to offer work. Some of the passengers were *'engaged by the proprietors of the cotton mills at Rothesay and Paisley'*.[80] According to *The Caledonian Mercury*, when the New Lanark contingent arrived in the village, they *'poured the blessings of them who were ready to perish on the head of their modest benefactor'*.[81] According to another newspaper report, when Dale discovered that there were a number of distressed families remaining in Greenock he *'wrote ... to find them out, to appoint a surgeon to visit them, and to furnish them with every necessary (sic) at his expense'*.[82]

Dale was establishing a reputation as a benevolent and compassionate man – a reputation which, alongside that of patriot, enlightened mill owner and Christian evangelist, was to remain with him for the rest of his life. *The Caledonian Mercury* was in no doubt as to his virtues:

> Is he not a patriot who has saved them to their country? Is he not a good citizen who undertakes to form them to habits of industry? Is he not a good Christian who provides the means of instruction for young and old, teaching them to fear God and honour the King.[83]

As was often the case with Dale, this offer was certainly one of benevolence and charity – on this occasion designed to relieve distress and stem Highland emigration – but an offer designed also to be one which would benefit both parties by providing workers for his mills. As a result of the *Fortune* episode, houses capable of accommodating 200 families were built and became known as 'Caithness Row'. Building work was completed by 1793 and the *Statistical Account* reports that *'a considerable number of Highlanders'* came to live in the village.[84]

Drawings & Elevations of Caithness Row. © Peter Robinson. (New Lanark Trust/I.G. Lindsay & Partners)

Dale was extremely concerned about the issue of emigration (temporary and permanent) from the Highlands, as were two of his partners in other business ventures – George Dempster and George Macintosh. They were members of a group calling themselves 'The Society for Preventing Emigrations to Foreign Parts'.

Dale's concern was one of the main reasons why he later became involved in the Spinningdale venture and why he and Macintosh retained an interest in it long after it was financially prudent to do. Similarly, Macintosh's Dunchattan dyeworks in Glasgow were famous for employing large numbers of Gaelic-speaking Highlanders who might otherwise have fled to North America.[85] George Dempster's strenuous efforts to provide employment, planned villages and decent roads in the Highlands were entirely due to concerns about the poor conditions and the increasing numbers who felt it necessary to emigrate.

Dale expressed some of his concerns about emigration in a letter to Alexander Campbell of Barcaldine (Carolina's brother-in-law) regarding a proposed mill in Argyllshire:

> I hope that this first attempt will be only an introduction to greater and more extensive manufactures in the Highlands which will give employment to all who are willing to remain in their native country & put a stop to emigrations which are equally hurtful to the country and to the poor people ... I shall reckon it one of the most happy circumstances in my life if I shall be so fortunate as to draw the attention of the people to Industry at home & I hope that the time is not far distant when all the people in Scotland that are willing to work will find full employment in every part of the country in various manufactures...[86]

He published a similar letter (this time to Col. Dalrymple of Fordell) in *The Scots Magazine* in October 1791.[87] Dale makes his views very clear. Emigration was '*no less hurtful to the poor people themselves than to the country*'. The Highlanders would do best for themselves if they were able to find work in their local area but if this were found to be impossible, it would be better for them and for the country '*to invite all that cannot find employment to come here, and they will be provided for*'.[88]

Caithness Row, 2014.

For the first few years (at least) in New Lanark, Dale was dependent on the Highland workers at a time when '*few Lanarkians could look upon the new enterprise with favour*'.[89] The local population, despite the employment opportunities offered by the mills, were slow to adapt to large-scale factory conditions of employment in buildings which resembled workhouses or prisons. They were often less than enthused by the new ways of working where work was increasingly regulated by rigid adherence to time disciplines. The Highlanders were equally unused to this way of working but had little choice in the matter. There is little doubt that this initial resistance to factory work in the new community created some tension in the village itself and between the village and the town.[90] W.A. Davidson, writing in 1828 and reflecting on the situation some years earlier, noted that the new houses in the village had to be let at a low rent because '*only persons destitute of employment, friends and character*' could take up employment there.[91] The initial resistance of the locals, combined with Dale's determination to stem Highland emigration, led him to advertise in newspapers in the Highlands, promising work for families in his cotton mills.[92]

In response to these adverts and to the general publicity aroused by the new cotton mills, workers appeared from various parts of Highland Scotland, including Argyll, where Carolina Dale's family connections with Jura would be well-known. By the late 1790s, it is likely that number reached 400 to 500. There were also '*several families ... driven from Ireland by the distracted state of that country who found 'immediate employment here*'.[93] Perhaps ironically, given Dale's views on emigration and certainly contrary to his intention, the parish minister of Strachur and Stralachan noted that '*the cotton manufactures, the printing & bleaching fields in the neighbourhood of Glasgow have drained this parish of a number of workmen*'.[94]

Further north and west lay the island of Barra (then known as Barray) where some of the local population also responded to the promise of permanent paid employment in New Lanark. Their experience was much less satisfactory, it would appear, than their neighbours from Caithness and Sutherland. Having been '*invited by Mr. David Dale to work in his cotton factory*', the Barra people did not stay long in the community:

> ...*Mr. Dale's terms not coming up to their expectations, some of them returned home, and many of them, from a change of diet and occupation, contracted distempers of which they died; many more prepared themselves for emigration.*[95]

This was a significant, if relatively unusual, event. The problem may have been caused by a number of factors. The minister may have been correct about the change of diet and work practices. As Nicolson & Donnachie suggest, the area was a long way from the sea and the supply of fish was limited (although Dale did manage to find some on occasion to feed his child apprentices) and the lowland diet in general would have been less healthy than that of the Western Isles. It may also have been the case that '*some fell victim to respiratory problems or malarial illnesses still prevalent during Lowland summers*'.[96] There would certainly have been language barriers, although, of course, there were significant numbers of Gaelic speakers already in the village. Their religious beliefs, although always tolerated (and encouraged) by Dale, who '*stipulated that all … workers should enjoy full freedom of religious opinion*', were not particularly well catered for.[97] According to one source, '*there lingered a strong flavour of the old Jacobite feeling, and of the old religious persuasion that gave it vitality*'.[98] The Highlanders were '*sometimes, though rarely … favoured with a sermon in Gaelic by preachers of the Church of Scotland*' – of little interest or use to Highland Catholics.[99] Consideration had been given to building a permanent church for Gaelic speakers '*at least for one half of the day*' but it would seem that this was once again to be based on Church of Scotland principles and, in any event, requests for financial support from the SSPCK to build a Gaelic chapel were refused.[100] This was not particularly surprising. The SSPCK, Presbyterian in creed, was committed to providing charity schooling. They were keen to print Gaelic editions of the Bible – Dale and Moncrieff agreed to receive public donations at the Royal Bank – but their position was somewhat ambivalent.[101] Schools were required to educate the Highlanders where the parish system was under severe pressure but there were other agendas, post-1745 and although Gaelic was often essential as a medium of instruction, English was ultimately the preferred language and the language of the Presbyterian Church.

Gaelic, therefore, was something of a necessary and temporary evil in the SSPCK's attempts '*to convert Highlanders to Lowland values*' – including Presbyterianism and the English language.[102] Given that schools were already well established in New Lanark and beyond, it would have been highly unlikely that the SSPCK would fund a Gaelic, Roman Catholic place of worship.[103] All of these factors may well have had an effect, although why they might affect the people from Barra more than the others and induce them to return to the island is a mystery.

On the other hand, the unfavourable account of events outlined in the *Statistical Account* report from Barra may have been something of a scare story spread by the minister and/or the laird, Mr. MacNeil, to reduce the numbers emigrating from the parish – a notion given some substance by the minister himself who reported that potential emigrants (and those returning from New Lanark who might have been tempted to stay only briefly in the parish) had been persuaded to think again:

> Mr. MacNeil, the proprietor, not only gave them and such as returned from Glasgow, lands but likewise money enough to purchase a new stock of cattle, and all the other necessary implements of husbandry. The spirit for emigration is now happily and totally suppressed.[104]

There may also have been the fact that, according to the rather stereotypical Lowland view of the Highlanders, the latter were particularly affected by the imposition of conditions of work which required confinement to one building, subject to the demands of regulated hours of work. This stereotype of the Highlander (which conveniently ignored the fact that Lowlanders were also unused to factory work) was certainly prevalent. William Davidson took the view that:

> ...the manners of the Highlander, accustomed to wander at ease on his native mountains, in the full enjoyment of personal freedom, ill-fitted him for the confinement of a room; and his ignorance of the local dialect operated as a bar to his improvement.[105]

Another observer went further and claimed that because of their *'entire ignorance'* of the business, the Highlanders' manners and customs were quite at variance with the employment and that the language barrier was an additional impediment. Accordingly, *'many left the place and desertion became so frequent that Mr. Dale determined to apprentice boys and girls to the business'*.[106] While it is certainly true that Dale required the services of apprentice children, there is no evidence that this was caused by the frequent desertion of large numbers of Highlanders. With the exception of the Barra group, most of the adult workers who found themselves in New Lanark stayed there and were well looked after.

Social conditions for everyone in the village were far in advance of anything else available in the late 18th century and this was entirely because Dale wished it to be that way. That is not to suggest, however that Dale micro-managed the everyday affairs of the mills and the community associated with it. In modern terminology, his role was more akin to that of a chief executive or managing director, planning and directing the business, not only of New Lanark but also the mills in Blantyre, Catrine and Spinningdale, while maintaining his position at the Royal Bank and as a City Magistrate and leading light in Glasgow's new Chamber of Commerce. The head office of the New Lanark business was in the warehouse in St. Andrew's Square in Glasgow and Dale was, of necessity, based there. Despite his busy schedule, one of Dale's New Lanark employees (John Wright, promoted to the Glasgow office in 1799), remembered *'the calm unruffled way in which Mr. Dale went through his very extended business'*.[107] This may well have been the case but, on one occasion, Dale clearly felt the pressure. In a letter to Dr. James Currie in 1792, Dale noted that the office of Magistrate was taking up more time than he would have liked and was (temporarily) preventing him from visiting the mills:

> *I have it not in my power to pay much attention to the works, the duties of my office here requiring almost my whole time and attention.*[108]

Similarly, it is not clear how often Dale visited the village. In a later letter to Dr. Currie, Dale mentions that he had not visited the mills for four weeks but it must be borne in mind that Dale's health by this time was causing concern. Despite Dale's four week absence, everything was progressing satisfactorily – *'they were all going about'* in the normal manner.[109] This minor 'aside' in a letter is important and indicates Dale's satisfaction with the way the business was operating. He was most certainly not the type of character to tolerate poor practice or inefficiency in business. Owen's claim that Dale wanted to sell the business a year later because it had not been managed *'with the necessary success he had expected'* seems to be quite inconsistent with reality, at least as things stood in 1799, although there had been some concerns in the first few years.[110]

It would have been impossible (and undesirable) for Dale to live in the village and manage the daily affairs of the factory and the community. He had a house in the village which he visited when he needed to be there and he kept a stable of thirteen horses in the village for use when he needed transport (for which privilege he paid the sum of £1. 6s. Horse Farm tax in 1797–1798) but the everyday running of the business was left to his half-brother James, in partnership with the very able and ever-inventive Mr. Kelly.[111] Robert Owen later claimed Kelly and James Dale did not work well together but there is no real evidence to support this view.[112] The two managers (Dale referred to Kelly as his 'Foreman') worked together for many years and created a very successful community before Owen dispensed with their services soon after his take over in 1800.[113]

However, Dale did initially have some serious concerns about James Dale's abilities. He revealed these concerns quite pointedly to Claud Alexander, his Catrine partner, in two letters written in 1788. In April of that year, Dale told Alexander that he *'would not go any further with Mr. Dale until we have proved him'*:

> *I have not such recommendations as to induce me to give him any place of trust. He is under no engagements ... If Mr. Dale does not answer we can soon be quit of him. In the meantime he will be useful in selling our jennies again whenever they are ready to spin ...*[114]

He went further in a letter at the end of 1788 when, clearly irritated by events, he wrote at length to Alexander about an embarrassing dispute raised by potential partners (the Clark and Houston families) regarding a contract. He was also concerned

New Lanark (Richard Stenlake, private collection)

New Lanark (Richard Stenlake, private collection)

about James Dale's management of the jenny house – presumably in New Lanark but possibly in Catrine where James may also have had some management responsibility:

> *...I am exceeding anxious to have the matter settled for if it is not settled in a few days Messrs Allan & McKay should have taken everything off James Dale's hand and shut up the jenny house as we are disgraced by its being carried on in such an unbusiness like manner.*[115]

Although James Dale eventually played an important part in the business and raised four children in the village prior to 1800, Dale clearly had little faith in him in the early days. James must certainly have improved or Dale would have been '*quit of him*' very early on and it is interesting to note that James was the last of Dale's immediate family to apply for a ticket as a Burgess in Glasgow (in April 1808).[116]

In any event, as far as New Lanark was concerned, William Kelly was undoubtedly the more prominent figure. This is perhaps unsurprising, given Kelly's mechanical skills at time when a lot of the mill machinery was still being made in the village.[117] Stewart notes that:

> *Mr. Kelly not only managed the work faithfully and efficiently but he also entered with enthusiasm into all the schemes which Mr. Dale organized for the well-being of the little Lanark community and was a loving and persevering co-worker in all Mr. Dale's benevolent undertakings.*[118]

While Stewart was probably correct about Kelly's role, the '*little New Lanark community*' he refers to was processing an average of 6,000 lbs of cotton per week in 1793 and was making an enormous amount of money.[119] It was achieving success nationally and, increasingly, internationally and it is fair to say that, while the mills were obviously well managed on a daily basis, the vision and direction of the project here and in Catrine and elsewhere were Dale's alone.

As a skilled managing director, Dale knew a great deal about the operation of cotton mills – including the machinery involved. Owen's assertion that '*Mr. Dale knew little about cotton spinning, having always left the management of his various mills ... to such managers as he could provide*' could not be further from the truth.[120] 'Mr. Dale' was well acquainted with the cotton spinning industry, from the micro to the macro. From the very earliest days, he was involved in several technical, mechanical and design issues associated with cotton mills. Many of his letters to Claud Alexander deal with issues which must have come from personal knowledge and experience. For example, in the period 1787–1795, Dale refers to a Mr. Abercrombie's offer to build the Catrine mill and makes it clear that he wants to have details of the plans and the actual dimensions of the mills and the houses. As might be expected, he queries the cost but, more importantly here, he also discusses the size of the stonework and the vents; the thickness of the walls and the siting of the windows and he refers to specific items of machinery (plates, wheels, rollers, spindles) being sent by Arkwright. Similarly, Dale's technical knowledge is revealed in some detailed discussion of sluices, wooden troughs and the need for '*pudling with clay*'.[121] Although Dale was not interested in using steam engines in New Lanark, he wrote to James Watt in Birmingham as early as 1790 regarding machine parts. On an equally practical level, Dale is well informed and well aware of the need for fire engines, buckets, slates and for insurance to cover all of this. Of critical importance to him also were the prices of raw cotton from various sources and the price of yarn twists across the country. Twist sizes and the prices for each were very important in a competitive market, particularly given the advances in Mule spinning, as indicated in Dale's letter to Claud Alexander in November 1789 which contained a list of the selling prices of cotton twist (the higher the number, the finer the yarn) and a note to the effect that 1,576 spindles were in operation in the daytime and 480 at night.[122]

All of these issues appear in Dale's letters and, given his position, they inevitably led him to discuss wider issues regarding the state of the cotton spinning business, not just in Scotland (where he liked to keep an eye on local competitors such as the Finlay family and the proprietors of the Renfrewshire mills) but also in Bristol, Liverpool, London and, in particular, Manchester – the centre of the English cotton industry.[123] In one of his letters to Alexander, Dale mentions writing to John Barton, the Manchester merchant who was later to be Owen's partner in the purchase of New Lanark.[124] As might be expected from a major

Braxfield Row (Richard Stenlake, private collection)

New Lanark Village Store (Richard Stenlake, private collection)

manufacturer, some of the problems of international trade and the state of the British economy feature in his correspondence. He was concerned with the East India Company's monopoly of trade and he noted that he and his fellow manufacturers required to '*fall upon some method to get Mr. Dundas* (the Secretary of State for the Home Department, or 'Home Secretary' with a particular interest in Scottish affairs) *to fulfill his promise of giving the inland consumpt.* (sic) *to the British manufacturer*'.[125] As a mill owner and a banker, the fragile economy of the cotton industry was never far from Dale's mind. Bankruptcies were common and, finances were almost at breaking point during the crisis of 1793.

Letter from Dale to Alexander, November 1789. Twist sizes and prices. (Glasgow City Council: Archives.)

Finally, Dale's correspondence reveals significant 'hands on' involvement in a number of important areas, eg., procuring pauper apprentices from the charity workhouses and negotiating their terms and conditions; his plans for housing all his employees and, as the mills became ever more successful, dealing with inquiries from like-minded entrepreneurs, philanthropists and public health officials.

There is only one conclusion which can be drawn from all the available evidence and that is that Dale, quite contrary to Owen's view of him, was exceptionally knowledgeable about the cotton spinning industry in all its manifestations and, further, that his leadership and overall management were second to none. Because of Dale, New Lanark was a huge success long before Owen visited the site – indeed, it is likely that Owen only visited the place because of its success. Just how major the New Lanark venture was can be illustrated in Table 3 – originally compiled by Nisbet.[127]

By 1795 there were some 55 water-powered spinning mills in Scotland but only three of these were valued at more than £10,000 each for insurance purposes. New Lanark was clearly the largest individual site, with an insurance valuation of £24,400, followed by Stanley at £10,500 and Ballindalloch at £10,300. Arkwright may have been the father of the industry but New Lanark employed more people than the three mills at Cromford and Masson combined.

Table 3: Value of Scottish Cotton Mills by Partnership Groupings c.1795

Partnership	Mill Value (£)	Total Insured
Geo. Houston & Partners	Johnstone Laigh (7,800), Calderpark (6,900), Cartside (7,800), Hag (5,000[a])	£27,500
Dunlop, Cochrane & Co.	Gateside (5,000[a]), Linwood (>7,000[a]), Arthurlie (5,800), Levern (7,500)	£25,300
David Dale & Co.	New Lanark: Mill one (5,900), Two (6,000), Three (6,000), Four (6,500)	£24,400
Robert Corse & Co.	Johnstone Old Mill (9,000), Elderslie Mill (4,000)	£13,000
Wm. McKerrel & Co.	St. Mirren Mill (5,000), Underwood Mill (7,800)	£13,000
George Dempster & Co.	Stanley Mills One and Two	£10,500
Ballindalloch Co.	Ballindalloch Mills	£10,300
Wm. & Robert Osburn	Thornliebank and Newfield	£10,200
Claud Alexander & Co.	Catrine Mills	£9,900

Main Source: Guildhall Library Insurance Policies. [a]Estimated. + Renfrewshire Partnerships.

(Extracted from S.M. Nisbet. (2009) 'The Making of Scotland's First Industrial Region: The Early Cotton Industry in Renfrewshire'. *Journal of Scottish Historical Studies* 29. 1, 1–28. Page25).

Unsurprisingly, 'the concern proved hugely remunerative'.[128] Dale 'acquired a large fortune' and became 'immensely rich'.[129] However, the wealth generated and the benefits accrued were clearly not confined to one individual. Dale became equally famous for his benevolence and his charitable works. These good deeds were not restricted to direct charitable efforts with individuals or specific organisations. The county of Lanark, for example, benefited in many ways. In 1791, *The Scots Magazine* was already intimating the county's indebtedness to Dale for 'its present flourishing situation'. The authors felt 'assured' that cotton goods at that time were 'annually manufactured in the county to the extent of two millions Sterling'.[130] Initial resistance from local landowners had been overturned and they were now increasingly keen to extend the system of manufactures:

> Finding ... that the mills were yielding large returns to the proprietor, many landlords soon evinced a desire to have similar establishments on their own estates.[131]

Even those landowners who had been positive about Dale's enterprise from the beginning were impressed by the sheer scale of its success. Sir John Lockhart Ross, whose family were always supportive, wrote to Dale in 1797:

I generally hope that you may long retain in your possession the works at new Lanark and reap the fruits of those exertions which have been so honourable to yourself and productive of such evident advantage to this part of the country.[132]

Modern commentators have been equally impressed by Dale's achievements. Devine refers to him as '*the greatest cotton magnate of his time in Scotland*', while Butt saw him as '*the outstanding cotton capitalist of the first phase of the factory age*'.[133] As might be expected, the great new enterprise attracted many visitors, then as now. As *The Gentleman's Magazine* noted, Dale was '*visited by the great and extolled by the learned*' and it is to those visitors that we now turn.[134]

References: Chapter 4

1   Stewart, G. (1881) *Curiosities of Glasgow Citizenship as Exhibited Chiefly in the Business Career of its Old Commercial Aristocracy.* Glasgow: J. Maclehose, pp.50-52.

2   Ibid.

3   Robertson, A.D. (1975) *Lanark: the Burgh and its Councils, 1469-1880.* Lanark Town Council. p.270. Braxfield gained notoriety for sentencing Thomas Muir to 14 years transportation for circulating Thomas Paine's leaflets. Braxfield, however had not always been so ruthless. He was one of the law Lords who in 1778 had dealt with the famous Joseph Knight case which had resulted in the finding that 'the state of slavery is not recognised by the laws of this kingdom and is inconsistent with the principles thereof ...' See Whyte, I. (2006) *Scotland and the Abolition of Black Slavery.* Edinburgh: E.U.P., p.32 and Dalrymple, D. (Lord Hailes) (1826) *Deacons of the Lords of Council and Session from 1766-91,* 2 vols. Edinburgh: Wm. Tait. Vol. II, p.779.

4   Sinclair, J. (ed) (1791-99) *The Statistical Account of Scotland, 1791-99,* 21 vols. Vol. XV, pp.22-23. See also Robertson, A.D. (1975) *Lanark: the Burgh and its Councils, 1469-1880.* Lanark Town Council, p.257.

5   Hume, J.R. (1971) 'The Industrial Archaeology of New Lanark', in Butt, J. (ed) *Robert Owen. Prince of Cotton Spinners.* Newton Abbot: David & Charles, pp.216-7.

6   Robertson, A.D. (1975) *Lanark,* pp.255, 257.

7   Liddell, A. (1854b) 'Memoir of David Dale', in Chambers, R. (ed), (1855) *A Biographical Dictionary of Eminent Scotsmen.* Glasgow: Blackie, p.162.

8   Sinclair, J. *Statistical Account,* Vol. XV, pp.22, 34.

9   Ibid., p.473.

10   Ibid.

11   Nisbet, S.M. (2008) *The Rise of Cotton Factory in Eighteenth-Century Renfrewshire.* British Archaeology Report, Series 464. Oxford: Alden Press, p.77.

12   Sinclair, J. *Statistical Account,* Vol. XV, p.35.

13   Donnachie, I. and Hewitt, G. (1993) *Historic New Lanark.* Edinburgh: E.U.P., pp.24-5.

14   Sinclair, J. *Statistical Account,* Vol. XV, p.35n. See also Donnachie, I. & Hewitt, G. (1993) *Historic New Lanark,* p.50 for an extract from the 1792 Patent document.

15   Donnachie, I. & Hewitt, G. (1993) *Historic New Lanark,* p.24.

16   Ibid., p.35. The authors estimate that the town's actual contribution only amounted to some 15% of the total number of 1,334 employees working in the mills in 1793.

17   *The Manchester Mercury,* 22nd February 1785, quoted in Fitton, R.S. (1989) *The Arkwrights: Spinners of Fortune.* Manchester: M.U.P., p.75.

18   *The Nottingham Journal,* 19th February 1785, quoted in Fitton, R.S. *The Arkwrights,* p.75.

19   Davidson, W. (1828) *A History of Lanark & Guide to the Scenery with a list of Roads to the Provincial Towns.* Lanark: Shepherd & Robertson, p.164.

20   Hume, J.R. (1971) *Industrial Archaeology,* p.217 and also Sinclair, J. *Statistical Account,* Vol. XV, p.34. This may have been written over a period of time from 1793. Normally, these returns were completed by the parish minister but in this case, Rev. James Gray had recently died and his successor, Rev. Robert Menzies from Edinburgh was appointed in December, 1793. As a new, non-local minister, he would not have been in a position to make a return for the *Statistical Account.*

21   Cowan, W.A. (1867) *History of Lanark and a Guide to the Surrounding Scenery.* Lanark: Robert Wood, p.88.

22   Hume, J.R. (1971) *Industrial Archaeology.* p. 218.

23   Ibid., pp.218-220.

24   Davidson, W. (1828) *History of Lanark,* p.164.

25   Ibid., p.89.

26   Fitton, R.S. (1989) *The Arkwrights: Spinners of Fortune.* Manchester: M.U.P., p.78. See also Fitton, R.S. and Wadsworth, A.P. (1958) *The Strutts and the Arkwrights 1758-1830. A Study of the Early Factory System.* Manchester: M.U.P., p.105.

27   *The Derby Mercury,* 12th May 1785. Quoted in Donnachie & Hewitt (1993), *Historic New Lanark,* p.37.

28   Fitton, R.S. (1989) *The Arkwrights,* p.87.

29 *The Gazeteer and New Daily Advertiser.* London, 26th February 1785.

30 Ibid. Dempster's Brother was Captain John H. Dempster of the East India Co. Vide infra Chapter 9.

31 Sinclair, J. *Statistical Account*, Vol. XV, p.35. Also Hume, J.R., *Industrial Archaeology*, p.218 and Fitton, R.S. (1989) *The Arkwrights*, p.77.

32 See also Lang, A.M. (1998) *A Life of George Dempster, Scottish M.P. of Dunnichen (1732–1818)*. Lampeter: Edwin Mellen Press, p.223.

33 Hume, J.R. *Industrial Archaeology*, p.226, Policy No. 519065.

34 Owen, R.D. (1874) *Threading My Way: Twenty Seven Years of Autobiography*. New York: Carleton & Co. pp.29–30.

35 Ibid.

36 Ibid., p.30.

37 Fitton, R.S. and Wadsworth, A.P. (1958) *The Srutts and the Arkwrights 1758–1830. A Study of the Early Factory System*. Manchester: M.U.P., pp.75–76.

38 Fitton, R.S. (1989) *The Arkwrights*, p.209.

39 Owen, R. (1857) *The Life of Robert Owen Written by Himself*. Vol. 1. London: Effingham Wilson. New impression (1967) London: Frank Cass & Co., p.71.

40 Ibid., p.54.

41 Ibid., p.83.

42 'Merchant Princes of England' (1865), in *London Society*. 8:47. November. p.467.

43 Sinclair, J. (1831) *The Correspondence of the Rt Hon Sir John Sinclair, Bart.*, 2 vols. London: Colburn & Bentley. Vol. I, pp.361–2.

44 Arkwright's son had taken over one of his father's relatively new mills in Manchester. When he sold out in 1786, there were 'several Ballances ... then owing from David Dale of Glasgow ...'. See Fitton, R.S. (1989), p.64.

45 David Dale to Claud Alexander, 7th April 1788. Mitchell MS 63/3. Vide infra Chapter 9.

46 Sinclair, J. (1831) *Correspondence*, pp.361–2. See also Fitton, R.S. (1989) *The Arkwrights*, pp.72–3.

47 Cooke, A.J. (1979) 'Richard Arkwright and the Scottish Cotton Industry', *Textile History*, X: 196–202, p.200. See also Donnachie, I. & Hewitt, G. (1993), *Historic New Lanark*, pp.29–30 for an apocryphal tale of Arkwright returning to Perthshire in 1787 where, as a souvenir of his trip, he *'bestowed his silver spectacles on Mrs. Buchanan, the mother of one of his favourite apprentices, Archibald Buchanan'*.

48 George Dempster to George Macintosh, 11th October 1803. Private Collection. See Lang, A.M. (1998) *A Life of George Dempster, Scottish M.P. of Dunnichen (1732–1818)*. Lampeter: Edwin Mellen Press, p.253.

49 Hume, J.R. (1971) *Industrial Archaeology*, p.217.

50 Sinclair, J. *Statistical Account*, Vol. 15, p.34.

51 *The Public Advertiser*, 20th October 1788 – Extract of a letter from Edinburgh. I am grateful to Lorna Davidson, Director, New Lanark Trust for this reference.

52 Hume, J.R. (1971) *Industrial Archaeology*, p.218.

53 Even after No. 1 Mill was rebuilt, it was some time before new machinery could be installed. Cullen estimates that approximately £2,000 had been spent in wages before the operatives went back to work. See Cullen, A. (1910) *Adventures in Socialism*. Glasgow: John Smith, p.9.

54 Hume, J.R. (1971) *Industrial Archaeology*, p.221.

55 Ibid., pp.220–221.

56 Ibid., pp.217–8. When Owen took over the mills, he resurrected the quarrel with the Edmonstones by filling in the gap, resulting in many years of dispute and legal actions over water rights.

57 Donnachie, I. & Hewitt, G. (1993) *Historic New Lanark*, p. 27.

58 McNayr, J. (1797) *A Guide from Glasgow to some of the most Remarkable Scenes in the Highlands and to the Falls of Clyde*. Glasgow: Courier Office, pp.225–6.

59 Sinclair, J. *Statistical Account*, Vol. XV, pp.35–36.

60 *The Edinburgh Magazine or Literary Miscellany*. Vol. II, London: Laurie & Symington, 1793. Frontispiece.

61 Sinclair, J. *Statistical Account*, Vol. XV, p.35. See also Guildhall Library MSS, Sun Fire Insurance policies 638322, 648656, 664114, 716403 cited in Hume, J.R. (1971) *Industrial Archaeology*, pp.221–222.

62 Hume, J.R. (1971) *Industrial Archaeology*, pp.221.

63 Ibid.

64 Sinclair, J. *Statistical Account*, Vol. XV, pp.35–37.

65 Ibid., p.38.

66 Ibid., p.40.

67 Ibid.

68 Sinclair, J. *Statistical Account*. Vol. VII, pp.574–5 quoted in Nicolson, M. and Donnachie, I. 'The New Lanark Highlanders: Migration, Community & Language 1785–c.1850', *Family & Community History*, 6/1, May 2003: 19–31, p.23. See also George Dempster to Grimur Thorkelion, 21st August 1788, in Fergusson, J. (ed) (1934) *Letters of George Dempster to Sir Adam Fergusson, 1756–1813*. MacMillan: London, p.194.

69 Nicolson, M. and Donnachie, I. 'The New Lanark Highlanders: Migration, Community & Language 1785–c.1850', *Family & Community History*, 6/1, May 2003: 19–31.

70   Devine, T.M. (1983) 'Highland Migration to Lowland Scotland, 1760-1860', *Scottish Historical Review*, LXII, 2nd October: 137-149, p.46.

71   *The Caledonian Mercury*, 20th October 1791.

72   Ibid.

73   Royal Highland Society. *Report of the Committee on Emigration*. Sederund Book, Vol. III, January 1802, pp.478-9.

74   Ibid.

75   *The Caledonian Mercury*, 20th October 1791. See also *Lloyd's Evening Post*, 27th October 1791. Dale learned of the Highlanders' plight from a letter written by Mr. Buist, the minister in Greenock.

76   Ibid.

77   Sinclair, J. *Statistical Account*, Vol. XV, p.40.

78   Royal Highland Society. Report, pp.478-9.

79   *The Caledonian Mercury*, 20th October 1791.

80   *The London Chronicle*, 22th October 1791.

81   *The Caledonian Mercury*, 20th October 1791.

82   *Lloyd's Evening Post*, 27th October 1791.

83   *The Caledonian Mercury*, 20th October 1791.

84   Sinclair, J. *Statistical Account*, Vol. XV, p.40.

85   Note however, while it might have suited employers to create a separate, secretive community behind high walls, speaking a 'foreign' language and guarding the secrets of the dyeing industry in Glasgow, this was not the case in New Lanark, where the intention was to create a community.

86   Dale to Alexander Campbell of Barcaldine, 18th August 1791. National Archives of Scotland (NRS): GD 170/1743/13 in Johnston, W.T. (2000) 'An Essay on David Dale' in W.T. Johnston (ed), *David Dale & Robert Owen Studies*. Livingston: Officina Educational Publications. Note: Campbell married Carolina's sister Mary on 22nd September 1785 in Edinburgh. See *The London Chronicle*, 29th September 1785.

87   Dale to Dalrymple, 20th January 1791, *The Scots Magazine*, October 1791, 53, 513-514. Also *The Glasgow Courier*, 27th October 1791.

88   Ibid.

89   Robertson, A.D. (1975) *Lanark*, pp.255.

90   Nicolson, M. & Donnachie, I. (2003) *New Lanark Highlanders*, p. 20.

91   Davidson, W., *History of Lanark*, p.167.

92   *The Glasgow Mercury*, 31st December 1791; *The Caledonian Mercury*, 3rd June 1806 and *The Aberdeen Journal*, 23rd April 1807. See Nicolson & Donnachie (2003) *New Lanark Highlanders*, p. 23.

93   Garnett, T. (1811) *Observations on a Tour through the Highlands and Part of the Western Isles of Scotland. A New Edition in Two Volumes*. London: John Stockdale. Vol. II, p.236.

94   Sinclair, J. *Statistical Account*, Vol. IV, p.571. See also Nicolson & Donnachie (2003) *New Lanark Highlanders*, p.24.

95   Sinclair, J. *Statistical Account*, Vol. XIII, pp.332-3.

96   Nicolson & Donnachie (2003) *New Lanark Highlanders*, p. 24.

97   Stewart, G., *Curiosities*, p.57.

98   Ibid.

99   Sinclair, J. *Statistical Account*, Vol. XV, p.41.

100   Ibid.,Vol. XVII, p.41. See also Nicolson & Donnachie (2003) *New Lanark Highlanders*, p.28.

101   *The Morning Chronicle*, London, 7th December 1802.

102   Smout, T.C. (1998) *A History of the Scottish People 1560-1830*. London: Fontana, p.209.

103   The SSPCK were keen to print Gaelic versions of the Bible but largely for the purpose of conversion to Presbyterianism.

104   Sinclair, J. *Statistical Account*, Vol. XIII, p.333. See also Nicolson & Donnachie (2003) *New Lanark Highlanders*, p.24.

105   Davidson, W. *History of Lanark*, p. 165.

106   Cowan, W.A. *History of Lanark*, p. 90.

107   Gourock Ropework MSS cited in Donnachie, I. & Hewitt, G. (1993) *Historic New Lanark*, p.52.

108   Dale to Dr. James Currie, Physician in Liverpool, 30th June 1792. I am indebted to Professor Edward Royle, University of York, for sending me a copy of this.

109   Dale to Dr. Currie, 9th July 1798. Copy courtesy of Professor Royle.

110   Owen, R. *Life*, Vol. I, p.50.

111   National Archives of Scotland. E326/10/4, p.103. In addition to his famous clock – still in the village – Kelly was the first person to apply power to Crompton's Mule in 1790 and, by 1796, had invented several methods of heating mill buildings, particularly the system of stoves and hot-air ducts.

112   Owen, R. *Life*, p.46.

113   Dale to Claud Alexander, 22nd December, Glasgow City Archives, MS 63/6. This letter had been missing for some years because it had been filed in the Chamber of Commerce papers. It has now been included in MS63.

114   Dale to Alexander, 28th April 1788. Glasgow City Archives, MS63/5.

115   Dale to Alexander, 22nd December 1788. Glasgow City Archives MS63/6.

116   His application is dated 12th April 1808. See Anderson, J.R. (ed) (1935) *The Burgesses and Guild Brethren of Glasgow, 1757–1846.* Edinburgh: J. Skinner & Co., p.249.

117   An iron founder (George Wilson) and a brass founder, (David Kelly – no relation to William Kelly) were both employed in the village. See Hume, J.R. (1971) *Industrial Archaeology*, p.240.

118   Stewart, G. *Curiosities*, p.64, Note 2.

119   Sinclair, J. *Statistical Account*, Vol. XV, p.37.

120   Owen, R. *Life*, p.59.

121   Dale to Claud Alexander, 14th February 1787. Glasgow City Archives, MS 63/1; Dale to Alexander, 7th April, 1788, MS 63/3; Dale to Alexander, 12th April 1788, MS 63/4; Dale to Alexander, 13th September 1793, MS 63/14.

122   Ibid., Dale to Alexander, 9th November 1789. MS 63/8.

123   Ibid., Dale to Alexander 24th April 1794. MS 63/18 and 27th August 1796. MS 63/19.

124   Ibid., 3th January 1794. MS 63/16.

125   Ibid., 13th September 1793. MS 63/14.

126   Dale to Richard Richardson, 7th September 1790: Dale to J.J. (unknown), 27th September 1790. Edinburgh City Archives West Kirk Charity Workhouse Minute Book Shelf 69, 9/41. Cited in Johnston (ed) (2000) *David Dale & Robert Owen Studies*. Livingston: Officina Educational Publications.

127   Nisbet, S.M. (2009) 'The Making of Scotland's First Industrial region: The Early Cotton Industry in Renfrewshire', *The Journal of Scottish Historical Studies*, 29.1: 1–28. Edinburgh: E.U.P., p.25. Cooke, A. (2010) *The Rise and Fall of the Scottish Cotton Industry, 1778–1914: The Secret Spring*. Manchester: M.U.P., p.43.

128   Stewart,G. *Curiosities*, p.54.

129   Liddell, A. (1854b) *Memoir*, p.64.

130   *The Scots Magazine*, 53, 1791, p.562.

131   Liddell, A. (1854b) *Memoir*, p.162.

132   MSS Gourock Ropework Co., 15th July 1797, cited in Donnachie, I. & Hewitt, G. (1993) *Historic New Lanark*, p.25.

133   Devine, T.M. (1999) *The Scottish Nation 1700–2000*. London: Penguin, p.115. Also Butt, J. (1977) 'The Scottish Cotton Industry during the Industrial Revolution, 1780-1840', in Cullen, L.M. and Smout, T.C. (eds) *Comparative Aspects of Scottish and Irish Economic and Social History, 1600–1900*. Edinburgh: John Donald, p.118.

134   *The Gentleman's Magazine*, August 1806, p.771.

Chapter 5: A Major Attraction

From the outset, David Dale's community attracted a great deal of attention, since large factories were unusual and New Lanark's location near the famous Falls of Clyde was, in many ways, unique. It is often assumed that New Lanark was made famous by Robert Owen – a view which Owen himself rather encouraged. In his '*Life*' he writes thus, referring to 1817:

> *I had been and was making great and substantial progress with my New Lanark experiment and it was now becoming widely known and attracted the attention of those in advanced stations at home and abroad.*[1]

While there is no doubt that New Lanark had an international reputation, visited by some 20,000 people between 1815–1825, Owen neglected to mention that the community under Dale had also attracted many visitors, including those in '*advanced stations*' – one of the reasons why Owen visited the village in the first place.[2] Indeed, as local landowner William Lockhart noted in 1795, a '*neat additional Inn*' had been built in the Burgh to accommodate visitors – '*which was much needed, as the resort of strangers to see the Falls of Clyde, the Cotton works etc. is very considerable*'.[3] The *Scots Magazine* of 1791, only a few years after spinning commenced, noted that that Dale's mills, situated as they were near the popular Falls of Clyde, were attracting '*universal attention*'.[4]

The Visitors' Book from August 1795 to October 1799, arguably the period when New Lanark was at its most successful during the Dale period, is an illuminating document.[5] Modern readers expecting to see a grand volume with carefully inscribed records will be disappointed in the small, rather untidy book containing a wide variety of entry styles and handwriting.[6] And yet, the book is of major interest, given the information it contains. On closer inspection, it soon becomes clear that Dale's New Lanark had achieved a national and international reputation long before Owen opened the New Institution in 1816. Between August and December 1795, 459 visitors are recorded. In the twelve months following and again in 1797, visitor numbers averaged 750 per year, falling to 660 in 1798 and 605 in 1799.

It is not possible to identify every single visitor but a closer look at some of the names and their addresses certainly emphasises the fact that the village was known well beyond the Clyde Valley.[7] Visitors came from far and wide. In the U.K., they visited from Scottish towns and cities such as Edinburgh, Glasgow, Perth, St. Andrews, Kelso and the county of Galloway. From England there were visitors from York, London, Cambridge, Oxford, Shrewsbury, Northampton, Southampton and St. Albans. Visitors came from a variety of backgrounds – ministers of religion, surgeons, academics, lawyers, soldiers, bankers (including John More, Dale's successor at the Royal Bank in Glasgow and a Mr. Buchan of the Bank of Scotland) and, naturally, entrepreneurs and cotton spinners. The landed gentry were also attracted by the new venture. Among the nobility were Henry Dundas, the Home Secretary, Minister for War and friend of Robert McQueen of Braxfield. Dundas visited in September 1798, accompanied by his family. The 'Lord Advocate of Scotland' who visited New Lanark in September 1795 was the Hon. Henry Erskine. Other distinguished visitors included Lord & Lady Clive; Sir John & Lady Stirling; Sir George & Lady Young; Lord Viscount Stepford; Lord MacDonald; Sir John Gordon and members of some of the local landowning families, including Lady Ross from Bonnington (Viscount Melville's niece); the Countess of Hyndford and such Enlightenment figures such as Henry (later Lord) Brougham and Henry Cockburn.

Perhaps most striking on an initial investigation is the number of visitors from abroad. Appendix 5 gives some general indication as to overseas visitors, i.e. those who gave their address as furth of the UK. Bearing in mind that Dale, unlike Owen, never left the country on any kind of proselytising mission, the list is fairly extensive for the period and is testament to the reputation of the village. Some of the overseas visitors are likely to have been expatriates on temporary visits back home from some form of colonial service on the sugar, rum and cotton plantations. Others were clearly merchants in their own right, drawn from burgeoning cities like New York and from various European cities by the success of a village which combined industry and philanthropy to produce a healthy profit margin. It is also interesting to see that Zachary Macaulay visited in October 1795. Macaulay was a Scot who, at the age of 16, had left Glasgow University in 1784 and set sail for a sugar plantation in Jamaica where he became an under-manager. He was a friend and supporter of Wilberforce and was himself to become an important figure in the abolitionist cause. He had returned to Britain in 1792 and would certainly have been aware of Dales' involvement with the anti slave-trade movement. At the time of his visit to New Lanark, Macaulay was 27 years old and Governor of the Sierra Leone settlement for freed slaves. As such, he would also have been aware of Dale's support for that particular venture.

Inevitably, by far the largest number of visitors came from the business community – predominantly, although not exclusively, the Scottish business community. Appendix 6 lists some of the visitors who had a commercial background.

This period represented an opportunity for merchants and entrepreneurs to diversify in the post-tobacco age. The tobacco trade, however, was not completely finished as a commercial venture and, more importantly, the tobacco merchants and their associates were experienced traders who had made (and sometimes lost) vast amounts of money from their entrepreneurial activities. They knew all about demand and supply, fluctuating prices and credit crises and were well positioned to join the new entrepreneurs like Dale in the textile industry. The sons and daughters of the 'tobacco lords' inherited not only vast fortunes but also a keen eye for business. In so doing, 'tobacco families' in Glasgow such as the Glassfords, Ingrams, Bogles, Buchanans, Dunlops and Dennistouns developed strong interlocking social and financial networks through marriage.[8] These families represented the social, financial and commercial elite of the city who were keen to be involved in the new commercial life of the city and as such it is no great surprise to find many of their names in the Visitors' Book.

In many ways, they had already 'diversified'. The Bogle, Oswald, Dennistoun and Buchanan families had extensive interests in sugar and rum. The Dennistouns were also involved in coal mining and (later) in cotton spinning. The Dunlops had extensive interests in cotton, linen, coal mining and banking. John Dunlop owned the Rosebank estate which Dale bought in 1800. William French also had interests in coal mining and the McCalls were involved in the linen industry and in brewing.[9]

Dale would have known them all personally, given his position in the city. Some of them (Bogle, Buchanan, Dennistoun, Dunlop, French and Wardlaw) had been among the original signatories with Dale in the establishment of the Chamber of Commerce 25 years earlier and at least two of them (William French and John Dunlop) had been or were to become Lord Provosts of the city.[10] Dale knew the Buchanans as fellow yarn dealers in the city and through their involvement with Arkwright. The Finlay family was also well-known and Wardlaw lived near Dale in Charlotte Street.

Not all of the visitors, of course, had formal connections with the tobacco and Caribbean trades. Many were interested in developing their interests in cotton spinning, banking or other businesses and, although they were not related to the tobacco families, they were the most successful businessmen of the day. Charles Macintosh and George Dempster were already involved with Dale in dyeing and in the Spinningdale venture. William Douglas was Dale's partner in the spinning mill in Newton Stewart and Claud Alexander was his partner in Catrine. The Gillespies and McIlwhams were wealthy cotton spinners – William Gillespie was a partner in the Turkey Red venture – and Scott Moncrieff and John More were closely involved with him in the Royal Bank. The Tennents were successful maltmen in the Drygate and Walter Graham was a highly-respected and popular rum merchant in the city – often to be found, with many of the others, in the Tontine Rooms.[11] Some were well-connected members of the Campbell family, notably the Campbells of Jura who had invested sums of money with Dale in the Royal Bank.[12]

News of New Lanark's success was spreading fast and was attracting national attention. It is interesting also to note the visit of James Watt of Birmingham in 1796. This was Greenock-born James Watt, pioneer of the steam engine who was working in Matthew Boulton's works in Birmingham at the time. Engines made by Boulton & Watt were proving popular in England, but Scotland was much slower to move to steam power. The purpose of Watt's visit is unclear but it is hardly surprising that he was drawn to Scotland's single most successful cotton spinning enterprise. If he was hoping to persuade Dale to convert to steam power, he was to be disappointed. Dale had been offered the opportunity to experiment with steam power looms some years earlier but had declined.[13] In fact, New Lanark continued to use water power long after other mills had converted to steam. Dr. Thomas Garnett, physician, natural philosopher, professor at Anderson's Institution in Glasgow (and subsequently at the Royal Institution in London), visited New Lanark in August 1798 as part of his famous *Tour of the Highlands*. He notes that New Lanark was '*a charming village built by Mr. Dale: his cotton mills are very handsome and the whole village, with its situation, particularly*

New Lanark from above. (New Lanark Trust)

striking'.[14] Like many visitors, Garnett was attracted to the power and the majesty of the various Falls of Clyde and his description is typical of that expressed by many (middle class) tourists:

> The situation of these works is very romantic; they are surrounded on all sides by high grounds, rising in the form of an amphitheatre, which effectively screen them from view, till we arrive in their immediate vicinity, when all at once, as if by enchantment, they burst upon the sight, and from the magnitude and grandeur of their appearance, produce a happy effect.[15]

Garnett talks of 'noble' falls, 'roaring waters and sublime horrors'.[16] James McNayr, writing in similar vein about the Clyde Valley, talks of 'the Eden of Scotland'; 'verdant vegetation'; 'enchanting softness'; 'rocks half clad in Nature's russet robe' and 'Nature's wondrous works'. The village of New Lanark, we are informed, 'is perhaps the most romantick in the island'.[17]

The area attracted William and Dorothy Wordsworth, who, with Samuel Taylor Coleridge as a travelling companion, visited in the summer of 1803 as part of their Scottish tour. As poets, Wordsworth and Coleridge were attracted to the Falls and the inspiration to be drawn from the natural world, as indeed was Robert Southey who visited some years later. There was more to the Coleridge/Southey connection, however. They had been friends since Oxford days in the early 1790s. Inspired by the French Revolution, they intended to set up a utopian community in the Susquehanna Valley in the USA and had progressed as far as planning the advance party when the idea fell through and Southey departed for Portugal in 1795. Robert Owen records that during college vacations at this time, Coleridge was an occasional visitor to Owen's 'circle of enquiring friends' (from the Litereray & Philosophical Society) in Manchester.[18] Coleridge also visited Derby where he became friendly with the Strutt family before attaching himself to the Wordsworths.[19] Despite Southey's absence, Coleridge continued to write a significant number of anti slave trade tracts for *The Watchman* and brought anti slave trade leaflets with him on the Scottish tour of 1803.[20] In fact, the Wordsworths and Coleridge were on friendly terms with Thomas Clarkson and supported his anti slave trade campaign. Whether they knew of Dale's involvement with Clarkson's campaign is less clear. The Wordsworths were impressed by the Falls and by the factory community but Coleridge – ill, drug-addicted and subject to fits and 'screaming dreams' throughout the tour – was less so.[21] In a reference to Coleridge's diary entry, Kyros Walker notes that New Lanark might have been expected to strike a chord in the heart of one who in his younger days considered living in a Pantisocratic commune in America. Coleridge, however, noticed only ... 'Huge Cotton Mills'.[22]

This was certainly a rare and exceptional reaction.[23] The area inspired many poets and artists before and after Coleridge. However, the romantic and spiritual view of the world to be found later in the work of the Romantic writers needs to be tempered in relation to New Lanark with, firstly, an Enlightened view of the emergent industrialisation process and the advancement of science and technology within that and, secondly, a practical view of the working and living conditions of factory workers, most of whom were women and children. Thomas Garnett, a major Enlightenment figure himself, while attracted by the scenery, also makes it clear that there was an other purpose to his visit, namely, to see the children at work.[24] This growing concern for the child workers and their living conditions was picked up by Thomas Bayley and others and led eventually to Parliamentary enquiries culminating in the various Factories Acts. Hence Garnett notes the existence of 'neat substantial houses, forming two streets, about half a mile in length, broad, regular and clean'.[25] Similarly, as his party is passing through the village, 'the children were just coming from their work to breakfast; on this account we did not stop as we wished to see them at work'.[26]

His detailed observations of the village have proved to be a valuable historical record over the years. However, although he was signed in as a visitor to New Lanark in 1798, many of Garnett's 'observations' (particularly in relation to the children) rely heavily on the *Statistical Account* and on James McNayr's comments published in 1797.[27] McNayr was at the time the publisher (and co-editor) of *The Glasgow Courier* and his *Guide from Glasgow* was printed by the Courier office in 1797. Assuming that their accounts were written and published in chronological order, it is reasonable to assume that McNayr visited new Lanark before Garnett but McNayr's name does not appear in the Visitors' Book. Alternatively, McNayr may simply have embellished the existing information in the *Statistical Account*.

Thomas Bayley (entered as 'Bialey') of the Manchester Board of Health visited on 14th September, 1798. Dale had responded to Bayley's 1796 questionnaire on conditions in New Lanark and it is likely that Bayley was gathering more evidence for the Board in their campaign for better factory conditions. If so, there could be no better place from which to gather evidence. There had always been strong connections between Glasgow and Manchester Chambers of Commerce, particularly in relation to cotton spinning factories and the New Lanark mills were certainly well-known throughout Lancashire.[28] The Manchester connection is crucial to the story of New Lanark because of Robert Owen's employment in the city prior to his New Lanark period. He was working for the Chorlton Twist Company and his associates in that venture included Messrs. Barton & Atkinson. The company had connections with Glasgow and the west of Scotland and it was Owen's job to visit twice a year to sell yarn to Scottish weavers.[29] It was quite natural that he should feel drawn to the New Lanark mills and his first visit is recorded as 9th March 1798.

Extract from New Lanark Visitors' Book showing Robert Owen's first recorded visit.
(University of Glasgow Archives Services. New Lanark Mills Collection.)

He returned with Barton and two others a few weeks later, on 16th May and again (on his own) on 15th June. For someone who was accustomed to visiting Scotland twice a year, this was quite a flurry of visits and Owen must have been impressed. Both Atkinson & Barton accompanied him on his next (recorded) visit a year later in July 1799 and Barton came back on his own in September of that year but by that time the deal was done and the mills were sold to the Chorlton Twist Company for £60,000. The management of the mills was to be Owen's responsibility.[30] In parallel with all of this, Owen's courtship of and subsequent marriage to Dale's daughter Caroline ensured that his ties to New Lanark would be particularly strong.[31]

New Lanark was a busy, profitable enterprise whose fame had spread well beyond Lanarkshire and was attracting what we would refer to today as 'tourists' (many with a variety of motives) visiting the Falls and the new model village. It is interesting to speculate (and it can be little more than that) on some of the other visitors whose names appear in the Visitors' Book. Could it be, for example, that the Mr. McGuffog who visited in August 1797 was James McGuffog, the Scottish-born Lincolnshire draper who employed (and looked after) the 10 year old Robert Owen for four or five years until 1784–1785? McGuffog had no family of his own (although there was a nephew) and, according to Donnachie, was a judicious buyer whose stock was the best that money could buy.[32] Given that he thought nothing of travelling to London and Stockport in his quest for quality cloth, it is possible that he came to New Lanark looking for fine yarns which could be 'put out'.

Similarly, there is some confusion about the various Gillespies and Douglases who visited New Lanark and disentangling these also leads to some speculation. James Gillespie of Anderston, who visited 8th November 1897, may have been a member of the eponymous family of spinners and weavers in the city of Glasgow. Alternatively, he may or may not have been the James Gillespie who visited on three other occasions (two with a Miss Gillespie) from 'Douglas Mill'. This small mill had been established c.1792 in the village of Douglas (named after Lord Douglas) in Lanarkshire, twelve miles from New Lanark when 'a company from Glasgow, consisting of natives of Douglas and men of industry and intelligence fitted up a small cotton spinning and weaving work' and he may have been looking to observe good practice.

It is likely that the 'Mr. Douglas', also of Douglas Mill who visited on 13th November 1797, was Campbell Douglas, who owned the mill and lived in a 'very good house' nearby.[33] It is quite possible, however, that this was a reference to William Douglas of Douglas Mills in Pendleton Lancashire. These mills had been in operation since the early Arkwright days and by 1792 were operating some 3,000–4,000 spindles.[34] What is interesting is that Douglas had been increasing his use of pauper apprentices (although he had only 27 in 1795) and may have been looking at Dale's arrangements for his apprentice children in New Lanark. Douglas took some of his pauper children from the London area 'but pauper children from as far away as Glasgow were placed in the Lancashire mills' and it is possible that he was looking to recruit new apprentices, albeit without making his intentions public.[35] It is to be hoped that he was unsuccessful because his harsh treatment of his child employees subsequently earned him the title of 'Black Douglas'.[36]

The 'Mr. Douglas' of Newton Douglas is clearly William Douglas (knighted in 1801), Dale's partner in the Galloway mill. It is not particularly surprising that Douglas should visit his business partner, given their common interests. However, Douglas may have been attracted to New Lanark at this time because Dale had let it be known that he wished to withdraw from some of his business ventures. He wrote to Dr. Currie in 1798: 'I have been rather indifferent in my health for some time past, and wish much to retire from the business'.[37] Ill-health would also explain why Dale was unable to attend the committee meetings of the Town's Hospital (where he was a director) for some four years. His health fluctuated quite significantly from then on and, although he was able to remain involved in most of his business and charity work, he was well aware of the need for what would be referred to today as 'succession planning'. That being the case, New Lanark was potentially on the market and was a very attractive proposition for anyone with sufficient finance or access to such, and it may be that Douglas had this in mind when he visited.

Other wealthy merchants visited, perhaps with a view to buying. The McCall brothers who were involved with Dale in the partnership with William Douglas were significant West India merchants with access to capital, but there were visitors from most of the wealthy merchant families in the city – other West India merchants such as the Bogles, Buchanans and Dennistouns but also the Dunlops, Finlays, Monteiths, Campbells, Tennents, Oswalds, all of whom were certainly in a position to form partnerships with a view to purchasing Dale's mills. Similarly, Robert Owen, while he may well have been sent by Messrs. Barton & Atkinson simply to do business with Dale, must have appreciated very quickly that New Lanark had huge potential for any individual or group who could afford the investment. Owen claimed that he knew immediately that New Lanark was the site for the great experiment which was already forming in his mind but this is at least open to question.[38]

It is entirely possible that some of the visitors were less interested in purchasing New Lanark than they were in discovering some of the secrets of a successful spinning business. On occasion, a few of these secrets could be made available to potential business partners in an attempt to attract their attention. Indeed, Dale noted that one such partner's 'chief reason in comming (sic) to us is that he might get good information respecting carding and he told me on Saturday that he has already produced much by this information that my foreman Mr. Kelly has given him'.[39] Interestingly, despite Kelly's generosity (or perhaps because of it), this particular partnership failed to materialise. Other visitors to the mills may have been interested in simply stealing some of its secrets. This type of industrial espionage was not uncommon at the time. The so-called 'Father of the American Industrial Revolution', Samuel Slater, had started out as an apprentice in Strutt's mills in Belper and, after emigrating to the U.S. (despite the fact that textile workers were prohibited from emigrating), set up America's first water-powered cotton mill in Pawtucket, Rhode Island in 1793, based entirely on the machinery and production methods in the Derbyshire mills. Since the Belper Mills used Arkwright's technology, Arkwright was understandably concerned (and always had been) about employees leaving his mills and taking their knowledge and experience with them, and even casual visitors were not allowed to look round any of his mills.[41] Other mill owners were less careful. The La Rochefoucauld brothers, sons of the Duc de Lioncourt, toured England in 1785, clearly intent on gathering as much information as they could regarding the new technology, sketching and recording as they went. They visited a cotton mill in Derby but were refused access to all the Manchester mills, which is perhaps unsurprising, given that a few years earlier, an M. de Grillon had visited some of the Manchester factories and had "made off with several good designs" and also some machine parts.[42] It is quite feasible that some of Dale's visitors, particularly from abroad, where there was considerable potential for new developments in spinning, were more than tourists – it has been suggested that John Aspinwall, an American and great grandfather of F.D. Roosevelt was one such visitor.[40] However, Aspinwall's diary entry for 1795 appears innocuous enough at first sight, moving from a description of the mills to a focus on the famous water-powered clock invented by William Kelly:

> Mr. Dale's great Cotton Mill ... four different buildings of five Storeys high having eight hundred windows and forming a front of six hundred feet. This Manufactory of Cotton yarn employs 1,300 people. There are about 12,000 spindles going in these mills. There is a remarkable clock with a face something larger than a common clock. It has five dials, one for the hours and minutes and seconds; one for the weeks; one for the months; one for the years; one for the ten years, the hand requiring that time to go once around. And all this goes by water and by which they regulate the Mill as the same wheel turns the Clock and the Mill.[43]

Perhaps this was an example of 18th century espionage or perhaps it was merely a diary observation. Perhaps William Douglas was not 'The Black Douglas' on the lookout for more child labour to exploit. Whatever the case, New Lanark certainly had the potential to attract the unscrupulous as well as the virtuous.

Donnachie has argued that New Lanark, with its combination of factory tourism and rugged wild scenery, spanning the eras of Enlightenment, Romanticism and Reform, holds a particularly significant place in the history of tourism and that the area offered all three eras in the one place.[44] While this would certainly apply to New Lanark under Robert Owen, much the same could be said of the Dale period. The area attracted not only businessmen and the new merchant classes but also Enlightenment figures from the world of science and technology, alongside anti slave trade campaigners and people with new ideas about freedom and working conditions not just in the U.K. but across Europe and the Empire. As the Romantic movement gained popularity, the Falls attracted poets and artists interested in the power of nature and the possibility of communitarian, utopian life. Running parallel to all of this were increasing numbers of people who were concerned about conditions of employment, factory reform and public health. All of these are observable in the Dale period.

Dale's 'tourists' were among the early pioneers of all of these issues. They were the people who were interested in new ways of producing things – the factory method; the social, economic and educational opportunities of a factory community; reform of the Poor Laws and public health through full employment. Dale himself was one of these men. His entire business career was built on a strong social conscience and a recognition that only a successful, profitable business could provide plentiful employment and humane living conditions while supplying enough cotton twist to satisfy the explosion in demand. In Owen's time, tourists came to New Lanark to see his famous educational and social 'experiment', centred on the New Institution and the village itself. But Dale's New Lanark was the foundation for much of these later success stories, whether or not Owen chose to recognise it. Dale's new factory community quickly established a reputation for humane conditions of employment, established schooling and enlightened social conditions:

> *This union of circumstances soon drew to Lanark vast numbers of strangers; and although a multiplicity of objects claimed their attention, no one was ever more pleasing than the neatness and order in which the boarders were kept.*[45]

The 'boarders' were Dale's pauper apprentices – one of the most vulnerable groups in society. It is to Dale's eternal credit that his reputation for benevolence, honesty and integrity was founded on his humane treatment of his workforce and, in particular, of the apprentice children. No biography of Dale would be complete without a close look at the living and working conditions of his employees, young and old.

References: Chapter 5

1   Owen, R. (1857) *The Life of Robert Owen Written by Himself*. Vol. 1. London: Effingham Wilson. New impression (1967) London: Frank Cass & Co., p.134.

2   Donnachie, I. (2000) *Robert Owen of New Lanark and New Harmony*. East Linton: Tuckwell Press, p.170. See also *New Lanark Visitors' Book 1821–24*. University of Glasgow Archives. UGD 42/7/1/2.

3   Sinclair, J. (ed) (1791–99) *The Statistical Account of Scotland, 1791–99*. Vol. XV, p.34.

4   *The Scots Magazine* 53, November 1791. p.563.

5   *New Lanark Visitors' Book 1795–99*. University of Glasgow Archives. UGD 42/7/1/1. I am also indebted to Prof. Ian Donnachie for his assistance in compiling this chapter.

6   It seems likely from the mis-spelling of several surnames that the guests did not enter their own names in the book and that different employees undertook this task at different times.

7   All the visitor information is based on the names listed in the 1795–99 *Visitors' Book*.

8   Devine, T.M. (1975) *The Tobacco Lords. A Study of the Tobacco merchants of Glasgow and their Trading Activities, 1740–90*. Edinburgh: John Donald, p.12.

9   Ibid., pp.177–184.

10   William French from 1778–1780 and John Dunlop 1794–1796. In earlier years, there had been a number of Provosts elected from the Buchanan, and Dunlop families.

11   Stewart, G. (1881) *Curiosities of Glasgow Citizenship as Exhibited Chiefly in the Business Career of its Old Commercial Aristocracy*. Glasgow: J. Maclehose, p.220.

12   Dale's nephew David Dale Junior – son of Dale's brother Hugh – also visited but there is some mystery as to the identity of John Dale and William Dale who visited in 1796 & 1797 respectively.

13   White, G. (1847) 'A Practical Treatise on Weaving by Hand and Power Looms. Intended as a Text Book for Manufacturers and Power Loom Engineers', *The New Quarterly Review or Home, Foreign & Colonial Journal*, Vol. 8. (2) January: 448–488. p.465.

14   Garnett, T. (1811) *Observations on a Tour through the Highlands and Part of the Western Isles of Scotland. A New Edition in Two Volumes*. London: John Stockdale Vol. 2, p.228. N.B. Originally published 1800 by Cadell & Davies.

15   Ibid., p.231.

16   Ibid., p.228–9.

17   McNayr, J. (1797) *A Guide from Glasgow to some of the most Remarkable Scenes in the Highlands and to the Falls of Clyde*. Glasgow: Courier Office, pp.215, 217–8, 231, 245.

18   Owen, R. (1857) *Life*, Vol. 1, p.70.

19   Fitton, R.S. and Wadsworth, A.P. (1958) *The Strutts and the Arkwrights 1758–1830. A Study of the Early Factory System*. Manchester: M.U.P., pp.174–5.

20 Walker, C.K. (2002) *Breaking Away. Coleridge in Scotland*. New Haven & London: Yale Uni Press, p.13.

21 Knight, W. (ed) (1904) *Journals of Dorothy Wordsworth*. 2 Vols. London: MacMillan. Vol. 1. pp.189–196, 200.

22 Walker, C.K., *Breaking Away*, pp.12–13.

23 However, when Southey met Owen on a visit to New Lanark in 1819 his personal opinion of him was not entirely complimentary. Owen is variously described as a kind of plantation manager, wielding absolute power, intent on destroying individuality of character. See Southey, R. (1972) *Journal of a Tour in Scotland in 1819*. (Facsimile). Edinburgh: J. Thin, pp.260–266.

24 Garnett, T. (1811) *Observation*, p.228.

25 Ibid., p.232.

26 Ibid.,p.228.

27 Ibid., p.235n.

28 Donnachie, I. and Hewitt, G. (1993) *Historic New Lanark*. Edinburgh: E.U.P, pp.42–43.

29 Owen, R. (1857) *Life*, Vol. 1, p.46. See also Donnachie, I. and Hewitt, G. (1993) *Historic New Lanark*, p.61.

30 Donnachie, I. (2000) *Robert Owen*, p.75.

31 The Visitors' Book shows a visit on 21st Sept 1798 by Arthur Spear and his sister. Arthur was a cotton broker in Manchester whom Owen had known for some time. His sister was a friend of Caroline Dale and both Spears acted as intermediaries in the Owen's courtship of Caroline. See Owen *Life* p.45–50.

32 Donnachie, I. (2000) *Robert Owen*, p.24.

33 Garnett, T. (1811) *Observation*, p.237.

34 *The Douglas Archives' A collection of Historical and Genealogical records*. http://douglashistory.co.uk/history/william_douglas8.htm

35 Ibid.

36 Presumably named after the 13th Century Scottish nobleman, known to the English as 'Black Douglas' because of his murderous incursions into the north of England.

37 Currie, William Wallace. (1831) *Memoir of the Life, Writings and Correspondence of James Currie*, 2 vols. London: Longman, Rees, Orme, Brown & Green, Vol. 1, p.162.

38 Owen, R. (1857) *Life*, Vol. 1, p.46.

39 Dale to Claud Alexander, 22nd December 1788. Dale/Alexander Correspondence. Glasgow City Archives, MS 63/6.

40 Donnachie, I. *Behold Dale's Works*. Unpublished paper.

41 Wrigley, W. (2011), 'Cromford Mills, Lea Mills and the Lumsdale Valley', *The Historian*, Autumn 2011, pp.26–31.

42 Scarfe, N. (1995), *Innocent Espionage. The La Rochefoucauld Brothers' Tour of England in 1785*. Woodbridge: Boydell Press, pp.62, 65.

43 Butt, J. (1967) *The Industrial Archaeology of Scotland*. Newton Abbot: David & Charles, p.65.

44 Donnachie, I. (2004) 'Historic Tourism to New Lanark and the Falls of Clyde, 1795–1830. The Evidence of Contemporary Visiting Books and related Journals', *Journal of Tourism and Cultural Change*, 2 (3): 145–162, p.160.

45 'Memoir of David Dale esq.', *Imperial Magazine*, 4:46 (1822: November) p.1069–70.

Chapter 6:
The Factory Community, Apprenticeship and Social Conditions.

The concept of the factory community was not Dale's invention. Arkwright and Strutt had established communities around their mills several years before New Lanark opened for business. Indeed, as Fitton & Wadsworth note, the Derbyshire factories were the first model for the factory community.[1] These communities operated on a number of important assumptions. Principal among these was the notion that the owner was responsible for everything. There was no Government or local authority contribution and there were no public services. Labour had to be attracted and retained and the more individuals who could earn a living, the less strain there would be on poor rates. Inevitably, the owners became patriarchal figures, subject to a greater or lesser extent to the 'benevolent feudalism dear to [their] generation'.[2]

Although smaller than New Lanark, the mills at Cromford and Belper were the centre of substantial communities. Cromford numbers peaked around 800 employees in 1789 and remained at that level for some years. Belper reached 600 employees by 1789 but thereafter numbers increased to 1,300 by 1802 – a rise matched by an equally steep increase in the number of houses built, from 433 to 873.[3] Such factory villages required the usual infrastructure of a working community – houses, roads, bridges, shops, inns and so on but they also required a social identity and this was certainly in existence in Cromford. Arkwright provided a lot for his employees, including a regular market (with prizes for the bakers, butchers etc. who produced the best market fare); an annual feast for 200 workers; two balls per year at the Greyhound Inn for families and regular choral concerts staged by the workers. There was much partying and dancing in the September festival of 'Candlelighting', when 500 men and boys paraded round the town, accompanied by a band.[4] 'Everything was the face of industry and cheerfulness', as one early traveller put it.[5]

In case this all got out of hand, chapels were built and Sunday schools established to cater for the morals of the people and to provide basic education. Fitton and Wadsworth's description of these schools as 'a cheap solvent of the twin problems of vice and ignorance' seems entirely appropriate.[6]

Strutt's Sunday school was established in 1784 and Arkwright's in early 1785. Very quickly, Arkwright's school was dealing with 200 children (50 at a time) every Sunday. In Belper, the local newspaper was fulsome in its praise of Strutt:

> We hear from Belpar (sic) that Mr. Strutt has, (with a liberality which does honour to the human heart) entirely at his own expense, instituted a Sunday School for the benefit of all the youth of both sexes employed in his cotton mill at that town; and provides them with all necessary books etc., for learning to read and write ... An example worthy of imitation by all whom Providence has blessed with Affluence ... it becomes the duty of every thinking person ... to hold forth an assisting hand ... to stop the tide of Immorality.[7]

In similar vein, Joseph Farington describes the chapel and Sunday school in Cromford:

> They came to Chapel in regular order and looked healthy and were decently cloathed (sic) and clean. They were attended by an Old Man their schoolmaster. To this school girls also go for the same purpose ... Whichever are not at Chapel are at School, to which they both go every Sunday both morning and afternoon. The whole plan appears to be such as to do Mr. Arkwright great credit.[8]

Committed as Arkwright was to the idea of 'community' and of supporting his workers and their children, there were limits. It was put to him that a factory was no place to form and prepare the female character for domestic life and that he ought to allow one half day per week 'to instruct the women in sewing and in their Christian duties'. Arkwright, however, said that he 'could not possibly allow his neighbouring competitors such an advantage over him as the sacrifice of half a day would prove'.[9]

Laudable as Sunday schools undoubtedly were, they were still in their infancy. In Glasgow in 1787, there were only eight Sunday schools (for some 400 children), paid for by the General Session, the Town Council and private donation. Paisley began to introduce Sunday schools from 1797.[10] Inevitably, they provided only the most basic education and fell well short of the schooling provided in New Lanark. Also, the Sunday school movement, particularly in England where there was no established parish school system, met with limited success. Although it is clear that Strutt and Arkwright included some reading and writing in their Sunday schools, this was not the case elsewhere. There was still considerable opposition to popular, mass education, which was considered a threat by some to the established order. This helps to explain the situation in Manchester in 1786 where it was forbidden to teach writing in any Sunday school in the town.[11]

It is also worth noting that the children in the Sunday schools were nearly all employed in the factories during the week and that some of them were as young as six or seven years old – as they were in New Lanark. According to Archibald Buchanan, children at Arkwright's mills in Cromford worked from 6 a.m. till 7 p.m. with only one hour for dinner and no regular timeslot for breakfast.[12] However, for some 22 years until 1792, Arkwright's mills operated a double shift, 23 hours per day until the demand for cotton appeared to fall and nightshifts were halted.[13] Night shifts were not uncommon. Robert Peel, later an enthusiastic proponent of factory reform, also operated a 24-hour system at the family mills in Radcliffe, near Manchester.[14] Parish apprentices there took turns in the dormitory beds.[15] At the Stanley mills in Perthshire, there appears to have been occasional night working. The children working there are described as being generally very healthy, despite being *confined at work in the mill for many hours of the day and at times during the night*.[16] In New Lanark at the time, there are no recorded instances of children working night shifts, although there is a curious reference to *1576 spindles going in the day time and 480 going during the night* in one of Dale's letters to Claud Alexander.[17] It is possible, therefore, that occasional night shifts may have been in operation – perhaps in periods of high demand. If that were the case, then it is likely that the children would have been required to work at their machines in the normal way.

There may have been no night shifts (or very few of them) in New Lanark but there were large numbers of young people employed there – so much so that when Charles Hatchett, a distinguished scientist and mining engineer, paid a visit in 1796 he formed an initial impression that the mills were *attended principally by children.*[18]

The use of child labour was part and parcel of the times and, while modern attitudes find it abhorrent, it was perfectly normal to employ children under ten years of age in cotton mills and bleachfields. Arkwright and Strutt were considered to be benevolent philanthropists and patriarchal mill owners at one and the same time and it is into this tradition which Dale fits. Large numbers of children (and women) were required and, although there was initial resistance and reluctance to join the new factory system of employment in Derbyshire, just as in Lanarkshire, there was as strong a tradition of child employment in other industries in the Derbyshire area. At Cromford, Arkwright could draw on the families of the lead miners of the area, just as at Belper Strutt could draw on those of the nailers.[19] This tradition may have reduced the supply problem somewhat, allowing Arkwright and Strutt to access a sufficiency of female and child labour and may also explain why Arkwright and Strutt (unlilke mill owners such as Oldknow and Greg in other areas) seldom had to use parish apprentices in their mills, although Fitton notes that *some few* such apprentices were employed.[20] In Scotland, George Dempster, one of the country's most charitable and philanthropic figures, concerned at all times with providing the means of employment to as many as possible, thought nothing of employing pauper apprentices in the Stanley Mills. By 1795, 300 of the 350 employees were women or children under sixteen years of age.[21] The minute book of the West Kirk Charity Workhouse in Edinburgh, notes that in 1797, *'a petition was presented from Messrs. Dempster & Co., cotton manufacturers, Perth, requesting that if there were any children fit for a Cotton Manufactory they might be sent to their Cotton Mill'.*[22]

In Aberdeen, Woodside Mills had a large building called 'The Barracks' which housed young indentured apprentices – almost certainly paupers or orphans – working in the calico printing works. The boys were called 'the bun boys' (bound boys) because of their indentured status.[23] Houldsworth's mill in the Anderston district of Glasgow (1801) housed 500 workers in barracks accommodation built by the company.[24] The Blantyre Mills had 60 'barracks' children – indentured orphans or pauper children aged eight to twelve years.

Indentures

In New Lanark and elsewhere, employment in the mills was based on an apprenticeship or indenture system where employees would contract themselves to an employer for a period of time. This is sometimes described as a 'bound apprenticeship' scheme where young apprentices were held in a legally binding agreement or contract. However, indentures were also part of the adult employment pattern and were a fact of life in many types of employment, from domestic service to mining. Archibald Davidson, one of the adult mechanics employed by Dale in the very earliest days of New Lanark and sent with ten other men and fifteen boys for training at Cromford, was an indentured employee. In Davidson's case, there was a legal agreement:

> ...between David Dale, merchant in Glasgow and Archibald Davidson, journeyman wright in Glasgow. The latter binds himself to the service of the former for ten years, for six days per week and twelve hours per day and to keep secret, under penalty of £5,000, the form, construction use or manner of working of any machines or engines lately invented by Richard Arkwright Esq. of Cromford.[25]

The agreement was signed on 12th January 1785 and discharged on 15th January 1795. Of those ten years, two were spent in Cromford before returning to New Lanark where he could expect to earn twelve shillings per week – a sum almost certainly fixed for the duration of the agreement. Pay rises would normally only be negotiated as part of a new indenture and, while Davidson's was a moderately well paid job, it was no more than that. It was certainly comparable with what was on offer to skilled men in Lanark at the time (and in Glasgow and Cromford where wages were very similar), at around eleven shillings per week for a spinner.[26] In 1793, for example, a Lanark stonemason could expect to earn ten to twelve shillings per week, a stockingmaker eleven shillings, a carpenter nine shillings and a labourer six to seven shillings. According to one source, 'Dale's male operatives earned about the same'.[27] Table 4 below shows some food prices in Lanark at the time and it would seem that wages were reasonable in term of their buying power.[28]

Table 4: Lanark food prices c.1793

Beef & Mutton	3½d.–4½d.	per lb. English
Veal	4d.–6d.	per lb. English
Lamb	5d.	per lb. English
Butter	8½d.–10d.	per lb. English
Hens	1s. 3d.–1s 6d.	each
Eggs	4d.–7d.	per doz
Sweet milk	2d.	per Scotch pint
Churned milk	¼d.	per Scotch pint

Wages did not rise a great deal over time. The *New Lanark Monthly Report Book & Wage Book* for 1801-1802 indicates that the average wage for a spinner was around ten shillings per week but some made as little as 7s. 4d., while others (relatively few) made up to fourteen shillings.[29]

Much is, quite justifiably, written about Dale's benevolence and philanthropy but Liddell's *Memoir of David Dale* indicates that when Dale decided that something was a purely business matter, he could, on occasion, be quite inflexible – as he was with Archibald Paterson, James Monteith and possibly Richard Arkwright.[30] Dale comes in for some rare criticism for his treatment of some of his (adult) 'servants'. 'Servants' should not be taken literally in the first instance, although Liddell does address the issue of Dale's personal servants in the same piece. Acknowledging that the custom of the time was to employ people on a period of indentured servitude at a fixed salary for the duration and also that Dale *'from time to time'* promoted employees who were particularly able:

> ...it was remarked at the time that he seldom, if ever, increased the salary in proportion to the greater responsibilities, nor in general would he allow the individual to leave till the end of the engagement, even when his doing so would have improved his circumstances.

Dale, was, of course, quite entitled to stick to the letter of the law as far as the 'contract' was concerned but Liddell argues that on these occasions, Dale did not act *'with that generosity which his great benevolence would have led us to expect'*.[32] In fact, Liddell goes further and offers the view that Dale's behaviour in these matters was *'considered by his best friends as rather sharp dealing'*. Dale, however, was not to be moved on the issue, preferring to adhere to *'the usages of trade of that day'*. Apparently, those affected by these decisions did not hold it against him and Dale did not lose the *'confidence and favour'* of his old staff. They spoke of him with the greatest of respect, which seems particularly generous of them. Likewise, Dale's *'confidential servants'* (domestic staff, presumably subject to the same conditions) were not hindered in their careers – *'most of them afterwards rose to commercial eminence'*.[33]

In New Lanark, the indenture system was gradually amended but the principles remained the same. A New Lanark indenture form (c.1790–1800) is shown opposite. This had to be completed by individuals on their own behalf or (more often) on behalf of their children.[34] Neither the number of years nor the weekly wage is specified but there was clearly no longer a need to be concerned about Arkwright's secrets and he is not referred to. The penalty for breaking the agreement is therefore reduced to five guineas – still a considerable sum but far from the ludicrous figure of £5,000 mentioned in 1785. All of this has to be borne in mind before it can be claimed that Dale's treatment of his workers was entirely original. Certainly, the provision of day schooling was relatively new, but the principle of the 'factory community' with indentured workers had been established for several years in England. Even the provision of day schooling in New Lanark may not have been entirely unique, since it is possible that William Gillespie's cotton mill in the North Woodside area of Glasgow (1784) had a school attached to it from the beginning. By 1797 the Woodside mill also had a 'Reading Society', paid for by the employees – as was the case in the Rothesay cotton mill.[35] Gillespie employed *'a master to teach the children through the week, to read'* and *'a preacher who publicly catechises and instructs the children'* on Sundays.[36] These reports were written in the mid 1790s and it remains unclear whether the teacher and preacher were in place as early as 1784, although it seems quite likely. Gillespie's school is described in The Statistical Account as a *'charity school'* and it is interesting to note that Dale supported a similar school in the Calton area, near his house in Charlotte Street. The master here had a salary of £15 per annum, although it is not clear how much of this was contributed by Dale.[37]

There was clearly a sense of community in the North Woodside area of the city (often referred to simply as 'Woodside' but not to be confused with Woodside Mill in Aberdeen), where the cotton mill formed a significant part of the community.[38]

> This [i.e. the cotton mill] with the people engaged in the bleachfield and otherwise, has made Woodside a considerable village, while it has become a seat of plenty and comfort, the happy consequence of industry and manufacture. Sensible to the advantages of religion and good morals, to promote the industry and happiness of the people, the benevolent proprietor pays particular attention to these ... he has also fitted up, and supports at his own expense, a place for public worship on the Lord's Day.[39]

Overall, then, it might be argued that Dale's efforts to establish a community in New Lanark were indeed improvements, but improvements on a model which had its beginnings in Cromford in England and possibly Woodside in Glasgow.

The general notion of 'charity schooling' was also well established by this time. Joan Simon argues that charity schools were those which were non fee-paying and which had as their aim the rescuing *'from idleness and irreligion the unemployed poor from 7–12'*,

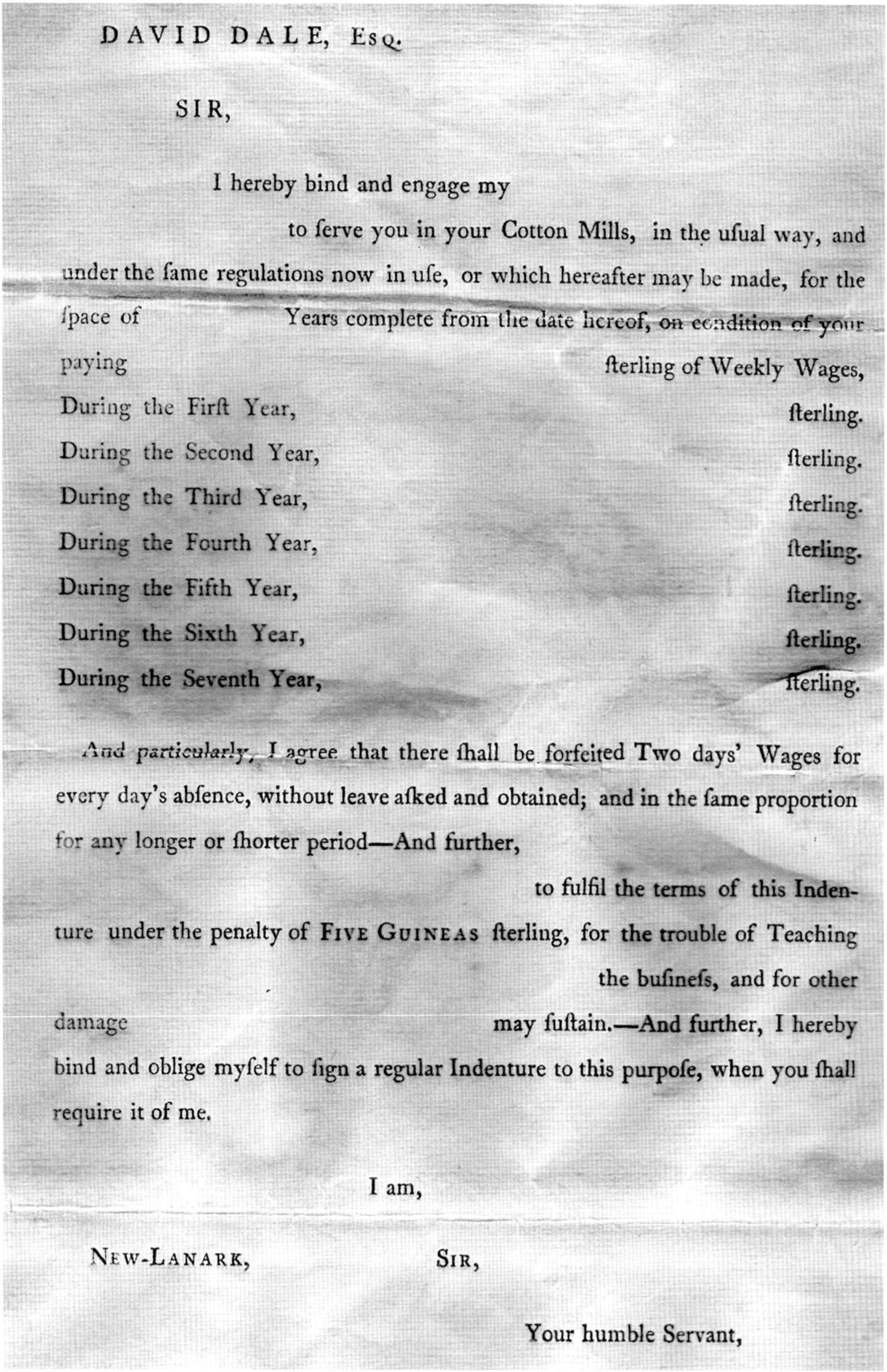

DAVID DALE, Esq.

SIR,

I hereby bind and engage my

to ferve you in your Cotton Mills, in the ufual way, and under the fame regulations now in ufe, or which hereafter may be made, for the fpace of Years complete from the date hereof, on condition of your paying fterling of Weekly Wages,

During the Firft Year, fterling.

During the Second Year, fterling.

During the Third Year, fterling.

During the Fourth Year, fterling.

During the Fifth Year, fterling.

During the Sixth Year, fterling.

During the Seventh Year, fterling.

And particularly, I agree that there fhall be forfeited **Two** days' **Wages** for every day's abfence, without leave afked and obtained; and in the fame proportion for any longer or fhorter period—And further,

to fulfil the terms of this **Indenture** under the penalty of FIVE GUINEAS fterling, for the trouble of Teaching the bufinefs, and for other damage may fuftain.—And further, I hereby bind and oblige myfelf to fign a regular Indenture to this purpofe, when you fhall require it of me.

I am,

NEW-LANARK, SIR,

Your humble Servant,

Blank indenture form, *c.*1790–1800. (Robert Owen Museum, Newtown).

i.e. not a parish school.[40] Such schools also had to provide clothes, food and books and set pupils on the path to a useful working life, normally by helping them to find employment.

Hutcheson's Hospital, founded 1641, certainly maintained, clothed and educated boys over nine years of age and bound them as apprentices, but only if these boys were sons of Burgesses and had attended an English school (i.e. a school which taught reading and some grammar) for six months before entering Hutcheson's. The idea of a free education for those who could afford to pay for it does not really equate with the notion of 'charity'.

The only major institution in Glasgow which came close to Simon's definition of charity school was the Town's Hospital, which clothed, fed, educated, nursed, lodged and employed pauper children. Even here, however, this must be set against the fact that it also housed lunatics, geriatrics and sick adults. The Town's Hospital, supported by the town council and the General Session, was a large institution with various functions and itself supported a number of small charity schools in the area.[41]

As far as Dale's involvement with charity schools is concerned, the only other information available is the *Statistical Account's* brief reference to the 'charity school' in the Calton area of Glasgow (near his house in Charlotte Street) to which he subscribed. Similarly, very little is known about his involvement in a *'Free School established in Glasgow for the Education of Poor Children'*, apart from the following:

> One of the schools is exclusively for the children of soldiers and sailors and was instituted in 1789 by the late Rev. Dr William Porteous ... and David Dale, Esq. Every year the children are furnished with shoes and stockings and they also receive books gratis.[42]

The system of schooling in New Lanark, on the other hand, is slightly more accessible. The point is that the idea of a factory community was not new; perhaps even day schooling in mills was not new; neither was the idea of 'charity schooling'. However, what *was* new was Dale's expansion of these ideas to produce a thriving community with a thriving school as well as providing charity for his workhouse apprentices. He provided a great deal for the people of New Lanark – much more than any other mill owner. In the village, 'factory community', 'school' and 'charity' came together for the first time in Britain. This is perhaps most evident in Dale's treatment of the pauper children.

Pauper Apprentices

No. 4 Mill was used '*as a store room for cotton wool, as workshops for the different tradesmen employed; and as a boarding house for 275 children who have no parents here, and who get their maintenance, education and clothing for work*' – i.e. without pay.[43] These were the children brought from the West Kirk Charity Workhouse in Edinburgh and the Town's Hospital in Glasgow, of which Dale became a director in 1787. Dale referred to them as 'boarders' to distinguish them from the children who stayed with their parents in the village.

The workhouse apprentices, in common with the other children, many of them as young as six, were 'bound' to their employer as part of the indenture system in much the same way as adults like Archibald Davidson, although the workhouse children's indenture period was invariably longer. Dale's letter to Bayley in 1796, which is discussed more fully later in the chapter, contains a great deal of information on the pauper apprentices. As far as their terms of engagement were concerned:

> The time of hiring differs with the different descriptions of children. Those who agree for a stipulated weekly wage, and who are generally such as live with their parents, are commonly engaged for four years; while such as are received from the workhouse in Edinburgh, or who are otherwise without friends to take charge of them, and who, in lieu of wages are maintained and educated, are bound four, five, six or seven years, according to their age, or generally till they have completed their fifteenth year. The mode of hiring is generally by contract of the parents or curators of the children in their behalf.[44]

Often, the children would work for a few years in cotton mills before the apprenticeship actually started. In one of Arkwright's mills, one boy started work at the age of six years and two months and worked in the card-room for four years before being apprenticed for seven years to learn '*the turning, filing and fitting up of wood, brass, iron, steel and every branch of machinery*'.[45] Young children were always required to prepare the cotton and card it (manually or on the carding machines) or to piece broken threads and clean the machines. The employment of large numbers of children (particularly workhouse apprentices) brought with it the problems of health, morals and discipline. Nor should it be assumed, as Butt points out, that these children were necessarily cheaper than home-based apprentices when the cost of feeding, clothing and educating them was taken into account.[46]

It is clear why Dale, in common with many English mill owners, employed pauper children.[47] Factory work was new and initially unpopular with the local population, north and south of the Border. At first, it was '*considered to be disgraceful to any father who allowed his child to enter the factory...*' and, until attitudes changed, the factories were worked by '*stranger children*' gathered together from the workhouses.[48] Attitudes did change in New Lanark. Dale's letter to Bayley noted that there were three sources of labour for the New Lanark mills – firstly the local '*native population*'; secondly, '*from families who have been collected ... from the neighbouring parishes and more distant parts of the country; or lastly from Edinburgh or Glasgow, by the number of destitute children these places constantly afford*'.[49]

It was also true that as technology advanced, fewer and fewer men were required in any event, the work being much better suited to women and children who could operate the lighter and faster machinery. Large numbers of women and children (particularly the latter) were required and, while Dale was quite correct in noting that '*the greatest part of the workers are lodged in their parents' houses in the village, in the immediate neighbourhood of the mills, or in the town of Lanark, one mile distant*', he might have added that there was still a shortage which could only be met by employing the workhouse children.[50] He might have further added that he always felt he had a Christian duty to provide paid work and security for these children, rather than leave them to the uncertainties of the workhouse.

Mill owners entered into contracts with the workhouse or similar charitable institution for children to work in the mills. The children themselves were either orphans or the sons and daughters of destitute parents who had placed the children in the care of the church or charity which operated the institution. As was often the case with Scottish 'charity', there were strict rules. When one parent objected to his children being sent out to any manufactory, the response from the West Kirk Charity Workhouse Committee in Edinburgh was swift and uncompromising:

> *...if any of the parents shall refuse to have their children disposed of as the Managers have determined, they must immediately remove them out of the house as having forfeited all title to this Charity, either for themselves or families.*[51]

When another parent requested that his daughter should not be sent to Lanark but kept in the workhouse until he could take her out, the request was summarily rejected.[52]

The workhouses were managed by powerful overseers sometimes referred to as 'Curators', 'Preceptors', 'Masters' or, simply, 'Managers'. In the case of the Town's Hospital in Glasgow, the Preceptor (William Craig) was, according to the original constitution, the '*one person with the principal superintendence*' of the workhouse'.[53] All the staff and inmates were responsible to him and he was responsible for ensuring that all the inmates were catered for according to the rules, and he supervised the day to day running of the institution. Much the same was true of the 'Master' in the Edinburgh Charity Workhouse and the West Kirk Charity Workhouse (also in Edinburgh) which supplied a considerable number of Dale's child apprentices. Samuel Kydd (writing under the pseudonym *Alfred*) notes that despite the efforts of the workhouse managers, parish apprentices in England often found themselves in difficult and dangerous situations during their indentured employment. Dale in New Lanark, however, is quoted as an exception.[54]

The accepted principle was that factory owners agreed to combine industrial training with moral and religious education, both of which were in limited supply (and had to be paid for by the public) in the workhouses. There was never any suggestion that these children would receive any regular wage for their work in the manufactories – indeed the workhouses forbade such a thing. The managers of the West Kirk Charity Workhouse in Edinburgh 'could not consent to any of them drawing weekly wages'.[55] Given that the workhouses received payment from the factory owners, the House Managers were keen to have these children employed. The Managers, however, had a continuing responsibility for the children throughout the apprenticeship, even if this was this often inadequately 'policed'.

The committee of the West Kirk, meeting on 5th October 1790, were keen to supply apprentices for New Lanark when their neighbouring institution could not:

> Mr. David Dale in Glasgow having proposed to the Managers of the Edinr. Charity Workhouse to relieve them upon terms advantageous to the house of as many children as they could spare for the purpose of employing them in his cotton manufactory, certain of the managers of this workhouse being informed that he could not be supplied from that quarter with as many as he needed, desired the master to enquire if he would accept upon the same conditions of what number might be allowed from this house.[56]

Dale had already written to the West Kirk a few days earlier, referring to an agreement in which 'the Managers ... would bind over about a dozen and a half of children to me on the same terms I give to the Edinr. Charity Workhouse', – terms which already included a guarantee that the children would be 'at no farther expence whatever' to the workhouse. Dale also guaranteed to 'cloathe the children completely when their Indentures expire'. Ever hopeful, he concludes his letter to the West Kirk by saying that he would 'take any number they chuse to send on the same terms'.[57] This was all acceptable to the Managers and they reminded Dale that his letter to the neighbouring Edinburgh Charity workhouse had included a reference to educating the children 'and they order this to be intimated to him accordingly'.[58] This all seems rather unnecessary since Dale's school had been operating for some five years.

Having thus satisfied themselves that terms and conditions were acceptable, the committee proceeded to identify some 25 boys and 24 girls who were 'inspected and ... judged sufficiently qualified to be bound over to him [Mr. Dale] accordingly'.[59] It is clear from a later meeting of the committee that 'inspected' and 'sufficiently qualified' were simply euphemisms for 'reckoned sufficiently strong'.[60]

Prior to their departure for New Lanark, the children were given a full set of new clothes which were obviously designed to last as long as possible. Boys and girls each received a hat and a night cap; three shirts (two coarse and one fine); two pairs of stockings; one pair of shoes; one pair of shoe buckles and a pair of sleeve buttons. The boys also received a new coat, waistcoat, breeches and two half neck kerchiefs while the girls each had a new gown, two petticoats and two neck kerchiefs. The workhouse arranged for the clothes to be made and supplied by a local man, Mr. Pratt, who estimated the cost of each set of clothes to be half a crown. Despite the fact that some of this cost might be defrayed by any money the children had earned by spinning wool in the workhouse, the committee immediately instructed Mr. Pratt 'to charge as much less as he found he could afford'.[61]

Other institutions were involved. It is well known that Dale was a director of the Town's Hospital and that apprentices from there worked in New Lanark, but there is very little other detail available from the records. The Statistical Account noted that the Town's Hospital clothed and educated all the boys and girls, '...upwards of 100 in number and when at a proper age, binds them apprentices to trades, or gets them into service.'[62] However, the same source, referring to the Town's Hospital expenditure for 1789, noted that £12. 11s. 7d. was spent on clothing only fourteen boys 'when bound apprentices' (down from a figure of 30 boys in 1780 but less than the 23 boys in 1790). There is no indication as to the place of employment and there is no mention of female apprentices.[63]

The Minutes of the Kirk Session of Corstorphine (Midlothian) are more revealing. They indicate that two local boys (William Finlay & David Ramage, aged eight or nine) were sent to New Lanark as apprentices in 1796. The parish minister was keen that an attempt should be made to have the boys placed 'in some of these Manufactories who ... cloath and educate them, requiring no recompense but their own labour for a certain period of years'.[64] This was far from an unusual practice, as many boys of that age were employed in the Manufactories carried on in the country.[65] The boys themselves would gain 'an advantage to themselves in *future life*', while the parish would also be conveniently relieved of the expense of caring for the boys. They would receive vocational training, and would be clothed, properly educated in reading and instructed in the principles of religion. Their travel expenses would also be met. Unsurprisingly, the Session agreed to the proposals and their clerk was ordered to write to Dale. It is worth noting that the proposal came from the church, not David Dale. It is also worth noting in this case that Dale employed an 'agent' – Mr. Anderson of West Bow, Edinburgh – who dealt with such enquiries. Two months later, the two boys were presented with a Bible from the Session and sent off to New Lanark for a period of six years. Three years later, a similar situation arose in Corstorphine Kirk regarding John Geddes, a parish orphan of unknown age. The minister agreed terms with Mr. Anderson and an indenture was signed '*binding the said boy to Mr. Dale for eight years to be fed cloathed and educated by Mr. Dale for said space of time*'.[66]

The *Edinburgh Magazine* was in no doubt as to the reality of the situation for all the child employees, boarders or not, and yet was still able to be positive about Dale's treatment of them:

> *The children who are employed in great numbers in this manufactory of cotton yarn are treated as tenderly and with as careful attention to their health and morals as the circumstances of their employment can permit.* [67]

The authors noted that the establishment of the mills had already improved the '*aspect*' of the village by its '*public spirited proprietor*', and that the environs were '*populous and their scenery beautiful and picturesque*'. Predicting a rosy future, it anticipated that new roads and canals would be built '*and opulence and improvement diffused all round*'. Dale, it seemed, was one of the merchants and manufacturers, '*who, improving their own fortunes, thus essentially serve their country are well entitled to that praise of patriotism which they never fail to obtain*'.[68] According to this view, providing employment to orphans and paupers (and Highlanders) who were found worthy of employment was '*by itself, a great boon to Scotland*'.[69]

The *Edinburgh Magazine's* view of the situation was relatively understated in comparison to some of the praise which was heaped on the proprietor of New Lanark. Dale was generally considered to be an exceptionally benevolent and philanthropic employer, particularly concerned in New Lanark with the welfare of the community and of its residents but similarly concerned about the general condition of employees and customers in his other business ventures and with the general wellbeing of all – as evinced in his charitable work and his religious beliefs. Thomas Garnett was effusive in his praise, noting the very low death rate among child employees in New Lanark and the fact that '*not one*' judicial punishment had been incurred. These were grounds for '*exultation*' on the part of the '*worthy owner*'.[70] He went further. Referring to the New Lanark community as a whole, he warmed to his theme:

> *What a number of people are here made happy and comfortable who would, many of them, have been cut off by disease, or, wallowing in dirt, been ruined by indolence... I never felt more gratified in my life. This scene formed a striking contrast to what I had witnessed in the Highlands.*[71]

Social Conditions

There were worse places to live in the 1780s. Liddell talks of '*comfortable dwellings ... good wages and constant employment*'. Cowan notes that the houses were all built according to a regular plan, '*combining economy with comfort*' at Lanark and the purpose-built houses in the village provided above-average accommodation. Some were slightly larger than others to accommodate differing family sizes and the houses were '*generally kept in good order*'.[72] The houses had slated roofs and internal ceilings – relatively new features which replaced the rural style of thatched roofed buildings sometimes shared with cattle and sheep.[73] Dale's tenants were also '*accommodated with gardens*'.[74] However, the Rev. John Aiton, writing a few years later, indicated that some of the original housing was less than desirable. Some of the houses had been built into the hillside and were '*earthed up*' on one side. He describes these as damp and uncomfortable. Overcrowding did nothing to help and, as a result, there was frequently '*a sickening indescribable effluvia, indicative of the want of ventilation*'.[75] Overall, although Aiton's comments were valid for parts of the village, it would appear from the many accounts of the place that Cowan's assessment was reasonably accurate, at least in terms of an 18th century community. He described it as 'a compact, handsome village, which for neatness and cleanliness is rarely to be met with'.[76] For good measure, Liddell adds that the population 'at all periods in its history' commended itself for 'decent, orderly behaviour'.[77] The Edinburgh Magazine summed up the popular view of both Dale and New Lanark:

> The mills and village of New Lanark ... of which he is the founder and sole proprietor, afford the most striking display of his opulence as a manufacturer and his benevolence as a man.[78]

Alcohol was available and, despite the fact that the people were generally honest, decent, religious, strict in their attendance on divine worship and 'industrious, if not remarkably so', they sometimes made free with the bottle. Drunkenness 'among the better class of inhabitants' was 'rather unusual' although the Statistical Account admits that it was less unusual as far as the other 'inhabitants' were concerned.[79]

There were opportunities for the community to meet, although there are no reports of markets, fairs and balls, with the exception of a report in the Glasgow Mercury of 13th January 1795. Interestingly, it is the pauper apprentices who seem to be having the best of times. The report is headed 'A Pleasing Instance of Health' and describes how 307 apprentices 'distinguished from the rest by the name of Boarders, that is provided by him with meat, clothing, schooling etc.' walked in procession from the village to the town of Lanark on New Year's Day, 1795 where they were toasted with punch supplied by the local magistrates. On their return to New Lanark, they were provided with dinner and the rest of the day was given over 'to dancing and conviviality'. It was clearly a very special annual event:

> They made a very fine appearance, the boys dressed in blue clothes with leather caps ornamented with fur and the girls in white muslins and black hats. This sight never fails to excite the most agreeable sensations in all who have an opportunity of seeing so great a number of orphans so comfortably provided for by industry.[80]

The following year, numbers had risen to 400 and once again, the children 'all newly clothed' in their blue suits or white frocks and caps, processed through the streets of the town, accompanied with music and the ringing of bells, to a place opposite the Black Bull where they were entertained with a suitable repast, before returning to the mills 'where they dined and spent the remainder of the day much to their own satisfaction'.[81]

Some years later, the apprentices, as Lorna Davidson points out, continued to reflect credit on the establishment.[82] When Dorothy Wordsworth visited in 1803, she came across the apprentice boys 'dressed all alike in blue, very neat' who were, she was informed, well instructed in reading and writing. She had already seen 'a flock of girls dressed in grey, coming out of the factory, probably apprentices also'.[83]

Drinking and dancing were also on offer on other special occasions. Nelson's victory at the battle of the Nile provided one such opportunity:

> At Lanark the victory was celebrated with similar demonstrations of joy. The town and mills of New Lanark were also illuminated. The children boarded by Mr. DALE at the works, amounting to upwards of 400, had a glass and a dance upon the occasion.[84]

It is to be wondered how 'a glass' (a euphemism for one or more glasses of whisky) would be productive of good health in young children but there are many accounts which indicate that the general health of the child employees (and the boarders in particular) was good. The Mercury article of 1795 concluded with a mention of the excellent health record in the mills and noted that 'the above fact is sufficient to prove that cotton mills are not prejudicial to health'.[85]

Personal and public health matters were of the utmost importance at this time, as the city of Glasgow suffered a prolonged epidemic of smallpox from 1787–1791.[86] Edinburgh fared no better with smallpox being the second biggest killer in the city (after consumption) in 1791.[87] Even after this date, the deaths from this disease ran into hundreds each year in Glasgow alone. Typhus fever was the other major scourge and there were outbreaks of cholera but these did not reach epidemic proportions until the late 1820s. As Maltby points out in relation to Manchester and the surrounding area, the towns and cities were adversely affected by the influx of people from largely rural areas who '*had no knowledge of the danger to health of large towns and of close confinement for long hours in mills*'.[88] There were no national or local authorities concerned with the health or housing conditions – nor did any control exist over the mills or the workers in them. This inevitably resulted in bad housing, poor sanitation, disease and excessively long hours of labour, especially in the case of children, '*resulting in physical weakness, ignorance and lack of right training*'.[89] Clearly, New Lanark was not Manchester but if a large mill complex in Scotland could sustain good, healthy living and employment conditions, then much could be learned from such a community. It might also be added that if the cities failed to address these issues by emulating good practice in places like New Lanark, then the consequences might be severe indeed:

> ...not merely a sanitary problem, or an industrial problem, or an educational problem but a great social problem, constituting, if left unsolved, a danger to the well-being of the whole community, and finally a danger to the future of the state.[90]

The relatively good health of the New Lanark residents is perhaps all the more surprising, given the primitive or non-existent sanitation facilities in the community. In the early years, the contents of chamber pots and dry closets were collected and literally piled up near the houses, awaiting collection by farmers who fertilised their fields with the solid waste. On a wet or hot (or indeed any other) day the situation must have been grim, although, in principle, fairly common in many communities in Scotland. (Water-borne sewage disposal was not introduced in the village until 1933.)[91] Such conditions were certainly common enough in Glasgow. In 1785, the Glasgow Magistrates gave notice that they had received an offer to '*carry off the whole dung and rubbish*' lying in the streets – '*provided the offerer should have the property of the dung*'.[92]

In 1796, the recently formed Manchester Board of Health had heard of Dale's great efforts at New Lanark and wished to hear more. Indeed, the Board felt it was '*natural*' that communication should be established with Dale – a man '*who had a wide renown as a humane and philanthropic employer of children*'.[93] Dr. Thomas Percival, (one of the founders of the Manchester Board) knew of Dale's schools, his abolition of night labour and his care for the physical welfare of his employees.[94] Percival may also have been aware that in Liverpool, another public health campaigner, Dr. James Currie, was equally interested in events at New Lanark. Currie had actually visited New Lanark four years earlier, in May 1792, and had noted that:

> The utmost cleanliness, health and order pervaded the whole manufactory. The children looked cheerful and happy with rosy cheeks and chubby countenances, and I found a variety of excellent regulations established for health, morals and knowledge.[95]

Currie was one of many visitors who noticed '*the neatness and order in which the boarders were kept*'.[96] He had purchased an estate in Moffat and was considering the erection of a cotton mill there, a matter which he had clearly discussed with Dale during his visit to New Lanark. Currie also seems to have been looking for a partner but Dale declined to be directly involved. It is possible that Currie may have visited Claud Alexander in Catrine a few years earlier in a similar search for a partner.[97]

After the trip to New Lanark, Currie noted that, although he had '*obtained nothing immediate*' from Dale, he had gained something '*in his acquaintance*' and the promise of ongoing advice from Dale, who advised that Currie's scheme was '*almost certain of success*' but that everything depended on good management.[98] After spending the day with Dale and dining with him, Currie returned to Moffat, clearly impressed with the information and advice he had received – '*I do not know that I have ever received a gratification more pure or more rational than this day produced*'.[99]

Currie wrote to Dale a few weeks after their May meeting, asking for further advice on the matter and also (presumably, given Dale's reply) making positive comment about New Lanark. As far as advising Currie, Dale replied, somewhat modestly:

...I have not as yet got matters brought to such a state of improvement at Lanark as to satisfy my own mind far less to be held out as a pattern for others to follow:[100]

He also makes his intentions clear:

...I hope to make such improvements in the course of a few months as to be able in some degree to unite the things which as you observe have been thought impossible to go on together 'the prosperity of the works and the health, morals &c.' of the people and if this cannot be done in some good degree I will [see/rue] the day of laying the foundation of the works in which I am concerned.[101]

At the first meeting of the Manchester Board on 7th January 1796, Thomas Percival spoke of the many sanitary measures necessary to prevent the spread of disease, including the need to improve '*the accommodation of those who are parochial apprentices or who are not under the immediate direction of their parents or friends*'.[102] A few weeks later, Thomas Bayley, their chairman, wrote to Dale asking for an account of the New Lanark mills, posing a series of thirteen questions related to health and wellbeing, particularly in relation to the children. Dale was proud of his achievements in the village and, always aware that public health matters were of great concern, replied personally and promptly. Appendix 7 contains the questions and Dale's very full reply. In any event, Dale would have known of Percival and Bayley from the earlier correspondence between the Glasgow and Manchester Chambers of Commerce. Of considerable significance here is the fact that one Robert Owen was a friend of Percival's and was a member of the Board of Health from its inception. It is entirely possible that, although Owen would have known of New Lanark's existence, he would have a learned a great deal more about the village and the humane conditions of its inhabitants from Dale's responses to Bayley's questions. The association between prosperity, decent living conditions and schooling for all children were therefore brought to Owen's attention as early as 1796 – two years before his first recorded visit to New Lanark.

Dale's responses and Lockhart's observations in the *Statistical Account* return three years earlier, along with other contemporary accounts, allow us to piece together a reasonable snapshot of life for the apprentices and other children. The *Statistical Account* in 1793 indicates that, of 1,157 people actually employed in the manufacturing process at that time, there were 795 children (68% of the workforce), of whom 275 were 'boarders' (normally aged between five and eight years at the beginning of a five to seven year apprenticeship) in No. 4 Mill. Lockhart notes there had never been fewer than 80 boarders in the previous seven year period.[103] There were a further 103 children living with parents in Lanark itself, leaving over 400 living with parents in the village at New Lanark.[104] Dale's own figures for the boarders in 1793 are slightly different. In response to Bayley's question (on typhus fevers), Dale lists the number of boarders between the years 1792 and 1795. Numbers here vary slightly from account to account but are generally around the 400 mark in the mid 1790s and this figure is maintained until 1801, according to an insurance policy taken out in March that year.[105]

Table 5: Boarders 1792–1795

Year	No.
1792	272
1793	288
1794	306
1795	384

A full breakdown of the age range and numbers of all the young people (aged seventeen and under) employed in 1793, and including the boarders, is illustrated in Table 6 – drawn from the figures in the *Statistical Account*.[106]

Table 6: Ages of the young people employed in the New Lanark Mills in 1793.

Age	No.
6	5
7	33
8	71
9	95
10	93
11	64
12	99
13	92
14	71
15	60
16	69
17	35

The boarders mixed with the other children and adults in the mill during working hours (6 a.m. – 7 p.m.), where they were employed in reeling or picking the cotton or mending any broken strands. The small hands of the women and children were well-suited to this type of work. During their day at the mill, workers had '*half an hour of intermission at 9 o'clock for breakfast and a whole hour at two for dinner*'.[107] Mills could be hot, dusty and dangerous places, especially in the summer months and Dale notes that, in addition to opening the top windows, ventilation and the circulation of fresh air were aided by opening '*air holes*' in the walls, six inches square and situated below each window, about 14 feet apart. General cleanliness of the workplace was maintained by '*frequent and constant*' brushing of the walls and floors, weekly washings of the floors and machinery with scalding water and '*washing the walls and ceilings of the rooms at least once a year with new slacked* (sic) *lime*'.[108] Dale certainly appears to have met his commitment to the charity workhouses in full. The children housed in No. 4 Mill were given regular and nourishing meals. Provisions were '*dressed in cast iron boilers*' and consisted of oatmeal porridge for breakfast and supper and '*milk with it in its season*'. In winter, the substitute for milk was a composition of molasses, '*fermented with some new beer, which is called swats*'.[109]

> For dinner, the whole of them have every day, in all seasons, barley broth made from fresh beef. The beef itself is divided among one half of the children, in quantities of about seven ounces English to each; the other half is served with cheese in quantities of about five ounces English each; so that they have alternately beef and cheese for dinner, excepting now and then a dinner of herrings in winter, and fresh butter in summer. To the beef and cheese is added a plentiful allowance of potatoes or barley bread, of which last they have also an allowance every morning before going to work.[110]

Dale took care to ensure that living conditions were as humane as the late 18th century would allow. In 1796, there were 396 boys and girls '*who get their maintenance in lieu of wages*' and they were accommodated in six apartments in No. 4 Mill. Dale informed Bayley that, '*of late, cast iron beds have been introduced in place of wooden ones*' but up until that point, the children slept three to a bed on wooden-bottomed beds on bed ticks filled with straw which were covered with a sheet. These were changed '*in general*' once per month. '*Above that, are one or two pairs of blankets and a bed cover, as the season requires.*'[111] Thomas Garnett noted that many of the children had provided themselves with boxes with locks, '*in which they keep their books, or any other little property to which they annex a value*'.[112]

To prevent the spread of disease, Dale ensured that:

> The ceilings and walls of the apartments are whitewashed twice a year with hot lime and the floors washed with scalding water and sand... The bedrooms are carefully swept and the windows thrown open every morning.[113]

This practice, as with many of those employed by Dale, was somewhat ahead of its time. More than twenty years later, Sir Richard Arkwright's son complained to the Parliamentary Committee (looking into the conditions of employment for children in factories) that the requirement that all rooms be whitewashed twice a year was one of the rules which he found 'troublesome' and which 'could answer no purpose', suggesting that his father's mills had not been used to this practice, although the younger Arkwright claimed that the Cromford mills were clean and in very good order and well ventilated.[114]

Inevitably the boarders occasionally became ill – a situation aggravated by long hours of work. When 'fevers or any epidemical distempers' appeared, the outbreak was contained by '...the immediate removal of the sick to a detached part of the house, and frequent sprinkling and fumigating of the bedrooms with vinegar'.[115] This approach contrasts sharply with some of the practices elsewhere. For example, when Robert Peel was asked in 1784 to stop night work because of an outbreak of 'putrid fevers' at the family mills, he felt that it was such an unprecedented request 'to deprive one House of privileges which are common to every other person in the business' that 'no man in his senses would have complied with it'.[116]

Dale's efforts met with considerable success. Between 1786 and 1795, only fourteen deaths occurred in total and there is a clear suggestion in Dale's letter to Bayley that the boarders in No. 4 Mill were healthier than the general populace.[117] He notes that there had been no outbreaks of typhus fevers in the boarders rooms 'for years' but that, during that time, such fevers had occurred in the village. He was also keen to point out that any such outbreaks originated outwith the New Lanark community:

> ...in no case, so far as circumstances afforded the means of judging it, did it appear to originate in the mills, or even to be communicated by the intercourse the workers had with each other.[118]

Clearly, public hygiene resulted in part from personal hygiene and the boarders were again well catered for. Clothing was provided and this was made, not surprisingly, from cotton. It is not clear whether these clothes were the kind of uniform he had provided for the boys sent to Cromford some years earlier, with brown cloth and red collars on their coats. It seems more likely that the Cromford uniforms had been specially made for the purpose. In the 1790s Dale informed Bayley that:

> The upper body clothing in use in summer, both for boys and girls, is entirely of cotton, which, as they have spare suits to change with, are washed once a fortnight. In winter, the boys are dressed in woollen cloth, and they, as well as the girls, have complete dress suits for Sundays. Their linens are changed once a week. For a few months in summer, both boys and girls go without shoes and stockings.[119]

Dale reports that the health of his pauper employees was good. The death rate was low and the boarders were certainly better provided for than they might otherwise have been in the workhouse. In fact, Dale went further and claimed that all of the children employed in the mills, boarders or not, were healthier than other members of their families who were at home:

> I am quite satisfied in my own mind that cotton mills, under proper management, are as favourable to health as any other employment. Indeed, it is observed by the parents of the children who work at my mills for wages, and are fed and lodged by their parents in their own houses, that the part of their family which works at the mills, is more healthy than the part that is at home.[120]

No other factory community in Britain offered these conditions. Dale was already leading the way in his treatment of these children but what really set New Lanark apart was Dale's commitment to a systematic, organised schooling system. This was intended for all the village children, but with a particular focus on the children in No. 4 Mill. It was a unique venture at the time and, given the numbers involved, an ambitious one.

The number of boarders remained broadly similar in the first few years under Robert Owen while their indentures were worked through. Appendix 9 has been compiled from figures in *The Monthly Report & Wage Book* for 1801–1802 and shows that they were working in various 'rooms' in four different locations, including the 'Old Mill' (the rebuilt No. 1 Mill), the '2nd Mill' (Mill No. 2), the 'New Mill' (No. 4) and the Jenny House (the original Mill No. 3).[121] It is also interesting to note that each of the five rooms in the 'Jeanie House' had a named person acting in what appeared to be a supervisory capacity. 'Martin'; 'J. Williamson'; 'J. Forrest' and 'James Collins' were in charge of Rooms 1, 2, 4 & 5 respectively, while 'D. Dale' was responsible for supervising those working in Room 3. There were only two individuals of that name who could have been involved, namely, Dale himself who was in poor health and who was spending much of his time in Glasgow or in his new country house in Cambuslang or David Dale Jnr., his nephew – not normally resident in New Lanark. There is also the possibility that the entry was simply a mistake and that it should have read '*J. Dale*' – Dale's half-brother who part-managed the mills with William Kelly.

Despite the harsh conditions in the cotton mills, the children in New Lanark were treated better than their contemporaries elsewhere. A fundamental part of their welfare at the time and an essential part of their future wellbeing, was the education provide by Dale and it is necessary now to look more closely at the schooling available in the village. Education was the keystone in Robert Owen's plans for a new society but it was a crucial element in Dale's New Lanark also when factory, school, community and charity came together for the first time in Scotland.

References: Chapter 6

1   Fitton, R.S. and Wadsworth, A.P. (1958) *The Strutts and the Arkwrights 1758–1830. A Study of the Early Factory System.* Manchester: M.U.P., p.98.
2   Ibid.
3   Ibid., pp.224–5.
4   Ibid., pp.99–100.
5   Bray, W. (1778) *Sketch of a Tour into Derbyshire & Yorkshire.* Preface & p.119. Quoted in Fitton, R.S. & Wadsworth, A.P. *The Strutts*, p.99.
6   Fitton, R.S. & Wadsworth, A.P. *The Strutts*, p.102. These schools at Belper and Cromford have to be seen in the context of the huge expansion in the number of Sunday schools in late 18th century England. The Sunday school in Manchester opened in 1784 and trebled its numbers to some 550 by 1788, and the total number of children attending Sunday schools in 1787 was approximately 250,000. The Scottish picture was somewhat different, owing to the tradition of the parish school and its emphasis on reading in order to be able to read the Bible. Sunday schools as such were only really organised after 1800 by evangelists like David Stow.
7   *The Derby Mercury*, 25th August 1785 quoted in Fitton, R.S. & Wadsworth, A.P. *The Strutts* p.102.
8   Farington Diary quoted in Fitton & Wadsworth, p.103. N.B. this refers to 1802.
9   Harford, J.S. (1820) *Some Account of the Life, Death & Principles of Thomas Paine.* 3rd Ed. Bristol, p.94n. Cited in Fitton, R.S. (1989) *The Arkwrights: Spinners of Fortune.* Manchester: M.U.P., p.7 n31.
10 Cooke, A. (2010) *The Rise and Fall of the Scottish Cotton Industry, 1778–1914: The Secret Spring.* Manchester: M.U.P., p.39.
11 Browning, M. (1971) 'Robert Owen as Educator', in Butt, J. (ed) *Robert Owen. Prince of Cotton Spinners.* Newton Abbot: David & Charles, p.56.
12 *Report of the Minutes of Evidence of the Select Committee on the State of Children Employed in the Manufactories of the United Kingdom*, 1816, pp. 8–9.
13 Fitton, R.S. (1989) *The Arkwrights.* Manchester: M.U.P., p.152.
14 Ibid.
15 Fitton, R.S. and Wadsworth, A.P. *The Strutts.* p.226.
16 Sinclair, J. (ed) (1791–99) *The Statistical Account of Scotland, 1791–99*, 21 vols. Vol. XVII, p.556.
17 Dale to Claud Alexander, 9th November 1789. Dale/Alexander Collection, Glasgow City Archives, MS 63/8.
18 Raistrick, A. (ed) (1967) *The Hatchett Diary – A tour through the counties of England & Scotland in 1796, visiting their Mines and Manufactories.* Truro: Bradford Barton, p.100.
19 Fitton, R.S. and Wadsworth, A.P. *The Strutts.* p.104. N.B. Nailers are described here as 'a tough and rather demoralised lot of domestic workers who survived there until well on into the nineteenth century'.
20 Fitton, R.S. *The Arkwrights*, p.153.
21 Sinclair, J. (ed) *The Statistical Account*, Vol. XVII, p.556.
22 West Kirk Charity Workhouse, Edinburgh. Monthly Meeting, 1st August, 1797. Edinburgh City Archives. Minute Book SL222/1/7. For Workhouse Minutes, see Laurie, A.E. and Young, N. (2009, 2013) *New Lanark's People. A Collection of Transcribed Archive material from over 70 Different Sources.* 2 Vols. Private CD Publication. New Lanark Conservation, Vol. 2. N.B. No reply is recorded to Dempster's request.
23 Morgan, P. (1886) *Annals of Woodside & Newhills.* Aberdeen: David Wylie, p.24. Cited in Cooke, A. *The Rise and Fall*, p.150.
24 Ure, A. (1835) *The philosophy of Manufactures*, London: C. Knight, p.393.
25 Davidson, H. (1910) *Lanark: A Series of Papers by the late Hugh Davidson, Writer.* Edinburgh, pp.x–xi.
26 Fitton, R.S. *The Arkwrights* p.187 and Sinclair, J. *The Statistical Account*, Vol. V, pp.505–6.
27 Robertson, A.D. (1975) *Lanark: the Burgh and its Councils, 1469–188.* Lanark Town Council, p.281.
28 Sinclair, J. *The Statistical Account*, Vol. XV, p.33n.
29 *The New Lanark Monthly Report Book & Wage Book, Dec 1801–Dec 1802.* University of Glasgow Archives. UGD 42/7/10.
30 Liddell, A. (1854b) 'Memoir of David Dale', in R. Chambers (ed), (1855) *A Biographical Dictionary of Eminent Scotsmen.* Glasgow: Blackie, p.175.

31 Ibid.

32 Ibid.

33 Ibid.

34 Courtesy of the Robert Owen Museum, Newtown. I am indebted to Pat & John Brandwood for their help and their permission to use this.

35 *The Monthly Magazine & British Register for 1797*. Vol. IV, July–December. London. 1798. p.277. Vide infra Chapter 7 on Rothesay.

36 Sinclair, J. *The Statistical Account*, Vol. XII, p.116n.

37 Ibid., p.122.

38 This mill is variously referred to throughout the existing literature: Gillespie's original 1770s linen and calico printing business and bleachfield was in the Anderston area, and some sources refer to his 'Anderston' mill. However, the 1784 cotton mill was on the banks of the Kelvin in Woodside, although sources disagree whether it can be described as North or South Woodside – the latter seems to be the more favoured option.

39 Sinclair, J. *The Statistical Account*, Vol. XII, p.116.

40 Simon, J. (1968) 'Was there a Charity School Movement?' in Simon. B. (ed) *Education in Leicestershire 1540–1940. A Regional Study*, Leicester University Press.

41 Vide infra, Chapter 13.

42 *The Morning Chronicle*, London, 23rd April 1817.

43 Sinclair, J. *The Statistical Account*, Vol. XV, p.36.

44 Vide infra, Appendix 7.

45 Fitton, R.S. *The Arkwrights* p.153.

46 Butt, J. (1971), *Robert Owen as a Businessman*, p.191.

47 According to Fitton & Wadsworth, *The Strutts*, pp.104-7, there is no evidence to suggest that Arkwright used parish apprentices, 'though they may have taken individual apprentices from overseers'. This rather contradicts Fitton's own reference in *The Arkwrights*, p.152. It does seem likely that parish apprentices were used on occasion.

48 Kydd, S. ('Alfred') (1857) *The History of the Factory Movement From the Year 1802 to the Enactment of the Ten Hours Bill in 1847*, 2 vols. London, Vol. II, pp.116-20.

49 Vide infra, Appendix 7.

50 Ibid.

51 West Kirk Charity Workhouse Minutes. Pro Renata Meeting, 5th October 1790.

52 Ibid., 1st July 1794.

53 Regulations of the Town's Hospital with the Original Constitution of the House, Glasgow, 1844.

54 Kydd, S. *History*, pp.116-20.

55 West Kirk Charity Workhouse Minutes, 6th October 1795.

56 Ibid., 5th October, 1795.

57 Ibid., 7th & 27th September 1790. Note: the Minutes are appended to the Minute of 5th October 1790.

58 Ibid., 5th October 1790.

59 Ibid.

60 Ibid., 1st November 1791.

61 Ibid., 5th October 1790.

62 Sinclair, J. *The Statistical Account*, Vol. V. p.528.

63 Ibid., pp.521-522.

64 Corstorphine Kirk, 5th April 1796. National Archives of Scotland, NASCH2/124/4 pp.572, 586. See Laurie, A.E. and Young, N. *New Lanark's People*, Vol. 2. See also Cowper, A. S. 'Corstorphine history: an eighteenth century vignette. William Finlay, David Ramage, John Geddes, and others not named, pauper children sent to the New Lanark Mills' in Johnston, W.T. (ed) (2000) *David Dale & Robert Owen Studies*. Livingston: Officina Educational Publications. Also, Davidson, L . 'The New Lanark Pauper Apprentices.' Unpublished Conference paper, 'The legacy of David Dale – Industry, philanthropy and Heritage', 4th November, 2006. Glasgow Caledonian University.

65 Ibid.

66 Ibid.

67 *The Edinburgh Magazine or Literary Miscellany 1793*. Vol. 2. London: Laurie & Symington, pp.6-7.

68 Ibid.

69 *London Society*. (1865) 8:47. November, p.469.

70 Garnett, T. (1811) *Observations on a Tour through the Highlands and Part of the Western Isles of Scotland. A New Edition in Two Volumes.* London: John Stockdale, p.236.

71 Ibid.

72 Cowan, W.A. (1867) *History of Lanark and a Guide to the Surrounding Scenery*. Lanark: Robert Wood, p.91.

73 Robertson, A.D. *Lanark*, p.282.

74   *The Edinburgh Magazine*, 1793, p.6.

75   Aiton. J. (1824) *Mr. Owen's Objections to Christianity and New View of Society & Education Refuted by a Plain Statement of Facts with a Hint to Archibald Hamilton of Dalziel*. Edinburgh: Jas. Robertson & Co., p.39.

76   Cowan, W.A. (1867) *History of Lanark*, p.91.

77   Liddell, A. (1854b) *Memoir*, p.164.

78   *The Edinburgh Magazine*, February, 1797.

79   Sinclair, J. *The Statistical Account*, Vol. XV, pp.41–42.

80   *The Glasgow Mercury*, 13th January 1795.

81   *The Edinburgh Magazine* Vol. 7, January 1796, p.75.

82   Davidson, L. *The New Lanark Pauper Apprentices*.

83   Knight, W. (ed) (1904) *Journals of Dorothy Wordsworth*. 2 vols. London: MacMillan. Vol. 1, p.196.

84   *The English Chronicle or Universal Evening Post*, 31st October 1798.

85   Donnachie, I. and Hewitt, G. (1993) *Historic New Lanark*. Edinburgh: E.U.P., p.49.

86   Glaister, J. (1886) *Epidemic History of Glasgow 1783–1883*. Glasgow.

87   *The Scots Magazine*, Vol. 53, 1791, p.572.

88   Maltby, S.E. (1918) *Manchester and the Movement for National Elementary Education, 1800–1870*. Manchester. M.U.P., p.13.

89   Ibid.

90   Ibid.

91   Hume, J.R. (1971) 'The Industrial Archaeology of New Lanark', in Butt, J. (ed) (1971) *Robert Owen. Prince of Cotton Spinners*. Newton Abbot: David & Charles, p.236.

92   Reid, R. (Senex) (1884) *Glasgow Past and Present*, 3 vols. Glasgow: David Robertson & Co., Vol. III, p.195.

93   Maltby, S.E. *Manchester*, p.16.

94   Ibid.

95   James Currie to Mrs. Greg & Miss Kennedy in Manchester. Liverpool, 27th May 1792. Quoted in Currie, William Wallace. (1831) *Memoir of the Life, Writings and Correspondence of James Currie*, 2 vols. London: Longman, Rees, Orme, Brown & Green. Vol. 1, p.161.

96   See 'Memoir of David Dale Esq', *The Imperial Magazine*, 4.46 (November 1822), pp.1067–1073, p.1070. Also *The Scots Magazine*, September, 1806, p.654.

97   Vide infra, Chapter 9.

98   Currie, William Wallace. (1831) *Memoir of the Life, Writings and Correspondence of James Currie*, 2 vols. London: Longman, Rees, Orme, Brown & Green. Vol. 1, p.162.

99   Ibid., p.160.

100 Dale to Currie, 30th June 1792. I am indebted to Prof. Edward Royle, York University for this information.

101 Ibid.

102 Maltby, S.E. *Manchester*, p.15.

103 Sinclair, J. *The Statistical Account*, Vol. XV, p.37.

104 Ibid., p.36.

105 Hume, J.R. *Industrial Archaeology*, p.225.

106 Sinclair, J. *The Statistical Account*, Vol. XV, p.37: N.B. There were no children aged five that year.

107 Vide infra, Appendix 7.

108 Ibid.

109 Ibid.

110 Ibid.

111 Ibid.

112 Garnett, T. *Observations*, p.234.

113 Vide infra, Appendix 7.

114 *Report of the Select Committee on the State of Children Employed in Manufactures*. *Parliamentary Papers*, 1816, (397) III, Children in the Manufactories, p.279. It is likely that Arkwright Junior was concerned that all rooms be whitewashed, not just the rooms with machinery.

115 Vide infra, Appendix 7.

116 *The Manchester Mercury*, 9th November 1784.

117 Sinclair, J. *The Statistical Account*, Vol. XV, p.37 indicates five deaths between 1786 and 1793, the year the report was written. There is some overlap however in numbers/years because between 1792–1795 there were nine deaths according to Brown, A. *History of Glasgow*, pp. 236-7.

118 Vide infra, Appendix 7.

119 Ibid.

120 Ibid.

121 *New Lanark Monthly Report & Wage Book, Dec 1801–Dec 1802*. University of Glasgow Archives UGD 42/7/10.

Chapter 7: Education and Schooling

David Dale's regime also provided education for the village children. The New Lanark children worked in the mills until 7 p.m., which was 'the hour for supper; in half an hour after at most, and as much sooner as possible, the teaching commences and continues until nine o'clock'.[1] Lockhart notes that this was at the proprietor's expense and one source, writing a few years later noted that 'the education of the young mind' was one of Dale's primary objects.[2] While this was undoubtedly true, the same source takes a realistic view of the situation:

> It cannot be supposed that the juvenile mind could be capable of intense application, after eleven hours hard labour through the day; and many of these young creatures were under ten years of age.[3]

This, we are assured, is not Dale's fault. Under the circumstances, he did everything he could 'and all that his benevolent mind prompted him to perform; but he could not afford to maintain 500 children without their remunerating labour'.[4]

Reports of the school are, in places, a little confusing. The *Statistical Account* quotes the number of teachers in 1793 as ten: three 'professed teachers' who taught during the day those children who were too young to work (generally those under six years of age) and seven assistants 'who attend in the evenings, one of whom teaches writing.'[5] This accords with an article in *The Annual Register* of the previous year, in which it is stated that ten schoolmasters were daily employed in teaching the children.[6]

Garnett, in his *Observations on a Tour through the Highlands* quotes ten teachers.[7] However, by 1796, teacher numbers had increased:

> The schools at present are attended by five hundred and seven scholars, in instructing whom sixteen teachers are employed; thirteen in teaching to read, two to write, and one to figure, besides a person who teaches sewing, and another who occasionally teaches church music.[8]

Thus the total was eighteen teaching staff, including one who was part time. Three of the teachers had lodgings in New Lanark.[9]

The education of such large numbers of pupils required careful organisation and planning if anything were to be achieved. Dale was quite specific as to what he wanted done. This was not to be the haphazard, superficial attempt at schooling to be found in 'adventure' schools, dame schools, song schools and the like in many parishes (and some towns) in Scotland. Nor was it to be the well-intentioned but severely limited type of schooling to be found in the Sunday schools of the day. In England, Arkwright and Strutt, for example, provided Sunday schools instead of day and evening schools.

The New Lanark curriculum compared favourably with that offered in the so-called 'charity schools' in Glasgow. For example, the sons (not daughters) of middle class Burgesses at Hutcheson's in Glasgow were being taught the three R's, grammar and church music, and were clothed twice a year.[10] New Lanark did not have grammar, but both boys and girls, poor or not, were taught to read – with some success. Thomas Garnett visited the day school for the youngest children and heard 'some little boys read in a very superior manner'.[11] They were also taught to count and to write. Church music was also on the curriculum. There is also one reference to singing and dancing. John Marshall, a Leeds flax-spinner, visited in September 1800 and noted that:

> Mr. Dale not only taught the children reading and writing but the polite accomplishments he had singing masters & one year actually employed 2 dancing masters to teach the factory girls to dance.[12]

While this may well have been the case, singing and dancing were much more obvious features of the curriculum under Robert Owen.

The girls were also taught a practical skill such as sewing, and, unlike many charity schools, no pupil was required to show evidence of attendance at an 'English' school. The Town's Hospital had a similar curriculum where the children were taught the three R's by the teacher (who also functioned as 'Chaplain'), for which he received £15 per annum. Church music was taught by his assistant (annual salary £5) as well as practical skills like tambouring muslin (embroidering on a frame), and, in particular, the manufacture of thread lace. Religion was taught in the form of catechising. It is worth noting that even in the workhouse, the children were taught by teachers, or at least persons with some claim to that title. The Hospital minutes show that applicants for the post of teacher/chaplain or his assistant had to be qualified and/or experienced. When a vacancy arose in May 1794 for chaplain and schoolmaster, there were three candidates – a teacher 'in one of the charity schools'; an assistant to a teacher of English and a schoolmaster from Stonehouse. All were examined on reading, spelling, English Grammar and their ability to recall and recite the Shorter Catechism. They also had to produce specimens of their 'writeing' (sic) and 'attestations of their ... success in teaching'.[13]

Given the status and relative importance of the teacher, it would have been surprising indeed if this had not been reflected in Dale's choice of staff for the New Lanark schools. New Lanark provided employment and a progressive system of schooling delivered by recognised teachers, with definite prospects for the employment of the children at the end of the process – and in a community which provided much better social conditions than the Town's Hospital. There was an attempt to establish a systematic, progressive elementary schooling system with professional teachers employed to deliver a curriculum, and all within a factory community. This was elementary education on an industrial scale for the first time.

What Dale called 'the mode of teaching' is explained thus:

> The course is divided into eight classes according to the progress of the scholars; to each of these classes one or more teachers are assigned, as the numbers in that stage of advancement may require.[14]

There were eight classes in total, with class number 8 being the highest or top class. The number of pupils in each class varied. In the First (or 'latter') class there were 65 'scholars', in the Second, 85; in the Third, 76 and in the Fourth, 65. The Fifth and Sixth classes each had 44; the Seventh had 51 and the Eighth, 80 children.[15]

Having grouped the children by ability (itself an example of established educational principles and practice), teachers were provided with a type of syllabus which benefited pupil and teacher alike:

> To the teachers is specified in writing, how far they are respectively to carry forward their scholars; which, so soon as they have accomplished, the scholars are transferred to the next highest class and the teacher receives a premium for everyone so qualified.[16]

Nothing was left to chance. A distinctive classroom methodology involving regular testing, competition, recognising achievement and rewarding successful pupils was also in evidence:

> In their respective classes, the teachers promote emulation in the usual way, by making the top of the class the post of honour, which is still farther kept up by the distribution of rewards every half year to such as, from an account taken once a fortnight, appear to have been most frequently uppermost.[17]

The notion of a 'premium' or bonus of some kind for teachers and pupils was not unusual at the time in the towns and burghs but was less common in the parishes. Dale could see this in operation in the Town's Hospital. The house teacher/chaplain could earn a premium (amount unspecified) every year 'on favourable report of the School Examination Committee in the month of December'.[18] Dale was a member of the committee which agreed that the house teacher/chaplain had been 'so successful in teaching the children that they were not only making ordinary but great progress in their education' and that, as a result, the teacher should be recommended to the Magistrates and Town Council for an additional payment in recognition of his 'diligence and attention with the duties of his office'.[19] It is likely that Dale operated a similar system in the charity school in Glasgow (for the children of soldiers and sailors) with which he was involved.[20] A newspaper report written in 1817 but apparently referring to the school during the Dale period, notes that a premium was given to the teachers '*for every child who is found qualified to leave the school.*'[21] In New Lanark, Dale was building on established good practice – albeit in a completely new setting.

Once the New Lanark pupils had successfully attained the eighth or top class, more time could be devoted to writing and other subjects. Dale wrote to Bayley in 1796 that the twelve boys and twelve girls in the highest class had all become good readers and could afford to spend half their time each night studying and practising writing. The remainder of the evening would be spent on arithmetic and sewing, '*except on occasional nights appointed for reviving their reading*'.[22] This is highly significant, given that in parish and burgh schools, writing was not always taught to everyone because there was an extra charge for it. For example, in Catrine, fees in the parish school were 1s. 8d. for reading, 2s. 6d. for reading and writing and 3s. for writing and arithmetic.[23] Where writing was taught separately, it was often more expensive than reading. The Kirk Session paid the fees of the very poorest children to enable them to learn to read but this benevolence was not always extended to the provision of writing.

Learning to write was, in many families, considered less important than learning to read. Being able to read meant access to scriptures in exactly the same way as it did in the parish school. The aim was to achieve universal literacy – a literacy not necessarily designed to liberate the mind but, in the words of John Knox, '*to foster the virtuous education and Godly upbringing of the youth of this realm*'.[24] Also, girls were often excluded from writing classes in favour of more 'domestic' practicalities such as sewing and tambouring. It is therefore highly unusual to find any school which provided writing for both boys and girls and which did so free of charge for a considerable number of pupils. It is also worth noting that 'arithmetic' normally meant something beyond the basics of addition, subtraction, and multiplication tables. In some parish schools where it was taught, arithmetic involved practical calculations to do with land surveying, volume, weights and measures of crops in the country areas or perhaps distances, times, tides and speeds in coastal areas (where navigation, geography and geometry might also be taught). Schools nearer some of the larger towns and burghs (where parish school legislation did not apply) offered bookkeeping. On that basis, it is reasonable to argue that in New Lanark, for example, 'arithmetic' may have been related to lengths, volumes, weights, profits etc. related to the cotton industry. Whatever the case, it is certainly true that Dale's schools introduced a new dimension to the Scottish education system.

Apart from the evening schools, there were two day schools (i.e. classes) for those under six years of age run along the same lines. No other mill owner (with the possible exception of Gillespie in Woodside) had provided a day school for the under-sixes in a factory community and certainly none had provided for such large numbers of children. These day schools, as well as the evening ones, were free for the boarders, except for the provision of one's own note book, although it seems likely that this would also have been provided, given that the boarders were not paid any wages. Interestingly, Robert Lyon, a New Lanark teacher who became a well-respected figure notes that Dale provided free education for the children of *all* the New Lanark employees.[25]

Garnett's observations on his tour of New Lanark illustrates some of the results:

> On going into the day school we heard some little boys read in a very superior manner. In the evening these three masters are assisted by seven others, one of whom teaches writing. There is likewise a person who teaches sewing to the girls, and another who teaches church music. The teachers have written instructions, pointing out how far they are to carry forward their scholars, before they are transferred to the next higher class. At dinner the masters preside over the boys at table, performing the office of chaplains and conduct them on Sundays to divine worship, where they sometimes receive instruction from their benevolent master. In the evening of Sunday, all the masters attend to teach, and give religious and moral instruction.[26]

As Garnett notes, there were also schools on Sundays. The boarders were expected to attend church in Lanark – for which Dale paid 36s. 6d. per year in seating costs – but, since only 150 could be accommodated there, '*they all go to it in rotation*', in their uniforms and led by their teachers.[27] Those who could not attend were kept busy in school until it was their turn and in the evenings, after public worship, '*the usual teachers spend regularly three hours in giving religious instruction, by causing* the scriptures to be read, catechising etc.'[28] What is perhaps less well known is that Dale also supported a Sabbath School in Lanark which was intended for 'young girls who worked in the cotton mills'.[29] The same source, however, also indicates that this religious instruction was intended for a wider audience, i.e. the children of what were referred to as 'the poorer classes'.[30]

The first of such schools in the town, the Sabbath School, was run by Mr. Gillespie, the English master in the Grammar School, under the supervision of the parish minister, the redoubtable William Menzies. Classes were held in the town hall and Dale paid Gillespie an annual allowance of £5 for teaching there.[31] There appear to be no records of any of the New Lanark boarders attending, although some of the village children may have been sent by their parents.

Good teachers were fundamental to Dale's scheme – '...indeed the anxiety of the proprietor to have proper teachers and instructors for children will ever redound to his honour', according to the Statistical Account.[32] Another source noted that Dale appointed the best instructors which the country could provide.[33] Dale's insistence on high standards is exemplified by Robert Lyon – a highly-regarded figure in his own right:

> We question if at any period since the institution of the establishment, so much good was done, as during this gentleman's incumbency. His was indeed a system of severe discipline but it was one of real and solid usefulness; for, to this day, his pupils are distinguished by accuracy of thought, eagerness of application and correctness of conclusion.[34]

Lyon held the post of teacher and then superintendent for more than 23 years from 1790 to 1814, i.e. during the last ten years of Dale's involvement and the first thirteen to fourteen years of Robert Owen's. Lyon's experience as a schoolteacher was quite different under each. He reports that, when he was employed by Dale, there were approximately 150 children attending the day school and somewhere between 600–700 in the evening school.[35] Under Dale:

> The progress of the young people was very considerable, and the plan adopted seemed to answer the benevolent intentions of the proprietor... Indeed the greatest attention was always paid to the school both by Mr. Dale and his managers. The children were publicly examined every six months and premiums were distributed to those scholars who had made the greatest progress.[36]

Interestingly, things were quite different under Owen. Lyon noted that, although free education continued and the day school was well-attended, the evening school 'fell greatly off'. Given that New Lanark was later to become internationally renowned for its Owenite educational system, what follows is quite surprising. According to Lyon:

> For ten years, Mr. Owen paid no attention to the school. In place of being examined once every six months, as in Mr. Dale's time, we had only three examinations in the course of thirteen years.[37]

There is also a suggestion from another source that Owen wanted rid of the evening school immediately following his installation as manager in 1800. John Marshall, referring to the evening school at this time, notes that 'the present proprietors it is said wished to give that up but could not because it was contracted for by Mr. Dale in the indentures'.[38] The situation improved a little during Robert Lyon's last two to three years in the village when Owen apparently paid more attention to the school (by which he almost certainly meant the day school). Mr. Lyon, however, did not think this attention was particularly advantageous, noting that Owen was always introducing new plans and particularly a new system of morals, 'of which he claimed the sole invention'.[39]

Education for Life

Dale was very concerned from the very beginning that his apprentice children should benefit from their time in New Lanark and, crucially, that the skills they had learned in the school room and in the factory should maximise their employment potential – wherever that employment might be found. He felt that, in some cases, the period of indenture was too brief and that the children would be too young to make sensible choices for the future. He appeared to think that age 15 was a good time to make those choices but this might involve the indenture period being extended in some cases. If that could be resolved, the children would be in a much better position to move on. In a letter to the Edinburgh Charity Workhouse in 1790, Dale makes a suggestion:

> ...were the Managers to extend the term of their indentures for 5 or 6 years I think I can promise to put them all in a way of gaining their bread. The Girls might all continue in the Mill & receive such wages as grown up women get – a number of the boys might remain in the Mill – others might be taught to work on the loom and those who were stout might be taught to spin either on mule or common Jennies – those that chose to go to the loom or to spin on Jennies behoved to enter into a new indenture but I would owe them journeyman wages – in this way I think I could provide for all the children that the Town may send out from time to time and if I am spared in life might have the pleasure of introducing the well behaved among them to such employment as to enable them not only to provide for themselves but to be useful to others.[40]

It can be argued that, as an employer, Dale was bound to benefit from a longer indenture period. However, the letter seems to be an expression of genuine concern for his child employees and a measure of his willingness to equip the children with useful, transferable skills and decent wages.[41]

Although Dale looked after the pauper children, the workhouses were technically responsible for their apprentices' welfare until the end of the indenture period. In essence, this simply meant that the institutions would ask for a report from the mill regarding the health and progress of the children. While this was potentially open to abuse, there is no suggestion that the reports from New Lanark were anything other than genuine. Had they not been, word would soon have reached the workhouses and the supply of child employees would have stopped. If they were to supply any more children, the workhouse managers had to be satisfied that the children were at least well treated and it seems that, for the most part, the West Kirk were satisfied with arrangements at New Lanark (although see below). Reports were submitted to the West Kirk Committee by Hugh Dick, a New Lanark employee who appears to have had a managerial responsibility (undefined in the documentation) for the children. The West Kirk Committee were more than satisfied:

> The Committee desired the Master to return in answer to Mr. Dick that they are highly gratified with his account of the children who were bound to Mr. Dale in 1790, that they have no objection to bind to him those of them who are willing for such another space of time as may be agreed on.[42]

Such reports give an interesting insight into the achievements and future earning potential of the children. In a letter to the West Kirk managers in 1795, Hugh Dick provides a brief report on the progress of 41 children whose apprenticeship had begun in 1790 and whose terms of engagement were on the point of expiring. Of the original 41, 15 boys and 16 girls remained, '9 having run away or been carried off by their parents and one only is dead'.[43]

It is interesting to note that nine children ran away or were removed by parents. A popular (and often accurate) view was that employment and schooling in the mill community had rescued these 'outcasts' from a life of potential vice and misery but there is little doubt that, benevolent as the regime may have been in terms of their treatment in New Lanark, young children were not necessarily appreciative of that fact and life could be very hard indeed.[44] They worked long hours and the boarders, in particular, were without parents to care for them. The Caledonian Mercury in an uncharacteristically inaccurate piece (almost certainly syndicated from elsewhere) observed that, because of the children's tender years, 'their tasks were light and each day certain hours were allowed them for play and amusement'.[45] This was very far from being the case. If the reports above about strict discipline in the schools are true, it is little wonder that 'the idea of servitude operated powerfully upon some of their minds' and that, before the period of indenture was complete, at least some of them 'took every opportunity to break away, although in every respect well-treated'.[46]

Although the number of 'runaways' was relatively small, their disappearance did cause problems on occasion, particularly for the workhouses who were responsible for their welfare until the end of the indenture period. The Minutes of the West Kirk

Charity Workhouse make illuminating reading in this respect. In March 1792, the master informed the committee that one James Paton *'was the second boy belonging to this House who had run off from Lanark within the space of a fortnight'*. Given that the workhouse *'had bound themselves to keep these children in the service of Mr. Dale'*, they appointed two individuals:

> ...to apprehend him by means of a street officer to commit him to the cells, to be kept there till the first return of the Lanark Carrier when he shall be sent home to his work.[47]

The errant youth was apprehended and returned to New Lanark in March 1792 but the following month, reports indicated that he had absconded again. There was still no sign of him in September of that year, by which time he had been joined by another frequent absconder by the name of George Herd. The committee simply could not find them but, by way of encouragement, the officers engaged in the search were to be allowed one shilling for apprehending each of them and committing them to the cells.[48] One boy managed to put some distance between himself and the New Lanark Mills. George Rentoul ran away in 1794 and was traced to Haddington. However, he refused to come back, *'declaring that, although he were at Lanark, he would take the first opportunity to run off'*. The committee decided to *'write to a man of business'* in Haddington to obtain a warrant from the Sheriff *'to apprehend him and send him hither'*.[49]

One or two boys were beyond redemption, it seems. Alexanderr Gunn was a frequent absconder from both New Lanark and the workhouse, being brought back on each occasion by *'humane people who observed his destitute condition'* as he wandered the streets. Eventually, he was held *'in a lockfast place'* until the committee could decide what to do with him. Finally, it was decided:

> ...that he was fit for nothing but the sea & referred it to Mr. Young and the Master to send him on board a Man of War or Merchant Ship as they should find most expedient.[50]

In Glasgow, the few surviving minute books of the Town's Hospital make no specific reference to New Lanark runaways but the principle of enforcing indentures was also high on their agenda. At a committee meeting in May 1796, the directors agreed that the House should *'prosecute before the Magistrates to force fulfilment of the indentures'*.[51] The problem was not confined to the mills in New Lanark. Arkwright had similar problems in his Derbyshire mills. There may have been few, if any parish apprentices but there were, nonetheless, runaways of (all ages) from the indenture system. In 1784, three men were on the run from the Wirksworth mill – an Oldham man aged 24, a Wirksworth man aged 27, both of whom had more than three years left to serve and a Blackwell man aged 28 who had two years left to serve. One of the runaways was an ex-soldier and one was wearing soldier's clothes.[52] It was common for adverts to be placed in local newspapers and if caught, the miscreants might well be brought before the Magistrates, as in New Lanark.

Troublesome as they were to the mill owners, runaways were relatively few in number and it would appear that Dale was either unaware of a problem or unwilling to see it as of any significance He wrote to Dr. Currie in August 1795, noting that there were more than 370 children in the boarding house, *'all in good health and seemingly growing every day more and more contented with their situation'*.[53]

For the majority who were *'contented'* and who chose to remain and fulfil the conditions of their apprenticeship, the future offered some options. Hugh Dick describes three *'classes'* or age groups of young people at various stages of their apprenticeship in 1795 – firstly, those around fifteen years of age (two boys and four girls); secondly, those between thirteen and fourteen (eight boys and nine girls) and those between eleven and twelve (five boys and three girls). For this group, at least, education had gone well. All, *'excepting four'* could read *'with considerable propriety'*. Nineteen of the children had been learning to write, *'in which some of them have made considerable proficiency'*. A few of the boys had begun *'to learn figures'* and some of the girls learned *'the use of the needle'*.[54]

It is important to note that, although many of the children were at the end of their apprenticeship, their time at New Lanark was not necessarily at an end:

A number of them propose of their own accord, to continue some time longer in Mr. Dale's service. Others wish previously to see and consult with their friends. And the rest say they wish to go to other trades, and private service.[55]

At this point, one of the few 'expectations' in the original contract with the workhouses came into play. Having paid the young people no wages during their indentured period, mill owners were expected to give each apprentice a small cash sum at the end of the apprenticeship. Interestingly, despite the West Kirk's wholehearted endorsement of Dale's treatment of his boarders, the sum on offer on completion had previously drawn some mild criticism from the workhouse's management committee.

…they would expect that the additional allowances to be given them at the expiry of the engagement to be somewhat higher in proportion than is stated in the letter.[56]

There was also no great rush for the young people to decide on their future. If they wished, they were entitled to return to the workhouse:

…the house shall be thrown open for their reception for a few weeks till they make up their minds to return to Mr. Dale, or have leisure to find out a different service.[57]

The fifteen-year-olds who opted to stay (and for whom employment could be found) in New Lanark could expect a starting wage of 3s. 6d. per week (about one third of that paid to an experienced adult spinner). However, Dale offered another option to all his pauper apprentices – that of staying as a boarder but with an annual allowance. The deal also included further schooling:

Were they or the others to continue on the same footing as they now are on, an additional allowance in money over and above their maintenance, cloathing and schooling, could be afforded them. To those of the first class, this would be about 13/- p. annum, to the 2nd, 10/- p. annum, and to the third 20/-. for two years.[58]

For many of these young people, the offer of continued board, lodging and schooling must have been an attractive offer, although they would have very little actual cash in their pockets. This was another example of Dale's 'practical philanthropy' – genuine charity and benevolence on the one hand, combined with business acumen in ensuring a continued workforce. Some clearly did stay on in some capacity or another, either as paid employees or boarders and one source noted that some of these apprentices eventually filled 'the most respectable situations about the manufactory', a situation 'which, while it reflects a lustre upon their early education, does no less honour to themselves'.[59] Those who left also appeared to have had a reasonable chance of success – some of them fared well in later life and occupied honourable and responsible situations in society, according to one local source.[60] Even Dale could not provide work for everyone, however. For those young people (boarding and non-boarding) who wanted to leave at the end of the indenture, the future was still promising:

…the workers, when too big for spinning, are as stout and robust as others. The male part of them are fit for any trade. A great many, since the commencement of the war, have gone into the army and navy, and others are occasionally going away as apprentices to smiths and joiners etc. but especially to weavers; for which last trade, from the expertness they acquire in handling yarn, they are particularly well fitted, and of course are taken as apprentices on better terms. The females generally leave the mills, and go into private family service when about 16 years of age. Were they disposed to continue at the mills, these afford abundant employment for them at reeling, picking etc. as well as to many more young men that ever remain at them.[61]

By modern standards, the living conditions, educational provision and terms of employment may appear primitive, but at the time they were ahead of anything being offered elsewhere. There is no available evidence to suggest that any other mill owner was providing as much for his child labourers. There were established 'communities' with houses, markets and Sunday schools in Cromford, Belper and Milford and it may be that Dale's community was modelled on these. Similarly, Gillespie's school may have been established in Glasgow, but there is no evidence to indicate that any other child employees in Scotland were as well provided for as Dale's New Lanark apprentices. Dale was justifiably proud of his scheme:

And when it is considered that the greater part of the children who are in the boarding house consists of destitute orphans, children abandoned by their parents ... and many who know not who were their parents ... it gives me great pleasure to say, that by proper management and attention, much good instead of evil may be done at cotton mills. For I am warranted in affirming that many now have stout, healthy bodies and are of decent behaviour who in all probability would have been languishing with disease and pests to society had they not been employed at Lanark cotton mills.[62]

He was entitled to be proud of his efforts and must surely have been concerned to hear, in July 1801, only 18 months after the business had been sold to Owen and his partners, that there had been some complaints from the workhouse. In the first instance, the terms offered to the West Kirk by Owen in July 1801 were deemed to be '*very disadvantageous to the Managers*', who were by then supplying James Monteith's (previously Dale's) Blantyre Cotton Works. So annoyed were the West Kirk Managers with Owen's proposals that they instructed their clerk to write to the Blantyre Mills to find out if any children were needed before they would consider sending any more to New Lanark.[64] Relations remained strained for some months. In August that year, one of the workhouse managers reported to the committee that there had been serious complaints made against the managers of the New Lanark mills. The precise nature of these complaints is never made clear other than the charge that the managers at New Lanark had '*not performed their engagements respecting the children who have been sent from the Workhouse*'.[65]

In October of that year, the West Kirk were considering the relative merits of letters they had received from New Lanark and Blantyre Mills, each containing proposals for indentured apprenticeships:

The proposals from Blantyre being much more favourable than those from the Managers of New Lanark Mills ... the Managers desired the Clerk to inform the Superintendant (sic) of Blantyre Mills that he would receive as many of the children as should suit his purpose on the terms stated in the letter.[66]

Things had not improved much by 1803, when proposals from New Lanark for taking some of the children as servants were mentioned to the West Kirk managers but, because the terms of engagement were too long, the proposals were unanimously rejected.[67]

Robert Owen eventually phased out the employment of pauper apprentices. Attitudes were changing and Owen had his own educational and social agenda to pursue. Dale, however, operated in a period when the employment of pauper apprentices was the norm and for him, their welfare and education were one of his principal concerns. One of his other principal concerns was to oversee the operation of a successful cotton spinning business and to ensure its continued profitability and success. New Lanark, the most successful large-scale manufacturing concern of its time was, however, only the most obvious example of Dale's entrepreneurial ventures. There were quite a few others.

References: Chapter 7

1   Dale to T.B Bayley, July 1796. Vide infra, Appendix 7.

2   Sinclair, J. (ed) (1791–1799) *The Statistical Account of Scotland, 1791–99*, 21 vols. Vol. XV, p.38. See also Davidson, W. (1828) *A History of Lanark & Guide to the Scenery with a list of Roads to the Provincial Towns*. Lanark: Shepherd & Robertson, p.166.

3   Davidson, W. *History of Lanark*, p.172.

4   Ibid.

5   Sinclair, J. (ed) *Statistical Account*, Vol. XV., p.40.

6   'Chronicle', *The Annual Register for 1792*, London: Otridge & Sons (1799), p.27.

7   Garnett, T. (1800) *Observations on a Tour through the Highlands and Part of the Western Isles of Scotland*. London: Cadell & Davies, p.235. Garnett says he gets his information from the *Statistical Account* and from McNayr's *Guide from Glasgow to the Highlands of Scotland*, but McNayr (p.239) says there were sixteen teachers in 1797. This is made more confusing by Thomas. Bernard in *The Reports of the Society for Bettering the Condition of the Poor* (1800), when he quotes sixteen teachers and says he is indebted to Garnett for the information.

8   Vide infra, Appendix 7.

9   Sinclair, J. (ed) *Statistical Account*, Vol. XV, p.39.

10 Cleland, J. (1816) *The Annals of Glasgow*, 2 vols. Glasgow: James Hedderwick. Vol. 1, pp.218-9.

11 Garnett, T. (1800) *Observations*, p.235.

12 Marshall, J. (1803) *Tour Book for Scotland and Ireland*. University of Leeds, Brotherton Collection. MS 200/62. 1800-1803.

13 Glasgow Town's Hospital. *Minutes of Directors' Quarterly Meetings, 1732–1816*. 15th May 1794 Glasgow City Archives, Rare Book No. 641983.

14 Vide infra, Appendix 7.

15 See Brown, A. (1795-1797) *History of Glasgow and of Paisley, Greenock, and Port-Glasgow, comprehending the ecclesiastical and civil history of these places, from the earliest accounts to the present time: and including an account of their population, commerce, manufactures, arts, and agriculture*. 2 vols. (1795, 1797) Glasgow: W. Paton. Vol. 2, p.234.

16 Vide infra, Appendix 7. A similar system may well have been in operation at the charity school in Glasgow for the children of soldiers and sailors with which Dale was involved. A newspaper report written in 1817 but apparently referring to the Dale period, notes that a premium was given to the teachers *'for every child who is found qualified to leave the school.'* See *The Morning Chronicle*. London, 23rd April, 1817.

17 Vide infra, Appendix 7.

18 Town's Hospital. Minutes, 15th May 1794.

19 Ibid., 20th August 1790.

20 Vide supra, Chapter 6.

21 *The Morning Chronicle*. London, 23rd April 1817.

22 Vide infra, Appendix 7.

23 Sinclair, J. (ed) *Statistical Account*, Vol. XX, p.161.

24 Devine, T.M. (1999) *The Scottish Nation, 1700-2000*. London: Penguin, pp.91-102.

25 Robert Lyon, Edinburgh, to Andrew Mitchell, 16th April 1816. See *Glasgow Association of Master Cotton Spinners Sederunt Book*, 1816. Glasgow City Archives, T-MJ100. Lyon is seen as a reliable source but his observation here lacks corroboration.

26 Garnett, T. (1800) *Observations*, p.235.

27 Robertson, A.D. (1975) *Lanark: the Burgh and its Councils, 1469–188[?]*. Lanark Town Council, p.255. Also, vide infra, Appendix 7.

28 Vide infra, Appendix 7.

29 Davidson, H. (1910) *Lanark: A Series of Papers by the late Hugh Davidson, Writer*. Edinburgh. p.221.

30 Ibid., p.247.

31 Ibid., pp.221, 247.

32 Sinclair, J. (ed) *Statistical Account*, Vol. XV, p.38.

33 Davidson, W. (1828) *A History of Lanark & Guide to the Scenery with a list of Roads to the Provincial Towns*. Lanark: Shepherd & Robertson, p.172.

34 Ibid., p.173.

35 Robert Lyon to Andrew Mitchell, 16th April 1816.

36 Ibid.

37 Ibid.

38 Ibid.

39 Marshall, J. (1803) *Tour Book*, p.188n.

40 West Kirk Charity Workhouse, Edinburgh. Monthly Meeting, 5th Oct 1790. *Minute Book* SL222/1/7. For Workhouse Minutes, see Laurie, A.E. and Young, N. (2009, 2013) *New Lanark's People. A Collection of Transcribed Archive material from over 70 Different Sources*. 2 Vols. Private CD Publication. New Lanark Conservation.

41 In fact, the Workhouse Committee paid little attention to Dale's request, although they did finally agree a few years later when Dale repeated it. It proved impossible to ascertain the dates of birth of many of the children and Dale subsequently asked that all apprenticeships should be of seven years duration, regardless of age on entry. The Committee initially refused but on 6th February 1798 it was agreed that all children should be bound until they were seventeen years of age *'but that for the last two years of their indenture he should have them employed occasionally at the loom, or at such other business as they might prefer'*. However, this caused some practical difficulties and in many cases, the apprenticeships continued to end at age fifteen.

42 West Kirk Minutes, September, 1790.

43 Letter from Hugh Dick to J. Linsay, Treasurer, West Kirk Charity Workhouse. See West Kirk Minutes. 6th October, 1795. The Minute of 5th October, 1790 shows 42 children (25 boys & seventeen girls) originally earmarked for New Lanark. Between 1790 and 1797, the West Kirk sent a total of approximately 100 children - 63 boys and 37 girls.

44 'Memoir of David Dale, Esq.', *Imperial Magazine*, 4:46 (1822: November) p.1069.

45 *The Caledonian Mercury*, 10th August 1799.

46 Davidson, W. *History of Lanark*, p.166.

47   West Kirk Minutes, 6th March 1792.

48   Ibid., 6th March, 3rd April & 4th September 1792.

49   Ibid., 4th March 1794.

50   Ibid., 5th April 1796.

51   Town's Hospital Minutes, 19th May 1796.

52   Fitton, R.S. and Wadsworth, A.P. (1958) *The Strutts and the Arkwrights 1758–1830. A Study of the Early Factory System.* Manchester: M.U.P., p.106.

53   Dale to Dr. James Currie, 8th August 1795. See Johnston, W.T. (ed) (2000) *David Dale & Robert Owen Studies.* Livingston: Officina Educational Publications.

54   Hugh Dick to J. Linsay, Treasurer, West Kirk Charity Workhouse. West Kirk Workhouse Minutes, 6th October 1795.

55   Ibid.

56   Ibid.

57   Ibid.

58   Ibid.

59   Davidson, W. *History of Lanark*, p.166.

60   Cowan, W.A. (1867) *History of Lanark and a Guide to the Surrounding Scenery.* Lanark: Robert Wood, pp.90-91.

61   Dale to Bayley. Vide infra, Appendix 7.

62   Ibid.

63   West Kirk Minutes. 7th July 1801.

64   Ibid.

65   Ibid., 4th August 1801.

66   Ibid., 6th October 1801.

67   Ibid., 1st March 1803.

Part 3

The Entrepreneur: Mills and Bills

Chapter 8:
Penicuik, Rothesay, Oban, Newton Douglas and Blantyre

Penicuik & Rothesay

There were several cotton mills in Scotland before those at New Lanark, and it is interesting to note David Dale's interest and involvement (directly and indirectly) with some of these.

There is some debate about which was the first Scottish cotton mill to be built. Bremner argues for Rothesay Mill but most commentators would argue instead that Penicuik, built in 1778, was the first.[1] Nisbet is correct to point out that the attempts made to establish which was 'first' are rather pointless in that much depends on when the mill in question was planned; when the first site was purchased; when the first yarn was spun; when the whole works were operating – and so on.[2] Nevertheless, there does seem to be some general agreement that Penicuik was the site of one of the earliest cotton mills. Sir John Clerk, the landowner, feued the land to Peter Brotherstone (one of the Managers of the Board of Trustees for Manufactures) as early as 1776. Brotherstone was an English businessman who had invented a carding machine and had formed a partnership with some Edinburgh bankers. The mill was designed and built under the direction of James Hackett, a former employee of Arkwright and an acquaintance of Hargreaves.[3] Initially a very small-scale venture, Brotherstone had it insured for £500 in 1777, one year before building work was completed.

Perhaps inevitably, once the mills began operating, Arkwright took issue with what he considered to be an infringement of his patent and sued unsuccessfully in 1778.[4] He was also unsuccessful in his attempt to sue the Rothesay Cotton Mill one year later – shortly after it began production. As for Dale, he appears to have had little direct interest in Penicuik, as far as can be ascertained, but he would certainly have been aware of its existence, and of Arkwright's involvement, especially the latter's unsuccessful court cases.

Dale took a more active (if short-lived) interest in the Rothesay venture. Although it ultimately became a fairly successful mill, Rothesay had a troubled history for the first few years of its existence. In 1779, James Kenyon from Sheffield set up the spinning operation in a converted flax mill. Bremner describes this as '*of small extent ... almost an insignificant concern*'.[5] This may or may not have been the case, but, as Nisbet points out, there was often confusion surrounding references to the Rothesay 'mill'. The small-scale operation (two water frames in a tiny lint-mill building) was only a temporary experiment while the larger mills were being built.[6] The first of these was completed in 1780.

Although Dale would have been aware of Arkwright's two failed attempts to sue for infringement of patent, it was not until some years later in 1785 – just as the water wheel was being installed at New Lanark – that Dale expressed any obvious interest in a partnership in the Rothesay concern. The owners (Kenyon and Robert Carrick, a Glasgow businessman) had fallen into bankruptcy and the mill was for sale at a price of £4,000.[7] Dale offered a sum of £2,000 but this was not acceptable to Carrick and Kenyon.[8] The enterprise proved difficult to sell and the price began to fall. Dale formed a brief alliance with Paisley textile merchants John and James Cochrane in an attempt to effect a purchase. The Cochranes went to Rothesay to inspect the dams, lades and mills and this resulted in an offer from the trio of £1,200. However, this offer was also unsuccessful and the mills were eventually sold for £1,500 to merchant Robert Morrice, despite an insurance valuation at the time of £4,475.[9] Several commentators have noted that Dale was a partner in the Rothesay venture but Nisbet demonstrates beyond doubt that this was not the case.[10] The mill was up for sale again five years later, shortly after the completion of an expensive second mill building. The mills were offered for sale in November, 1790 and mention is made in the advertisement, not only of the new machinery, apartments and tools, but also of the favourable situation:

...having at all times a large supply of water, with a powerful fall – more than sufficient to turn 4,000 spindles... The near vicinity of the large and populous town of Rothesay is also of great advantage to the work – not only for procuring a number of hands – but likewise in affording a ready conveyance by water carriage...[11]

The mills did prosper and the *Statistical Account* one year later noted that 300 people were employed.[12] During the boom year of 1792, the mills were operating 24 hours per day.[13] Although Dale was never actively involved, it is clear that he spotted the potential of the business at an early stage and in fact, there was a New Lanark connection at a later stage with Rothesay, in that William Kelly, Dale's manager at New Lanark, and a considerable figure in his own right, became a partner in the Rothesay mills in 1800 and remained there until his retirement in 1826.[14] Kelly may have adapted some of the educational practices he had seen in New Lanark. Instead of evening schools, some instruction was given to the Rothesay children during the working day – a practice apparently borrowed from Mr. Birkbeck of Settle in Yorkshire:

The children taken thus, singly, for eight or ten minutes in rotation, are much better taught and their instruction comes to them under the appearance from labour and is therefore more willingly received.[15]

This mode of teaching did not adversely affect the quantity of work '*on the whole*' and any potential loss was more than compensated for by the positive effect on the morals and conduct of the children.[16] There had been a common library or Reading Society in the mills during the mid 1790s.[17] Employees (and some of the local population not employed in the mill) paid a small annual subscription and, by 1804, they had created a library of some 600 books, which had '*a beneficial effect on the manners of all the persons employed by supplying amusement for their leisure hours*'.[18]

Oban, Argyllshire

In the early 1790s, Dale's concern about the plight of the Highlanders and, in particular, the mass emigration which was taking place, found expression in his commitment to the mill at Spinningdale in Sutherland. However, this was not his only attempt to address the problem. The *Statistical Account* for the united parish of Kilmore and Kilbride noted in 1791–1792 that '*a small branch of the cotton manufacture*' had recently been introduced into the area '*by Mr. David Dale of Glasgow*' and that '*other gentlemen of enterprise and public spirit*' had it '*in contemplation to establish works of the same kind*'.[19] Information on this mill (near the town of Oban) is generally difficult to source but there is some surviving correspondence which sheds a little more light on Dale's motives and it does seem that *The Glasgow Herald* was accurate in its view (some years later) that the Spinningdale and Oban factories were opened expressly as a means of giving work to starving Highlanders.[20] Dale himself is quite clear about this. In his letter to Alexander Campbell of Barcaldine in August, 1791, Dale talks of his '*first attempt*' at a cotton manufactory in '*Argyleshire*' (sic) and hopes that this;

...will be only an introduction to greater and more extensive manufactures in the Highlands which will give employment to all who are willing to remain in their native country and put a stop to emigrations which are equally hurtful to the country and to the poor people who foolishy imagine that they are to be better in America.[21]

These views, of course, applied equally to the factory at Spinningdale. Referring to Argyllshire specifically, Dale continues to Campbell:

I have no doubt of your giving every encouragement to people to settle on your estate by assisting them to build houses for holding looms and if the present weavers in Argyleshire are properly assisted in this way I hope their number will be increased threefold in the course of twelve months and if I am spared I will employ them all.[22]

News of Dale's interest in Oban and the surrounding area spread quickly. Other members of the landed gentry began to see the potential, both in spinning and in weaving cotton. Donald Campbell of Sonachan (also near Oban), a wealthy landowner, wrote, apparently at the behest of the Duke of Argyll, to Murdoch Maclean of Lochbuy on the island of Mull, asking for

Maclean's opinion as to 'how far it may be for the advantage of Mull to encourage the weaving of cotton (sic) there'.[23] Campbell himself was somewhat sceptical. Local opinion, it seems, was that:

> Mr. Dale will establish other Branches of the Cottan (sic) manufacture in this Country but should the weaving of cottan webs (sic) not answer their expectations, no doubt they will drope (sic) that Branch ... and in that event it is natural to suppose, those bred to that weaving Bussiness (sic) will follow that lucrative trade to the Lowlands.[24]

Maclean's reply to Donald Campbell is not recorded but, in September, 1791, on receipt of Campbell's letter, MacLean wrote immediately to Dale, offering his help if it were required, and extolling the virtues of Mull, where there were 'many situations very well calculated for the setting of manufacters' (sic).[25]

However, Dale's response later that month may have dashed Maclean's hope somewhat. Despite the fact that Dale clearly states his intention to have 'a manufactory for spinning wefts established near about the place where my foreman is to reside' i.e. in the Oban/Nether Lorn area, what follows appears at first sight to contradict this, although Dale was always clear that any involvement in the Highlands was primarily to provide employment in the cotton industry in general, not necessarily confined to spinning:

> The only branch of Manufacture which I propose at present introducing into the Highlands is weaving of cotton cloth. I have already begun to give out webs to the weavers in Nether Lorn and its Neighbourhood and my instructions to the young man which I have sent there to manage the business is to employ every sober industrious weaver who wants to work and to encourage and assist him in teaching apprentices...[26]

The situation is clarified when Dale goes on to spell out, not for the first time, his thinking behind this (and his subsequent involvement in Spinningdale):

> '...my design in doing this is to introduce industry and give employment to the people which I hope will in time extend through the Highlands and prepare the way for the introduction of other Manufactures beside the Cotton. I cannot at present say when nor to what extent I shall be able to carry on this business but if nothing unforeseen happens to prevent me I intend visiting some parts of the Highlands next summer with the view of contributing my mite towards giving employment to the people which may probably induce others to make similar exertions and in time help to prevent emigrations which in my opinion are equally hurtfull (sic) to the people themselves and to the country'.[27]

As far as can be ascertained, the mill was built some twelve miles from the town of Oban. It seems likely that the manager was a Mr. Alex. Hunter, whom Maclean of Lochbuy sought out in his continuing efforts to establish a mill on Mull, or at least, as Hunter put it, to establish 'some part of our manufactory' on the Maclean estates.[28] Hunter offered to provide a manager if Maclean could provide suitable land and workers. Interestingly, Hunter also notes that the Duke of Argyll's initial scepticism had been won over and that the Duke would now 'offer anything I will reasonably ask if I'll only allow a part of the Business to be carried on on his grounds'.[29] However, Maclean attempted a rather sharp business manoeuvre by asking Dale to help with the cost of setting up the business on Mull. Maclean claimed to be enthusiastic about the whole venture 'but for the inconvenience at this time of advancing money for the Building' and asked Dale for 'one or two hundred pounds' towards the cost.[30] He also wanted Dale to 'furnish the necessary looms and other utenceles for the prentices (sic) and a proper allowance for their support...'.[31]

Dale, however, was having nothing to do with a scheme which would establish and maintain a new and precarious business at his expense, while Maclean remained risk-free. Dale's reply was succinct:

> I never advance any money to build houses for Manufacturers, having need for all the money I can command for carrying on the Works which I am engaged in on this Account.[32]

Dale's involvement with the Oban mill thereafter is not recorded, nor is the date of his withdrawal from the venture but, in any event, by this time (1792), he had become much more involved in his other, better known, Highland scheme at Spininngdale. Even so, his business activities continued to extend far and wide and while he was committed to New Lanark, Blantyre, Catrine in the central belt and Oban and Spinningdale in the north, he took on another mill venture at the other end of the country.

Newton Douglas

Dale wrote to his friend, George Dempster in 1791 regarding a Mr. McDowall of Garthland who was apparently 'very keen to introduce manufactures into Galloway and proposes building a manufacturing Village'.[33] In fact, Dale formed a business partnership, not with McDowall but with Sir William Douglas (1745–1809) in a small cotton spinning enterprise in Newton Stewart, Wigtownshire. Douglas was a wealthy landowner who had made his fortune in tobacco and was one of the few who had successfully diversified into manufacturing and banking.[34] Quite how Dale became involved in the project is unknown, as is the true extent of his involvement. James & John McCall, Glasgow merchants were also partners in the venture but the precise details of the partnership have not survived. Douglas himself was a very influential character and was well connected to the nobility – so much so that the town of Newton Stewart was renamed Newton Douglas in his honour in 1792 (although the designation was only used for a few years) and Douglas was eventually knighted in 1801.[35] The following extract from Lloyd's Evening Post explains the situation in September 1792:

> We are informed that a cotton mill is to be erected and manufactories introduced into Newton Stewart by William Douglas Esq. of Castle Douglas, proprietor of the town and contiguous estate. This town has of late rapidly increased and the inhabitants display a spirit of industry truly laudable. By a charter from the king, lately obtained, this town is to be called in the future Newton-Douglas.[36]

Royal Charter was granted three months later.[37] Shortly thereafter, in early 1793, the firm of Douglas, Dale & McCall established a spinning mill in the town, at a cost quoted in one source as £10,000.[38] Unfortunately, the extent of Dale's involvement in the operation and management of the mill is unclear but it seems likely that, given his many other major interests, it was relatively minimal. There is no record of him visiting the mill, although he retained a financial interest until the early 1800s, when the mill employed 177 people.[39] At that point, Robert Owen advised his father-in-law to withdraw from the venture, along with his interests in Catrine, Spinningdale and Stanley.[40] This may well have been sound advice in relation to Newton Douglas. A detailed inventory drawn up five years after Dale's death indicates that at the time of Dale's death in 1806, Sir William owed him £6,378.[41]

Blantyre

While New Lanark was in the early stages of establishing itself as a pioneer of industrial cotton spinning, Dale was not content to focus all his energies on one location. He was wealthy enough to take up or to create other options. Such was the case with the Blantyre Cotton Mill which Dale established in 1787. Information on Blantyre in the early days (i.e. during the period of Dale's ownership) is extremely scant, although there is a suggestion that it was Dale's interest in Turkey Red dyeing which led him to build Blantyre in the first place.[42] It was certainly the case at a later stage during the Monteith family's stewardship that Blantyre was the site of both spinning and dyeing and it is possible that some Turkey Red dyeing was established on site as early as 1787 (given that the partnership with Macintosh and Papillon in Dalmarnock had been established two years earlier). However, there is very little, if any, evidence to substantiate this.

All that can be noted with any certainty is that, while New Lanark was in its infancy, Dale had the mill built in Blantyre for the same, or similar purposes – the spinning of cotton. Details of the operation of the Blantyre Mill between 1787–1792, when it was sold to James Monteith, are equally scarce and, as a result, the Statistical Account of the parish becomes the only significant source of information for this period, and even this provides little in the way of detail. The Rev. Stevenson, writing in 1791 (when Dale was still the owner of the mill) appears to suggest that the population of the village was in the region of

1,040 and that it was making "*continual and rapid progress and as the machinery is not nearly completed ... [is] still daily increasing*".[43] There is little information on the business, although some of the minister's account of life in the village indicates a strong resemblance to events in New Lanark. Approximately 368 people were employed in the mill, of whom 60 were 'barracks children', employed in Blantyre as bound apprentices and who were fed, clothed, lodged and educated by the mill owner, as in New Lanark. The child apprentices were generally orphans or pauper children, generally between eight and twelve years of age:

> They are generally bound to the work by their relations for a few years; and are fed, clothed and lodged by the proprietor of the mill. He has a schoolmaster employed in teaching them in their spare hours; a surgeon to attend them when sick; and much praise is due to such a guardian of youth for his attention both to their health and education.[44]

There is certainly evidence that Monteith later used one of Dale's sources for child apprentices in Blantyre. The West Kirk Charity Workhouse monthly meeting of February, 1799 makes this clear. The Managers had received '*a memorial*' on behalf of James Monteith of Blantyre Cotton Works, '*requesting the Managers to allow him such a number of children for his Mills as they may think proper, upon the same terms as those upon which they have been in use to send children to Mr. Dale's Cotton Works*'.[45] The Managers, having first satisfied themselves that Dale did not, at that point, require any more child employees in New Lanark, agreed to send Monteith some six girls and five boys, aged between eight and eleven years. In making their decision, the committee took into consideration 'the warm recommendation produced in Mr. Monteith's favour and the ample attestation of the attention and care he pays to the children at his works'. Later that year, the same Managers received a visit from the Superintendent of Blantyre Cotton Mills who picked out the children he wanted – in this case, six boys aged between eight years six months and ten years six months.[46] The West Kirk continued to supply Blantyre with children for at least another four years.[47]

Blantyre Mill (Richard Stenlake, private collection)

Later accounts of Blantyre credit James Monteith with establishing the school and the (relatively) healthy living conditions but the evidence suggests that Monteith may have inherited these from Dale. It does appear that Dale had a school built in Blantyre at roughly the same time the school was being built in the Catrine mills. It seems highly likely also, that the *Statistical Account* reference to a schoolmaster in Blantyre being employed to teach the children '*in their spare hours*' and of a surgeon '*attending them when sick*' refer to the period when Dale was in charge.[48] Similarly, there are clear echoes of New Lanark in the minister's comment that, despite the potentially unhealthy conditions in cotton mills, 'only two have died' in Blantyre since the mills had been built:

> Great care indeed is taken, to keep the house and machinery as clean as possible; fresh air is carefully thrown in; and tar is burnt, to remove or counteract the noxious smell of the oil, that must necessarily be used about the machines.[49]

His observations about the care taken to promote healthy conditions is much in line (apart from the tar-burning) with Dale's response to the Manchester Board of Health regarding New Lanark. Since the *Statistical Account* referring to Blantyre was published in 1792 (the year Blantyre was sold), and the minister's account was written sometime in 1791, it is highly unlikely that Monteith bought the mill, established a schoolmaster and a system of feeding, clothing and lodging and had houses built, all in time for inclusion in the *Statistical Account*. Thus the evidence, such as it is, points to Dale as the provider of such a system between the years 1787 and 1792. It seems clear that New Lanark, Catrine and Blantyre all had a system of schooling from the very earliest days and that the common denominator in all of this was David Dale.

What is beyond doubt, however, is that as New Lanark expanded, Dale's business empire expanded with it. However, for reasons which are unclear, he felt the need to sell the Blantyre Mill and concentrate on his other new development at Catrine in Ayrshire. Perhaps he anticipated the conflict with France and the dire commercial consequences of that or perhaps he decided that New Lanark and Catrine together offered the best prospects of success and sufficient challenge in themselves or perhaps he simply received an offer he could not refuse. Whatever the case, Blantyre was sold to James Monteith in 1792.

It is worth commenting briefly on Dale's relationship with the Monteith family. In the course of his life, Dale was involved with many of the major merchant families in Scotland – most notably the Buchanans, the Finlays and the Monteiths. His connection with the Monteiths dates from his earliest days in Glasgow. Both Dale and James Monteith Senior (the father of James Monteith of Blantyre Mill) began their careers importing linen yarns from France and Holland. Monteith Senior began weaving in Glasgow's Anderston district and became one of the city's famous 'wee corks' – small manufacturers who bought linen yarn and then either wove it themselves or put it out for weaving by hand.[50] Born in 1734, he was a contemporary of Dale's and subsequently became the '*first manufacturer in Glasgow who gave out a web of cotton yarn to be woven into cloth in imitation of the East India muslins*'.[51] So fine was the quality of the muslin that Monteith had one embroidered with gold and sent to Queen Charlotte. His move into cotton was very successful and he '*ultimately came to be called the father of the cotton trade in Glasgow*'.[52] Monteith and Dale were both part of the group of manufacturers who met Arkwright on his momentous visit to the city in 1784.

Monteith was the father of six sons, three of whom became prominent businessmen, not only in the family business but in their own right. The eldest, John, founded his own cotton firm and established the first power loom in Scotland (in Pollokshaws) in 1801. The third son, Henry, was even more successful – as a mill owner, entrepreneur, Lord Provost of Glasgow and Tory M.P. for Linlithgow. However, it is Monteith's second son, James, who continued his father's direct connection with David Dale. There is a dearth of information on the operation of the Blantyre Mill prior to Monteith's purchase in 1792. Most of the accounts of the period simply note that James Monteith Junior appeared in 1792 and took it off Dale's hands. However, as with New Lanark and Catrine, Dale could not be an on-site manager and it may well be the case that the young James Monteith was Dale's manager during the period prior to the sale. Dale hints at such in a letter to his Catrine partner, Claud Alexander, in August 1789:

> Mr. Monteith at Blantyre is going to spin lower numbers than formerly ... and I have no doubt that when Mule spinning comes more general, Mr. Monteith will be obliged to go much further with his numbers...[53]

Events surrounding the sale to Monteith – described as '*sedate and somewhat reserved in his manners*', even as a young man, are easier to access.[54] Dale sold the mill in 1792 but by 1793, the industry was in crisis. The war with France had begun, trade was in decline, cotton prices were falling and in Glasgow, three banks (The Glasgow Arms, The Merchant and Thomson's) collapsed. Even the Royal Bank '*quaked and trembled*'.[55] Monteith, '*quite in despair*' at the prospect of trying to keep up payments on the Blantyre Mill, '*begged and entreated*' Dale to annul the sale but Dale refused.[56] However, what seemed to be a hard-headed business decision on Dale's part ultimately made Monteith a fortune. Monteith was forced into manufacturing his own cloth (perhaps guided by his father) and sending it to be auctioned by Messrs. Wheelhouse & Whitfield in London. Much to Monteith's surprise, this was extremely successful and he is reported to have made the huge sum of £80,000 in five years.[57] Indeed, Robert Reid, writing some years later, refers to him as '*our first cotton lord*', – perhaps reminiscent of Glasgow's famous 'Tobacco Lords' – an image strengthened by the following description of Monteith arriving in Glasgow from the Blantyre Mill (and one which contrasts with the earlier image of the '*somewhat reserved*' gentleman already alluded to):

> *Figure to yourself a portly gentleman of forty; five feet nine inches high, walking with a slow and rather heavy step, dressed in a neat round hat, powdered hair and long cue, white neckcloth, Duke of Hamilton striped vest, blue coat and gilt buttons, yellow buckskins and top boots.*[58]

As Reid points out, Monteith made a fortune '*nearly as rapidly as our former tobacco lords*' but not, like the tobacco lords, by holding large stocks during a crisis but by holding no stock at all.[59] By 1798, he was able to move into the first mansion built in Miller Street in the city centre.

Interestingly, Monteith seems to have been the only Glasgow merchant who was successful in this way. When Dale realised what was happening, he tried to do exactly the same, using the same auction house and even having a room set aside on their premises exclusively for his own goods. Reports suggest, however, that Monteith had cornered the market. Dale, it seems, was too late '*and was not supposed to have been successful in this department of his business*'.[60]

James Monteith of Blantyre died in 1802 but the mills were taken over by his brother Henry and stayed in the Monteith family for many years. David Livingstone, arguably Scotland's most famous missionary explorer, was born in 1813 in Shuttle Row, now a National Trust property and site of the David Livingstone museum. For Dale, the sale of Blantyre in 1792 allowed him to concentrate on his other spinning enterprises elsewhere, most notably in Catrine, Ayrshire.

Livingstone's Birthplace, Blantyre. (Before it was Restored). 41080. JV.

David Livingstone's birthplace. (Richard Stenlake, private collection)

References: Chapter 8

1   Bremner, D. (1869) *The Industries of Scotland. Their Rise, Progress and Present Condition.* London: Black. Reprint (1969), Newton Abbot: David & Charles, p.279. See also Nisbet, S.M. (2004) 'Early Cotton Spinning in the West of Scotland, 1778–1799: Rothesay Cotton Mill', *Transactions, Buteshire Natural History Society,* XXVI: 39–47. Also Donnachie, I. and Hewitt, G. (1993) *Historic New Lanark.* Edinburgh: E.U.P. and Cooke, A. (2010) *The Rise and Fall of the Scottish Cotton Industry, 1778–1914: The Secret Spring.* Manchester: M.U.P.

2   Nisbet, S.M. (2004) 'Early Cotton Spinning in the West of Scotland, 1778–1799: Rothesay Cotton Mill', *Transactions, Buteshire Natural History Society,* XXVI: 39–47, p.39.

3   Cooke, A. *Rise and Fall,* p. 29. Donnachie, I. & Hewitt, G. (1993) *Historic New Lanark,* p.11.

4   Nisbet, S.M. (2008) *The Rise of the Cotton Factory in Eighteenth-Century Renfrewshire.* British Archaeology Report, Series 464. Oxford: Alden Press, p.62.

5   Bremner, D. *Industries,* p.279.

6   Nisbet, S. (2004) *Early Cotton Spinning,* pp.41–42.

7   Nisbet, S.M. (2008) *The Rise of the Cotton Factory,* p.107.

8   See Introduction to the 1969 reprint of Bremner's *Industries of Scotland,* edited by J. Butt and I. Donnachie.

9   Signet Library Session Paper 411/62. I am extremely grateful to Dr. Stuart Nisbet for his assistance and for contacting me with this information. See also Cooke, A. *Rise and Fall,* p.45.

10 Bremner, in his *Industries of Scotland* and, more recently, W.T Johnston (*Dale and Owen Studies*) are quite clear that Dale was a partner, However, see Nisbet, S.M. 2004, p.43n.

11 *The Glasgow Courier,* 22nd November 1790.

12 Sinclair, J. (ed) (1791–1799) *The Statistical Account of Scotland, 1791–1799,* 21 vols. Vol. I, p.305.

13 Nisbet, S.M. *The Rise of the Cotton Factory,* p.70.

14 Donnachie, I. & Hewitt, G. (1993) *Historic New Lanark,* p.54; Cooke, A. *Rise and Fall,* p.108.

15 Aiken, A. (ed) (1805) 'Reports of the Society for Bettering the Condition of the Poor'. Vol. IV: 323–5 in *The Annual Review & History of Lit for 1804.* Vol. III. London: Longman, Hurst, Rees & Orme. p.324.

16 Ibid.

17 *The Monthly Magazine & British Register for 1797,* Vol. IV, July–Dec 1798, London, p.277. N.B. this article lists two such societies in 'Rothsay Cotton Mills' (sic).

18 Aiken, A. (ed) *Reports,* p.324.

19 Sinclair, J. (ed) *Statistical Account,* Vol. XI, p.132.

20 *The Glasgow Herald,* 27th August, 1886.

21 Dale to Alex Campbell of Barcaldine, 18th August 1791. National Archives of Scotland (NAS): GD.170/1743/13, in Johnston, W.T. (ed) (2000) *David Dale & Robert Owen Studies.* Livingston: Officina Educational Publications.

22 Ibid.

23 Donald Campbell to Murdoch Maclean, 2nd September 1791. NAS. GD.174/1460/1, in Johnston, W.T. *David Dale.*

24 Ibid.

25 Murdoch Maclean of Lochbuy to David Dale, 10 September, 1791. NAS. GD.174/1460/2., in Johnston, W.T. *David Dale.*

26 Dale to Murdoch Maclean of Lochbuy, 22nd September 1791. NAS. GD 174/1460/3., in Johnston, W.T. *David Dale.*

27 Ibid.

28 Alexander Hunter to Murdoch Maclean of Lochbuy, 17 October, 1791. NAS. GD.174/1460/4., in Johnston, W.T. *David Dale.*

29 Ibid.

30 Murdoch Maclean of Lochbuy to David Dale, 5th March 1792. NAS GD.174/1460/5., in Johnston, W.T. *David Dale.*

31 Ibid.

32 Dale to Murdoch Maclean of Lochbuy, 12th March 1792. NAS. GD.174/1460/6 in Johnston, W.T. *David Dale.*

33 Dempster, G.S. *The Papers of George Soper Dempster,* 19 vols. University of Toronto, MS Coll. 126. UT Vol. 3. Accession No. 35452, 21st December 1791. (Also catalogued as *The Dempster Papers. A Collection of Letters & papers relating to George Dempster of Dunnichen.* 19 Vols. MS Coll. 126.)

34 Donnachie, I. & Hewitt, G. (1993) *Historic New Lanark,* p.31.

35 *The British Gazette & Sunday Monitor,* 5th July 1801.

36 *Lloyd's Evening Post,* 24th September 1792.

37 *The Scots Magazine,* (54), December 1792. p.623.

38 Lloyd Jones, M. (1889) *The Life, Times & Labours of Robert Owen.* London: Swann, Sonnenshein & Co., p.212. However, readers are advised that this source can often be unreliable.

39 Cooke, A. *Rise and Fall,* p.147.

40 Owen, R. (1857) *The Life of Robert Owen Written by Himself*. Vol. 1. London: Effingham Wilson. New impression (1967) London: Frank Cass & Co., pp.72–75.

41 Cooke, A. *Rise and Fall*, p.177.

42 Cullen, A. (1910) *Adventures in Socialism*. Glasgow: John Smith, p.10.

43 Sinclair, J. (ed) *Statistical Account*, Vol. II, p.216.

44 Ibid., pp.216–17.

45 West Kirk Charity Workhouse Minute Book. Monthly Meeting, 5th Feb 1799, Edinburgh City Archives, SL222/1/7. See Laurie, A.E. and Young, N. (2009, 2013) *New Lanark's People. A Collection of Transcribed Archive material from over 70 Different Sources*. 2 Vols. Private CD Publication. New Lanark Conservation, Vol. 2.

46 Ibid.

47 Ibid., 4th February 1800; 7th July 1801; 6th October 1801; 2nd October 1804.

48 Sinclair, J. (ed) *Statistical Account*, Vol. II, p.216.

49 Ibid., p.217.

50 Reid, R. (Senex) (1884) *Glasgow Past and Present*, 3 vols. Glasgow: David Robertson & Co., Vol. III, p.316. See also Cooke, A. *Rise and Fall*, p.17.

51 Ibid., Vol. III, p.317.

52 Ibid., pp.317–18.

53 Dale to Claud Alexander, 26th August 1789. *Dale–Alexander Correspondence, 1787–1797*. Glasgow City Archives, MS 63/7.

54 Reid, R. (1884) *Glasgow*, Vol. III, p.319.

55 Ibid., p.301.

56 Ibid., Vol. II, p.51.

57 Ibid., Vol. III, pp.301–2.

58 Ibid., pp.312; 302.

59 Ibid., p.302.

60 Ibid.

Chapter 9: Catrine, Spinningdale and Stanley

A clearer picture of Dale's involvement in cotton spinning outside New Lanark can be seen in his partnership with Claud Alexander of Ballochmyle in the establishment of the Catrine Cotton Works in Ayrshire.

Claud Alexander (centre) with his brother, Boyd.

Alexander himself is an interesting figure. He had been a senior employee of the East India Company and had spent seventeen years in India as Paymaster General of the company's armed forces – a prestigious and influential position. Advance notice of his return to the U.K. was posted in the London newspapers in April 1786 and his ship finally docked in August that year.[1] As a senior civil servant, he moved in elevated social circles. A year after his return, for example, he was elected a member of the Society for the Encouragement of Arts, Manufactures & Commerce in London. Other members included various dukes, earls and baronets.[2] Although he did not return from India until August 1786, Alexander had instructed his attorney in Scotland to look at estates coming on to the market with a view to procuring one for him which was suitable for 'improvement'. Ballochmyle (or Ballochmyl) was bought for him in 1785 prior to his return.

Alexander and his sister, Wilhelmina, moved in to the 'elegant mansion house ... fit for the immediate reception of a large family with suitable offices of every kind' and this marked the beginning of a long and successful family relationship with the area – all the more so, given that he had no previous experience as a landowner or as a mill owner.[3] Robert Burns lived on the nearby Mossgiel Farm and Wilhelmina found enduring fame as Burns' *Bonnie Lass of Ballochmyle* after a chance encounter between them on the Ballochmyle estate. The family connection with Burns does not end there. Burns was the Deputy Master of the local Freemasons' Lodge and was in the Chair when Claud Alexander was admitted as an Honorary member in July 1787.[4] However, some years later, Burns wrote vitriolically about Claud Alexander and his brother Boyd.

By 1788, Alexander had finally sold his 'large pucka-built upper roomed house' in Calcutta, married Eleonora Maxwell, eldest daughter of Sir William Maxwell of Springkell and had joined 'the patriotic Mr. Dale of Glasgow' in establishing the new and vitally important factory community of Catrine – all of which 'with a rapidity, taste and judgement ... rarely ... exceeded by a man of equal fortune'.[5]

Some sources claim that construction work on the mills began in 1786 but correspondence between Alexander and the neighbouring landowner – one James Boswell – in early 1787 refers to construction commencing in the spring. Richard Arkwright recommended his millwright, Thomas Lowe of Nottingham and Lowe subsequently built and installed four water wheels 'at different parts of the building with a divide fall of 48 feet'.[6] The *Statistical Account* also refers to 1787 and there is some early correspondence which would seem to confirm that building work was in its early stages in 1787.[7] This exchange of letters is also useful in indicating Dale's considerable and detailed involvement in the management of the project.

A Mr. Abercrombie wrote to Dale in February 1787 offering to take on 'the erection of the Cotton Mill at Ballochmyle':

...on the following manner That is to direct & oversee the cutting the Canal or lead including the Dam compleat to the Mill. The building the House the water wheel & principal Machinery brought up as far as sufficient to begin to place the spinning frames & the apparatus thereto belonging upon such principles as Mr. Dale shall point out

This I undertake to direct oversee & get executed with as much dispatch & economy as circumstances will admit & to give all my attention during the time for Mr. Alexanders interest both at the Mill & otherwise for the sum of £250 upon your allowing me proper operative powers to execute the same[8]

Dale wrote to Alexander some four days later and seemed less than impressed by Mr. Abercrombie's offer, and in particular, his prices:

I think them rather too high & we must therefore look out for some other person unless he can be brought to more reasonable terms I wish much to see you here so soon as your conveniency will admit of it. The Stanley Company have no plans of their houses they have sent the dimensions of some of them but we shall be very little wiser thereby but there will be no difficulty in getting proper plans. I have not seen nor heard from Mr. Abercrombie since he sent his proposals. I suppose he wishes to make himself a necessary man, & I suspect that the want of proper instruments was not the reason of his returning here but that he wished to make a bargain for himself before any thing further was done.[9]

Even at this early stage, Dale appeared to be very much in charge of events and was arranging to have plans copied of the houses at the Stanley Mill in Perthshire. In Catrine, building work continued into 1788 and in April that year in a letter to Alexander, Dale discusses in some detail not only the price per foot of the stonework but also the payment of the stonemasons and the positioning of the windows and vents. It is clear that, although he was taking some advice from his half-brother James regarding building work, Dale was not yet convinced of James's worth as a business partner David Dale therefore became directly involved in drawing up the plans for the carding house and the jenny (or 'jeanie') house (eventually opened in 1790).[10] Alexander obviously depended a great deal on Dale's expertise in a number of areas. In similar vein, both Dale and Alexander were again supported by Arkwright. Dale wrote to Alexander in April 1788, informing him that Arkwright had sent two boxes of machine parts, comprising plates, wheels, rollers for two spinning machines and an additional 48 spindles.[11]

The mill was not yet fully operational, as Dale noted a few days later in another letter to Alexander. Once again, Dale's experience and expertise are crucial, not only in terms of practical technical knowledge and advice regarding the machinery but also in terms of his knowledge of the cotton business in general:

> ...I am of opinion that it was a wrong measure to shut the sluices & leave the water in the mine all night had the water passed through the mine in the manner that it will do when the works are finished & the Mill going, I have no doubt that it would have continued to answer the purpose in the same manner it did before the sluices were shut & the longer that the water had run in that way the chinks in the side of the sluice next the brae would have filled up with the slime & earthy parts of the water. the carry[i]ng wooden troughs through the mine will be expensive though no doubt they will be effectual & therefore that measure must be pursued in our present situation I am receiving Acc[oun]ts every day from England of some Cotton works giving over business & the greatest part of them all have stoped spinning in the night there is not the least doubt of the business comming round at last. I think matters will settle here with respect to any more Bankruptcies, & I have great hopes that next year there will be a brisk trade the Fustain business is at present exceeding brisk in Manchester notwithstanding of the late Bankruptcies & there are several persons from Manchester now in this place wishing to buy Cotton Wool but the holders have advanced the price I am however of opinion that the advance in the price of wool will be of short duration so long as the Muslin & Callicoe trade continues in the present situation.[12]

By 1789, the water wheels were turning, business was progressing and the partnership with Claud Alexander seemed to be working well. The jennies in particular were making 'excellent yarn':

> ...they will cut out the water spinning above N° 80 perhaps N° 60. indeed Mr. Clark at the Bridge of Johnston thinks that Jennie Spinning will cut out water spinning altogether. I think that this will not be the case, yet there is no saying what improvements may be made as no person imagined that the Mules would have made such an astonishing progress 2 year ago... I am doing every thing in my power to push on the Machinery of the Mill at Catrine.[13]

Despite Dale's obvious seniority in terms of experience and expertise, there was a real sense of partnership. For example, regarding a contract with the Houston family, Dale told Alexander that he had no objection to signing the contract but decided not to do it until Alexander had had a chance to look over it and give it his approval.[14]

The mill was built at the centre of the proposed village square. It had five storeys plus attics, and houses were built around it.[15] The tiny houses had thatched roofs, although Dale would have preferred to have used slate for this purpose, especially after a fire in 1792 which destroyed four of the houses, '...but perhaps these kind of houses will not admit of the expense of a slate roof.'[16] As Dale knew all too well, fire was always an issue in both the mills and local housing, which in turn raised the question of insurance by the proprietors. Dale had some interesting observations, based on his experience at New Lanark:

> ...I shall write for a fire Engine if you please but there is not the least chance of our getting one from the Insurance office they did not pay one shilling of the expenses of the one I have at Lanark nor did they give me the leather buckets though I have above £20,000 Insured there & the Engine & Buckets cost me above £150. I have 6 doz: of Buckets Consider what

kind of engine you would have & the number of Buckets against the time you come to Glasgow. I cannot learn for some time what the prices of wood are likely to be they are little fallen yet

I leave every thing about the road & water &c to you & shall be pleased with whatever you do...[17]

The term 'Fire Engine' has sometimes been used to refer to James Watt's steam engines, where the steam had been generated by fire or heat.[18] However, Dale did not use any of Boulton & Watt's engines in any of his mills and he does appear here to be referring to a different kind of 'engine', i.e. a machine for use in extinguishing fires. As a further precaution, Between 1795 and 1797, Claud Alexander took out three insurance policies – two with Sun Insurance and one with Royal Insurance (worth £1,795, £1,797 and £4,350 respectively), although there may well have been additional policies.[19]

The 'jeanie factory' was built to house 76 'mule jeannies' and by 1793 the total population of the village had reached nearly one thousand. By the time the Rev. Robert Steven came to write the return for Catrine in the *Statistical Account* in 1796, he noted that the community had grown from two to three thatched houses in 1783 to a thriving community with a total of 1,350 souls.[20]

Most importantly, the company provided a school – much like New Lanark although on a smaller scale. Quite when it was built is unclear but it was certainly in existence at the time of Rev. Steven's return for the *Statistical Account*:

The company pay a very laudable attention to the morals and education of the youth. They have built a large school-room, and appointed a schoolmaster with an annual salary of £15 and a free house ... for which he teaches the children employed in the work from 7 to 9 o'clock in the evening.[21]

One source states that this schooling was also available to adults, but there is no other evidence for this.[22] One wonders how many children would attend in the summer months when there was so much work to be done in the fields.

During the day, the company schoolmaster taught children aged nine or under, for which he received an additional £15 per annum. It would appear that the children, although they may have been bound apprentices, were not paupers or orphans:

Children are not admitted into work under nine years old and they all lodge with their parents and friends. It is but justice to add that both young and old enjoy uniformly good health. The different apartments are kept as clean and free of dust as possible...[23]

The master's assistant (who earned £5 per annum) was employed during the day in the twist mill as an under-clerk. On Sundays, master and assistant met the children, catechised them and conducted them to church. A Chapel of Ease, '*esteemed a great ornament to the place*', built in 1792, was financed by Alexander.[24] Although attempts were made at a local subscription in essence this failed and the church remained Claud Alexander's own property. On his death, it passed to his son who sold it to the congregation in the late 1800s. With considerable additions this has survived and is now the Parish Church in Catrine, although it is believed that part of the churchyard was sacrificed to accommodate the mill lade extension and new aqueduct constructed by the engineer Fairbairn in the 1820s.

It is interesting to note in comparison that the parish schoolmaster's situation was less desirable. His salary for teaching 25 to 30 pupils, including emoluments for his duties as Session Clerk, totalled no more than £20 per annum. Even worse:

...he has a school and a dwelling-house, both among the most wretched that are to be found in any cultivated country... The school is by no means in a flourishing state and there is but little probability of its ever being so, till better provision is made for the matter.[25]

Mill Street, Catrine, looking towards Twist Mill, Catrine, *c*.1903. (Richard Stenlake, private collection)

It would appear that the factory school in Catrine was in much better order than the parish school. The factory school was similar to the one at New Lanark in a number of ways, e.g. day schooling, an evening school from 7 p.m. to 9 p.m., a combination of master and part-time assistant, and Sunday meetings in the school. Education and health were priorities. However, there were one or two important differences: the day school charged for instruction; the pupils were aged up to nine years, not six years, as at New Lanark and the Catrine pupils were not pauper children or bound apprentices obtained from an overseer. Also, the school seems to have been on a smaller scale, since only one master and one assistant were employed, which suggests that the subjects offered for study would be more limited. This would seem to be quite natural, as the spinning at Catrine was on a smaller scale than at New Lanark. Exactly where this large school-room was in Catrine is difficult to ascertain. The *Statistical Account* map below does not show it as a separate building, but nothing definite can be read into this, given the crude nature of the map. It is also possible that it was situated in one of the five storeys or attics of the mill.

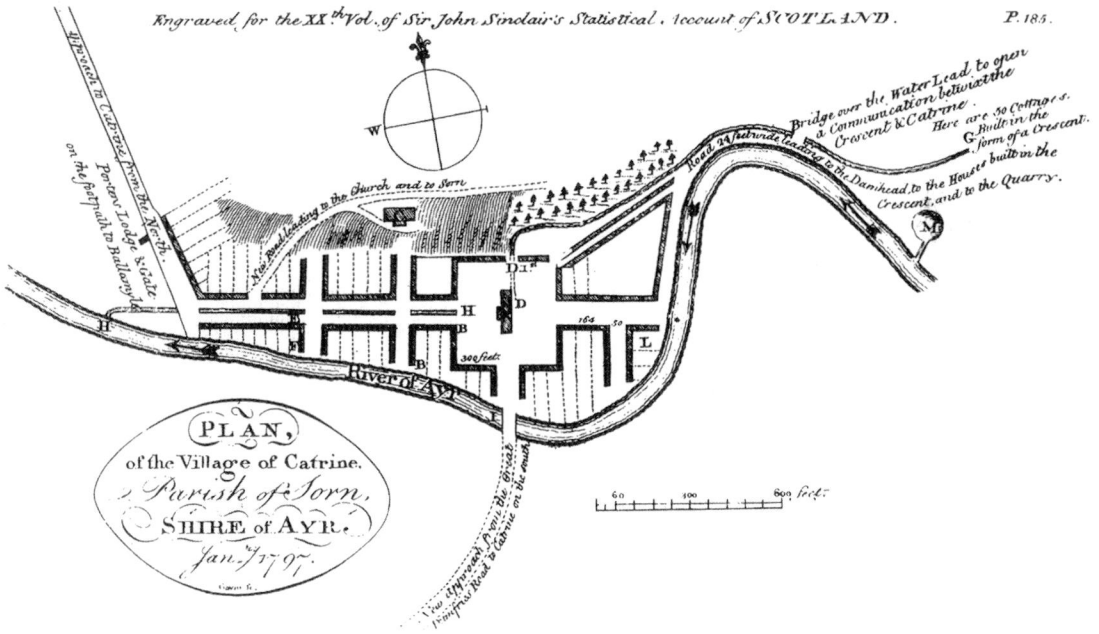

The *Statistical Account of Scotland* Vol. XX.

EXPLANATION.

A, The twist-mill, in the centre of a square of 300 feet. The great wheel has a fall of 29¼ feet.

B to B, The jeanie factory; the carding and roving in which is performed by the water after it comes from the twist mill, the lade from which is all arched.

C, The church.

DD, Is an aqueduct-bridge, which conveys the water from the hill to the top of the twist-mill wheel.

E, Is the corn-mill, and is also worked by the tail-water of the twist-mill.

F, Is a situation feued for a wauk or fulling mill.

From G to D 1st, Is the water brought from the dam to the aqueduct-bridge.

H to H, Is the tail-water from the twist-mill; it is arched until it passes through the square, and then runs through the centre of the principal street, with bridges over it opposite to the three cross streets.

I, Is a proposed bridge over the river Ayr, to communicate with the Dumfries road.

L, A brewery.

M, A fine free-stone quarry.

N. B. The proprietor of the village of Catrine does not feu to the river side, but has reserved the ground along the river for a walk, 12 or 15 feet broad, for the health of the inhabitants, and which he is now facing with a stone and lime wall.

Information on schooling generally is also scarce and it is interesting to find that some fifteen years later, Archibald Buchanan, the new manager, states that business had increased, but is a little vague about the provision of schooling. He states that 'we have three schools at present, I think, in the village', and that 'one of these schoolmasters is paid by the company to teach for one hour each day after work and on Sundays'.[26]

Mill Street, Catrine from Twist Mill, c.1903.

It is difficult to know exactly what this means. It is possible that 'we' refers to the Catrine people, which would imply that only one school was attached to the factory, in which case the incidence of schooling had decreased since the time of Dale and Alexander, with only two hours' instruction being given and no assistants mentioned. If the 'we' refers to James Finlay & Co., then the incidence of schooling had increased. Given that Buchanan could be precise about the hours and salary of the company schoolmaster but is unsure about the number of other schools, it is possible that Buchanan was referring to three schools in the village as a whole. What is not in question is Dale and Alexander's commitment to providing basic schooling on a regular and sustained basis.

Although the village is described as 'thriving' in 1796 and there are many references to the abundance of work, good wages and comfortable living conditions, the population in 1796 had actually declined from a high of 1,601 in 1793.[27] This was not an uncommon occurrence, according to the parish minister. The 'scarcity of hands all over the country' which he referred to was almost certainly due to the frequent fluctuations in cotton pricing and trading and, more particularly, the war with France.[28] In New Lanark, for example, after a period of stable recruitment and employment, there were serious trading problems. Dale refers to great distress being suffered by many English firms in 1793.[29] New Lanark and Catrine could not hope to escape the overwhelming commercial crisis of that year.[30]

Dale refers to financial pressures in a number of letters to Alexander throughout 1793. In June that year, there had been a problem over the sum of £6,000 due to be transferred to Dale and Alexander from a firm of solicitors but which had disappeared. In a time of financial difficulty, even Dale was feeling the strain:

> ...the disappointment has very much discouraged me and I much fear that I will be obliged, contrary to both my inclination and interest to discharge a number of work people as the weekly wages of Lanark & Catrine Mills is very considerable besides discharging a number of engagements which I am under by bills for Cotton works...[31]

It appears that he may have been forced to bow (at least temporarily) to these pressures, and to lay off some of his workforce. *The Morning Chronicle* noted the change in fortune for Dale and his employees, although it is not clear whether this refers to New Lanark, Catrine or both. The newspaper is clear enough about the loss of employment but there is little firm evidence to corroborate this, at least in 1793:

> *These and circumstances have so much changed, that instead of giving employment to new hands, he has of late been obliged to turn off many of his old ones. Such are the blessed fruits of our glorious war.*[32]

In September, 1793, Dale noted that trade had not revived as much as expected and that he (along with other British manufacturers) was concerned about cheap Indian imports – a point he wished to take up *'with Mr. Dundas, to fulfill his promise of giving the Inland consumpt. to the British manufacturer'*.[33] Banks were also in a precarious position, which in turn affected the manufacturers. Dale warned Alexander in November that Thomson's Bank had gone under and that, consequently, he should take none of their notes.[34]

As the war continued, the situation did not improve and Dale wrote that even *'Mr. Arkwright and the great spinning houses'* had been forced to reduce their prices – *'very low to make sales on this account'*.[35] In March 1794, Dale was forced into a corner yet again. His personal anguish at having to turn people out of work is very clear but the whole Catrine enterprise was under threat:

> *...it took a good deal of thought to bring myself to write to you on a subject that I knew must give you much pain you cannot have a greater aversion than I have to throwing the people out of employment but alas what can I do I believe there are few individuals in the nation that have made greater exertions than I have done to carry on the works in which I am engaged & to shew you how much I am inclined to continue to do this to the utmost of my power & even beyond my power I will try to carry on the works for another month, & you may therefore defer doing any thing more in reducing the spinning for a little unless this can be done with care & without pain. Cotton wool is actually scarce both here & in England & for my part I am at a loss where to find wool fit for the Mills...*

> *...in the mean time I thought it necessary to write you by post to prevent as much as in my power any uneasiness which my orders (which you may be sure were given from mere necessity) may have given you. so much do I feel averse to such measures that I would willingly try and part with some thousand Pounds of my property to prevent it*[36]

Again, it is not clear whether Dale did actually reduce his workforce. Although these letters were written in 1793 and 1794, these were not the only occasions which saw Dale under financial pressure. In a letter to Dr. James Currie, Liverpool physician and public health campaigner, Dale reflected on events in New Lanark in 1790, when business and prices had slumped:

> *My greatest concern in the midst of the wreck of 1790, next to being able to pay everyone what I owed, was the keeping together the people and particularly, the Children, which I have hitherto effected, though not without difficulty.*[37]

Despite all the financial pressures, the Catrine community, although similarly prone to the effects of poor trading conditions, was in a relatively good position to weather the commercial ups and downs of the period. During the Dale/Alexander partnership, very hard times were the exception rather than the rule. For those who were looking for work, Catrine was certainly as good a place as any (and much better than most) in which to be employed and drew workers from far and wide, sometimes to the detriment of other villages, such as Auchinleck, which saw a decline in its population *'owing in some measure to the Muirkirk iron & coal tar Works but more especially to the cotton mill at Catrine, which have attracted inhabitants from this parish'*.[38]

Of Catrine's 1,350 population in 1796, 445 persons were employed in the twist mill, 118 of whom were under twelve years of age, although no-one under nine years of age was employed in the mill. Of the remainder, 128 were between twelve and twenty years and 200 were aged twenty or older. There were 5,240 spindles in operation, with one overseer and two clerks.[39] A further 200 were employed in the jeanie factory, 43 of whom were under twelve years of age and 72 between twelve and twenty years of age. The population also included (fifteen in total) clockmakers, smiths, millwrights and mechanics and there were some

275 women employed in picking cotton at home. Weaving was described as being in its infancy but there were 91 looms in operation, apparently (and not unusually) separate from the rest of the factory, where the weavers were mainly employed by the cotton manufacturers in Glasgow and Paisley. The spun yarn was sent to Glasgow weekly by the company's carrier.[40]

Community spirit seems to have been strong in the village and this was helped by Alexander's provision of some 15 to 25 acres which he prepared for the villagers in order that they might plant potatoes for their own consumption in the winter. The villagers paid him a small sum and young and old spent their summer hours after work in the fields.[41]

Similarly, Alexander provided a number of enclosures near the village, let out at something of a loss to himself, on a long lease, for those who wished to keep milk cows. Most of the villagers had been inoculated against smallpox, which was not the case in the villages elsewhere in the parish where the people saw it as 'implying an impious distrust of Divine Providence'.[42] If any of the company's employees were accidentally hurt in the Company's service, they were entitled to medical assistance while on full pay.[43] There was also a corn mill and a brewery. The latter was let to 'a very respectable gentleman' from Kilmarnock with the intention of reducing the consumption of whisky – with some success.[44] Illness did occur, of course, most often in the form of fever. During this period, Dale was in regular correspondence with Dr. Currie. Although Currie had been impressed by the health of the villagers in New Lanark, he nevertheless sent Dale a copy of a book on the treatment of fevers, for use when the need arose.[45] Dale wrote to Currie thanking him for the book which had been 'of great use at Catrine':

> Very soon after I received your book Mr. Alexander wrote me that a fever had got into the village. I sent him the book and desired him to cause the Surgeon to follow the directions therein and he informed me that their doing so has been attended with good effects.[46]

It is just possible that Currie and Claud Alexander may have met – possibly as early as 1788. Dale wrote to Alexander in April of that year, advising him not to lend money, interest-free for two to three years to 'a physician' who, in Dale's estimation, did 'not propose to follow any other business'.[47] Dale was always polite to Currie and appreciated his enthusiasm but was cautious about investing in him financially.

c.1903.

In any event, Catrine was becoming something of a model village and there were tentative plans to increase its status. Dale spoke personally to Lord Braxfield, the Lord Justice Clerk 'with support to the expense of writing Catrine into a burgh of barony'. Braxfield estimated the cost to be £100–£150 'and he did not see any difficulty in getting it done'.[48]

However, it was not possible for just anyone to turn up in Catrine in the expectation of employment and even those who were fortunate enough to be employed had to behave themselves. Dale and Alexander had a business and a community to run and a profit to make. Alexander is reported as giving every encouragement to the sober and industrious but 'he dismisses the riotous and idle as unworthy to eat the Company's bread'. To prevent the inclusion of 'worthless' people, certificates were required from the parishes in which they had previously lived. Notwithstanding the vagaries of war and commerce, those who were successful could expect to find good wages, where they would be well lodged and fed and clothed in a comfortable manner.[49]

The entire works at Catrine were sold to James Finlay & Co. in 1801, not long after Dale sold New Lanark to Robert Owen. Alexander wrote to his brother in May of that year regarding the sale of the mills (Appendix 8). This seems to have been a particularly busy period for Alexander. He had been 'hurried back' from Edinburgh the previous month to complete the handover:

> '...but all my troubles began from that period and I have scarcely written to any person since then excepting to Mrs A and to my friend David Dale. However as it is the last year's trouble with the mills I do not begrudge it ... you say many of my friends are making enquiries for me and express their surprise at my seldom making an appearance in London but those friends know not what I have all to do, else their surprise would cease. However, every year after this, I shall have less to do & then.'[50]

Archibald Buchanan (a cousin to the Finlay family) took over as manager in Catrine. As a young man, he had spent eighteen months with the Arkwright family in Cromford learning how to manage a cotton mill. On his return, the Buchanan family installed him first as the manager at Deanston and then Ballindalloch before sending him to Catrine as resident and managing partner in 1802.[51] David Dale's health was beginning to decline and the sale of New Lanark and Catrine were significant disposals and, apart from his involvement with the Stanley mills, marked the beginning of his withdrawal from the business world, often guided by Owen. Claud Alexander outlived Dale by three years and died in 1809 but the mills went from strength to strength under Buchanan and the Finlays.

Spinningdale

Spinningdale Mill. (Richard Stenlake, photograph.)

Dale was involved for a number of years in what has been described as '*a unique and courageous venture*' in the cotton mill at Spinningdale on the Dornoch Firth in Sutherland.[52] He was one of three significant figures here – the others being George Dempster, on whose land the mill and village were situated and George Macintosh (1739-1807), Dale's friend and business partner in the Turkey Red dyeworks in Glasgow.

Dempster had borrowed money to buy the country estate of Skibo and the adjoining estate of Pulrossie (the ownership of which he subsequently transferred to his brother, Captain John Dempster). Friends warned Dempster, still an M.P. and committed to his Dunnichen estate in Angus, that the Sutherland venture would be a millstone round his neck. According to James Guthrie of Craigie:

> *...the lands are already exhausted by bad management, the tenants beggars, their houses ruinous, everything about it daily growing worse, its immense distance, impracticable to yourself in winter and nobody in the north to manage it for you whose fidelity you can rely on ... there will be a loss of money which you will feel very sensibly...*[53]

Dempster, ever the rose-tinted optimist, remained unmoved and was determined to pursue his commitment to improving the lot of the Highland people and to any scheme '*for encouraging the Highlanders to remain at home*'.[54] He had some experience as a partner in the Stanley mill but for this venture he needed experienced (and wealthy) partners. Macintosh and Dale, both of whom he already knew well, could provide the necessary experience, the finance and the moral support, committed as they already were to relieving distress and reducing emigration. Macintosh visited Skibo in 1791 and shortly thereafter he and Dale became involved as partners in the scheme. In fact, both Dale and Macintosh had been involved in relieving distress some years prior to this in the early 1780s when they had attempted to relieve the worst effects of famine in the area by sending a cargo of food for the starving Highlanders.[55] Both were businessmen but it is very clear that profit was not the motive here. Macintosh wrote to one of his colleagues assuring him that the Spinningdale venture was '*more from patriotic motives than that of profit*'.[56] In similar vein, Dale wrote to Dempster, noting his approval of '*the landed gentlemen interesting themselves in what must not only promote their own interest but the interest of the nation in general*'.[57] Indeed, it would seem from a letter published in *The Scots Magazine* in 1791 that Dale would have been happier if the locals had been involved in the spinning of wool rather than cotton but so great was his concern about the level of poverty and the extent of emigration, that he agreed to proceed:

> *...I have, for some time past, been devising every method I could think of, to contribute my mite towards preventing these emigrations, which are no less hurtful to the poor people themselves than to the country; and I have been making attempts to introduce a branch of the cotton manufacture into the Highlands, which I find will soon spread, and employ a number of people; but I wish to see a plan executed that would enable the people in the Highlands and Islands to work up their own wool, and I do not despair seeing an establishment of this kind, which is better suited for the Highlands than any other manufacture. But though such a plan were already established, it would be too slow in its operations to produce that immediate relief to the poor people that their present situation requires; for I have certain information that there are now persons traversing the Islands, to entice the poor people to go to America...*[58]

He was firmly of the view that emigration was as undesirable as it was avoidable. However, if all else failed and they could not find employment, the best thing for them and for the country would be to accept Dale's invitation to come to New Lanark, where they would be well provided for.[59]

Even Dempster was aware of the difficulties involved – to the extent that he had a clause written into the partnership agreement that clearly stated that 'public spirit' was the motive behind the venture. To make doubly sure that partners knew what they were buying into, he added that Spinningdale '*never, probably, will prove so profitable to the other partners as undertakings of this kind, situated immediately under their own eye*'.[60]

By late 1791 the plans were finalised for a cotton mill and village at Spinningdale and a linen manufacture and village nearby. Originally, the two planned villages were jointly referred to as 'Balnoe' and the company was known as 'The Balnoe Company'.

However, by 1794, the nomenclature had changed. Dempster explains in a letter to Sir Adam Fergusson that, although the Balnoe Company name remained, 'Spinningdale' now referred to the cotton venture and 'Balnoe' to the linen venture.[61]

Things began promisingly enough, all things considered. Dempster wrote to Fergusson in late 1791 that Skibo and Pulrossie were *'lying together ... at present fast asleep ... wanting nothing but houses and inhabitants ... a plan for a cotton manufacture in it is on the point to being carried into execution with our Glasgow partners'*.[62] Similarly:

> By Mr. Dale and Mr. Macintosh[e]s assistance we are on the point of introducing a branch of the cotton manufacture into the Captain's new seaport Ballnoe – Galic name of Newtown (Balnoe), (Balnuich) – where 15 or 16 lots are already taken and which will have the appearance of a town by next year.[63]

It is worth noting here that Dale's involvement may not have been entirely confined to finance and moral support, essential as these were. There is some evidence that he was influential in drawing up the plans for the mill and the community, as he had been in New Lanark & Catrine. In a letter to Dempster in December 1791 Dale enclosed a plan of Balnoe, adding that he hoped to live to see it executed.[64]

To begin with (c.1792), Dale and Macintosh each took £200 in shares (later increased to £300) in the Balnoe Company; the Dempsters £200 each and there were fourteen other shareholders (including significant Glasgow names such as Robert Dunsmore, Robert Bogle and William Gillespie) with £100 each. Dale's involvement was crucial from the start. Indeed, he and Macintosh became the *'leading and most faithful partners in the undertaking'*.[65]

Spinningdale Mill. (David McLaren, photograph.)

The foundation stone was laid in June 1792 and the aims were quite explicit, as a newspaper report of the time makes clear:

> This day, the foundation stone of a cotton manufactory was laid at Spinningdale in the county of Sutherland by John Barclay Esq. This business is established by George Dempster Esq. of Skibo and a number of patriotic gentlemen in Glasgow and the neighbourhood with the laudable intention of preventing emigration by employing the people of this so long neglected country at home. It is hoped that the example of the philanthropic gentlemen will be followed by others establishing woollen and other manufactures in the neighbourhood.[66]

Building work progressed well enough. Dempster wrote to Sir Adam Fergusson in September of that year and seemed very pleased with progress – '*...our cotton mill goes on charmingly*'. He was keen to outline to his friend the potential for a warm-air heating system for the mill, similar to the one installed in his house on the Dunnichen estate.[67] Much of the management of the entire venture (then and subsequently) was left to Macintosh who visited frequently from Glasgow, supported by Dale (although Dale never visited) – sometimes to the annoyance of George Dempster's seafaring brother. Captain John Dempster was seldom at home but clearly had some reservations about the influence of the Glasgow partners:

> *...but why and how will your Mr. Macintosh and Mr. Dale say what's reasonable? I am determined to be satisfied at all events.*[68]

Building work was largely completed by 1794 and included '*barracks for the work people*', two weaving houses (totalling 20 looms), a smithy, a wooden bridge and the four-storey mill itself.[69] Dempster described the building as '*a palace cotton mill*' built by '*our Glasgow friends*'.[70]

However, all was not well, even at this early stage. Spinningdale was being developed but the linen venture in Balnoe had not been successful and the entire project was already in financial difficulty. Macintosh had already advanced a further £588 and Dale a further £398. In addition, The Balnoe Company owed the sum of £659 to the firm of Dale and Macintosh, £728 to the Bank of Scotland and £745 '*in bills payable*'.[71] Additional partners had to be found if any more houses were to be built. Both Dale and Macintosh sent weavers and spinners from Glasgow to encourage the local population and Macintosh was of the view that this would '*have the effect of getting hands plentyer in Sutherland as it convinces the poor ignorant natives in the County that the encouragement there is fully as good as in Glasgow*'.[72] Nevertheless, employers were always concerned with morals (i.e. the good behaviour) of their employees and the indenture system was in operation in Spinningdale, despite the urgent need to recruit local labour. More in hope than in expectation of long-term employment, perhaps, indentures were signed and these included conditions as to an employee's conduct. The apprentices had to agree, among other things, to abstain from '*debauched company and from playing at idle and expensive games*'.[73] Whether this abstinence was effective or not, the reality, according to Macintosh, writing a few years later, was that there was a lot of '*idleness and dissipation*' amongst the workforce and that consequently, production levels were, at best, only one half to two thirds of what would be expected elsewhere.[74]

The war with France resulted in trade which fluctuated and frequently stagnated. Times were bad for all manufacturers and only the strongest could ride out the storm. Even before building work was fully completed, there was a distinct possibility that the business would have to be sold. In a letter to Dempster, Macintosh tried to take an optimistic approach. He felt that the factory could make a profit if some of the partners would contribute more. Money was in short supply, however, and few businessmen could afford to risk what little capital they had. As Macintosh correctly observed, '*Mr. Dale and myself – with Mr. Gillespie and Mr. R. Bogle are the only people at this moment whose hands are at liberty to act*'.[75]

Macintosh also noted that the Glasgow partners were likely to be '*displeased*' at the prospect of abandoning the venture and noted, quite pointedly, that the Sutherland partners lacked the '*spirit and activity*' of their Glasgow counterparts.[76] Nevertheless, even Macintosh came to the conclusion that the business would need to be sold if no additional workers could be found locally and no further capital could be raised.[77]

Perhaps inevitably, the Spinningdale project collapsed after only a few years. Macintosh blamed the indolence of the workers and poor management but there were other problems such as poor trading conditions, low output and the distance from markets. Dempster remained optimistic about Spinningdale but began to spend more time on his Dunnichen estate. By 1797 all the partners had withdrawn, with the exception of Dale and Macintosh. Given that they knew they were unlikely to make any money from their continued involvement, it is a testament to their commitment to the cause that they continued the struggle into the new century. However, when Owen visited Spinningdale (ostensibly at Dale's request) with Macintosh in 1802, he found that '*the locality was unfavourable for extension or for a permanent establishment.*' According to Owen, Dale sold his interest in it shortly thereafter '*and induced Mr. Macintosh to follow his example*'.[78]

In fact, however, Dale and Macintosh held on for some time after Owen's visit, requesting (via Thomas Telford) some government aid for the embattled Highland community. Only when this was refused did they finally withdraw in 1804, despite Dempster's rather unrealistic assessment of the situation. Having visited the site prior to its final demise, Dempster, the eternal optimimst, maintained that he had never beheld '*a busier or more enchanting scene*' and that it was '*surely to the Times that so well-conducted an undertaking fails of success*'.[79] By '*the Times*' he was presumably referring to the economic uncertainties engendered by the Napoleonic wars. Whatever the cause, Dempster was forced to recognise that the venture was finished and he wrote to Macintosh that he would '*lament sincerely the Fall of Spinningdale*'.[80]

The mill was subsequently sold in 1805 for £2,000 to a Mr. McFarlane of Glasgow, described by Macintosh as '*a bred spinner*'.[81] There was a serious fire in 1806 and the mill was never rebuilt. The shell of the building still remains.

Macintosh drew a suitable veil over events thus:

> *Mr. Dale and myself lost a great and heavy sum – however it does not hurt us tho' it is much to be regretted... Thus my friend has all our patriotic schemes and endeavours ended in the meantime.*[82]

For David Dale, of course, this was one of his last '*patriotic schemes and endeavours*' – but not quite the end of his involvement in the cotton spinning business.

Stanley

Owen's advice to sell up would certainly have made sense in relation to Dale's involvement with the Stanley Mill in Perthshire. Owen claims to have advised Dale against it.[83] However, Liddell argues that, far from advising against it, Owen encouraged Dale to invest in the project which was to lose him some £60,000.[84]

In fact, Dale was never a formal partner and did not become involved financially with Stanley until 1801. In order to explain the loss of his money it is necessary to look briefly at the history of the mill. George Dempster's name appears again in this context. He was the local M.P. and had persuaded Arkwright, (who had been given the Freedom of the City of Perth), and others to put up money for the mill in 1785 on 70 acres of land feued from the Duke of Atholl, who was supportive of the plan. As in New Lanark (and Spinningdale), men and young children from Stanley went to Cromford to learn how to operate the machinery.[85] In the event, Arkwright withdrew from the venture (in 1787), but by 1795 the mill was employing 350 people, 300 of whom were women or children under 16, and there were 100 families in the village. The mills (one cotton and one flax) were valued at £10,500 – second only to those at New Lanark. However, the war and the rising price of cotton affected Stanley very badly, and when the flax mill was burned to the ground in 1799, the company was forced to put the mills on the market, which had a drastic effect on the village.[86]

One final attempt was made to resurrect the mills in 1801 when two Glasgow merchants, James Craig and James Mair, bought the business for £4,600, with Dale providing financial support.[87] By 1803, Mair had left but Dale continued to support Craig, paying £1,533 for the privilege. Since Dale left many of his business affairs at this time to Owen, it is reasonable to assume that Owen approved, however briefly, of this financial support. However, the mills were never profitable and between 1803 and 1806, Dale supplied some £24,270 of working capital in an attempt to keep the business going.[88]

Whether or not Owen advised his father-in-law to withdraw, it begs the question as to whether Owen and Dale knew how much money was being pumped into Stanley. The true nature of the problem was not finally uncovered until 1817, and only then because the Royal Bank were pursuing Dale's successor, John More, for bankruptcy. It seems clear that, after Dale's death, James Craig continued to draw on the estate – the money being provided by John More, who was one of the Trustees. Apparently, More advanced Craig a further £15,996 until he withdrew from the venture in 1811. Archibald Campbell of Jura was also an unwitting investor in Stanley. More used money from Campbell's Royal Bank account to continue to prop up Stanley, just as he did with the money from Dale's estate.[89] The mills closed in 1814. All in all, Stanley is estimated to have cost Dale over £40,000.[90] Thus, although Liddell's figure of £60,000 seems inflated, there is no doubt that this enterprise cost Dale and his estate a great deal of money. Robert Owen's role in all of this is at least questionable. The sums of money involved were enormous and the key to Dale's financial affairs lie in his connection with the Royal Bank of Scotland, alluded to here and earlier in the book. For a fuller understanding of Dale's affairs, it is essential to understand his role in the Royal Bank's Glasgow agency.

Stanley Mill (David McLaren, photographs.)

References: Chapter 9

1 *The Morning Chronicle & London Advertiser*, 3rd April 1786.

2 *The Gazeteer & Daily Advertiser*, London, 11th June 1787.

3 *The London Chronicle*, 24th August 1782.

4 Lodge Tarbolton/Kilwinning St. James No. 135 met in Mauchline on that occasion. Online at www.thefreemasons.org.uk/tarbolton135/history.htm

5 *The Calcutta Chronicle & General Advertiser*, 27th March 1788; Sinclair, J. (ed) (1791–99) *The Statistical Account of Scotland*, 1791–99, 21 vols. Vol. XX, pp.165, 176.

6 Fitton, R.S. (1989) *The Arkwrights: Spinners of Fortune*. Manchester: M.U.P., p.80.

7 Sinclair, J. *Statistical Account*, Vol. XX, p.176.

8 Copy of bid by Mr. [Charles?] Abercrombie, 10th February 1787. *Dale–Alexander Correspondence*. Glasgow City Archives: MS. 63/2.

9 Ibid., MS. 63/1. David Dale to Claud Alexander, 14th February 1787.

10 Ibid., MS. 63/3. David Dale to Claud Alexander, 7th April 1788.

11 Ibid.

12 Ibid., MS. 63/4., 12th April 1788.

13 Ibid., MS.63/7., 26th August 1789.

14 Ibid., MS. 63/7., 26th August 1789.

15 Sinclair, J. *Statistical Account*, Vol. XX, pp.184–5.

16 Ibid., MS. 63/9., 23rd January 1792.

17 Ibid.

18 See Reid, R. (Senex) (1884) *Glasgow Past and Present*, 3 vols. Glasgow: David Robertson & Co. Vol. III, p. 283.

19 Nisbet, S.M. (2008) *The Rise of the Cotton Factory in Eighteenth-Century Renfrewshire*. British Archaeology Report, Series 464. Oxford: Alden Press, pp.158-60.

20 Sinclair, J. *Statistical Account*, Vol. XX, pp.176-77.

21 Ibid., p.180.

22 *James Finlay & Co. Manufacturers & East India Merchants 1750–1950* (1951), Glasgow: Jackson & Son. pp.56-7.

23 Sinclair, J. *Statistical Account*, Vol. XX, p.177.

24 Ibid., p.181.

25 Ibid., p.181.

26 *Report of the Minutes of Evidence taken before the Select Committee on the State of Children Employed in the Manufactories of the United Kingdom, 1816*, (397) III, p.10.

27 Sinclair, J. *Statistical Account*, Vol. XX, p.178.

28 Ibid., p.179.

29 Dale to Alexander 23rd March 1793. *Dale–Alexander Correspondence*. Glasgow City Archives, MS. 63/10.

30 Reid, R., *Glasgow*, Vol. II, p.51.

31 Dale to Alexander, 6th June 1793. MS. 63/13.

32 *The Morning Chronicle*, London, 17th August 1793.

33 Dale to Alexander, 13th September 1793. MS. 63/14.

34 Ibid., 1st November 1793. MS. 63/15.

35 Ibid., 30th January 1794. MS. 63/16,

36 Ibid., 24th March 1794. MS.63/17.

37 Dale to James Currie, 8th August 1795. See Johnston, W.T. (ed) (2000) *David Dale & Robert Owen Studies*. Livingston: Officina Educational Publications.

38 Sinclair, J. *Statistical Account*, Vol. XX, p.180.

39 Ibid., pp.176–78.

40 Ibid.

41 Ibid.

42 Ibid., p.143.

43 Ibid., pp.182, 184.

44 Ibid., p.177.

45 This may have been a copy of Currie's own *Medical reports on the Effects of Water, Cold and Warm as a Remedy in Febrile Diseases ...* written in 1797.

46 Dale to J. Currie, 9th July 1798. I am grateful to Professor E. Royle (University of York) for sending me a copy of this letter.

47   Dale to Alexander, 28th April 1788. MS. 63/5.

48   Ibid.

49   Sinclair, J. *Statistical Account*, Vol. XX, pp.180, 183.

50   Claud Alexander to Boyd Alexander, 1st May 1801. Richard Stenlake Collection.

51   Cooke, A. (2010) *The Rise and Fall of the Scottish Cotton Industry, 1778–1914: The Secret Spring.* Manchester: M.U.P., p.33.

52   Calder, S.B. (1974) *The Industrial Archaeology of Scotland.* University of Strathclyde: Unpublished M.Litt thesis, p.150.

53   James Guthrie of Craigie to George Dempster, 13th November 1786. See Lang, A.M. (1998) *A Life of George Dempster, Scottish M.P. of Dunnichen (1732–1818).* Lampeter: Edwin Mellen Press, p.240.

54   George Dempster to Mackenzie of Seaforth, 25th January 1789. *The Dempster Papers. A Collection of Letters & Papers relating to George Dempster of Dunnichen.* 19 vols. MS. Coll. 126. University of Toronto, Thos. Fisher Rare Book Library, Vol. 2. Accession No. 35451. The collection is also catalogued as Dempster, G.S. *The Papers of George Soper Dempster.* Note: the cataloguing of these papers is often confusing. The University of Toronto's Volume numbers differ from the originals used by G.S. Dempster. Readers are advised to use the more reliable Accession Numbers.

55   Stewart, G. (1881) *Curiosities*, p.79.

56   George Macintosh to Dugald Gilchrist, 2nd April 1792. Quoted in Calder S.B. (1974) *Industrial Archaeology*, p.163.

57   David Dale to George Dempster, 21st December 1791. *Dempster Papers*, Univ. Toronto. Vol. 2 Accession No. 35452.

58   Dale to Col. Dalrymple of Fordell, Glasgow, 10th October 1791, in *The Scots Magazine*, October 1791, 53, pp.513–514. Vide supra, Chapters 4, 6, 7.

59   Ibid.

60   Sinclair, J. *Statistical Account*, Vol. VIII, p.382. Dempster was the author of the supplementary statement listing the various partners.

61   George Dempster to Adam Fergusson, 27th November 1794, in Fergusson, J. (ed) (1934) *Letters of George Dempster to Sir Adam Fergusson, 1756–1813.* MacMillan: London, p.253.

62   Ibid., 14th October 1791, in Fergusson, J. *Letters*, p.208.

63   Ibid., 2nd November 1791, in Fergusson, J. *Letters*, p.208.

64   David Dale to George Dempster, 21st December 1791. *Dempster Papers*, Univ. Toronto. Vol. 2 Accession No. 35452.

65   Calder, S.B. (1974) *Industrial Archaeology*, pp.166a; 163–4.

66   *The Glasgow Advertiser & Evening Intelligencer*, 18th–22nd June 1792. Quoted in Calder, S.B., *Industrial Archaeology* p.169.

67   George Dempster to Adam Fergusson, 9th September 1792, in Fergusson, J. (ed) (1934) *Letters*, p.223.

68   John Hamilton Dempster to George Dempster, 12th April 1792. *Dempster Papers*, Univ. Toronto. Vol. 3. Accession No. 35452.

69   Balnoe Company Balance Sheet, 1st November 1794 in Calder, S.B., *Industrial Archaeology*, p.170.

70   George Dempster to Adam Fergusson, 27th November 1794, in Fergusson, J. *Letters*, p.25.

71   Cooke, A.J. (1995) 'Cotton and the Scottish Highland Clearances – Spinningdale, 1791–1806', *Textile History*, XXVI: 89–94, p.91.

72   George Macintosh to George Dempster, 18th January, 1794. Univ. Toronto, Vol. 4, Accession No. 35453.

73   National Archive of Scotland. (N.A.S.) Sheriff Court, 9/28/1, fol. 1. Indenture between Andrew McPherson & the Balnoe Spinning Co., 9th November 1793. Quoted in Cooke, A. (2010) *Rise and Fall*, p.165.

74   Macintosh to Dempster, 11th December 1805. *Dempster Papers*, Univ. Toronto. Vol. 8. Accession No. 35456.

75   George Macintosh to George Dempster, 18th January 1794. *Dempster Papers*, Univ. Toronto. Vol. 4. Accession No. 35453.

76   Ibid.

77   Ibid.

78   Owen, R. *Life*, p.75.

79   George Dempster to George Macintosh, 11th October 1803. Private Collection quoted in Lang, A.M. (1998) *A Life of George Dempster*, p.253.

80   Ibid.

81   Macintosh to Dempster, 11th December 1805. *Dempster Papers*, Univ. Toronto. Vol. 8. Accession No. 35456.

82   Ibid.

83   Owen, R. *Life*, pp.59, 71–75.

84   Liddell, A. (1854b) 'Memoir of David Dale', in R. Chambers (ed), (1855) *A Biographical Dictionary of Eminent Scotsmen.* Glasgow: Blackie, p.167.

85   Cooke, A. (2010) *Rise and Fall*, pp.32–33.

86   Cooke, A.J. (1977) *Stanley: its History and Development.* University of Dundee Extra-Mural Dept. pp.11–18.

87   Cooke, A. (2010) *Rise and Fall*, p.52.

88   Cooke, A.J. (1977) *Stanley: its History and Development*, pp.11–18.

89   Cooke, A. (2010) *Rise and Fall*, p.178

90   Cooke, A. (2010) *Rise and Fall*, p.52.

Chapter 10: 'Dainty Davy', Scott Moncrieff and The Royal Bank of Scotland in Glasgow.

That Dale was a major figure in the cotton industry is not in question. What is less well documented, however, is his involvement and relationship with Robert Scott Moncrieff (1738–1814) in the establishment and initial success of the first Glasgow branch of the Royal Bank of Scotland in Glasgow in 1783. This partnership and friendship was a crucial foundation stone for much of Dale's subsequent success, placing him, as it did, in an extremely powerful position to advance credit to other entrepreneurs in Glasgow and beyond – and allowing Dale himself to access substantial credit facilities.

How then, does a Glasgow importer of linen yarn from a humble background in rural Stewarton find himself appointed to such an important position – one in which the bank's future in the west of Scotland depended? Certainly, Dale had money – his new mansion in Charlotte Street testified to that – and he had influence in the city as one of the founders of the new Chamber of Commerce and he was undoubtedly well connected. What was missing was a direct link to the Royal Bank itself and this was securely established when Dale married Anne Carolina Campbell, the daughter of the bank's famous Chief Cashier, John Campbell (c.1703–1777) who had steered the bank safely through the troubles of the Jacobite Rebellion.

John Campbell by William Mossman (1759). (Reproduced by kind permission of the Royal Bank of Scotland plc © [2015])

Given the marriage and the family connections, it is no great surprise that Carolina's successful and entrepreneurial husband joined the 'family business' five years later – a connection from which Dale could not fail to benefit personally and professionally.

There is reason to suppose her father's connection with the Royal Bank of Scotland as Director led to Mr. Dale's appointment as agent of that establishment in Glasgow and this increased his commercial credit and command of capital.[1]

Until 1783, the Royal Bank of Scotland (founded 1727), unlike the Bank of Scotland (founded 1695), had no branches outside Edinburgh. Both were public or 'professional' banks founded by Royal Charter or Act of Parliament and their business was exclusively banking, in contrast to the operation of the private banks such as the Ship Bank and the Arms Bank in Glasgow, which were really offshoots of the owners' other business. Some years later, during one of the several crises which affected the banking system, Dale was at pains to reassure Claud Alexander, his partner in the Catrine mills, as to the security of both the Bank of Scotland and the Royal Bank, pointing out that the former had been established by Act of Parliament and the latter by Royal Charter and that *"several gentlemen of the first respectability in the law hold stock in the Royal Bank and all of them considered themselves as safe as those that hold Bank of Scotland stock..."*.[2] Dale was certainly correct about the *'gentlemen of the first respectability'*. In 1789, for example, the Governor of the Royal Bank was the Duke of Buccleugh with Lord Ellick as his Deputy. Other Governors included the Lord Justice Clerk, distinguished lawyers and various members of the aristocracy.[3]

The first Glasgow branch of the Royal Bank with Scott Moncrieff and David Dale as joint agents was established in September 1783 in Dale's own linen shop in Hopkirk's Land (High Street), near the Trongate in Glasgow. Prior to that date, Dale had allowed a watchmaker to share the tenancy of the shop but this arrangement was swiftly ended and the branch was established, with the intention of providing service for merchants and businessmen. The bank paid £2. 10s. annually in rent and Dale continued *'his ordinary business as a linen draper on the other side of the shop'*.[4] The Bank's head office was in Edinburgh and the branch was run as an 'agency' which meant that the branch was not known as the Royal Bank of Scotland but by the name of the agents – in this case *'Scott Moncrieff and Dale'*. Agents were appointed by head office but (as later events proved) were left largely to their own devices, although Moncrieff sent a written report almost every day to William Simpson, his Chief Cashier (similar to Chief Executive) in Edinburgh, outlining events in general terms.

Robert Scott Moncrieff was the principal agent. One year older than Dale, he was from an established, professional, middle-class family in Edinburgh. At the time of his appointment, he was Deputy Receiver General of Customs and Receiver of the Land Tax for Scotland and was therefore used to dealing with matters of finance. Dale, as a self-made entrepreneur from Stewarton was from a rather different background.[5]

It would be fair to say that Moncrieff was better known as an eminent banker than a Glasgow merchant, although he purchased membership of the Merchants' House as Burgess in August 1785, two years before the bank's move to St. Andrew's Square.[6] In the same year he became a director of the Chamber of Commerce and remained so for some seven years. However, although he did attend a number of meetings, his involvement seems to have been fairly minimal.[7] He was certainly aware of the wider business issues but his entrepreneurial experience was rather limited. He did have some business experience of his own and was an early partner in the well-known and extensive business enterprise of the Monteith family, whose principal interests included linen and cotton and whose offices were in St. Andrew's Square, the subsequent home of the Royal Bank agency, following the move from High Street. Apparently, Moncrieff was a nervous businessman, averse to risk-taking, preferring instead *'a small, snug*

Right: Robert Scott Moncrieff, Treasurer of the Orphan Hospital (1772–1781). Henry Raeburn, oil on canvas. (On loan from the Dean & Cauvin Trust; City Art Centre, Edinburgh Museums & Galleries)

business with steady profits and sure'.[8] When Monteith's business expanded rapidly (and his applications to the Royal Bank for increasingly substantial discounts became more frequent), Moncrieff became *'nervously alarmed'*, even although there had been no losses, *'and wished to withdraw from the co-partnership'*.[9] The precise date of Moncrieff's nervous exit is unclear but may have been in 1792 when the Monteiths established the Pollokshaws mill.

As far as the Royal Bank agency was concerned, what Moncrieff required was a partner who was financially stable, known to the Royal Bank establishment, with a detailed knowledge of the business affairs of the local merchants and who could therefore make decisions as to their creditworthiness. Dale met all of these criteria (and more) and was therefore eminently suitable.

To establish the Glasgow agency, Moncrieff and Dale had to find the significant sum of £10,000 as a bond or guarantee for the bank. This they did by borrowing the money from businessmen on the east coast of Scotland. The bond was not refunded until 1804, when the Directors expressed their *'fullest conviction'* that Dale and Moncrieff had conducted the business *'with ability as well as the strictest integrity'*.[10]

In 1783, business in Glasgow and the west of Scotland was entering a period of rapid expansion and the demand for credit was high. The banks provided credit through straightforward cash credits or overdrafts and also, principally, through Bills of Exchange. From the late 1790s, for example, cash credits of £500–£1,000 were given in advances to Glasgow mill owners and a wide range of cotton manufacturers. Robert Owen had cash credit worth £1,000.[11] One commentator noted that *'we know so little of how David Dale financed his own interest in cotton spinning'*.[12] Given Dale's family connections, perhaps the answer is not too difficult to find.

The major form of credit was the bill of exchange. These had their roots in medieval times when they referred to a written promise to a pay a person in another town a sum of money. Every bill of exchange involved a short term loan, usually with interest. The principle was similar in the late 18th century. This type of credit transfer meant that the bank would agree to lend Merchant A the money to buy goods from Merchant B to sell on to Merchant C. Merchant A would be charged interest on this loan and all he had to do was to write out a simple note promising to pay Merchant B by a certain date (usually three months), thus allowing time to obtain payment from Merchant C. Merchant B, however, would be out of pocket for three months so if he required payment before that, the bank would normally agree to pay him the full amount less a 'discount' of between 5% and 7%. When the three months had expired, Merchant A would be presented with the full bill for payment. Where there was any doubt about anyone's ability to pay, such bills would not be paid before the agreed date, i.e. no discounting would take place. The Royal Bank Glasgow agency was apparently very successful in issuing bills of exchange. These were discounted weekly on Tuesdays and Fridays but by 1800 anything from 200 to 400 were being discounted on a daily basis. Customers placed their bills a day or so before discounting in a wooden box with a slit which stood on the counter:

> *At the close of business for the day, the bills were examined by the 'first accomptant' who, after due enquiry and with due reference to the agents, extracted those elegantly described as 'not convenient for discounting'. Those to be paid were to be marked with the appropriate rate of discount … the bills being collected by the customer in due course.*[13]

If the agency was discounting up to 400 bills a day, the office in the High Street must have been a very busy place indeed – so busy, in fact, that larger premises had to be found and the agency was forced to move to new premises in St. Andrew's Square, where Dale had his Glasgow warehouse and offices. The building of the Square began in 1787 and Burgh records show that the Town Council were quite glad to be rid of the ground in January of that year.[14] They took the view:

> *…that Mr. Dale should have the south east corner of the two steadings on the south side of the square, adjoining thereto, and that Mr. Scott Moncrieff should have the two steadings on the east end next to the south corner at the above prices. The committee think that the Royal Bank and Mr. Dale taking the above Steadings will induce others to purchase and it will be for the interest of the town to get to quit of so much back ground.*[15]

However, matters moved slowly and it was some time before building work was complete. There was a lane running through the ground in question and in October 1790, before taking possession, the Magistrates and Council required Dale to build 'an arched entry or close of six and a half feet broad' to allow access.[16] Burgh records note that Dale was to take entry to the 'lott of ground' in St. Andrew's Square on Whitsunday 1791. However, Dale must have been impatient because he took possession on Whitsunday 1790, a full year earlier than agreed. As a result, he was reported to the Magistrates and Council. This is somewhat ironic, given that he was himself to become a Magistrate the following year. Perhaps unsurprisingly, there is no evidence of any action being taken against him in 1790.[17]

In any event, by the 1790s, St. Andrew's Square was fast becoming a prestigious area, housing 'the best and wealthiest of the city', where the 'dwellings both for commodiousness, beauty and ornament', were 'well worthy' of the city's 'rank and fashion' at the time – an area 'in its heyday, both for gentility and business... Liveried lackeys and gay equipages leant life and animation to the Square in those days'.[18] The Royal Bank had its office and manager's house in the two tenements in the south east corner of the square and there were sentry boxes for the soldiers who, 'with loaded musket and bayonet, guarded the treasure...'.[19]

By 1800 the Glasgow agency was doing business worth a million pounds per year, and by 1802 this figure may have reached two million pounds.[20] This was a truly incredible amount of money, particularly given the fluctuations in trading conditions and the vagaries of the banking business, to say nothing of events in revolutionary France. For example, in 1793, when Britain declared war on France, banks were collapsing and there was a huge demand for credit. Checkland argues that the Royal Bank was 'perhaps the chief culprit in the immense extension of credit'.[21] As it turned out, the banks were rescued by government grants, but not before William Ramsay, one of the directors, was moved to write thus about the Glasgow branch:

> We have been ruined by Scott Moncrieff and Dale who ought to have managed the Glasgow branch with more safety and prudence than they have done.[22]

Government grants meant that Ramsay's assessment was exaggerated but it does indicate how much the success of the entire Royal Bank depended on the business transacted in the Glasgow branch.

Cotton was also a risky business and was subject to frequent crises in supply and demand – a fact not lost on Moncrieff, the ever-prudent professional banker. The agency gave large cash credits to cotton manufacturers for the purchase of cotton and for trading in cotton goods but the mill owners sometimes invested it in buildings which were much more difficult to dispose of should the bank be forced to take possession. When his friend, cotton manufacturer James Paterson, failed in 1803, leaving the bank with huge debts, Moncrieff referred to the cotton spinning industry as 'that vile manufacturing trade'.[23] This was not the first time he had let his feelings be known about the uncertainties of cotton spinning. As early as 1791 Dale noted in a letter to George Dempster that 'Mr. Scott Moncrieff is still complaining but no worse than when you was (sic) here'.[24]

There can be no complaint, however, about the success of the agency from its establishment in 1783 until 1803/1804 when John More took over. The move to St. Andrew's Square did not, however, alleviate the pressure on the agents and their thirteen staff. In October 1801, Moncrieff wrote to Chief Cashier William Simpson, noting that 'the office was just as full today ... and the crowd so great at the accountant's window that they smashed one of the panes in pieces'.[25] The following month, in a similar letter to Simpson, he notes that there were shortages in the tellers' accounts on occasion, 'but such were the mobs on Tuesday and Wednesday that it is not to be wondered at'.[26] The bank was forced to find new premises a few years later and purchased a mansion house in Queen Street.

The Dale/Moncrieff partnership worked very well indeed, despite (or possibly because of) the fact that they played very different roles. The two men became close friends and developed great respect for each other's talents and abilities. Moncrieff was the banker who dealt with the business of the branch – the accounts and the staff – and he kept head office informed on a regular basis. He was well known for his tendency to 'growl' or grumble at customers, but his bark was certainly worse than his bite, which the public soon discovered.[27] Many of the decisions to invest in a business, to advance credit or to discount bills were his but he simply could not have achieved success without Dale's advice on the commercial viability of many of the local businesses, many of which depended on Dale's personal contacts through the Chamber of Commerce and New Lanark. Dale was a very well-connected entrepreneur and Moncrieff depended on him more for his local knowledge than for his hands-on role as a banker. This was just as well, since Dale had little time to devote to the world of banking directly, although he did appear in the office as often as he could. When Dale was unable to attend, Moncrieff visited him regularly for advice on discounting some of the more potentially troublesome bills. Dale was busy forging a career as entrepreneur in New Lanark and Catrine and it is true to say that by 1801 he had become, as far as the Glasgow agency of the Royal Bank was concerned, 'a combination of advisor, patron and favourite uncle'.[28]

Royal Bank of Scotland, Queen Street, Glasgow, c.1812.

There is evidence that Dale allowed his customers a longer repayment period than was normal at the time and also that he used his position at the Bank to his advantage. For example, he sold large amounts of cloth to Messrs. William Stirling and Sons at twelve months' credit which he then discounted 'at his pleasure' – the long credit period securing a valuable customer.[29] Neil Munro, in his History of Royal Bank describes Dale's approach to banking as 'a leisure-hour recreation, like a game of golf'.[30] This seems unlikely but there is anecdotal evidence to suggest that Dale did adopt a rather relaxed and benevolent approach on occasion. When a young client presented a forged Bill:

> Mr. Dale then pointed out to him the risk he put his life in by such an act, destroyed the bill, that no proof of his guilt should remain, and finding that he had been led to it by pecuniary difficulties, gave him some money, and dismissed him with a suitable admonition.[31]

However, had Dale been quite as relaxed and inattentive as Munro suggests, he would have been a poor business partner. Scott Moncrieff's letters between 1801 and 1803 provide a more accurate account of the business partnership and the personal friendship between them. Moncrieff clearly held Dale in the highest regard. Throughout his correspondence with William Simpson in Head Office, Moncrieff constantly referred to Dale as 'the honest man' or 'the good man', although there is an uncharacteristically informal (and inexplicable, given Dale's physique) reference to his partner as 'dainty Davy'.[32] The 'honest *man*' label may have come from an incident later related by Dale's grandson, Robert Dale Owen.[33] There is also anecdotal evidence that he may have occasionally taken pity on young clients who found themselves in '*pecuniary difficulties*'.[34] Nevertheless, however discriminating and liberal Dale appeared in granting loans to industrious, prudent traders, he is reported as possessing the '*firmness to resist*' speculators.[35]

Throughout the 1790s, Dale suffered from increasing bouts of ill-health and in 1801 he added to his property portfolio by purchasing a new country residence, Rosebank, in Cambuslang. Moncrieff was a frequent visitor and occasionally John More would join them – '*Mr. Dale will have us go out and take our dinner at Rosebank*'.[36] Moncrieff was clearly impressed by the country estate and the house, particularly a new range cooker pioneered by Sir Benjamin Thompson, Count Rumford:

> *I was at Rosebank on Saturday and saw a Rumford kitchen Mr. Dale has erected there – it is curious to see what boiling, roasting and baking can be carried on by a mere handful of coal.*[37]

The following month he wrote once more that he was '*going out to Rosebank literally to eat mutton roasted in the Laird Rumford kitchen*' and later of the Rosebank estate: '*such a crop of oats and potatoes as Mr. Dale has I never saw, particularly the potatoes*'.[38] The entire correspondence 1801–1803 contains many references to dining at Rosebank.

That he was a family friend was also borne out in Moncrieff's apparent support of Robert Owen's courtship of Dale's daughter during the 1790s and his role in persuading Dale that the match would be a suitable one.[39] In this he was assisted by his wife, Margaritta (sic) – something of a local beauty if Raeburn's portrait is accurate – who befriended the young Anne Caroline. As a friend, Scott Moncrieff was concerned later, when, after only a few days' illness, '*poor young David Owen, Mr. Dale's grandson died at Lanark*'.[40] Moncrieff is concerned for the family and for Dale and his additional comments about Dale and Owen also indicate a close friendship with the Dale family:

> *In comes Mr. Owen to tell me the honest man is arrived back from Lanark and is to be with me at 7. He* [Owen] *is a clever lad, far from being sanguine or speculative.*[41]

Similarly, later that year, with reference to the birth of Robert Dale Owen:

> *...in comes Mr. Dale and Mr. Owen to announce Mrs. Owen being safely delivered of her son.*[42]

It is clear from the correspondence that the frequent visits to Rosebank were visits to a friend but also to a business partner who was frequently ill and therefore unable to come into the office in St. Andrew's Square. It is equally evident that they were playing to their respective strengths.

Moncrieff believed that Dale's ongoing illness was due to gout, although it was later attributed to 'dropsy', a condition with similar symptoms.[43] In December 1801, Moncrieff refers to Dale's '*swelled foot ... which prevents him coming out. I hope it is a fit of the gout which will remove all his other complaints*'.[44]

Left: Margaritta MacDonald, Mrs. Scott Moncrieff (d.1824). Henry Raeburn, oil on canvas (c.1814). National Galleries of Scotland.

When Moncrieff visited a few days later he found that Dale had been in great pain all night.[45] By 9th January, 1802, Dale was very much improved but intermittent illness continued throughout the year and explains why his attendance at the bank was variable. Moncrieff was tolerant of the situation and seemed genuinely concerned for 'the honest man' – noting Dale's illness on several occasions and that he was 'sorry to find it so'.[46] In any event, Dale had never been a frequent attender at the bank:

> He frequently does not come in on Saturdays ... he has not for above a month come in to the Tuesday morning's work...[47]

However, it is also clear that he did make considerable effort to come into town to deal with some of the bills, even though he was clearly unwell:

> He came in for a little this forenoon – he is much dispirited and he cannot tell me what the matter is with him. I am afraid it is some ghoulish complaint affecting his whole frame and he will not be right till he gets a smart fit.[48]

After a twelve month period (October 1802 to October 1803) where no mention was made of Dale's ill health, the problem reappeared but Dale still made the effort to come to town:

> I was glad to see him creeping into the office again this morning ... he himself felt so sick he was not able to write and he went immediately back to Rosebank.[49]

Again, Moncrieff reverted to his regular visits to Rosebank for advice about the bills: 'I hope he will be able to look over the Bills with me in the evening and I shall go down to him for that purpose' – and one month later in December 1803: 'I saw him in good spirits this morning and told him he would be bright with the Bills'.[50]

Throughout the correspondence, whilst there is strong emphasis on the personal, there is also considerable emphasis on the need for Dale's input on these bills. For example, Moncrieff had been reluctant to accept some London bills but had eventually done so on Dale's advice: 'he [Dale] thought, as the Bills were so very good, it was better to take them than let them go to another bank'.[51]

Where Dale knew the client concerned, he was prone to take a fairly benevolent view of their creditworthiness – a fact not unnoticed by Moncrieff who observed that 'Mr. Dale certainly serves his customers on the easiest terms'.[52] For example, Dale accepted a bill from a Mr. Lindsay which helped the latter's company 'after they were in their difficulties'. Dale 'had some knowledge' of the man and by doing so he also helped another client obtain money due from Mr. Lindsay.[53] Moncrieff, far from being troubled by this relaxed approach, relied on this kind of information and seemed very positive about it. Referring to Dale once again as 'the honest man', Moncrieff clearly valued the work of his partner: '...what a mercy it is to me in the midst of so much trouble that he is so easy'.[54]

At times, however, affairs in the wider world were not so 'easy'. Claud Alexander wrote to his brother Boyd in May 1801 (Appendix 8), concerning the possibility of a French invasion:

> 'I think it looks by the news papers as if Buonaparte (sic) intended an invasion of this kingdom. It is certain that he made such an extravagant demand as is mentioned in the newspapers before he would treat for peace'.[55]

An invasion was an ever-present threat and the Glasgow agency had to make contingency plans. In October 1803, Moncrieff informed head office that three strongboxes containing important documents had been made ready and had been stored in 'Mr. Dale's warehouse and so [we] are ready for Bonaparte'.[56] If the enemy did invade, there was talk of moving the boxes to the basement of a house owned by Bob Gray, a local mine owner and Royal Bank customer. Dale was, however, unconvinced by the plan and was 'for going to New Lanark with them'.[57] In the event, it can only be assumed that the boxes stayed in Dale's St. Andrew's Square warehouse until the threat passed.

By 1803, Moncrieff, then aged 65, had had enough of the vagaries of the financial sector with its various crises and signalled his intention to retire. He had sold his large Edinburgh property ('*three flats and a sunk storey, comprising of seven rooms, besides kitchen, cellars, various light closets and other conveniences*') in 1801 and had presumably bought something smaller.[58] He may have been spending more time in Edinburgh because he had established a partnership with a John Robertson '*under the firm of Scott Moncrieff and Robertson*'.[59] The firm was later involved in selling sugar from Jamaica.[60]

Moncrieff, however, was concerned about how Dale – his friend and colleague – would fare in any new arrangement the Royal Bank might make for their Glasgow agency. Dale was an adviser, not a banker – a fact that Dale himself knew very well. In fact, Dale had never taken his full allowance from the bank, for the simple reason that he felt he did not deserve it.[61] In any event, Dale was old and frequently unwell and it seemed unlikely that John More (who had been involved in the Glasgow agency since 1801 and who was expected to take over) would want Dale as a partner.

However, Moncrieff also knew that, given his friend's longstanding involvement with the agency and his significant contribution to its success, Dale would be hurt and offended if he were to be merely cast aside – although Dale was unlikely to say so himself. In November 1803, Moncrieff raised this matter in a letter to Simpson:

> ...*I could not get the honest man to say a word as to the arrangement that would please him – he said that he would be as well pleased to be out altogether but he thought it would be in the interest of the bank his remaining a year or so. I can easily see he has a desire to remain in the ostensible management and would perhaps be hurt if he was put out. His being merely in the way of advocacy would not I suspect please him, tho it would be the most proper plan for he can never take any charge or labour as he never did.*[62]

In a very similar letter in the same month, Moncrieff reiterated the point that it would be '*absurd*' to give '*honest David Dale*' any official responsibility in the new management of the agency, given that Dale had never taken complete charge of all the bills or of the money. Also, there might seem to be '*an impropriety in his name being on the Firm merely for giving his advice*'.[63] In both letters, he suggests that Dale be given an emolument. In the meantime, Dale remained silent on the matter saying only that he '*would not like to be responsible*'.[64]

The bank compromised and decided to allow Dale to stay as an adviser '*for a while at least*' under John More – something that Moncrieff felt would please Dale.[65] The bank followed this one month later with a payment of five hundred pounds to both Moncrieff and Dale on the occasion of Moncrieff's retirement. Moncrieff seemed very surprised to receive anything for his own efforts – '*never was anything more unexpected by me*' and claimed it was '*disproportionate*' to his merits.[66]

Dale reacted to his own emolument in similar fashion, thanking the bank for '*their handsome present ... and for their approbation of my conduct which I value more than the money*'. He claimed it was more than he '*either deserved or merited*' and noted modestly that his '*worthy colleague ... had all the trouble and fatigue of the business, which he attended to with unwearied diligence*'.[67] He noted that he would continue to give his '*best advice*' to John More, '*who I always thought was the only person I knew that would fill up Mr. Scott Moncrieff's place in the branch here*'.[68] Given later events surrounding John More's embezzlement of the bank's money (and that of the Dale estate), it is ironic that Dale's assessment of More was so positive here. He was clearly taken in by More, as he was with James Craig, the persistently ineffective and inefficient manager of the Stanley Mills in Perthshire, where Dale had a substantial financial investment. (He did have concerns about Craig but he disregarded these because of his friendship with the man.) A younger Dale, the one who had dealt sharply with business partners who had outlived their usefulness (such as Paterson, Arkwright and Monteith) would not have made that mistake.

As it turned out, Dale took very little to do with the new agency in the remaining two years of his life. He was quite unwell and effectively retired from all direct involvement in business and handed over the management of his remaining investments to Robert Owen. In a sense, however, Dale's involvement with the Royal Bank and with More continued for many years after Dale's death. The bank eventually discovered that More had been making extravagant investments using Royal Bank money and money from the Dale estate, where he was one of the trustees. More continued to invest good money after bad in the Stanley Mills, where he was a partner, and he enjoyed a flamboyant lifestyle:

> On Saturdays and holidays a splendid equipage with a black servant ... drove up to the bank to convey the manager to his rural home at Wellshot, which he had erected and surrounded with a vinery, a flower garden, and romantic walks and bowling green at an expense of £17,000 ... but it would take a man of princely fortune to occupy it as Mr. More did, the style of his housekeeping may be learned from the fact that he possessed upwards of 1,200 ounces of silver plate.[69]

Unfortunately, he ran up a debt of some £94,267 in the process.[70] It took some years for Dale's daughters to be compensated for money which More had stolen from their father's estate and during that time, family relationships were undoubtedly strained. Campbell of Jura even accused Owen of mismanagement of the Jura funds previously handled by Dale, and there may well be some truth in this. It is doubtful if we will ever know the full financial machinations which followed Dale's death but is certainly true to say that during his active involvement with the Royal Bank, the company prospered, as did a very large number of businesses in the west of Scotland. There can be no doubt that 'the honest man' played a very significant part in their success.

There can also be no doubt that Dale's access to credit for his own business affairs contributed in no small part to his success. His fortune came from his ownership of New Lanark and his partnerships in cotton mills across the country. As might be expected of a man with such entrepreneurial talents, he also had significant business interests in and around Glasgow. Many of these were related to the cotton industry but, as we shall see in the next chapter, many were not – and not all of them were entirely successful.

References: Chapter 10

1   Liddell, A. (1854b) 'Memoir of David Dale', in Chambers, R. (ed), (1855) *A Biographical Dictionary of Eminent Scotsmen*. Glasgow: Blackie, p.164.
2   David Dale to Claud Alexander, 25th May 1793. *Dale-Alexander Correspondence, 1787–1797*. Glasgow City Archives. MS. 63/11.
3   *The London Chronicle*, 10th–12th March, 1789.
4   Reid, R. (Senex) (1884) *Glasgow Past and Present*, 3 vols. Glasgow: David Robertson & Co. Vol. 1, p.477n.
5   Reed, R. (2006) 'David Dale and the Royal Bank of Scotland, Glasgow Agency.' Unpublished conference paper, 4th November 2006, Glasgow Caledonian University. *The Legacy of David Dale – Industry, Philanthropy and Heritage*.
6   Anderson, J.R. (ed) (1935) *The Burgesses and Guild Brethren of Glasgow, 1757–1846*. Edinburgh. J. Skinner & Co., p.142. Moncrieff's son, John Scott Moncrieff, took advantage of his father's membership and enrolled the same day as 'son of Robert Scott Moncrieff, Burgess & Guild Brethren'.
7   He was a member of only one committee during those seven years – a committee in July 1788, charged with looking at the 'bounty' on lumber. See *Glasgow Chamber of Commerce Minutes*. Glasgow City Archives, Mitchell Library. TD 1670/1/1.
8   Reid, R. (Senex) (1884) *Glasgow*. Vol. II, p.72.
9   Ibid., p.73.
10 'David Dale, Scottish Banker, Benefactor & Industrialist, 1739–1806', *The Three Banks Review*, Number 45. March 1960: 38–44. p.42.
11 Cooke, A. (2010) *The Rise and Fall of the Scottish Cotton Industry, 1778–1914: The Secret Spring*. Manchester: M.U.P., p.49.
12 Checkland, S.G. (1975) *Scottish Banking: A History, 1695–1973*, Glasgow: Collins, p.230.
13 *Three Banks Review*, p.34.
14 Reid, R. *Glasgow*, Vol. III, p.198.
15 Burgh Records, 30th January 1787. See Renwick. R. (ed) (1913) *Extracts from the Records for the Burgh of Glasgow with Charters and other Documents*. Vol. 8, 1781–95. Glasgow. p.216.
16 Ibid., p.666
17 Ibid., p.380.
18 Reid, R. (1884) *Glasgow*, Vol. 1, p.129.
19 Ibid.
20 Checkland, S.G. (1975) *Scottish Banking*, p.146.
21 Ibid., p.219.
22 *William Ramsay's Diary*, 4th May 1793. Quoted in Checkland, S.G. *Scottish Banking*, p.219.

23 Moncrieff to Chief Cashier, William Simpson, 26th October 1803. Quoted in Checkland, S.G. *Scottish Banking*, p.231.

24 *The Dempster Papers. A Collection of Letters & Papers Relating to George Dempster of Dunnichen (1732–1818)*. University of Toronto. MS. Collection 126. Vol. 3. 21st December 1791. Accession No. 35412.

25 Moncrieff to Simpson, 10th October 1801. R.B.S. Archives: RB/837/406.

26 Ibid., 7th November 1801. RB/837/443.

27 Reid, R. (1884) *Glasgow*, Vol. 2, p.229. Vol. 3, p.374.

28 Reed, R. *David Dale*.

29 Reid, R. (1884) *Glasgow*, Vol. III, pp.372–3.

30 Munro, N. (1928) *The History of the Royal Bank of Scotland, 1727–1927*. Edinburgh: Clark Ltd., pp.150–151.

31 Liddell, A. (1854b), *Memoir*, p.175.

32 Moncrieff to Simpson, 9th January 1802. R.B.S. Archives: RB/837/532.

33 R.D. Owen relates an apocryphal tale about his grandfather discovering a young man stealing gooseberries from the garden in Charlotte Street. Dale is reputed to have hailed the intruder initially as an '*honest man*' before admonishing him and allowing him to leave with the berries. According to Owen, '*when the story got wind, David Dale's notion of* an honest man *excited many a smile among those who loved him*'. See Owen, R.D. (1874) *Threading My Way: Twenty Seven Years of Autobiography*. New York: Carleton & Co., p.38.

34 Liddell, A. (1854b), *Memoir*, pp.174–175.

35 Ibid., p.174.

36 Moncrieff to Simpson, 27th September 1801. R.B.S. Archives: RB/837/384.

37 Ibid., 6th April 1802. RB/837/152.

38 6th May 1801. RB/837/212 and 22nd July 1801. RB/837/296.

39 Owen, R. (1857) *The Life of Robert Owen Written by Himself*. Vol. 1. London: Effingham Wilson. New impression (1967) London: Frank Cass & Co., p.53. See also Donnachie, I. and Hewitt, G. (1993) *Historic New Lanark*. Edinburgh: E.U.P., p.75.

40 Moncrieff to Simpson, 13th March 1801. R.B.S. Archives: RB/837/114.

41 Ibid., 22nd June 1801, quoted in *Three Banks Review*, No. 48. December 1980. pp.36–45.

42 Ibid., 7th November 1801. RB/837/443.

43 National Records of Scotland. Old Parish Registers: Deaths, 644/01 0600 0362, Glasgow.

44 Moncrieff to Simpson, 8th December 1801. RB/837/480.

45 Ibid., 10th December 1801. RB/837/482.

46 Ibid., 9th October 1802. RB/837/843.

47 Ibid., 17th August 1802. RB/837/776.

48 Ibid., 11th October 1802. RB/837/844.

49 Ibid., 21st October 1803. RB/837/1476.

50 Ibid., 28th November 1803. RB/837/1395 and 5th December 1803. RB/837/1405.

51 Ibid., 18th May 1801. RB/837/214.

52 Ibid., 19th August 1802. RB/837/779.

53 Ibid., 20th August 1803. RB/837/1262.

54 Ibid.

55 Claud Alexander to Boyd Alexander, 1st May 1801. Richard Stenlake Collection.

56 Moncrieff to Simpson, 22nd October 1803. RB/837/1345.

57 Ibid.

58 *The Caledonian Mercury*, 25th October 1800.

59 Ibid., 25th October 1802.

60 Ibid., 11th October 1804.

61 Reed, R. *David Dale*.

62 Moncrieff to Simpson, November 1803, no day date. RB/837/1459.

63 Moncrieff to Simpson, November 1803, no day date. RB/837/1458.

64 Moncrieff to Simpson, 9th November 1803, RB/837/1375.

65 Moncrieff to Simpson, 14th November 1803. RB/837/1382.

66 Moncrieff to Simpson, 15th December 1803. RB/837/1421.

67 Dale to Simpson, 24th December 1803. RB/566.

68 Ibid.

69 Reid, R. (1884) *Glasgow*, Vol. I, p.129.

70 Checkland, S.G. *Scottish Banking*, p.298.

Chapter 11: Glasgow Businesses, Land and Property

Turkey Red

It is worth reiterating that Dale had been a significant businessman in Glasgow for some years prior to the building of the New Lanark mills. Indeed, Liddell notes that even before Dale's arrival in Glasgow, he had turned his back on the 'sedentary occupation' of weaving in Paisley, despite it being 'the most lucrative trade in the country', in favour of the entrepreneurial career of a linen merchant in Glasgow, which he pursued with great success.[1] Given this entrepreneurial drive, it is no surprise to learn that Dale had other business interests in and around the city throughout his life. These were, of course, on a smaller scale than the massive industrial developments in New Lanark and Catrine but, with the exception of the Barrowfield Coal Company, they were all successful ventures.

The most significant of these was his involvement with Charles Macintosh and Pierre Papillon in the Turkey Red dyeing industry in the city. Macintosh, as has already been indicated, was his friend and his business partner in the Spinningdale mill. A successful businessman in his own right, Macintosh had established a major shoemaking business in Glasgow in 1777 which employed 500 people. He also began to manufacture a purple dyestuff ('cudbear') in the Dennistoun area of the city.[2] This lichen-based dye was used largely to dye wool and silk and required the addition of large amounts of ammonia which was supplied by collecting 2,000 gallons of human urine every day, gathered in 1,500 iron-bound casks dispersed among the manufacturing and tradesmens' houses in Glasgow and the suburbs.[3] The dyeing industry was a particularly secretive one, since new developments were being discovered all the time. To protect his business, Macintosh had his factory enclosed behind a 10-foot high wall and tended to employ only Gaelic speakers as a further protective measure.[4] His walled estate also contained his mansion house – 'Dunchatten'.

In 1785 Dale joined Macintosh in a new dyeing business – still in its infancy in Great Britain but one with enormous potential for the cotton industry. The new dye was known as 'Turkey Red' – a brilliant red dye which attached itself firmly to cotton yarn and which remained relatively unaffected by washing and sunlight. In this venture they were joined by Monsieur Pierre Papillon from Rouen in France, with whom Macintosh had been in contact. They built '...an extensive dyehouse in Dalmarnock ... where cotton is dyed real Turkey Red, equal in beauty and solidity to East India colours'.[5] The dye itself was made from the roots of the madder plant and originated in Turkey and Greece. Depending on the mordant or chemicals used with it, madder could produce a range of colours from pink, through purple and brown to nearly black. The most valuable colour, however, was the bright, fiery 'Turkey' or 'Adrianople' red.[6] It was often known in Glasgow at a later date as 'Dale's Red'.[7]

The French had been experimenting with Turkey Red since the 1750s but the business only became profitable from 1776 when two Paris merchants hired a number of Greek dyers directly from Adrianople and set up a colony around an existing dyehouse in Darnetal in northern France and from this centre, Turkey Red became firmly established in the Rouen area.[8]

In the early 1780s, one of the Rouen dyers, Pierre Jacques Papillon, visited Manchester with a view to emigrating and starting Turkey Red production in the UK. (Such was the secrecy involved, he travelled under the name of 'Cigale' – the English Translation of which is 'grasshopper'.) The Manchester merchants, however, were already in negotiation with another French émigré dyer – a Monsieur Louis Borelle (variously referred to subsequently in various documents as Bureil, Basil, Burell) and did not encourage Papillon. Borelle came to Manchester but Macintosh stepped in quickly and in 1785 persuaded Papillon to come to Glasgow and join the Dale/Macintosh partnership in Dalmarnock on the banks of the Clyde. Papillon agreed and thus became 'the first successful Turkey Red dyer in Britain'.[9]

The first advertisement for Turkey Red dyeing appeared in *The Glasgow Mercury* of 15th December, 1785:

> DALE and MACINTOSH have now got their Dyehouse finished, and are just begun to dye cotton yarn Turkey Red, for the Manufacturers at large, at 3s. per lib. Weight. The excellency of this colour is already known here, as it has been tried

and found to stand the process of bleaching when woven along with green linen or cotton tarn, without impairing, but rather increasing its beauty and lustre. The yarn is received in by Mr. McDonald at Messrs Macintosh and Murdoch's warehouse in Trongate, in quantities not less than 60 lib. At one time, from one person... To accommodate the Manufacturers in general, Mr. Dale will keep an assortment of this dyed cotton at his warehouse, which he will sell, with the addition of 3s. per lib. for the dyeing to the original price.[10]

Papillon knew what he was about because the business in Dalmarnock was extremely successful – more so than Borelle's dyeworks in Manchester.[11] The dye-making process was as complex as it was malodorous and involved a lengthy process of washing, steaming, boiling, wringing and the use of various unpleasant chemicals such as salt of alumina, ammonia and bulls' blood. Bremner notes, with some understatement, perhaps, that the workers involved:

...have the most unhealthy and disagreeable occupation. They have to stand over the cistern of scalding, steaming liquor and keep the yarn in constant motion by shifting and turning about the rods on which it is hung.[12]

The government, keen to encourage Turkey Red in Great Britain, offered a premium, or prize of £2,500 as an incentive for anyone skilled enough to bring the process (still considered to be something of a mysterious and secret affair) to the country. Papillon and Borelle apparently agreed to share the premium but in 1787, it emerged that Borelle had disappeared with all the money. Papillon petitioned the Board of Manufactures who were sympathetic and asked George Dempster to investigate on their behalf.[13]

Glasgow Chamber of Commerce was also concerned about the matter. Dale and Macintosh attended meetings of the Chamber (where they were both directors) in January and February 1787, where they learned that the Government had purchased the secret of dyeing Turkey Red *'according to the method practiced by a certain Mr. Basil'*, (by which they meant Borelle) – a blow to Papillon's claim.[14] This had been done *'for the good of the public'* and the secret formula and method could be viewed by anyone who applied to do so.[15] However, a few weeks later, the Chamber took a slightly different stance. In the interim, H.M. Treasury had advised that the secret should not be made public just yet. The Chamber compromised and agreed that it could be made available to any members who wanted to see it but anyone who saw it would be exhorted *'not to give it away or allow a copy to be made'*.[16]

Given that Dale and Macintosh had been using Papillon's improved version of the 'secret' process for two years, they may have been surprised at this news. More importantly, Dale must have known all about this issue as he was deputy chairman of the Chamber at the time and Macintosh followed him as deputy chairman the following year.[17] If the Government had decided that the discovery was attributable to Borelle, then Papillon could not claim the money or dream up any plans for patenting the process. His presence in Dalmarnock was therefore not entirely essential. Papillon's position was perhaps not helped by the fact that George Dempster, M.P. was himself an Honorary Member of the Chamber of Commerce (enrolled almost certainly because of his political connections) and was undertaking his inquiry at a time when both Dale and Macintosh were in very influential positions.[18]

Although the Dalmarnock business prospered, the partnership itself ran into some difficulties within a year or two. This was apparently because of Papillon, who seems to have been *'troublesome and contumaceous'* and was, *'both by nature and education, unfitted to stand the keen scrutiny of the shrewd Highlandmen'*.[19] He was making himself unpopular with Dale and Macintosh and a few months later, things came to a head. In the summer of 1787, Macintosh wrote to his son Charles (*'a very able chymist'* who was later to give his name to the popular waterproof raincoat):[20]

Papillon has now left us entirely. We could not manage his unhappy temper. I have made a great improvement in his process. I dye in twenty days what he took twenty five to do, and the colour better. We paid him his salary up to October, so as to be quite clear of him.[21]

Any concerns they might have had after Papillon's departure about profitability and their newly-found source of prosperity proved to be unfounded.[22] Papillon continued as a dyer in Glasgow, setting up in one of the nearby streets and is said to have retired in 1799, having accrued a fortune of some £20,000. However, he does seem to have been involved with his son in some business ventures in London after this date.[23] Although Papillon continued to dispute the ownership of the 'secret', he posed no threat to Dale and Macintosh's profits. In 1802, the Royal Bank of Scotland described their Turkey Red business as '*a most profitable concern and easy on us*'.[24] However, Dale and Macintosh were interested in selling the business at that point. A new manager, John Matheson from Dornoch (Macintosh's home area) was engaged in June 1802 on a salary of £50 per year with a free house and coal. His terms also provided for a 2.5% share in the profits for three years and 5% thereafter.[25] Matheson notes that he was only offered one quarter salary in advance in case Dale & Macintosh sold the works, '*which they had in view when I engaged with them*'.[26] In fact, Matheson remained with Dale & Macintosh until the works were sold in 1805 to Henry Monteith, Bogle & Co., who renamed it as Barrowfield Dyeworks and extended the buildings.[27]

Coal

The Barrowfield/Dalmarnock area of the city was part of the Barony Parish, where, according to the local minister, coal was in plentiful supply. What he called the '*cheapest of fuels*' was '*of the utmost importance to the comfort of the inhabitants*'.[28] Across the whole parish, coal worth £30,000 was produced annually. The minister hoped that coal prices could remain low because high coal prices would be damaging on at least two levels. The local people required it for domestic fuel but it was also becoming increasingly important as an industrial fuel for the new steam engines which were already powering factory engines. Although Dale used water power in all his mills and had no use for coal as a power source, here was a business opportunity on his doorstep – one which would turn a respectable profit and which would also allow him to combine profit with philanthropy if he could provide coal at a cheap price for those who really needed it.

This was not Dale's first attempt to involve himself in the coal business. He had been unsuccessful a few years earlier when he had been actively engaged in prospecting for coal around the town of Lanark. He began his search in 1787 in the Lanark Moor (Muir) area and also in the adjoining Caldwellbank and Bankhead areas but the search yielded nothing, although he was allowed '*the benefit of the Muir for heather or diviots*' for thatching his New Lanark buildings.[29]

By 1792 there was still no sign of coal but he was given the right to take '*free stone*' from Caldwellside:

> ...*upon the application of D.Dale, merchant in Glasgow, they* [Town Council] *have allowed and hereby allow Mr. Dale the privilege of winning and away tak[e]ing of free stone from any part of that part of the Moor called Caldwellside ... and hereby allow him six years thereof free of rent for indemnifying him of the expence he may be put to sinking of putting Doun for the same.*[30]

Nothing daunted, Dale turned his attention to Glasgow. He entered a partnership with Robert Tennant and David Todd, both merchants in the city, and together they bought shares in the Barrowfield Coal Company.[31]

Newspaper reports of the time took the view that Dale's motives were entirely philanthropic. He is described as a '*public-spirited citizen*' who, in partnership with '*other respectable gentlemen*', bought into the Barrowfield Coal Company '*with the avowed purpose of relieving the inhabitants of this city and neighbourhood from the apprehension of any unnecessary rise in the price of so very essential an article*'.[32] While it seems likely that Dale did want to provide cheap coal for families at a time of escalating prices, he also wanted to make a profit from the commercial side of the business. During his lifetime, numerous attempts had been made to extract coal from the Barrowfield estate, owned by John Orr, Glasgow's Town Clerk – the only proviso being that no pit be sunk within 100 yards of James Dunlop's cotton mill. However, none of these attempts were successful and Barrowfield proved to be '*the grave of more than one Glasgow fortune*'.[33] This ill-fated venture is reported to have cost Dale and his partners some £20,000 and Liddell in his *Memoir* described it as a '*total failure ... owing to the soil being a running quicksand, which could not be overcome, although the shaft was laid with iron cylinders*'.[34]

Although Dale's involvement in Barrowfield seems to have begun around 1792, it is not clear when he disengaged from the partnership. Efforts to extract coal, however, continued for many years after his death, with limited success. A map of 1823 shows a working 4,000ft long from Barrowfield, west under Glasgow Green, almost to the river.[35] It runs near the east end of

Monteith Row and is only 700 yards from Dale's House in Charlotte Street. The seam is named 'Dale's Dyke', although it is not clear whether this was because Dale was actively involved with the Barrowfield Coal Company up until his death in 1806 or merely because he was still a well-remembered figure in the area.

This business failure, uncharacteristic as it undoubtedly was for Dale, was painful and expensive but hardly '*disastrous*', as suggested by John Mitchell in the *Glasgow Herald* some years later.[36] It seems likely that Andrew Liddell's assessment of the situation is more accurate when he noted that Dale, Tennant and Todd were co-partners in this '*unfortunate project*' but that '*together they held a comparatively small share*'.[37]

Inkles

There is some (limited) information about Dale's involvement in a number of other business ventures in Glasgow – two of which were associated with textile manufacturing. He was a partner, with his brother-in-law, John Campbell, his nephew, David Dale Junior and Glasgow merchant Robert Reid (who later wrote for the *Glasgow Herald* under the pseudonym of 'Senex') in a small-scale cotton business '*largely concerned with the manufacture of cotton cloth*' in the centre of Glasgow.[38] It seems most likely, given the location, that this was a business for printing cotton cloth. Reid notes that in 1790 he went to Dale's establishment (probably his warehouse) in St. Andrew's Square to learn the muslin manufacturing business (presumably the financial side of it) '*and shortly afterwards into the warehouses of Dale, Campbell, Reid & Dale for a like purpose, having previously paid a weaver of the name of Paterson the sum of £10. 10s. for instructing me in the operative part of weaving*'.[39] *Jones' Directory* lists two High Street addresses which are relevant here. Dale is listed as having a cotton twist wareroom above No. 18 and a warehouse above No. 31 (sharing the space with Dalglish, Hutcheson, Steel & Co., linen printers).[40] It seems likely that either or both of these are the warehouses referred to by Robert Reid. At the time, in addition to the normal retail trades, there were some fifteen premises listed as '*warehouses*' and ten as '*warerooms*' in the High Street, nearly all of which were related to the cotton or linen trade – yarn merchants, calico & linen printers and cotton twist and inkle warehouses.[41]

Glasgow was one of the first cities to establish looms for producing 'inkles' (or 'incles') – originally a type of linen tape – and in the 1790s these still formed a very significant part of the cotton business in the city.[42] Dale was certainly involved in an inkle factory (probably with a small number of looms) and warehouse, trading under the name of Campbell, Dale and Co. from premises in the Ramshorn ground in what is now Ingram Street, just off the High Street. According to one commentator, this business began in 1785 and Burgh records indicate that his partners were Robert Dunmore, Alexander Grindlay (or Grimlay) and a Mr. Crawford.[43] John More, writing exactly one year after Dale's death, mentions two other names as partners in the inkle business – 'Clathick' (possibly John Coates, later Campbell of Clathick, merchant and Lord Provost of Glasgow 1784–1786) and Archibald Campbell, '*not the Carolina merchant but what is called Jamaica Archie*'.[44] Mitchell, however, notes that Dale's inkle business traded simply as 'Campbell, Dale and Co.' and his business printing cloth traded as 'Dale, Campbell, Reid & Dale'.[45] The second Dale here is David Dale Junior, Dale's nephew who was '*put into business in Glasgow*' by his uncle.[46] It is more likely, however, that Messrs. Dale, Campbell, Reid and Dale produced cloth destined specifically for the printfields, rather than printing the cloth themselves.[47]

Regardless of the company name, Stewart describes the businesses as '*highly remunerative*'.[48] There is also mention in *Jones' Directory* of one more warehouse, (possibly cotton twist) associated with 'Rankins, Dale & Co' on the south side of Trongate, '*by No. 17*'. However, it is likely that the Dale family member here is Hugh Dale who was a partner (with William & Robert Aitken) in Rankine, Dale & Co. who operated the Crofthead Mill in Neilston, Renfrewshire. and who also had a regular supply of French cambric for home or export sale available from their Glasgow warehouse.[49]

Fire Insurance, Land, Property and Other Interests

Scott Moncrieff's letters to head office reveal yet another business interest of Dale's and one which he bought into only three years before his death. In March 1803, Moncrieff informed Simpson about Dale's latest venture:

Mr. Dale has been much taken up some days past with all the rich folks here, forming a society for insuring against fire – it is all settled – their capital 100m [thousand] all to be paid down – not to be sent to the funds but lent out on good security at home – the sum paid in Glasgow, Paisley, Greenock etc. for insurance annually must be very great and they expect to get the most of it. He bids me ask you if [Gilbert Innes of] Stow and Mr. R[amsay] will take a share.[50]

This was the Glasgow Fire Insurance Society which Dale and 26 others (including Alex Oswald, Gilbert Hamilton, John Stirling, James Buchanan and Archibald Grahame) set up in 1803. The company had capital amounting to £100,000, divided into 400 shares of £250 each.[51] Shares were offered in May of that year and Appendix 10 illustrates the individual shareholdings of the first directors. Eleven shareholders, including Dale, the Oswalds, John McIlwham, Kirkman Finlay and Archibald Grahame each held six shares, the maximum held by any individual at that stage.[52] This was a significant investment in a company which, despite its name, was not merely concerned with insuring properties against loss. It was equally interested in *insuring sums of money against lives* and in selling and buying *annuities on lives* and the Charter was to run from 10th March 1803 until 1st June 1813.[53] The original shareholders were joined a few weeks later by some 60 others from around the country, e.g. Edinburgh, Perth, Kirkcaldy and London. The company was to hold £10,000 above capital stock in reserve against losses and the nine directors, of whom Dale was one, were subject to annual election. One of the shareholders, David Denny, described as a *merchant in Glasgow* was employed by the directors as a full-time secretary and, as a salaried employee, was not subject to election.[54]

In October 1803, Dale and the other directors of the Glasgow Fire Insurance Company were entered in the Glasgow Burgh Register of Sasines as purchasers of two tenement buildings in George Street and part of a building on the corner of Glassford Street and Wilson Street - presumably as potential office space.[55] The company began to advertise on a regular basis in *The Caledonian Mercury*, promising to insure property *on the most liberal terms*. The intention was to compete with the London insurance houses and the public were encouraged to put their faith in the directors because of *the extent of their capital and the responsibility of the Members*.[56]

Although based in the centre of Glasgow, they quickly appointed agents in Paisley, Greenock, Dumbarton, Perth and Dundee. By 1805, John More, Dale's successor at the Royal Bank, joined the company and by that time the number of agencies had expanded to include Edinburgh, Leith and Port Glasgow.[57] Although Dale's involvement ended with his death in 1806, the company survived until 16th July 1811 when, on account of its *not answering the expectations of the proprietors*, it was dissolved and the existing business transferred to the Phoenix Fire Insurance Company in London, who agreed to secure any losses.[58] The company proved to be more successful and, by 1816, had established no less than 22 branches across Glasgow.[59]

Right: Glasgow Fire Insurance Society Notice. *Caledonian Mercury*, 31st March 1804.

GLASGOW FIRE INSURANCE SOCIETY
Established for Insuring against Losses by Fire.

THIS Society will Insure, on the most liberal terms, all Property commonly insured by the Offices in London.

Where losses occur, the Society will pay the full amount without deduction, with the utmost promptitude and liberality.

The extent of their Capital, and the responsibility of the Members, afford to the Public the most ample security for the fulfilment of their engagements.

Losses by Fire from Lightning will be made good by the Society. And for the terms and conditions of the various insurances, the Public are referred to the Society's printed proposals, which may be had by applying at their Office, opposite the Exchange, or to any of their agents.

Common Insurance,	from	L. 100 to L. 3000	a 2s.	Per Cent. Per Ann.
Hazardous,		100 to 1000	3s.	
Double Hazardous,		100 to 1000	5s.	

DIRECTORS.

David Dale,	Alexander Oswald,
Gilbert Hamilton,	John Stirling,
Walter Ewing M'Lae	Archibald Smith,
John M'Ilwham,	Archibald Graham,
James Buchanan,	DAVID DENNY, Sec.

AGENTS.

THOMAS KINNEAR & SONS,	Edinburgh.
David Walker,	Perth.
Ebenezer Anderson,	Dundee.
Alexander Dunlop,	Greenock.
Alexander Campbell,	Paisley.
John Denny,	Dumbarton.

Land and Property

The Registers of Sasines also provide a substantial amount of information on Dale's other land and property deals in Glasgow between 1780 and his death in 1806. There are two registers which are relevant here – one for the Burgh of Glasgow and one covering the Barony and Regality of Glasgow.[60] There are many entries which include Dale's name but not all are directly related to his own personal ownership (or transfer) of land and property. For example, ten of the 28 'Dale' entries in the Burgh Sasines are as a trustee on behalf of others, with no direct connection to property transactions in his own right or in partnership with others. The remaining eighteen are a mixture of properties already discussed here (Charlotte Street, St. Andrew's Square and the Fire Insurance properties in George Street, Glassford Street and Wilson Street) and a number of others. The Register indicates that Dale bought land (extent unspecified) in Bell's Wynd in 1793. He also owned land in St. Enoch's croft which he sold in 1800. Most of the land and property owned by him in the Burgh was registered between 1803 and 1805 and in many of these entries he is registered as a 'Director' – sometimes solus and sometime with others. For example, in October/November 1803, his is the only name listed (as director) as owner of two houses and ground at the north end of Stirling Street – also 260 square yards of ground and buildings in Great Glassford Street.

In 1804, Dale, and four others bought a considerable amount of land in Charlotte Street and beyond (the Dovehill grounds) from John Burnside, Dale's neighbour and himself a prominent businessman.[61] Part of this was land adjoining Dale's own property and was used to extend the grounds of his house. He was still dealing in property between February and April, 1805 but generally as a partner, e.g. a steading house in Ingram Street was sold by Dale, William Perry, Alex. Bryce and Andrew Miller to a Mr. Colin Gillespie. Campbell, Dale & Co. sold 572 square yards of land in Craignaught Yard to Ralph Wardlaw. The same company owned the inkle factory and other property on the Ramshorn lands, and had done so for many years. Given the central situation of these properties, they would normally have been entered in the Glasgow Burgh Sasines but for some reason they appear in the Sasines for the Barony and Regality – along with other property dealings undertaken by the company. They show that *Campbell Dale & Co. of the Incle Factory* were involved in a number of property transactions between 1786 and 1791, including the purchase of land in part of the Ramshorn area in 1786, the acquisition of tenements from the Stirling family in 1789 and the subsequent disposal of two parts of the Ramshorn lands – an unspecified amount in 1790 to John & Matthew Perston, merchants and *2,885 square yards & houses theron to John and Robert Tennent, maltmen* in September 1791.[62]

The Register of Sasines for the Barony & Regality of Glasgow indicates an equally extensive portfolio of land and property held personally by Dale and others. Some of these deals were struck just days before Dale died and many were subsequently sold over a period of time. It is possible that Dale was still buying and selling properties one month before his death but it is also more than possible that he was ill and that the management of his portfolio had passed into the hands of his son-in-law. Whatever the case, it is clear that the portfolio was very extensive indeed. Given the haphazard nature of some of the Sasines, and the fact that only Glasgow is referred to here, Dale's portfolio was almost certainly more extensive than outlined here.

Table 7: Barony and Regality Sasines – David Dale & Partners

Register of Sasines*: Barony & Regality (Extracts)

Feb 14, 1784
Part of lands of Willowcare. David Dale from James Finlay.

Jul 4, 1785
Tenements, north side Dalmarnock Road. David Dale from John Orr of Barrowfield.

May 3, 1787
Part of lands of Willowacre. David Dale from James Finlay.

Oct 19, 1789
Lands in Dalmarnock. D. Dale, G. Macintosh – feued from Thos. Buchanan.

Nov 3, 1792
6.5 acres in Ruchill. David Dale from Wm. Gibson.

Sept 13, 1803
Lands and housing in western Shettleston known as Parkhead (£20,000) D. Dale of Rosebank, Wlt. Ewing McLae, Wm. Wardrop, Robt. Dennistoun, Jas. Farrie, Allan Smith – from Robt. Gray of Westmuir.

Jan 27, 1806
8 acres in Barrowfield. David Dale of Rosebank ....

Mar 15, 1806
333 sq yards in Clyde St. & lnd. & tenements part of Parson's Haugh or Rankins Haugh, David Dale & behoof of David Dale & Co. from James Hart.

*NB. Date of entry into the register, not the date of transaction.

It is certainly true that Dale was involved in other business ventures and partnerships during his life and it is likely that more of these will come to light as time moves on and evidence gradually emerges. For the moment, because of the dearth of evidence, it is possible to identify only one or two of these.

The Clydesdale Inn

This well-known landmark in Lanark dates back to the 1790s and David Dale was one of the original shareholders. His name appears in the first Minute Book of the Clydesdale Inn on 30th April, 1791.[63] The intention was to build a new inn on land directly opposite the Black Bull, as a rival to it. There were four 'proprietors' (i.e. initial subscribers and shareholders) at the first meeting, namely: David Dale; Sir James Stewart Denholm of Coltness and Newarthill; William Honeyman, the Sheriff Depute of Lanarkshire and John Bannatyne of Castlebank, a businessman and Provost of Lanark. Building costs were estimated at £1,200 and this sum was to be raised by subscription. Shares were £50 each and Dale took one share. Money was slow to appear, however, and the council (whose initial shareholding was only six shares) had to support the venture financially. Building began in February 1792 and a year later it was described as 'nearly finished'. Interestingly, Dale did not actually pay his £50 until 1794.

It seems that Dale's involvement was minimal. He held one share and although that was not an insignificant amount of money, it was not going to overburden his finances. He did not attend any further meetings and, as far as can be ascertained, did not mandate Owen or anyone else to attend on his behalf. It is possible that Dale simply saw the new inn as a viable and worthwhile project which he might support. As ever, there was a potential benefit for him in that any visitors who came to view the New Lanark mills might well wish to stay a little longer if they could be accommodated in a new and clean establishment – a 'neat additional inn' as it is referred to in the Statistical Account.[64] Dorothy Wordsworth, for example, visiting in 1803 did not wish to stay in the Black Bull, finding it 'the abode of dirt and poverty'.[65] She much preferred The New Inn, as it was known. It was later (c.1825) renamed 'The Clydesdale Inn'.

Canals and Slates

Dale had an interest in the new canal systems which were being built at the time. In fact, as early as 1783 he had bought a few shares (worth £19. 2s. & 8d.) in the nascent Forth & Clyde Canal project but little is known about this investment. There is also relatively little known about his involvement as a shareholder in the later canal project designed to link Loch Gilp with

Loch Crinan – the Crinan Canal. In July 1792, Dale and five others were asked by the Chamber of Commerce to look into the viability of such a project. There is little recorded after that until November 1802 when, in a letter to the Chief Cashier in Edinburgh, Scott Moncrieff mentions that Dale had bought fifteen canal shares belonging to a Mr. Logan at a cost of £250 – 'a grand bargain' according to Moncrieff.[66] The price appears to have risen because a month later, Dale was offered only ten shares for the same price. Moncrieff told Simpson that he did not think Dale would be interested in the deal.[67] Dale was, however, more interested in Royal Bank shares and sent a message to Simpson, via Scott Moncrieff, expressing a wish to buy £1,000 of Royal Bank stock.[68]

Finally, it is possible that Dale may have been involved in transporting slate, although it more likely that he was simply a customer. In May, 1782, the following advertisement appeared in *The Glasgow Mercury*:

> *To Shipmasters*
> *Vessels are wanted, during the Spring and Summer, to carry Easdale slates from the quarries to the Frith (sic) of Forth. Enquire at Messrs David Dale & Co. merchants, Glasgow, John Campbell, Esq., writer to the Signet, Edinburgh and Mr. Archibald Campbell, Easdale, by Inverary.*[69]

A similar advertisement appeared the following week but the River Clyde had now been included and there was a greater sense of urgency 'as there is a demand for the slates, it is expected of those who are willing to freight their vessels that they will apply immediately'.[70]

Doubtless, Dale was involved in other business ventures extending well beyond the city of Glasgow and the mills at New Lanark, important as those certainly were. As details emerge, they will only serve to confirm that he was a very significant figure in the commercial life of Scotland at the time.

Dale had a number of profitable businesses throughout the country and a healthy portfolio of land and property which earned him a great deal of money. Undoubtedly, the bulk of his fortune came from the cotton industry, principally from the mills in New Lanark. As a man of devout Christian views, concerned with the moral conduct of his employees and as a man committed to charitable acts and to the public good, it cannot have escaped his notice that his fortune depended on raw materials picked by men, women and children who were forced to live and work as slaves. This 'inconvenient truth' had been largely ignored by Glasgow's tobacco lords and by the sugar and rum merchants of the city's 'West India Club' whose vested interests apparently blinded them to the realilty of the situation. Even if they had recognised the existence of the problem, there is little to suggest that many were prepared to do anything about it. True to form, David Dale does not fit this mould. To date, very little has been written about New Lanark's involvement with slave cotton and nothing at all on Dale's work with the Glasgow Society for the Abolition of the Slave Trade. These issues will be addressed in Chapter 12.

References: Chapter 11

1 Liddell, A. (1854b) 'Memoir of David Dale', in Chambers, R. (ed) (1855) *A Biographical Dictionary of Eminent Scotsmen*. Glasgow: Blackie, p.162.

2 Cooke, A. (2010) *The Rise and Fall of the Scottish Cotton Industry, 1778–1914: The Secret Spring*. Manchester: M.U.P., p.126.

3 Sinclair, J. (ed) (1791–99) *The Statistical Account of Scotland*, 21 vols. Vol. XII, pp.113-4, p.127.

4 Cooke, A. (2010) *Rise and Fall*, pp.126-7.

5 Sinclair, J. (ed) *The Statistical Account*, Vol. XII, p.114.

6 Cliffe, W.H. (ed) 'Turkey Red in Blackley: A chapter in the History of Dyeing'. Online at http://www.colorantshistory.org/TurkeyRed.html

7 Stewart, G. (1881) *Curiosities of Glasgow Citizenship as Exhibited Chiefly in the Business Career of its Old Commercial Aristocracy*. Glasgow: J. Maclehose, p.76. See also *Memoirs & Portraits of 100 Glasgow Men* (1886) Glasgow: James MacLehose & Sons, Vol. II, p.220.

8 Cliffe, W.H. *Turkey Red*.

9 Ibid.

10 *The Glasgow Mercury*, 15th December 1785.

11 Cooke, A. (2010) *Rise and Fall*, p.127.

12 Bremner, D. (1869) *The Industries of Scotland. Their Rise, Progress and present Condition*. London: Black. Reprint (1969), Newton Abbot: David & Charles, p.300.

13 Board of Manufactures to George Dempster, 20th March 1788. National Archives of Scotland: NG 1/3/15. See Johnston, W.T. (ed) (2000) *David Dale & Robert Owen Studies*. Livingston: Officina Educational Publications.

14 Ibid., p.74.

15 *Glasgow Chamber of Commerce Minutes*. Glasgow City Archives. TD 1670/1/1, 9th January 1787.

16 *Chamber of Commerce Minutes*, 14th February 1787.

17 He was elected Chairman in January 1806, two months before Dale's death.

18 Dempster had been enrolled as Honorary Member on 13th April 1784. He was a member of a committee formed in October that year to look into linen & cotton manufacturing but otherwise he took little direct part in the Chamber's affairs.

19 Stewart, G. (1881) *Curiosities*, p.73.

20 Sinclair, J. *Statistical Account*, Vol. XII, p.115.

21 Stewart, G. (1881) *Curiosities*, p.73.

22 Ibid., p.74.

23 Cooke, A. (2010) *Rise and Fall*, p.127. See also *The Early London Gas Industry*, online at http://marysgasbook.blogspot.com/2009/08/eat-london-customers-for-sal-ammoniac.html

24 *The Three Banks Review*, 1960, pp.38-9. Quoted in in Donnachie, I. and Hewitt, G. (1993) *Historic New Lanark*. Edinburgh: E.U.P., pp.31-2.

25 *Diary of John Matheson of Dornoch*. Glasgow City Archives. TD164.

26 Ibid.

27 Note: It is also interesting to note that Dale may well have combined cotton spinning and Turkey Red dyeing at his cotton mill in Blantyre. The early period of the Blantyre Mill is extremely difficult to research but at least one commentator is convinced that the interest in dyeing was Dale's main reason for his involvement there and that both spinning and Turkey Red dyeing were in operation on the same site. See Cullen, A. (1910) *Adventures in Socialism*. Glasgow: John Smith, pp.10-11.

28 Sinclair, J. *Statistical Account*, Vol. XII, p.111.

29 Robertson, A.D. (1975) *Lanark: the Burgh and its Councils, 1469–1880*. Lanark Town Council, p.255.

30 Ibid., pp.275-6.

31 Todd was a partner in Todd, Shortridge & Co., linen printers in Argyle Street and was also a partner in Todd & Stevenson, cotton spinners, who had mills at Bridge of Weir and Springfield near Glasgow.

32 *The Glasgow Courier*, 2nd February 1792.

33 Mitchell, J. 'An Old Glasgow Worthy'. See *The Glasgow Herald*, 27th August 1886.

34 Liddell, A. (1854b) *Memoir*, p.164.

35 McLelland's Map of Barrowfield & Coal Workings, 1823.

36 Mitchell, J. *Old Glasgow Worthy*.

37 Liddell, A. (1854b) *Memoir*, p.164.

38 Liddell, A. (1854b) *Memoir*, p.163.

39 Reid, R. (Senex) (1884) *Glasgow Past and Present*, 3 vols. Glasgow: David Robertson & Co., Vol III, pp.494-5. Note: Reid set up briefly on his own as a muslin manufacturer but eventually moved into his family's mahogany/furniture business.

40   *Jones's Directory or Useful Pocket Companion* (1787) Glasgow: J. Mennons.

41   Ibid.

42   Sinclair, J. *Statistical Account*, Vol. V, p.503. Note: The linen tape was exported to America and became known as Scotch Tape.

43   Renwick. R. (ed) (1913) *Extracts from the Records for the Burgh of Glasgow with Charters and other Documents.* 11 vols. Vol. VIII, Glasgow, pp.155-6.

44   J. More to William Simpson, 17th March 1807. R.B.S. Archives. RB/837/1569.

45   Mitchell, J. *Old Glasgow Worthy.*

46   Liddell, A. (1854b) *Memoir*, p.174.

47   Eyre-Todd, G. (1934) *A History of Glasgow*, 3 vols. Glasgow: Jackson, Wylie & Co. Vol. 3, p.315. Also Liddell, *Memoir*, p.163n.

48   Stewart, G. (1881) *Curiosities*, p.54.

49   Nisbet, S.M. (2008) *The Rise of the Cotton Factory in Eighteenth-Century Renfrewshire.* British Archaeology Report, Series 464. Oxford: Alden Press, pp.143; 162–3. See also *The Glasgow Courier*, 13th December 1791.

50   Moncrieff to William Simpson, 2nd March 1803. R.B.S. Archives. RB/837/1016.

51   Cleland, J. (1816) *Annals of Glasgow.* 2 vols. Glasgow: James Hedderwick. Vol. 1, p.406.

52   Glasgow Fire Insurance records. 12th/13th/24th May 1803. University of Glasgow Archives. UGD 71/1/5.

53   Ibid., Deed of Accession, July/August 1803. UGD 71/1/4.

54   Ibid.

55   Sasine dated 12th October 1803. Glasgow Burgh Register of Sasines. Vols. 45–87. Glasgow City Archives, B10/2.

56   *The Caledonian Mercury*, 31st March 1804.

57   Ibid., 11th April 1805. Note: More continued to act for the heirs of the Dale family in the affairs of the company. Given More's financial dealings elsewhere, this may not have been to the family's advantage.

58   Cleland, J. (1816) *Annals.* Vol. 1, p.406.

59   Ibid.

60   Register of Sasines, Burgh of Glasgow. Glasgow City Archives. B10/2. Also Register of Sasines, Barony & Regality of Glasgow. Glasgow City Archives. T-SA 5/1/1-2.

61   The other partners were James Rodger, David Lamb, Andrew Sibbald and Robert Blair.

62   *Register of Sasines, Barony & Regality of Glasgow.* Glasgow City Archives. T-SA 5/1/1-2

63   I am indebted to Thomas Davidson of the Lanark & District Archaeological Society for much of the information on the Clydesdale Inn.

64   Sinclair, J. *Statistical Account*, Vol. XV, p.34.

65   Knight, W. (ed) (1904) *Journals of Dorothy Wordsworth.* 2 vols. London: MacMillan, Vol. 1, p.190.

66   Moncrieff to William Simpson, 19th November 1802. R.B.S. Archives. RB/837/885.

67   Ibid., 22nd December 1802. RB/837/930.

68   Ibid.

69   *The Glasgow Mercury*, 1st May 1782.

70   Ibid., 8th May 1782.

Part 4
Slavery and the Slave Trade

Chapter 12: David Dale and the Abolition Movement

The New Lanark mills were in operation at the height of the national (and international) debate on slavery, the first part of which culminated in Parliament's decision in 1807 to abolish the trading of slaves. Cotton mills all over England and Scotland relied on imported raw cotton and cotton spinners and factory owners depended directly or indirectly on the labour of slaves and other plantation workers. Until fairly recently, this has not been widely discussed by academic and other writers interested in the history of cotton spinning in Scotland. As far as New Lanark is concerned, the Owen family's views on slavery and Robert Dale Owen's involvement with Frances Wright in Nashoba are relatively well-known but little has been written, for example, about David Dale's involvement with the Glasgow Society for the Abolition of the Slave Trade.[1]

This is surprising, given the context in which New Lanark was operating. Britain was, by far, the biggest imperial power in the late 18th and early 19th centuries. By 1815, the British Empire had 41.4 million people under its rule and by 1820 encompassed one-fifth of the world's population and the Scots played a highly significant part in that.[2] The Glasgow 'Tobacco Lords' have been well researched and they were so successful that they virtually monopolised the entire British tobacco trade. Slave colonies in Brazil, Maryland and Virginia accounted for almost the entire output of New World tobacco and imports to Scotland by the mid-18th century exceeded those of Bristol, Liverpool and Whitehaven combined.[3]

By the later part of the 18th century, sugar (along with rum and molasses) had taken over the dominant role in the empire – and with it the trade in human beings as slaves. By the end of the Napoleonic Wars in 1815, the West Indies accounted for 60% of the transatlantic sugar trade but the slave population of these islands had been extensive long before that time.[4]

During the period 1781–1790, the demand for sugar and related products led to the West Indies taking 95% of the African slaves brought to the New World and it was sugar which shaped the very nature of the Atlantic slave system as the West Indies became the trade centre for the New World.[5] This was not entirely surprising. Conditions in the sugar plantations were even more arduous and disease-ridden than those on cotton or tobacco plantations but there was more profit in sugar than in cotton or tobacco. Cotton certainly was exported in volume from the West Indies to Great Britain and although these imports were significantly greater than those from the North American colonies (at least before the huge expansion in the cotton trade during the 1830s), they were nevertheless eclipsed by the imports of sugar, rum, molasses and syrup. This is borne out in the Glasgow figures. Table 8 below shows the transatlantic imports to Glasgow for 1790, 1800 and 1805.[6]

Table 8: Transatlantic Imports to Glasgow

Goods	1790	1800	1805
Coffee (cwts)	228	7,584	18,879
Sugar (cwts)	132,690	187,510	311,342
Rum (gallons)	224,232	670,889	484,570
Tobacco (cwts)	94,400	37,030	16,451
Cotton (cwts)	24,399	53,422	75,195

As might be expected, given the prior involvement of Scottish merchants during the tobacco era (and their complicity in the slave trade), Scottish entrepreneurs were not slow in involving themselves in the new trade in sugar and cotton and thus, in the slave trade indirectly. Sometimes, the involvement was much more direct, as in the case of Richard Oswald, who owned his own slavery 'station' in Bance (sometimes 'Bunce' or 'Bunse') Island at the mouth of the Sierra Leone river.[7]

What Devine refers to as 'the relentless penetration' of the empire by Scots doctors, educators, plantation overseers, army and government officials, merchants and clerics which had been ongoing for a very long time (four sugar refineries had been built in Glasgow between 1667 and 1700 and Port Glasgow became a major centre for the trade), found a new expression in the post-tobacco era.[8]

Bance Island.

Many merchants, officials and overseers emigrated from Scotland to the West Indies and were enormously influential in their new situations. William MacDonald and James Milliken from Glasgow were both owners of sugar plantations in St. Kitts, as was Robert Cunningham of Glengarnock.[9] The majority tended to return within a few years, unlike many of those who emigrated to the U.S., where they were more inclined to stay and to set up home. In the process, they took their technical knowledge and skills with them, despite the British government's best efforts to legislate against the transfer of ideas and despite the home manufacturers' best efforts to maintain a high level of security. Samuel Slater, an ex-apprentice of Strutt in Belper, introduced water frames to the U.S. via Pawtucket, Rhode Island, in 1790. Thomas Marshall, the manager of Arkwright's Masson Mill, left to manage a mill in New Jersey in 1791.[10]

Whether they found themselves in the West Indies or North America, however, the Scottish merchants built on and expanded the existing merchant networks established by a previous generation of Scots. For example, the great merchant families such as the Dunlops, the Bogles, the Cunninghams and the Glassfords with whom Dale did business were not merely exporters and importers, hugely significant as those roles were. They were also proprietors of merchant houses and, as such, were able to provide capital to planters for new plantations – or to supply the ever-increasing demand for domestic and other 'store' goods in the colonies (including the plantations), particularly the North American colonies. The stores themselves often granted credit to planters. Output was increased by hiring more slaves rather than improving modes of production and there is no doubt that capital from Glasgow merchant houses was used to support this.[11]

Thus the network of trade established by a relatively small elite of tobacco lords became a much larger network of partnerships in the post-tobacco age but a network which was still dominated by large merchant houses and by people with whom Dale would certainly be acquainted, either personally or professionally. Nathaniel Jones' 1787 *Directory* lists several of Dale's business interests in Glasgow, including 'cotton twist warerooms' in the High Street and an inkle warehouse in Ingram Street.[12] His Charlotte Street neighbours included a tobacco merchant and at least three textile merchants and his involvement as Depute Chair of the Chamber of Commerce involved him in close contact with Pat Colquhoun, Lord Provost and one of Glasgow's most influential figures. In turn, the Chamber of Commerce also brought him into contact with the Trades & Merchants Houses. There he certainly met with all the famous merchants of the day. The list is too long to detail here but included figures such as Robert Houston, Robert and Richard Bogle, Richard Denniston, George Oswald, George McIntosh, the Stirling family and the Buchanan family – all members of a sub-group known as 'The West India Club', which had been meeting since 1781, prior to the formal establishment of the Glasgow West India Association in 1807.[13] Dale was clearly very well connected.

The West India merchants traded extensively in cotton, rum and sugar. Four merchant houses in particular (the Houstons, Dunmores, Gardens and McKays) handled 2,146 of the 3,200 hogsheads of sugar imported to the Clyde in 1781.[14] The McCall family owned three plantations in Trinidad; Bogle Scott & Co. had an estate in Grenada; Robert Dunmore and Robert McKay each had estates in Jamaica; John Campbell & Co. had two estates in Grenada and five sugar plantations in British Guiana and Alexander Houston & Co., despite some trading difficulties, still managed to own property in the West Indies valued at £139,000 in 1800.[15] Whether it was sugar, rum or cotton, profits were indisputably the result of slave labour and the West India merchants would require some persuading to alter that situation. They were a powerful group and formed by far the largest group of merchant councillors on the Town Council. Devine notes that in 1790, ten of the thirteen Council members had interests in the Caribbean trade.[16]

Slave Cotton

Dale's raw material and the source of his fortune is most likely to have come primarily from the West Indies, North America and, to a lesser extent, India (via the East India Company), all of which relied on slave labour. In this respect, Dale was in exactly the same situation as all the other factory owners in Great Britain.

In 1793, Dale wrote to Claud Alexander of Ballochmyle, his business partner in Catrine Cotton Works, referring to cotton wool from Domingo, *'the kind usually spun at the Water Mill'*.[17] In a similar letter to Alexander in March 1794 when times were clearly hard for the Catrine enterprise, Dale seemed clear that East India wool was unsuitable for the job. Dale observed that:

> *...cotton wool is actually scarce both here and in England and for my part I am at a loss where to find wool fit for the Mills I am quite clear that the East India wool is totally unfit for this purpose and even the small quantity of a 12th part put into it hurts the quality of the yarn...*[18]

However, while it might appear that East India cotton was unsuitable – James Monteith of Anderston had had similar problems with 'clouded yarns' from the same source – large amounts of it were still imported.[19] It would also be too simplistic to argue that the West Indies and, to lesser extent, the U.S., (prior to the 1820s) were the only sources of raw cotton, although they were clearly important. In fact, in 1781, the total imports of cotton wool into Great Britain were 5,198,778 lbs, none of which came from North America, *'or at least only a few bags from Georgia into London'*.[20] It was not until 1784, one year after the Treaty of Independence that U.S. cotton began to appear. Even then, it was such a rare occurrence that when an American ship arrived in Liverpool, British customs seized the cargo on the grounds that such a vast quantity had never been grown in that part of the world.[21] Interestingly, *'Archibald Campbell was the first who imported American cotton into Glasgow. He imported then only a few bags by way of trial.'*[22] Table 9 is taken from *The Scots Magazine* some five years later and indicates the origin of the raw material.[23]

Table 9: Source of Cotton Imported to G.B. (lbs) 1789

Foreign West Indies	239,803
Turkey	4,668,231
East Indies	2,101,104
Demerera	1,345,702
French Settlements	6,143,623
Brazil	4,755,635
Spanish West Indies	93,726
West Indies, per Ireland	52,794
Georgias	18,964
Africa	1,626
Bahamas	377,980
Bermudas	5,800
British Settlements	9,988,986
Other parts	705,921
Into Scotland from British West Indies	1,700,000
Total	**32,209,895 lbs**

The total figure, as can be seen from the above, was 32,209,895 lbs in 1789. By 1800 this figure had reached 56,010,732 lbs and by 1806, the year of Dale's death, the total was 58,176,283 lbs.[24]

The export figures for U.S. cotton (Table 10 below) indicate how important it was to become, after a relatively slow start.[25]

Table 10: U.S. Cotton Exports, 1791–1833

Year	Lbs
1791	189,316
1795	6,276,300
1800	17,789,803
1805	40,383,491
1810	93,874,201
1815	82,998,747
1820	127,860,152
1825	176,439,907
1833	322,215,122

This is not to suggest that all the U.S. cotton was necessarily destined for the United Kingdom but it is worth noting that the figures for 1832, for example, indicate that approximately 73% did come to the U.K. and amounted to seven times the amount of cotton from all the West Indies combined.[26]

The New Lanark *Report* and *Wage Books* of the time indicate the amount of raw cotton held in each of the mills.[27] The cotton is listed by type but since it was the habit to refer to the wool (at least in part) by the geographical area of export, it is relatively straightforward to point to the source. No *Report Books* are available for the period prior to 1801 but it is entirely reasonable (allowing for the considerable increase in the amount of U.S. cotton in the first few years of the 19th century) to assume that the *sources*, if not the *amounts*, of raw cotton 1790–1800 were broadly similar to those of 1801 to 1807.

U.S cotton was slow to establish itself in Great Britain but by 1795 there were clear signs that 'American Georgia' cotton had gained a place in the Manchester market.[28] The increasing importance of U.S. cotton appears to be evident in New Lanark just a few years later, although the figures vary from mill to mill and from month to month. The *Report Books* indicate that there were three major sources of raw cotton for the mills: the U.S., the West Indies and South America – all of which depended on slave labour. The *Report Book* for December 1801 to February 1802 indicates that there were significant amounts of U.S. cotton, namely Georgian (probably black seed, Sea Island, coastal cotton), 'Bowed' Georgian (green seed, upland cotton) and 'Orleans' cotton.

The U.S. figures varied each month and in the early 1800s were sometimes exceeded by imports of cotton from the West Indies and South America. Tables 11 and 12 indicate some of the fluctuations in stockholding. It is clear, however, that stocks of U.S. cotton were always significant and that they increased during 1801 to 1806, although the West Indies and South America remained important.

Table 11: New Lanark Mills.
Source of Raw Cotton: Dec 31st 1801–Feb 28th 1802

	U.S. (lbs)	West Indies/South America (lbs)
No. 1 Mill	5,055	14,598
No. 3 Mill	4,610	1,006

Table 12: Source of Raw Cotton: Annual Total 1806–1807

	U.S. (lbs)	West Indies/South America (lbs)
No. 1 Mill	314,263	48,902
No. 2 Mill	264,056	94,962

The West Indian cotton came from almost every significant Caribbean island in the chain from St. Domingo south to Trinidad and Tobago, including the Bahamas, the Grenadines, Tortola, St. Croix, Antigua, Jamaica and Guadeloupe. Further, the *Report Books* show that a significant amount came from Central and South America, including Panama, Demerera in modern Guyana, the Orinoco delta in Venezuela, Surinam, Colombia (Giron and Carthagena) Brazil (Pernambuco) – again, all places which depended on slave labour.

Raw cotton, from whatever source, arrived at major ports such as London, Liverpool or Glasgow. Little is known about where Dale bought his raw cotton for the New Lanark mills but it seems highly likely that he would draw on a number of sources, possibly including the Cotton Exchange in Manchester. With 1.7million lbs of West Indies cotton coming into Scotland, it is equally likely that he bought some of it locally and there is some evidence that Manchester dealers also bought cotton in Glasgow. In a letter to Claud Alexander in 1788, Dale makes this clear:

> I think matters will settle here with respect to any more Bankruptcies, & I have great hopes that next year there will be a brisk trade the Fustian business is at present exceeding brisk in Manchester notwithstanding of the late Bankruptcies & there are several persons from Manchester now in this place wishing to buy Cotton Wool but the holders have advanced the price I am however of opinion that the advance in the price of wool will be of short duration so long as the Muslin & Callicoe trade continues in the present situation.[29]

Glasgow merchant Alexander Campbell dealt locally in imported cotton.[30] Dale was a partner with the Campbell family, along with Robert Reid, a wealthy muslin merchant who as a young man had joined Dale briefly in St. Andrew's Square before commencing '*a shipping business to Jamaica*' for a few years, eventually taking over his father's lucrative business in mahogany furniture.[31] Campbell owned warehouses in Glasgow, which might suggest that Dale had some direct involvement in importing cotton or, more likely, that he bought it from a number of sources, including local ones, and warehoused it in Glasgow, along with the finished cloth.

Raw cotton was certainly for sale in Glasgow and had been for a number of years. For example, in 1758 *The Glasgow Journal* advertised '*Leeward island cotton by the bag or in larger quantities...*' to be sold at Joseph Angus's cellars in Bell's Wynd.[32] Cotton at this time was regularly retailed in single bags, having been imported from London, '*the principal market for the article*':

> NOTICE – At the Carron Warehouse, Glasgow, to be owned, seven bags of cotton; one marked i.e. the other six of different marks; brought from London on the 'Glasgow'...[33]

The first public auction that can be traced was advertised in *The Glasgow Journal* of 24th February, 1765:

> To be sold, by public roup, upon Monday the 28th of February inst., at 12 o'clock, at the callender of Messrs Gray and Co., Bell's Wynd of Glasgow, three bags of cotton, and forty tons of fustick, which will be shown there any time betwixt and the roup, by Mr. James Anderson.[34]

Later, during Dale's time at New Lanark, there were certainly cotton brokers and retailers in Glasgow. Jones' *Directory* in 1787 lists many yarn merchants and twist dealers but there are two cotton dealers also mentioned – one James Sharp with a business at 126 Gallowgate and a Mr. John Durnbell whose business address is shown as Charlotte Street, making him a neighbour of Dale's.[35] Dale seems to have been involved with a Mrs. Mary Brown, widow of a local shoemaker with extensive business interests in the city and one of Glasgow's principal cotton brokers.[36] Following the death of her husband, she was unsure how best to dispose of her husband's shoes and leather and '*applied to David Dale on the occasion*'.[37] Dale's advice was to make up shoes suitable for the market in the West Indies and then '*to consign the whole to a respectable West India house for sale in the West Indies*'. Dale would '*run halves*' with her in this venture.[38] Significantly, the stock was shipped to the West Indies '*upon joint account, with instructions that the produce of the sales should be remitted in cotton*'.[39] When the cotton arrived, Dale proposed sending it to a local broker for sale but Mary Brown took on the job herself and sold it at a good price '*and immediately thereafter she commenced the business of a cotton trader*'.[40] Reid offers an eye-witness account of Mrs. Brown:

> I have seen Mary bustling about with a large leather pocket at her side, containing samples of cotton, ready to show to any spinner or speculator whom she might meet. She thought nothing of bargaining offhand for thousands of pounds. Mary did not care for the company of ladies, or to talk about flounces, tucks, bowknots, trimmings, skirts or edgings; but preferred the company of gentlemen, and to discourse with them upon the merits of the long and short staple, of Surats, Surinams, Pernams, Sea Islands and Bowed Georgias. Mary really was a remarkable woman and I believe she passed more money through her hands than any woman in Scotland ever did.[41]

Her success, however, was fairly short-lived and she clearly over-extended herself. She '*most unluckily became an extensive speculator in cotton yarn upon her own account*' and the business collapsed in March 1794.[42] Eight days later, in a letter to Claud Alexander, Dale mentions some bankrupt stock which may well have belonged to Mary Brown and he indicates another possible cause of her failure:

> The cotton advertised to sell belongs to a Bankrupt Estate I bought several parcels out of it long ago and would have continued buying it had I been allowed to [stock, sack?] it but a great deal of it is of very bad quality.[43]

Mary Brown's commercial demise, however, was not the end of cotton-dealing in the city. Dale still had access to firms such as J. & G. Buchanan & Co., who had been established for some time. Also, Mrs. Brown had, on occasion, been joined by Archd. Calder & Co. and Jo. Aitken & Co. when they purchased cotton direct from the importer, Messrs. Leitch & Smith. There is also mention of one Archibald Sorely who, like Brown, became a successful broker, '*but became an extensive cotton speculator and dealer in 1799 and failed for a large sum*'.[44] Interestingly, in the same year, Dale's manager at New Lanark, William Kelly, '*commenced cotton broker and spinner*'.[45]

Given the obvious involvement of Dale and other merchants in the cotton and sugar trade with the West Indies and North America, and given the fortunes that were amassing to many merchants in the city of Glasgow, there can be no doubt that all involved were at least aware that their profits were built on slavery. There may not have been many Glasgow merchants or Glasgow ships directly involved in trafficking slaves from Africa (which could not be said of places like Liverpool, Whitehaven or Bristol, for example) but there is no escaping '*the deep involvement of the Scots in a colonial economy which could not have functioned without an entrenched and expanding system of slave labour*'.[46] At the same time, however, it cannot be denied that pressure from the increasingly public anti-slavery movement was beginning to reach Glasgow and the other major cities in Scotland. What becomes important, then, is where people like Dale stood on the question.

Dale and Abolition

'It is pretty well known that slavery existed in Scotland in early times. David II manumitted a slave in 1368...'[47]

There may well have been slaves in Scotland in the 14th century, although there are several definitions of slavery and there is a considerable difference between chattel slavery and the forcible exportation of human beings on the one hand and indentured service, domestic or otherwise, on the other. Brion Davis argues that chattel slavery must always be distinguished from varieties of servitude and dependence.[48] However, it is not always so clear in practice. For example, it might be argued that, until 1799, colliers and saltworkers in Scotland were enslaved by the company which virtually owned them. Colliers' children were not technically bound to the colliery for life, unless they worked for a year and a day. However, on the birth of a child, many parents accepted money 'on account', effectively enslaving the children from birth.[49]

Iain Whyte estimates that there were approximately 70 black slaves in Scotland in the late-18th century, compared with some 15,000 in England.[50] The Scottish slaves (or perhaps the more accurate term might be 'former' slaves) were mostly in domestic service. Conditions for these servants were sometimes better than those left behind on the plantations. There are cases where 'masters' paid for their servants' clothes, medical attention, schooling and apprenticeships. Sometimes, baptism was also paid for but this was less common because baptism was often taken to mean salvation from the *'heathenism'* of black culture and, with it, manumission. In 1760, John Glassford, the Tobacco Lord and largest ship owner in Glasgow, had his family portrait painted and this included a young black male servant. However, when attitudes changed, the black servant was erased from the painting, illustrated below.[51]

John Glassford & Family. Archibald McLaughlan, 1767. (© CSG CIC Glasgow Museums & Libraries Collections)

However, lest too comfortable a picture of domestic service is being portrayed here, it should be remembered that there were eight recorded slave sales in 18th-century Scotland and these included, in 1766, two eleven-year-old boys, one nineteen-year old female slave (Peggy), along with her one-year-old child.[52] In 1769, '*a handsome black boy, about 13*' was advertised for sale in *The Edinburgh Advertiser*.[53]

In similar vein, Archibald Buchanan of Glasgow, wealthy and influential cotton spinner purchased one 'Ned Johnston' in 1763 who subsequently claimed he had been '*subjected to severe and cruel usage*' and that he had been '*suspended from the joists of a byre and beaten with rods 'till the blood ran from many wounds in his body*', because he had done something to displease his master.[54] Local people helped him to escape and he gained his freedom from the Magistrates in Glasgow.

Ned Johnston was only one of a number who ran away or were subject of a dispute between owners and masters. In Perth, Lord Oliphant had a black slave called John Loudon or 'Quashy', who ran away in 1733.[55] These cases frequently ended up in court. When 'Jamie Montgomery', for example, was threatened with being forcibly returned to Virginia after a period of apprenticeship as a joiner in Beith, he refused to go and fled to Edinburgh. Those who wished to send him back planned to '*make a penny of him, reducing him again to slavery*'. It is hardly surprising that his situation in Beith was infinitely preferable to that in the colonies.[56] Branding, bone-crushing, amputation, castration and blinding were not at all uncommon as punishments. In Barbados, killing a negro attracted a fine of only £15 and it was not until 1783 that St. Kitts made it illegal to cut off '*any limbs or members or otherwise disable*' slaves.[57] In the West Indies, it was lawful to kill '*The King's negroes*' if they ran away. The crime of theft was punishable by death, transportation, dismemberment or other punishment '*at the discretion of two justices and three freeholders*'.[58]

In Scotland, there were several cases where the local community came to the aid of runaway or beleaguered slaves, sometimes, rescuing them and helping them flee to the city. In the case of one negro boy, David Spens, it was, perhaps ironically, the colliers and saltpanners on the east coast who, in 1769, raised enough money for his baptism and freedom.[59]

Importantly, the Court of Session, after discussing the famous case of Joseph Knight (a Jamaican slave in Perth who had resisted attempts to keep him in service) finally decided in 1778:

> That the state of slavery is not recognised by the laws of this Kingdom and is inconsistent with the principles thereof, and finds that the regulations in Jamaica concerning slaves, do not extend to this Kingdom, and repels the master's claim for perpetual service.[60]

Times were clearly changing and with them, attitudes to the trading of slaves and, more slowly, to the institution of slavery itself. As a committed Christian, it could be argued that Dale's position should have been clear. But, as will be argued later, there were many in the Church (both Established and Dissenting) who condoned slavery and, on occasion, actively supported it. Whether Dale chose to acknowledge it or not, he was indirectly associated with slavery, in common with all the other factory owners, sugar importers etc. in the city, in that his profits depended indirectly upon it. However, unlike many of the merchants in the city at the time, (in particular the West India merchants), Dale was prepared to take a leading role in the growing abolitionist lobby, albeit aware that caution was required if he were to avoid alienating himself from the very business community he hoped to influence and thereby threaten the welfare of his workforce in New Lanark.

On the one hand, Dale was a powerful figure in his own right. As owner of New Lanark and with growing business interests elsewhere, he was certainly an influential figure in the city. Indeed, many of the city's businesses were literally indebted to him, courtesy of the credit facilities of the Royal Bank. Here, as in all other business matters, Dale combined his Christian ethics with shrewd business acumen. On the other hand, however, he could not afford to lose the support of friends, colleagues and partners in the city and beyond. If business was to flourish, mutual support was necessary. This support was provided through a network of clubs, societies, churches, professional institutions, employers' organisations and business networks.[61] Powerful men such as Colquhoun, Houston, Buchanan, Bogle and many others were involved with Dale in the Merchants House, Trades House, Magistrates' committees, charitable commissions and coffee houses. However, many of these individuals, while they were members of the Chamber of Commerce, were also part of the twenty-strong exclusive 'West India Club' (sometimes known as 'The Pig Club' after the name of the hostelry in which they gathered) which was dedicated to safeguarding their interests in that part of the world.[62] Dale was not a member of this club and his efforts on behalf of the Abolitionist movement would certainly have raised some eyebrows among them.

There can be no doubt that all involved were well aware that slavery contributed to their profits. Colquhoun, for example, a close associate of Dale in the Chamber of Commerce, had spent some considerable time in the tobacco and cotton business in Virginia before returning to Glasgow in 1766. The Houston family were also well aware of the importance of slaves to their prosperity. Alexander Houston's son, Andrew, was a partner in the family business which eventually failed. One of the causes of his downfall:

> ...was in consequence of his having, in partnership with some others, entered into an immense speculation in slaves, when the total abolition of slavery was at first seriously agitated, and seemed likely to be immediately accomplished; but as the measure was delayed, the loss occasioned by the fall in the price of negroes, by the expense of keeping them, and by deaths amongst them, brought ruin to the speculators.[63]

It is clear, therefore, that Dale required to steer a difficult course between support for abolition on the one hand and the possibility of alienation from colleagues and potential bankruptcy on the other.

The campaign for abolition had been a nationwide issue since May 1787 when Thomas Clarkson (1760–1846) joined a twelve-man committee chaired by Granville Sharp, 'with Mr. Wilberforce as their chief in Parliament, with Pitt, Grenville, Fox, Dolben, Windham etc. as his colleagues'.[64] Thus William Wilberforce (1759–1833) and other members of the so-called 'Clapham Sect' in London began their campaign in earnest, often against predictably stiff opposition from vested interests such as the West India merchants but also, on occasion, less predictably, from the established Church in both England and Scotland. It is worth noting that the non-conformist tradition was a powerful influence throughout the campaign against the slave trade. Of the original twelve members of Sharp's 1787 committee, nine were Quakers. In many parts of the country (including Scotland) the campaign was often led by dissenters and evangelicals. Dale was no exception to this.

The London Abolition Committee raised the profile of the anti-slave trade campaign later that year when Wilberforce persuaded Clarkson to visit Bristol, Liverpool and Manchester to obtain more information on the slave trade in anticipation of a public enquiry. In fact, a number of provisional committees had already been established and Clarkson was charged with establishing more, under the supervision of the London society. In total, Clarkson made seven journeys between 1787 and 1794 and covered some thousands of miles across Britain. Clarkson and the provincial committees were warned against making their meetings too public and too obvious. Given events in America and France, it was important not to further alarm the public with thoughts of universal manumission.

Granville Sharp (1735–1813) was also heavily involved in the Abolition movement, particularly in the creation of the St. George's Bay Company in 1787. This was an ambitious programme intended to repatriate black Africans (former slaves who were destitute in London) to Sierra Leone, 'where it was expected they would have it in their power to turn their industry to proper account'.[65] Clarkson became involved at this stage and the avowed intention was to establish a 'free' colony where former slaves and colonists could trade unhindered – '...one of their primary objects is the abolition of the slave trade'.[66]

Largely at Sharp's expense, a ship was fitted out and more than 400 people, including 300 of London's black poor and various officials, clergy and tradesmen set off to establish 'Granville Town' on the cost of Sierra Leone, where land could be bought cheaply from local tribal leaders.[67] Inevitably, the first settlement ran into major difficulties. Disease, strife and conflict with local slave traders all took their toll and in 1789 only 64 members of the new colony remained.

At home, parliamentary progress towards abolition was delayed time and time again. The numbers arguing for immediate abolition of the trade were growing but they remained outnumbered by the gradualists. The Commons, heavily influenced by

Henry Dundas, prevaricated time and again, insisting on yet more evidence. In 1789, twelve resolutions were laid before the House but, again, more evidence was requested. In 1791, the House voted against Wilberforce and so Clarkson and others continued their tours across the country.

It was against this general backdrop that The Glasgow Society for the Abolition of the Slave Trade was founded in January 1791. Dale accepted the role of chairman, thereby making his opposition to the slave trade a matter of public knowledge.

Anti-slavery image based on Josiah Wedgwood's medallion of 1778. (Library of Congress)

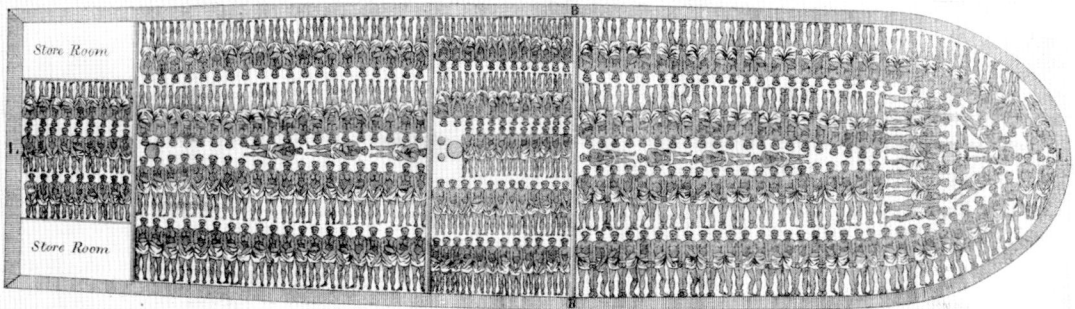

Stowage of the British slave ship *Brooks*, c.1789.

Clarkson came to Scotland later the same year and '*was received with great respect*'.[68]

> Mr. Clarkson (whose zeal in the offices of humanity have (sic) been so conspicuous on the subject of the slave trade) was received in Scotland with that attention his philanthropy so much entitles him to, and that the gentlemen of Glasgow provided a public dinner to do the more honour to their benevolent guest.[69]

Given that the Glasgow Society was formed that year with Dale as its chairman and, given that he was one of the most prominent of '*the gentlemen of Glasgow*', it seems almost certain that Dale would be present at such a dinner. However, despite eventually gathering evidence from some ten or twelve who, '*much to their honour, came forward of their own accord*', Clarkson's view of his time in Scotland was less than enthusiastic:

> This tour was the most vexatious of any I had yet undertaken; many still refused to come forward and be examined, and some on the most frivolous pretences; so that I was disgusted, as I journeyed on, to find how little men were disposed to make sacrifices for so great a cause. In one part of it, I went over nearly two thousand miles, receiving repeated refusals. I had not secured one witness within this distance. This was truly disheartening.[70]

Clarkson may also have been disheartened to learn that, of the 1,800 subscribers to the recently formed Sierra Leone Company, only nine were domiciled in Scotland. Of the nine, five are relevant here, namely: David Dale, Scott Moncrieff, Robert Grahame and John Campbell.[71]

This venture, heavily influenced by Wilberforce, Sharp, Thornton and Clarkson himself, was an attempt to pick up the pieces of the St. George's Bay Company and establish a 'Freetown' in Sierra Leone. Not only was the intention to establish a colony without slavery, where '*blacks and people of colour*' would have equal rights and equal treatment in all respects with whites, the subscribers themselves were also expected to be morally committed to the Abolitionist ideal.[72] One of the subscribers, C.B. Wadstrom, noted the '*purity*' of their motives and described them as '*the first promoters of the civilisation of Africa, who have done so much honour to this age, to this country and to mankind*'.[73] However, as might be expected:

> ...they trust that they are not too sanguine in looking forward to considerable and growing profits resulting from and connected with, the increasing prosperity of the country under their jurisdiction.[74]

As in many other aspects of Dale's life, the combination of social conscience and business acumen were clearly visible here. Shares were £50 each and Dale took five; John Campbell (most probably Dale's brother-in-law) took two and Robert Grahame (secretary of the Glasgow Abolition Committee) and Scott Moncrieff took one each.[75] Dale's stake seems modest but this was not at all unusual. The majority of the shareholders held fewer than five shares each. Granville Sharp, the major figure in the early days of the Sierra Leone movement held five shares. Sir Richard Arkwright held three; Thomas Clarkson, William Pitt and William Wilberforce each had ten.

It was decided that the company should be incorporated by Act of Parliament. Unsurprisingly, '*to the passing of this Act, the greatest opposition was made by the slave merchants and West India planters*'.[76] However, Henry Thornton, one of the Clapham sect was an M.P. and was a significant figure in guiding it successfully through Parliament in 1791.[77]

Despite Clarkson's pessimism about the Scottish contribution to the Abolitionist cause, he can have had no complaints about Dale's efforts. In 1791 the Sierra Leone Company was incorporated by Parliament with Dale as one of the few Scottish shareholders. Earlier that year, the Glasgow Society for the Abolition of the Slave Trade had been formed – three years after the larger and always more influential Edinburgh Society (the terms 'Society' and 'Committee' seem to be largely interchangeable at this time).[78] By 1792 there were five committees in total – Edinburgh, Glasgow, Paisley, Perth, Aberdeen. That same year, there were 185 Scottish petitions to Parliament (from a total of 572 across Britain) – a significant rise from the 1788 figure of only sixteen petitions from Scotland.[79]

Whatever Clarkson's view of events in Scotland, David Dale was elected as chair of the Glasgow Society in 1791. Unfortunately, all records relating to this society seem to have disappeared. It is obvious, however, that Dale's status among the merchant classes must have been considerable, given his own business interests and his position as banker and financier. Clearly, a careful course would have to be steered if the aims of the Society were to be achieved. The fact is, however, that he did agree to tread such a path at a time when its direction was only vaguely mapped out and when, eleven years prior to Abolition, opposition was everywhere to be found.

The Glasgow Society's first job was to publicise the London Society's *Abstract of Evidence* on the slave trade. There were several versions of the original 128-page document. Whyte notes that the Edinburgh Society produced a 25-page summary of the *Abstract* in 1792, which was prefaced by *A Short Address to the people of Scotland on the Subject of the Slave Trade* and that, although the intention was to distribute it throughout Scotland, most of the printing was funded by the Edinburgh Society itself.[80] However, a full year earlier, in January 1791 the Glasgow Society apparently agreed to pay for its own printing and to append to it a copy of the infamous drawing illustrating the stowage of human cargo on board a British slave ship.

Glasgow's version of the pamphlet was entitled *An Address to the Inhabitants of Glasgow, Paisley and the Neighbourhood concerning the African Slave Trade, by a Society in Glasgow* and was printed by Alex. Adam in Glasgow in January 1791. The preface reads as follows:

> Glasgow, 18th Jan. 1791
> At a Meeting of the Society in Glasgow for co-operating with the other Societies in Britain, in effecting the abolition of the Slave-trade: DAVID DALE, Esq. in the Chair.
>
> There was read over to the Meeting, a paper on the Slave-trade, intended to be addressed to the inhabitants of Glasgow, Paisley and the neighbourhood, which being considered, is approved of, and ordered to be printed at the expence of the Society, and a copy of the Section of the Slave-ship, published by the Society in London, to be annexed to every Copy of the address
>
> (Signed) DAVID DALE
>
> N.B Papers for obtaining Subscriptions, are appointed to be lodged in the Royal Bank Office; and the Tontine Coffee-room, Glasgow.[81]

This was a very public commitment to the abolition movement, particularly from a prominent member of the merchant class in the relatively early days of the Scottish campaign. It was also a fairly bold move to link the campaign, firstly, with the Royal Bank, provider of finance and credit to other merchants and, secondly, with the Tontine, meeting house of the Glasgow merchants.

The paper itself details some of the sufferings endured by those enslaved. Significantly for a pamphlet aimed at Glasgow merchants who profited from trade with the West Indies, it goes on to address the West India lobby directly, and offers a number of arguments. Firstly, it argues that, '*if the trade be founded on iniquity*', it ought to be abandoned, whatever the consequences. Secondly, it is suggested that the slave trade was as impolitic as it was unjust. Thirdly, any '*inconveniences*' attending abolition would be inconsiderable and temporary. Finally, in time, abolition would be advantageous to trade.[82] The paper was referring to the trading of slaves, not the institution of slavery itself. If slaves were treated well, such amelioration would mean that they would reproduce and there will be no need for a slave trade. The Society rejected completely the idea that slaves should be treated harshly and simply replaced with new ones imported from Africa. '*This system is so contrary to every sentiment of humanity and religion that it must be rejected with abhorrence*'.[83] To mollify the West India lobby in the city, the issue of emancipation was firmly dealt with:

> ...the present rude and uncultivated state of the slaves does not admit the thought. All that is just now in contemplation is to put an end to the importation of fresh slaves into the British West Indies.[84]

However, in time, slaves might expect:

> ...a higher degree of liberty. A state of well-regulated vassalage would be an important step in the process; this at length might give way to the enjoyment of the full rights of freemen. Should that day ever arrive, there is every reason to believe that the prosperity of those islands, and the happiness of their inhabitants, would go hand in hand.[85]

Dale and his Committee were well aware of what they referred to as 'powerful opposition from the contracted views and prejudices of interested persons' but the paper ends with a rallying call for support (including financial) from the inhabitants of Glasgow, Paisley and the neighbourhood 'whose manufactures and trade are, by the blessing of God, in so thriving a condition', and is nothing if not optimistic in hoping that even those involved in trade with the West Indies would also contribute, refusing to believe that, 'in this enlightened age, a narrow selfishness and a sordid attention to mere profit and loss has taken such a hold of mankind as to deaden their feelings of right and wrong and to render them indifferent to the sufferings of their fellow creatures'.[86]

According to The Star, a London newspaper, the committee (or 'The Glasgow Society' as it was often called) met again in April 1791, with Dale in the chair, resolving among other things, to express their gratitude to Wilberforce and his supporters in Parliament 'who displayed the most generous and enlightened sentiments in the vindication of liberty and truth'. The committee re-stated their opposition to the trade, referring to it as a 'disgrace to the nation of Great Britain' and resolved that the Glasgow Society would 'cheerfully contribute to defray what further expense may be requisite for seconding the intentions of those able and public-spirited members of Parliament' who remained loyal to the cause. They also resolved in the meantime to make a further remittance to Mr. Granville Sharp, chairman of the London Society, of one hundred guineas.[87] The notice was signed by Dale.

William Dickson.
Friends Library, London.
© Religious Society of Friends in Britain.

There appears to be no extant information on the work of the Glasgow Committee until almost exactly one year later, when William Dickson (1757–1823), a Scot originally from Moffat and a former Secretary to the Governor of Barbados, was sent by the London Committee (principally by Clarkson) to distribute the Abstract, with the intention of increasing the number of Parliamentary petitions from Scotland.

Dickson was in Scotland from 5th January until 19th March, 1792 and travelled considerable distances, visiting (and often re-visiting) some 38 towns, from Inverness in the north to Kirkcudbright in the south.[88] Given that he often described the roads as 'shocking' or 'execrable', this was quite a feat.[89] Dickson's diary of the trip is illuminating. There are 'Instructions' from Clarkson, in which Dickson is warned that arguments should be confined to abolition, not emancipation, which was clearly in harmony with Glasgow's Address the previous year. Any Scottish committee which might be formed should not attempt to go it alone but should take their lead from the Edinburgh and Glasgow Committees. Dickson was further cautioned against persuading people to sign petitions. Signatures should seem to come from individuals' own personal feelings after having read the *Abstract*.[90]

At first sight it might seem unnecessary to caution Dickson in this way. He was well aware, for example, of the bloodshed which the slave rebellion had caused in the French colony of Saint Dominique. The '*Domingo affair*', as he called it, had damaged the cause of abolition. Events in France had not helped matters and he reminded himself '*not to touch on the French Revolution*'.[91] Perhaps, however, Clarkson was aware of Dickson's sometimes impatient and occasionally intemperate and mercurial nature. There seems to be little doubt from Dickson's *Letters on Slavery* of 1789, that he was a gradualist but there are several occasions in his diary where he appears to portray himself as a supporter of immediate abolition, something which Dale and Moncrieff may have sensed in him, Dale more so than Moncrieff. Dale was certainly more cautious in his dealings with Dickson. Dickson was undoubtedly capable of some fairly extreme views, bordering occasionally on the bizarre. In his *Hints to the people of the United Kingdom in General and Northern Britain in Particular on the Present Important Crisis and some Interesting Collateral Subjects*, albeit written a few years later in 1803, readers are treated to various diatribes on the glories of the British Constitution, an attack on the unnecessary, outlandish luxuries of modern times such as butcher meat, calicoes, muslins and silks (woollens were preferred) and the '*miserable outlandish slop called tea*', before the paper descends into an hysterical call to arms against Napoleon.[92]

Dickson arrived in Edinburgh on 9th January 1792 where he was a dinner guest of Dale's brother-in-law, John Campbell. Dale was in Edinburgh at the time and Dickson was introduced to him:

> In company with Mr. Dale, Mr. Sherriff (Leith), Mr. Alison (who introduced me) and other Gentl. (and ladies) all friends to our cause.[93]

The strategy was clear. Edinburgh, as the largest and most influential committee would be the centre of Dickson's business and he would proceed from town to town, using letters of introduction from members of each committee. To that end, the Edinburgh Committee formally wrote to Dale and the Glasgow Committee, asking that they meet with Dickson. Consequently, Dickson set off for Glasgow on 17th January, armed with two letters – one for Dale, and one for the Committee. Given that he had already dined with Dale in Edinburgh, this may seem strange but was clearly designed for public consumption, i.e. to avoid giving any impression that petitions were being organised or promoted.

There are hints that Dickson's impatience (even at this stage) with the gradualist approach was problematic and it was obviously contrary to the spirit of Clarkson's instructions. It is certainly true that Dale and Moncrieff (who was also heavily involved with the Glasgow Committee) were generally wary of overstating the case – as Dickson suggests:

> Waited on Mr. Dale & Mr. Moncrief (sic) who, mentioning C[ampbell]'s letter on Sugar and F[rench] R[evolution] said he was afraid his honest zeal would hurt our cause.[94]

At the committee meeting the previous evening, Dale had been in the chair but, according to Dickson:

> ...he and Mr. S. Moncrief left us very early and before I had started my business fully. Rather disappointed at this but told business was the cause.[95]

Despite his disappointment with Dale and Moncrieff, Dickson was able to conclude that the committee members present (nine in total, including Dale and Moncrieff) were '*all hearty friends*'.[96] A week later, he dined '*at Mr. Monteith's*' in St. Andrew's Square, Glasgow.[97] Although it is not clear which member of the family he is referring to, the family's main offices were in St. Andrew's Square under the name of John Monteith & Co. Whether this was merely a social event or an expression of the family's support for abolition is not clear but there are no further mentions of any of the Monteiths in Dickson's diary.

In fact, Scott Moncrieff appears to have been more helpful than Dale. Dickson certainly encountered Moncrieff more often – sharing breakfast and tea with him on several occasions during January 1792. On his return to Glasgow from Kilmarnock, Dickson again had more success with Moncrieff than with Dale:

> Applied to Mr. S. Moncrief and Mr. Dale, along with Mr. Pattison for letters [of introduction] to Paisley. Mr. Dale could not but Mr. S[cott] M[oncrieff] gave me one to Revd. Mr. James Alice.[98]

Moncrieff actually gave Dickson several letters of introduction but was cautious when Dickson raised the possibility of including Greenock (a major port of entry for materials from the West Indies) in his tour. Moncrieff thought Greenock 'not to be attempted'.[99] Dale is not mentioned in this exchange and it may simply be that he left Moncrieff to deal with day-to-day matters relating to Dickson, in the same way that he left Moncrieff to look after much of the Royal Bank work. However, it may also be that Dale recognised Dickson's zealous approach and its potential to damage the gradualist cause. Dickson was sometimes prone to outbursts in public, despite his concern about the effect of issues such as the Domingo affair and the French Revolution on public sentiment. At dinner with one Hector McNeill and others (with whom Dickson was barely acquainted), McNeill offered a toast to gradual abolition. Dickson wrote in his diary, 'I drank to immed[iate]'.[100]

Nevertheless, the Glasgow Committee did help Dickson contact many influential people across Scotland. Many of them were clergymen and others were influential in other ways. Copies of the *Abstract* were distributed across the country, although there were often problems with the supply lines. Not all the letters of introduction were well received, even by the clergymen. Doctor Dalrymple in Ayr, for example, was 'cold' and 'had objections' and was apparently worried about Magistrates with connections to the West Indies.[101] Similarly, Glasgow Magistrates could not be persuaded to petition, even although Dale was one of them at this time. Dale's friend, business partner and fellow philanthropist, George Dempster, whom Dickson visited at the latter's home in Dunnichen, Forfar, 'was not ... very keen', although the reason is not entirely clear. Dickson simply observes that Dempster had scruples about compensation to planters.[102] There was, however, support from the churches, towns and cities across Scotland, led by Edinburgh and Glasgow but also strongly supported by Aberdeen, Perth and Paisley.[103] Whatever Dale's personal opinion of Dickson, the Glasgow Society played its part during Dickson's tour and it is worth looking at what exactly Dale was putting his name to. At a General Meeting of the Society on 1st February 1792, with Dale in the chair, the members resolved;

> ...that the traffic in the human species is founded on the grossest injustice, is attended with the utmost cruelty and barbarity to an innocent race of men and is productive of ruin and desolation of a country which the efforts of the well-directed industry of Great Britain might contribute to civilise.[104]

On Commerce and the Enlightenment:

> [the slave trade] ... is directly repugnant to the primary laws of nature, so it can neither be palliated from any views of commercial advantages or public expediency and that its continuance, in this enlightened age, is disgraceful to the nation and utterly inconsistant (sic) with the profession of Christians.[105]

The Glasgow Society was aware that, despite considerable opposition and delay nationally, they were swimming with a new tide and that 'men of the highest rank, influence and political knowledge' all agreed in expressing their 'abhorrence and detestation of this infamous traffic'. They argued that the nation at large was against it and that there was a 'great mass of evidence' being laid before the House of Commons. Despite the strong language throughout, the resolution makes it clear that they are proposing gradual abolition of the trade which would, in time, lead to a 'moderate and gradual regulation and improvement in the condition of the slaves...'. The statement, signed by Dale, concludes by 'loudly' calling on:

> ...all ranks and descriptions of persons whose hearts are not dead to the feelings of nature, to the precepts of morality and to those duties and charities inculcated by the mild and pure and beneficent spirit of the Christian Religion to come forward

and to join the general voice of supplication to Parliament in favour of so many of our fellow creatures, the victims of a horrible traffic which can subsist only by the unceasing ravages of treachery, rapine and murder.[106]

It is clear that Dale was very obviously (and very publicly) associated with the cause, a view perhaps endorsed by the statement from the secretary, Robert Grahame, which followed it. When Dale left the chair, the meeting:

...resolved unanimously that the thanks of the meeting be given to the Chairman for his unwearied and manly support of views and measures fraught with so much humanity. And that the present Resolution of this Society be immediately published in the Glasgow, Edinburgh and London newspapers.[107]

Another copy of the document was to be produced and lodged in '*a proper place*' in the city, so that all might sign up. In fact, several copies were made of what was then referred to as *The Petition of the Society in Glasgow for the Abolition of the Slave Trade* and these were lodged in the Session Houses of the Tron Church, the Chapel of Ease and the Relief Church in the Dovehill. They were available for signing '*every lawful day between the hours of one and three afternoons*'.[108]

At almost exactly the same time, the Edinburgh Society lodged copies of its own petition in three city churches and both Edinburgh and Glasgow Societies sent their petitions to Parliament the following month, Glasgow's appearing in the business of the House on 28th March.[109] At this time, petitions were a daily event; twenty two came before the House on 28th March, four of which were from Scotland. It is not clear how many signatures the Glasgow petition contained but it was certainly well short of Edinburgh's 10,885 signatures – a total '*exceeded in any city outside London only by Manchester*'.[110]

On April 17th, some two weeks after Parliament expressed its notional support for abolition of the trade on 2nd April 1792, *The Star* newspaper reported another meeting of the Glasgow Society where members had expressed their gratitude to (and continued support for) Wilberforce, Pitt, Fox and others '*for their generous and public spirited exertions*'. Interestingly, the Glasgow members stated their opposition to partial or gradual abolition, believing that plantation owners were likely to '*employ every expedient to retard or prevent such a measure*' arguing that total abolition was the only way to avoid '*endless disputes and inextricable difficulties*' between governments. The paper published a copy of the Society's resolution signed by Dale as chair:

That it is the duty of every friend of humanity and justice to guard against every attempt for misleading the people by false appearances of gratifying their wishes, and to use all Constitutional means for procuring the real, speedy and effectual Abolition of a Trade which now stands condemned by the decision of our National representatives, a decision so strongly supported by the voice of the people, that we can have no doubt that it must be carried into immediate execution – Signed by desire, and in the name of the Meeting.[111]

These were strong words in the early, optimistic days of the Abolition campaign and, given that Dale personally favoured gradual abolition, it is interesting that he allied himself so strongly with the cause of 'immediate' abolition. As the fight continued, vested interests were mobilised, and real concerns were aired about social unrest in Britain and France. It is not difficult to understand why the 'gradualist' approach to Abolition became more appealing.

An Enlightened Age?

The Glasgow Society's resolution talks of an '*enlightened age*' but there is a debate to be had regarding the extent to which any age can be called 'enlightened' which allowed the slave trade to exist for so long and which seemed so reluctant to abolish it. It is also essential to remember that 'emancipation' was nowhere on the horizon, even in 1807, and that it took a further 27 years before the government outlawed the institution of slavery, while at the same time feeding the Lancashire mills, the power houses of the Industrial Revolution, with huge amounts of slave cotton.

In late 18th-century Scotland, as elsewhere, it was perfectly acceptable to profit indirectly from slave cotton and sugar (as it had been a generation earlier with tobacco) and yet condemn the trading of slaves with all its brutality. Some established Enlightenment figures did condemn slavery outright – Adam Smith and Francis Hutcheson, for example – and there were many figures from the Established and Dissenting churches who spoke out against it or who were at least prepared to support Dickson in his quest for petitions to Parliament.

However, there was certainly what might be called a 'duality' of view here. Scots, many of them with a church connection, were owners and managers of slave plantations. They were also plantation doctors, administrators, merchants, overseers and clergymen. The capital for such ventures came from banks such as the Royal Bank of Scotland. Linen from the east coast was woven into cloth (and made into clothes) for slaves in the West Indies. Bandanas made in Glasgow and dyed in Dale's Turkey Red factory were sent to the slave colonies. It would seem, as Devine argues, that 'eminent Scots had little difficulty with slavery'.[112] Presbyterianism itself may have had a part to play in explaining why Scots in the West Indies embraced slavery so enthusiastically:

> With its stern rules, invigilation and penances, the Kirk had evolved a type of Scot uniquely fitted to serve the empire as officer, or policeman, overseer, manager; a Scot with an inbred instinct for harrying the unregenerate poor, or Negroes, or natives, for their own good as well as his employer's.[113]

On another level, despite the fact that academics, economists and philosophers condemned it, figures such as David Hume who was hugely influential in Europe and the U.S. (where he found support from Alexander Hamilton and James Madison), was sometimes less than committed to the abolitionist cause, at least at this point. Hume had claimed that there was 'a uniform and constant difference' between peoples and that negroes were naturally inferior. According to Hume, 'there never was a polished society but of the white race, to which all others are naturally inferior'.[114] Further:

> There never was a civilised nation of any other complexion than white, nor ever any individual, eminent either in action or speculation. No ingenious manufacturers among them, no arts, no sciences. There are negro slaves dispersed all over Europe, of which none ever discovered any symptoms of ingenuity.[115]

These may not in themselves be arguments for slavery per se but were inevitably seized upon by those who wished to validate it. This kind of view had a precedent. John Locke's efforts at a Constitution of Carolina had asserted the rights of every 'Freeman' of Carolina to 'absolute power and authority over his slaves', while at the same time asserting freedom of conscience, trial by jury and the right of any man to 'lawfully kill another who attempts to make a slave of him'.[116] William Dickson refers to this as an 'abominable jumble of slavery and absurdity'.[117]

This dualism or tension inevitably found its way in to the culture and literature of the time, including Scottish culture. The work of Robert Burns is a good example of this. Burns' 'egalitarian' work is well known, e.g. his celebration of common humanity in A Man's a Man for a' that, and The Slave's Lament and many other poems. However, Burns was poised to leave Scotland in 1786 to become a bookkeeper (often a synonym for 'overseer') on a plantation in Port Antonio, Jamaica. Almost penniless and in the midst of an emotional crisis involving Jean Armour, he wrote of his difficulties in trying to forget Jean and her 'ingratitude and perjury'. What he refered to as 'the grand cure' for his woes is the ship which was to take him out to Jamaica.[118] It was only the publication of the Kilmarnock edition of his poems and its subsequent success which prevented his departure.

The ability to hold two philosophically competing or contradictory views was not a uniquely Scottish phenomenon, although it might be argued that there was something in the Scottish psyche which lent itself to 'dualism'. R.L. Stevenson a century later undoubtedly raised the issue in Dr Jekyll and Mr. Hyde and, a further 50 years on, 'Caledonian Antisyzygy' (the combination of opposites) reappears as a theme in Scottish writing:

...a reflection of the contrasts which the Scot shows at every turn, in his political and ecclesiastical history; in his polemical restlessness; in his adaptability, which is another way of saying that he has made allowance for new conditions; in his practical judgement, which is the admission that two sides of the matter have been considered ... we need not be surprised to find that in his literature the Scot presents two aspects which appear contradictory...[119]

There may well be some mileage in this but the explanation for the 'duality' is likely to be more prosaic:

...despite educated and enlightened Scots having a philosophical distaste for slavery, social and economic factors could outweigh this and enable many of them to accept a living through its fruits.[120]

Duncan Rice offers a similar view:

In short, Scotland was a society whose intellectual and religious leaders had turned against slavery, without developing the slightest conception that anything should be done about it.[121]

Rice argues further (and convincingly) that the slave trade was never going to be abolished as long as the argument against it remained intellectual and secular. In such circumstances, there was no compulsion to apply it in practical terms against such an established institution.[122] Until the evangelists of the late 18th century began to impact on things, and until economic forces indicated that slavery was becoming less viable, little could really change. Significantly, all three elements were in place from the 1780s in Scotland, when Dale was beginning his career in earnest.

As the century wore on, attitudes to the slave trade clearly began to change – influenced by economic and religious (particularly evangelical) arguments against it. Dale could have ignored it, as many did for a long time. He was not directly involved in the trading of slaves. But, as so often in his life, he took a principled and public stand, albeit a 'gradualist' approach to the slavery issue. It is difficult to see what more he might have done, given the political, social and economic climate of the time. He was not an international Enlightenment figure of the stature of Adam Smith or Robert Burns (whose *Slave's Lament* rings rather hollow) and he was not a politician, yet he was part of an Enlightenment movement prepared to challenge the trading of slaves and to use what influence he had to make a stand, while trying to remain in business.

It is also worth noting that this 'dualism' was most certainly not confined to Scotland or to Europe. British observers of events in France during the Revolution were well aware that the '*white slaves of France*' had burst their bonds.[123] They were equally well aware of the Terror which followed – a Terror undertaken in the name of liberty, equality and fraternity. James Elmes, referring to the slave uprising in Domingo referred to the French as '*pretended advocates of liberty, equality and the rights of man whose wild, murderous cause the negroes did but imitate*'.[124]

While Dale may have had one eye on his own business interests, he did speak out against slavery and he did work towards abolition. This was far in excess of the efforts of major figures across the Atlantic – figures who might have been expected to take a leading role in the abolition of slavery in the New World. The American Colonies had fought for freedom from the 'slavery' of British rule, inspired by noble ideals such as the rights of man, liberty and freedom. Both George Washington and Thomas Jefferson, however, were slave owners and Washington, in particular, was reluctant to give them up. He '*persisted in it till the day of his death*'.[125] Dickson (never one to understate a case) berated those Americans '*who bawl about liberty and equality at a democratic meeting and then go home and flog their slaves*'.[126] He saw Washington as President of the USA, asserter of the Rights of Mankind '*and slave-holder in Virginia*' with '*the sword of Liberty*' in one hand '*and with the other, a whip*'.[127] Washington had other detractors who saw him as a land speculator and '*an aloof Virginia gentleman*'.[128] Both Washington and Jefferson, while ostensibly republicans were, according to some, ultra conservatives, prone to ceremonial trappings.[129] In addition, Brion Davis notes that Washington '*never ennobled the anti-slavery cause with a touch of his enormous prestige*' and failed to support even the most cautious of Quaker campaigns against the slave trade.[130] It seems that Samuel Johnson was prescient indeed when he noted as early as 1758 that slavery was nowhere more patiently endured than in countries once inhabited by '*the zealots of liberty*'.[131] A few years later, referring almost certainly to Washington and Jefferson, he asked pointedly:

How is it that we hear the loudest yelps for liberty among the drivers of negroes?[132]

The ability, then, to hold apparently conflicting views in the mid/late 18th century was not confined to Scotland, Great Britain or Europe, it would seem. Many came to change their views as the abolition and then emancipation movements gathered strength. There would seem to be nothing unusual in agreeing the principle of abolition while profiting directly or indirectly from the trade at this point in history. It is to Dale's credit that he was prepared to ally himself with the national movement to abolish the trade, fully aware that the institution of slavery was the real source of the problem, but equally aware that the powerful merchants in the city could and would move only gradually. Public opinion, the fluctuating price of slaves, the influence of the churches – all made the 1807 abolition increasingly likely (albeit as a first step) but in the 1790s, things had to move slowly. Above all, Dale's involvement with the abolitionists was entirely consistent with his moral view of the world and his willingness to take a public stand on important ethical and social matters, while at the same time ensuring that his business was successful enough to keep his workforce in employment and to sustain his influential position in the city and beyond.

References: Chapter 12

1   With the exception of a passing reference in Iain Whyte's important work on Scotland and black slavery. See Whyte, I. (2006) *Scotland and the Abolition of Black Slavery*. Edinburgh: E.U.P..

2   Devine, T.M. (2004) *Scotland's Empire 1600–1815*. London: Penguin, p.xxiv.

3   Ibid., pp.69–70.

4   Ibid., p.221.

5   Brion Davis, D. (2006) *Inhuman Bondage. The Rise and Fall of Slavery in the New World*. Oxford: O.U.P., p.104.

6   Adapted from Cooke, A. (2012) 'An Elite Revisited: Glasgow West-India merchants 1783–1877', *Journal of Scottish Historical Studies*, 32.2, November: 127–165, p.129. This is itself an adaptation from Jackson, G. (1995) 'New Horizons in Trade', in Devine, T.M. and Jackson, G. (eds), *Glasgow, Volume I: Beginnings to 1830*. Manchester. M.U.P., p.219.

7   Corry, J. (1807) *Observations Upon the Windward Coast of Africa*. London: G. & W. Nicol, facing p.33.

8   Devine, T.M. *Scotland's Empire*, Intro, xxvii. See also Rice, C.D. (1975) *The Rise and Fall of Black Slavery*. London: Macmillan, p.145.

9   Orr, W. 'Slave Labours' in *The Scotsman* (Weekend p.3), 30th June 1990. Cited in Whyte, I. (2006) *Scotland and the Abolition of Black Slavery*. Edinburgh: E.U.P., pp.15–16.

10   Ibid.

11   Devine, T.M., *Scotland's Empire*, pp.73–79.

12   *Jones's Directory or Useful Pocket Companion Containing an Alphabetical List of the Names and Places of Abode of the Merchants, Manufacturers, Traders and Shopkeepers in and about the City of Glasgow Compiled as Accurately as the Time Allowed Would Admit*. Published by John Mennons Editor of *The Glasgow Advertiser*, September 1787.

13   Devine, T.M. (1978) 'An 18th Century Business Elite: Glasgow-West India Merchants, c.1750–1815' in *Scottish Historical Review*, Vol. 57. pp.40–67, p.54.

14   Ibid., p.42.

15   Ibid., p.44.

16   Ibid., p.53.

17   David Dale to Claud Alexander, 25th May 1793. *Dale–Alexander Correspondence, 1787–1797*. Glasgow City Archives. MS 63/11.

18   Dale to Alexander, 24th March 1794, *Dale–Alexander Correspondence*, MS 63/17.

19   Reid, R. ('Senex') (1884) *Glasgow Past and Present*, 3 vols. Glasgow: D. Robertson. Vol. III, p.374.

20   Ibid., Vol. III, pp.379.

21   Burton, A. (1984) *The Rise and Fall of King Cotton*. London: BBC/Deutsch Ltd., p.49.

22   Reid, R. *Glasgow*, Vol. III, p.370.

23   *The Scots Magazine*, 1790, p.164, cited in Reid, R. (1884) Glasgow, Vol. III, pp.369–70.

24   Baines, E. (1835) *History of the Cotton Manufacture in Great Britain*. London: Fisher, p.347.

25   Ibid., p.302.

26   Ibid., pp.303 & 367.

27   *New Lanark Monthly Report & Wage Book, including Boarders. 1801–02* Gourock Ropeworks MSS. University of Glasgow Archives UGD 42/7/10 Also *Report Book* - monthly, 1803–1808. Gourock Ropeworks MSS. University of Glasgow Archive UGD 42/7/11.

28   Daniels, G.W. (1916) 'American Cotton Trade with Liverpool under the Embargo and Non-Intercourse Acts'. *American Historical Review*, Vol. 21, January 1916, p.276.

29 Dale to Alexander, 12th April, 1788. Glasgow City Archives. MS 63/4.

30 Reid,R. (1884) *Glasgow*, Vol. I, p.370.

31 Ibid., Vol. I, pp.494-5.

32 *The Glasgow Journal*, 4th December. 1758 in Reid, R. (1884) *Glasgow*, Vol. III, p.370.

33 *The Glasgow Journal*, 11th September 1766, in Reid, R. (1884) *Glasgow*, Vol. III, p.371.

34 Cited in Reid, R. (1884) *Glasgow*, Vol. III, p.370.

35 *Jones's Directory*, 1787.

36 Reid, R. (1884) *Glasgow*, Vol. III, p.283.

37 Ibid.

38 Ibid.

39 Ibid.

40 Ibid., p.284.

41 Ibid.

42 Ibid.

43 Dale to Alexander, 24th March 1794. Glasgow City Archives. MS 63/17.

44 John Aitcheson to Robert Reid, 2nd February 1855. Quoted in Reid, R. (1884) *Glasgow*, Vol. III, p.284.

45 Ibid.

46 Devine, T.M. *Scotland's Empire*, p.74.

47 Reid, R. (1884) *Glasgow*. Vol. II, p.168.

48 Brion Davis, D. (1975) *The Problem of Slavery*, p.39.

49 Orr, W. *Slave Labours*, p.3.

50 Whyte, I. (2006) *Scotland*, p.11.

51 Ibid., pp.13-14.

52 *The Edinburgh Evening Courant*, 30th August 1766; 27th September 1766; 6th December 1766. Quoted in Whyte, I. (2006) *Scotland*, p.14.

53 *The Edinburgh Advertiser*, 20th January 1769. Quoted in Whyte, I (2006) Scotland, p.14.

54 Orr, W. *Slave Labours*, p.2.

55 Ibid.

56 Whyte, I. (2006) *Scotland*, p.17.

57 Orr, W. *Slave Labours*, p.3.

58 Elmes, J. (1854) *Thomas Clarkson: A Monograph, Being a Contribution towards the History of the Abolition of the Slave Trade and Slavery.* London: Blackader & Co., p.195.

59 Whyte, I. (2006) Scotland, p.22.

60 *The Caledonian Mercury*, 17th January 1778, quoted in Whyte, I. (2006) *Scotland* p.18.

61 Cooke, A.J. (2009) 'The Scottish Cotton Masters', *Textile History*, 40(1): 29-50.

62 Cooke, A. *An Elite Revisited*, p.140. See also *Glasgow Chamber of Commerce Minutes.* 25th May 1784 where the Chamber remits the matter of sugar taxes (raised by Glasgow sugar merchants) to the West India Club requesting that the Club draw up a petition to be sent to the Lord Advocate. Glasgow City Archives. TD 1670/1/1.

63 Reid, R. (1884) Glasgow Vol. I, p.156.

64 Elmes, J. *Thomas Clarkson*, pp.142-145.

65 *The Scots Magazine.* 53, 1791, December. p.579.

66 Wadstrom, C.B. (1794) *An Essay on Colonization, Particularly Applied to the Western Coast of Africa.* (Two Parts.) Darton & Harvey, London. Part 1, p.120.

67 *The Gentleman's Magazine*, 58:6 (1788: December), p.1177 records the official purchase '*for ever*' of '*all the land, which is contained from the Bay, commonly called Frenchman's bay but by these presents changed to St. George's Bay, coastways up the River Sierra Leona, to Gambia Island, and southerly, or inland, form the river, five and twenty miles*'. This land was '*in behalf and for the sole benefit of the free community of settlers, their heirs and successors, lately arrived from England and under the protection of the British Government*'. The sale was agreed with one Chief referred to as 'King Tom' and a Chief Pabongee & Queen Yamacoaba who all marked the document with a cross. The 'presents' amounted to approximately £50 in value and included eight muskets, one barrel of gunpowder, some lead, iron, rum, tobacco and 24 laced hats.

68 This according to the diaries of Katherine Plymley, whose brother Joseph (Archdeacon Joseph Plymley, later Corbett) was a friend of Clarkson's and a member of the London Committee. See K. Plymley *Diaries, 1791-2*, Shropshire County Council Archives, MSS. 1066/4, p.6.

69 Ibid, p.6. Extract from Joseph Plymley's report '*in the Shrewsbury paper*'.

70 Clarkson, T. (1808) *The History of the Rise and Progress of the African Slave Trade by the British Parliament, 2 vols.* London: Longman, Hurst, Rees & Orme. *New Impression*, (1968) London: Frank Cass. Vol. II, p.196.

71   List of Subscribers in Wadstrom, C.B. (1794) *An Essay on Colonization, Particularly Applied to the Western Coast of Africa, with some free thoughts on Cultivation and Commerce. Also brief descriptions of the colonies Already Formed or Attempted in Africa, including those of Sierra Leona and Balama.* Two parts. London: Darton & Harvey. Part two, pp.341-353. The other Scots included two clergymen, one Excise Officer and two whose occupations are unknown.

72   Wadstrom, C.B. (1794) *An Essay on Colonization*, Part one, p.20.

73   Ibid., Part one, p.174 & Part two, p.340.

74   Ibid., Part two, p.23.

75   Ibid., List of Subscribers, Part two, pp.341-353.

76   *The Scots Magazine*, 53, 1791: December, p.580.

77   Following the Act, the numbers in Freetown were increased by an influx of black settlers from Nova Scotia - former slaves who had joined the British forces during the American Wars with the promise of land and freedom at the cessation of hostilities. Lt. John Clarkson, R.N., brother of Thomas, led the Nova Scotians to Freetown in 1792. The company survived, despite some major problems, until 1807 when it was succeeded by the African Institution. For more details, see C.B. Wadstrom, *An essay on Colonization*.

78   *The Caledonian Mercury*, 9th February 1792 refers to the Edinburgh Committee being formed in 1788.

79   Whyte, I. (2006) *Scotland*, p.85.

80   Ibid., p.88.

81   *An Address to the Inhabitants of Glasgow, Paisley and the Neighbourhood concerning the African Slave Trade, by a Society in Glasgow.* Glasgow: Alex Adam. January, 1791.

82   Ibid.,p.11.

83   Ibid., p.12.

84   Ibid., p.13.

85   Ibid., p.14.

86   Ibid., pp.14-15.

87   *The London Star*, 29th April 1791.

88   See Whyte, I. (2006) *Scotland*, p.92 for a map of Dickson's travels.

89   Dickson, W. *Diary of a Visit to Scotland 5th January–19th March 1792 on behalf of the Committee for the Abolition of the Slave Trade* (Friends Library, Temp MSS. 10/14). See entries for 28th February & 14th March 1792.

90   These instructions are handwritten inside the back cover of Dickson's Diary.

91   Dickson, W. *Diary*, 5th February 1792.

92   Dickson, W. (1803) *Hints to the people of the United kingdom in General and Northern Britain in Particular on the Present Important Crisis and some Interesting Collateral Subjects.* Edinburgh: Oliver & Co., pp.12-13.

93   Dickson,W. *Diary*, 9th January 1792.

94   Ibid., 19th January 1792.

95   Ibid., 18th January 1792.

96   Ibid., 18th January 1792.

97   Ibid., 26th January 1792.

98   Ibid., 23th January 1792.

99   Ibid., 23th January 1792.

100   Ibid., 17th January 1792.

101   Ibid., 21st January 1792.

102   Ibid., 7th February 1792.

103   See Whyte, I. (2006) *Scotland*, Chapter 3 for a fuller account.

104   *The Caledonian Mercury*, 9th February 1792.

105   Ibid.

106   Ibid.

107   Ibid.

108   *The Glasgow Courier*, 9th February 1792.

109   *House of Commons Journal*, Vol. 47, 28th March 1792.

110   Whyte, I. (2006) *Scotland*, p.89.

111   *The Star* (London), 17th April 1792.

112   Devine, T.M. (2004) *Scotland's Empire*, p.244.

113   Kiernan, V. 'Scottish soldiers and the conquest of India', in G. Grant & G. Simpson, (eds) (1992) *The Scottish Soldier Abroad, 1247-1967.* Edinburgh: John Donald, p.98, quoted in Devine, T.M. (2004) *Scotland's Empire*, pp.248-9.

114   Hume, D. (1753) *Essay on National Characters*, quoted in J. Elmes, *Thomas Clarkson* p.20.

115   Ibid.

116   Locke, J. (1669) *Fundamental Constitutions of Carolina*. No. 110 and *Treatise of Government* (1690), Chapter 3, quoted in Dickson, W. *Hints to the People*, pp.35–36.

117   Dickson, W., *Hints*, p.35.

118   R. Burns to David Brice, 12th June 1786 quoted in Bold, A. (ed) (1993) *Rhymer Rab, an Anthology of Poems & Prose by Robt Burns*. London: Black Swan, p.275.

119   Gregory Smith, G. (1919) *Scottish Literature*. London: Macmillan, pp.4/5 quoted in Bold, A. (1983) *Modern Scottish Literature*. London: Longman. N.B. Hugh MacDiarmid (C.M. Grieve) popularised the notion in the 1920s and 30s.

120   Whyte, I. *Scotland*, p.57.

121   Rice, C.D. (1983) 'Archibald Dalzel, the Scottish Intelligentsia, and the problem of Slavery', *Scottish Historical Review*, Vol LXII, 2: No. 174: October, p.121.

122   Ibid., p.133.

123   Elmes, J. *Thomas Clarkson*, p. xvii.

124   Ibid., p.240.

125   Dickson,W. *Hints to the People*, p.34.

126   Ibid., p.35.

127   Ibid., p.34.

128   Thistlethwaite, F. *The Great Experiment*, pp.24, 36.

129   Ibid., p.55.

130   Brion Davis, D. *The Problem of Slavery*, p.170.

131   Johnson, S. (1758) 'The Idler', No. 11, 24th June.

132   Johnson, S. (1775) 'Taxation, no Tyranny'.

Part 5

Philanthropy, Benevolence and Public Office

Chapter 13: Glasgow Charities, the Benevolent Magistrate and the Town's Hospital

It is difficult to separate Dale's provision of schooling from his charitable, philanthropic activities because in many ways they are one and the same thing. Although there was an agreement with the Edinburgh and Glasgow workhouses to provide reasonable conditions of employment, Dale exceeded these and provided a planned and coherent system of schooling for all his child employees, in parallel with living conditions which were in advance of anything to be found elsewhere in Britain at the time. To say that it was merely a reflection of a philanthropic or charitable nature is to ignore his shrewdness in business matters and his desire for a return on any form of investment, including philanthropic or charitable investments.

Also, the idea that Dale was simply a rich merchant who gave his money to deserving causes is too simplistic. It is true that he was more than sympathetic to requests from Dempster to help the unfortunate Highlanders in Spinningdale, and once again at New Lanark when *The Fortune* was shipwrecked. It is true also that he paid his workers' wages when the first mill was burned down. However, it should be borne in mind that business matters were often foremost in Dale's mind. The shipwreck was fortuitous in that it provided workers for New Lanark at a time when most of the local people were against this form of employment, which also helps to explain why Dale paid their wages after the fire. His donations to the British and Foreign Bible Society were plentiful, but this is hardly surprising, given his strong Christian faith. Similarly, as a figure with considerable social standing in the community, public gestures of a philanthropic nature would, to a certain extent, be expected of him and were bound to enhance this status.

However, it would be equally wrong to construe every philanthropic or charitable gesture or every attempt to provide his workers with more than was strictly necessary as some kind of carefully constructed investment plan. As with all 'philanthropic' acts, the return on investment could (and did) take a number of forms – including financial, personal and religious and sometimes a combination of all three.

By 1789, only six years after he moved into Charlotte Street, Dale's reputation as a philanthropist was already well established. Richardson's *Guide to Loch Lomond* is dedicated to Dale:

> To David Dale. In testimony of that esteem due to a character so truly respectable; illustrated by many acts of private and public beneficence tending, on the one hand, to soothe the distressed indigence and, on the other, to accelerate the progress of arts, trade and manufactures, this Guide to Loch Lomond is most respectfully published.[1]

Richardson was equally effusive about what he saw as Dale's philanthropic efforts in New Lanark, even at this early stage:

> The benevolence and utility of this institution is above all praise: and when the importance of Mr. Dale's immense colonial establishment is considered in a commercial point of view, it must be acknowledged that language does not afford appropriate terms to depict his merits.[2]

By 1806, the year of his death, this reputation for philanthropy and benevolence had spread far and wide:

> His ear was never shut to the cry of distress; his private charities were boundless; and every public institution which had as its object the alleviation or prevention of human misery in this world or in the world to come, received from him the most liberal support and encouragement.[3]

It is worth investigating how this reputation came about. Dale did certainly contribute to a wide range of small-scale, private charitable societies, often giving small sums on a regular basis. However, there were also much more public gestures of support, financial and otherwise, for good causes, ranging from donations to support the construction of new roads to extensive and public involvement with some of the city's most significant institutions such as the Royal Infirmary.

At the lesser end of the scale, he was happy simply to donate varying sums of money to what he considered to be deserving causes (and there were many to choose from) at home and abroad. In 1788 he sent money to a religious group in Belgium known as the Protestant Union (or, as *The Morning Chronicle* had it, the 'Protestants of Ostend') who were looking to build a Protestant church and maintain a minister in the face of opposition from the local Catholic population.[4] The Protestants accused the Catholics of creating '*unmerited and opprobrious stigma*' against the Reformed faith by '*weekly asserting that it is a political scheme and promoted only with interested and sinister views*'.[5] In response, some 30 supporters in England and 22 in Scotland rallied to the Protestant cause. The Scottish supporters (including James Finlay, James McIlwham and William Shortridge) each donated one guinea. Dale and William Gillespie, however, gave double that amount.

Dale also supported a military charity dedicated to '*affording a Provision for the Families of Warrant Officers, Seamen and Non-commissioned Officers in the Naval and Military Services as may fall by sickness or chance of War in the West Indies*'.[6] This was a fairly substantial organisation, funded largely by deductions from servicemen's pay. There were 52 subscriptions from Glasgow merchants, most of whom had interests in the West Indies. The biggest contributions (£30 each) came from the biggest merchant families – the Houstons, Stirlings, Buchanans, Dennistouns and Bogles. The vast majority of the individual subscribers gave only one or two guineas. Dale's contribution, however, was five guineas.[7]

In 1798, he sent a very respectable sum of ten guineas to the committee in Inverness who were raising funds for what was to become the Royal Northern Infirmary, built between 1799 and 1804.[8] A few years later, just months before he died, he sent a similar sum to Perthshire where there had been calls to support the growing Academy movement. The 'Perth Seminaries' were intended to be large, elegant buildings dedicated to a new curriculum which would include the usual grammar and English, but which would be expanded to include languages such as French and, most importantly, science subjects. Scott Moncrieff also supported this cause and contributed five guineas, half of Dale's subscription.[9]

Closer to home, Dale took a more active part in some of Glasgow's emerging institutions and charitable causes – often being named as a director or manager because of his financial contribution. Sometimes he was happy to leave the running of these organisations to others. More often than not, however, he became very actively involved with these groups and with the causes they espoused.

The Glasgow Humane Society

In 1790 Dale became a director of the newly-formed Glasgow Humane Society. According to two sources, a sum of £500 had been provided by Lawrence Coulter (whose family had helped to fund the Bridewell) '*for restoring Animation suspended by Drowning*'.[10] The first meeting of the founders took place in the Tontine Tavern on 16th August, 1790 where the aim was to elect office-bearers and to discuss how to raise more funds by subscription. The minutes record the election of Gilbert Hamilton as president, Dr. Robert Cleghorn as secretary and Robert Simpson as treasurer.[11] Although the extant minutes do not record the election of the other directors, the *Glasgow Mercury* did so. William Craig, David Dale and Gilbert Shearer became directors and Lawrence Coulter was named as an extraordinary director because of his brother's financial legacy.[12] It is interesting to note that the original capital of the Humane Society is declared as £200, which suggests that the original figure of £500 may be incorrect.[13]

Any individual who subscribed one guinea per year was eligible for election as a director and any public body subscribing £10 could nominate one of their number as a director. It seems that Dale was not on this occasion representing any public body and was involved in a personal capacity. He contributed one guinea per year, although more important would be his expertise as a fundraiser. He did live very near the banks of the Clyde and would have been aware of the dangers posed by the river. Dale was elected president of the Humane Society in 1792–1793 and again in 1793–1794.[14]

There was certainly a need for financial support. The Society had sent out 50 subscription papers but only eight were returned and although the total raised from these eight people came to a very respectable £83. 12s. 6d., more would be required.[15] The town council, meeting two days later, agreed to subscribe £10 and gave permission for the society to build a boathouse on the banks of the River Clyde *within the Green of Glasgow* but this was to be built at the society's own expense. Council support was not particularly evident. It took them five years to give permission to the Humane Society to build a covered place for mooring a boat with a room built over it to hold all the equipment necessary and *for the more conveniently performing their operations upon the bodies* of persons pulled from the river. Again, however, this was to be at the Humane Society's own expense.[16] The council was to have control over the building and could remove it at any time.[17] There was no return for Dale's money or time, except perhaps in terms of social recognition, so this appears as a genuinely charitable gesture.

Contributions such as these were private and, although recorded in minute books, were not particularly evident to the public. Although Dale *shunned the ostentatious display of benevolence* when it came to charitable work, it was often quite impossible to do so, especially if the charitable deeds were public works with institutions or aimed at large groups of people.[18] It was one thing, for example, to chair (as Dale did) a small group of eleven Glasgow merchants with the intention of raising money to build a statue in honour of that *illustrious statesman*, William Pitt, but it was quite another to charter ships and distribute food to starving people without the public knowing about it.[19] Similarly, as a man very much involved in the commercial, legal and public life of the city, it was extremely difficult to do good works and keep a low public profile although some of his affairs were better known than others. In April 1791, for example, he was asked by the chamber of commerce to consider the viability of a new road between Lanarkshire and England – a matter *of considerable importance*, according to the chamber minutes, but one which would not in itself attract much attention at that stage.[20] However, the situation was quite different a few months later. In November of that year, Dale chaired a meeting in Hamilton of the major landowners in the county of Lanark. Their purpose was to consider a draft Bill for the new Clydesdale road – *so much admired for its beautiful and picturesque scenery and so hugely beneficial to the numerous manufacturers ... establishing in the upper part of the County*. At that meeting, Dale *generously subscribed* £700 – a huge sum of money and one which was reported in many of the newspapers of the day.[21]

Much the same situation applied to his attempts to relieve famine and distress by supplying meal or grain at a reduced cost or, more often, gratis.[22] The first recorded instance of this was in March 1783 when he offered help to the poor of his native Stewarton:

> On Thursday and Friday last, Mr. David Dale, merchant here, opened sales of a quantity of meal made from pease, which he has imported for the relief of the poor, at the low price of ten pence per peck. His generosity and benevolence upon the present occasion has been exemplary. He sold the bulk of the pease at the market price but gave five bolls to the hundred to societies who purchased that quantity. He purchased meal to supply the working poor of the Parish of Stewarton, his native place, selling it at one penny a peck below what it cost him. The humane reader will feel pleasure in being informed of the liberality of this worthy citizen, whose private charities are not outdone by the most opulent of fortunes.[23]

Three months later, Dale bought more pease meal and beans from a James Brown of the Camlachie (Meal) Society. Between June and July he bought a total of 55 bolls of pease meal and 25 bolls of beans. The market price of both commodities had rocketed and the purchase cost Dale £98. 15s., although he paid only £35 cash at the time, the remainder to be paid at a later date.[24] The intended destination of this aid is unclear but it could have been an additional supply for Stewarton, Glasgow itself or Spinningdale.

In Spinningdale, the situation was so grave in 1783–1784 that the government had to send food.[25] When George Macintosh heard about the famine, he and Dale *and several Glasgow friends whose hearts were ever open to the appeal of want* sent money and five bolls of white pease which were distributed at cost or free amongst 80 people.[26] Several years later, Dale was involved with Macintosh in establishing the spinning mill there, in itself more an act of charity than anything else.

According to Andrew Liddell, Dale chartered several ships during the famine years of 1782, 1791–1793, and 1799. These were sent to America, Ireland and '*the Continent*' to buy grain and meal which was sold at cost price or less, '*thereby in great measure averting the threatened famine and preventing a still greater advance in prices*'.[27] The situation seemed to be particularly bad in 1799–1800 when there was a disastrous failure of the crops in Scotland, not helped by severe restrictions imposed by the Corn Laws. In Glasgow, the merchants and town council imported food to the value of £117,500 which they then sold as quickly as possible, losing £15,000 in the process.[28] Dale took matters into his own hands and sent a ship to America with orders to bring home as much grain (of any type) as could be had. The ship returned with Indian corn, then little known in Scotland and we are told that '*many a hungry family blessed the benevolent Magistrate*'.[29] In Lanarkshire, the Duke of Hamilton called a meeting in December of the local noblemen, gentlemen, and heritors to try and find a way of supplying the principal market towns in the county with grain and meal '*by voluntary subscriptions or otherwise*'. Both Dale and Owen attended the meeting but there is no record of what transpired as a result. Interestingly, it appeared that although the Duke was concerned about hunger in the County, he was equally concerned about the restlessness – '*tumults and illegal practices*' – which resulted from the high price of grain.[30]

Bridewell

Liddell, in his *Memoir of David Dale* simply notes that Dale was a frequent visitor to the Bridewell where he preached the Gospel to the inmates.[31] While this was undoubtedly the case, there is much more to Dale's involvement with offenders than preaching to them and donating money – significant as these were.

As early as 1786, Dale had been a supporter of John Howard's views on penal reform. To begin with, this support took the form of a donation of two guineas to a fund being raised for the purpose of erecting a statue to Howard. When Howard made it clear that he did not approve of the idea, the subscribers continued to raise money in the name of 'The Howardian Fund', dedicated to prison charities and reform. This was supported financially by a number of Glasgow businessmen (e.g. the Houstons, Buchanans and Finlays), and academics (John Anderson) although, true to form, Dale's contribution was double that of the other contributors.[32]

Less well-known is the fact that Dale subsequently became an important figure in bringing the new 'Bridewell' concept to Glasgow. For many years there had been (and there would continue to be) a prison for those convicted of criminal offences. For those who were poor or orphaned, sick or mentally ill, there was the Town's Hospital but the Bridewell was a new element in the penal system. In June 1789 Dale chaired a committee established by the town council with the purpose of '*procuring information on the subject of establishments for the punishment of crimes and reformation of criminals by means of bridewells and other places of confinement, at hard labour*'. The other members of the committee are not named but the report is signed by Dale as chairman.[33]

The committee had been considering reports from Oxford and Norfolk about a new and apparently successful scheme which dealt with offenders by way of Bridewells. The institution in Norfolk had gained a reputation as a model for such establishments, largely due to publicity engendered by Sir Thomas Beevor of Norwich, some of which reached Dale's committee. Thomas Bayley of Manchester, later involved with New Lanark, also contributed to the debate and the publicity. Beevor, '*influenced by Mr. Howard's book*' outlining the poor conditions in prison, had set up a '*Bridewell and Penitentiary House*' in Norfolk as an alternative.[34] Here, offenders (men and women, although the sexes were kept apart) were housed in solitary confinement in '*airy, neat and healthy cells*'.[35] Paid work (bunching hemp, spinning yarn and weaving cloth) was provided, although this had to be undertaken in the cells and the cost of the inmates' maintenance was deducted from their weekly wage. The aim was for '*a thorough reformation in their manners whereby they may ... become useful members of society*'.[36] They were short-term prisoners, incarcerated for a few days or, at most, a few weeks for offences which were minor but which still required punishment.[37] The house was run by a governor and other staff and the local magistrates were required to visit regularly and report to the local council. Penitence and reform were key principles – hence the weekly church services conducted by a local clergyman.

Dale and his committee were very impressed by this alternative to prison. The report makes it clear that he and the others felt that prison tended to ignore the element of reform and often made prisoners 'more profligate and vicious than before'.[38] Bridewells, it seemed, offered a real prospect of reforming character without the danger of what it called 'contamination' from those 'more experienced in wickedness' and the committee were in no doubt that such a system could work in Glasgow:

> ...how many fellow creatures may we not flatter ourselves will be rescued from vice and misery by the well-directed endeavours of the magistrates of so populous a city as Glasgow – the very idea must expand the heart of every benevolent being.[39]

The committee members were enthused by the idea. Dale reported that they were happy to impart 'such pleasing information' and that they wished to investigate further.[40] They must have done this with some speed because the *Statistical Account* reports that Glasgow's first Bridewell 'for the punishment and correction of lesser offenders' was established in 1789, the same year as Dale's *Report*.[41] According to this version of events, a granary building near the High Street was converted to 64 cells and run on exactly the same lines as the Bridewell in Norwich. Members of the town council, already required to visit the prison on a regular basis, now also had to include the Bridewell in their visiting schedule.

In fact, the Bridewell may have been located in a number of different buildings between 1789 and 1799. James Cleland's chronology of events seems more likely. He notes that the first Bridewell was an old manse which was 'fitted up as a house of correction for vagrants and women of dissolute character'.[42] It seems that the sentences were no longer restricted to a few weeks or months, however. *The Glasgow Courier* reported in December 1791 that a weaver in Glasgow had been sent to the Bridewell for twelve months for stealing shoes from a shop in the Saltmarket.[43] The original Bridewell building was too small and in 1793, inmates moved to the granary building referred to in the *Statistical Account*. The concept of a Bridewell must have found favour because the number of inmates increased and in 1799, helped by a significant legacy from the Coulter family (merchants in the city), the foundations were laid on the north side of Duke Street for a purpose-built Bridewell with 126 cells, a chapel, work room, public kitchens, an infirmary and store – all surrounded by a high wall.[44]

Dale, an enthusiastic supporter of the scheme, contributed the considerable sum of £250 to the 1799 project, a donation which the council recognised (somewhat understatedly) as 'a generous benefaction'.[45] The interest on this sum was to be applied 'in all time coming' towards a salary for a chaplain to the Bridewell.[46] The Bridewell embodied much that Dale believed in – Christian charity combined with a Calvinist approach to work. Redemption and a reformed character were the rewards for honest work. He may have had some reservations about the recommended periods of solitary confinement but at least these allowed for periods of reflection and penitence and, as the system established itself, more time was allowed for communal work.

Although he could not visit the Bridewell every week, Dale did visit occasionally to inspect on behalf of the council but more often to preach at the Sunday service. He may also have visited prisoners in the city's somewhat overcrowded jail in the Tolbooth, near the town hall. Before the new Bridewell was built, the *Glasgow Courier* reported in December 1791 that a gentleman of the city, 'justly distinguished for his benevolence' had 'added to his other various charitable donations by providing money to be used for purchasing a weekly waggon-load of coal to keep the prisoners warm in the Tolbooth jail'. Given Dale's concern about the effect of high coal prices on the poor and his impending purchase of the Barrowfield Coal Company, it is highly likely that the gentleman in question was David Dale. The *Courier* paid tribute to the mystery man:

> Of this gentleman it may truly be said, 'He hath a tear for pity, and a hand open as day for melting charity'.[47]

Overcrowding in the Tolbooth was eventually relieved when the jail and guard house were both rebuilt in 1810.[48]

The Magdalen Society

Dale's interest in prison reform also found expression in his support for the Magdalen Society, initially in Edinburgh (where John Campbell, his brother-in-law, was the secretary) and latterly in Glasgow, although Dale never lived to see the Glasgow Magdalen 'Asylum' (i.e. 'refuge') finally built in 1812. The charity, notorious in later centuries for its cruel and abusive treatment, started life innocently enough in England in 1758 and was originally dedicated to rehabilitating 'penitent prostitutes'.[49] The Scottish branch of this institution first appeaed in Edinburgh in 1797. It aimed to provide an asylum for 'dissolute women who might have a desire to return to the paths of virtue'.[50] Work was provided and, while this sometimes took the form of sewing and knitting, the women were mostly employed in laundry work – washing and dressing clothes for families outside the (high) walls of the institution. In Edinburgh, 90 women were received between 1797 and 1804. Of these, 33 had been placed in service or 'creditably settled in the world'; nine had been restored to their friends; two had died 'penitent and grateful' leaving 24 still in the house.[51] This charity was well supported financially by a substantial number of people, most of whom gave between one and three guineas. Dale and Robert Owen are recorded as giving £5 each during 1804.[52]

There are some key ideas associated with such a charity. Like the Bridewell, penitence is necessary for reform (perhaps even more so in the case of the Magdalen Society) and gratitude should be expressed for such charity. Naturally enough, these were both associated with a substantial religious input, eg., Scripture reading, thanksgiving, prayer. However, despite the rather stern air about it, the charity was well supported, largely because of its intention to reform and also because it offered practical help for women who were often sick or who had been abandoned in the streets. Reading was taught, and not merely through the medium of religious tracts. Books were provided which conveyed 'some amusement with instruction' and every attention was paid 'to promote their comfort, along with their improvement'.[53] The high wall was not, apparently, intended as a prison wall but more a recognition that the aims of the institution could not be achieved 'amid the bustle of active life'.[54]

The Glasgow branch of the Magdalen Society, although formed in 1801, did not purchase a building plot (behind the High Church) until 1804. It is possible that Dale (and Owen by this time) may have been involved, although there is little in the way of documented evidence. From Dale's perspective at least, the idea that individuals could be 'reclaimed from those vices which rendered them hurtful to the community' was one that he could fully support.[55] In Glasgow, however, Dale did not live to see the new building. Unspecified construction problems delayed matters and it was eventually completed on a different plot of ground some eight years later, in 1812, six years after Dale's death.[56]

The Magistrate

Dale's support for good causes and his relatively liberal approach to the treatment of offenders was often reflected in his duties in the public courts as a magistrate, where he 'won the golden opinions of his fellow citizens as he tempered justice with mercy'.[57] One source notes that he served for many years as a magistrate but there is no evidence for this.[58] It is known that he served on the bench between 1791–1792 and again in 1794–1795 because council records show that he had been elected as a bailie during those periods and the bailie generally served ex-officio as magistrates, although the position of people like 'River Bailies' in this respect is unclear.[59]

Exactly how many magistrates there were is also less than clear. Prior to 1801, there were three principal bailies from the merchants' ranks and two from the trades ranks but there may have been others drawn from the ranks of the town council. More significant is the fact that the job was exceptionally time-consuming and often very difficult. The *Statistical Account* for the City of Glasgow in 1793 noted that it was 'very laborious service' and that the difficulties attending to it were 'every day increasing' because of 'the irregularities of a numerous, increasing and opulent community'.[60] When Scott Moncrieff was appointed bailie/magistrate in October 1790, he refused the position and was fined the sum of £40 for doing so.[61] This was not a particularly unusual situation. It was sometimes difficult to find enough councillors and magistrates – 'proper persons of the merchant rank' – to fill the necessary positions, despite the fact that individuals were fined for refusing to accept the nominations and elections.[62] The *Statistical Account* reported that the duties were so demanding, many simply preferred to pay the fine.[63]

Dale was not one to shirk civic duties but he certainly found the position demanding. In a letter to Dr. Currie in June 1792, Dale wrote that his duties as a magistrate were taking up most of his time and attention and that, as a result, he had been rather neglectful of the mills in New Lanark.[64] It seems unlikely that Dale was ever unaware of events in New Lanark but it is not surprising that he was under pressure, given that the magistrates were involved in a wide range of activities. They were required to be present at every meeting of the town council and to chair numerous council committees. They had to attend every civic ceremony and procession (and there were many of these) dressed in their full court attire, including gold chains of office and they were undoubtedly pivotal figures in civic life. The number of magistrates was increased in 1801 but, prior to that date, there is little doubt that Dale and his colleagues were under pressure.

On the bench, he earned the reputation as a just and fair-minded individual. Never given to understatement, Robert Alison wrote some years later that 'the poor blessed him and affectionately distinguished him by the title of the benevolent magistrate'.[65] It is worth noting that the same people were responsible for physically attacking Dale (and others who were not licensed preachers) during the various ecclesiastical disruptions of the period – some of which are discussed in Chapter 15. Dale's grandson, Robert Dale Owen, took the view that magistrates at the time were men of unblemished integrity, strict honour and unblemished integrity – 'incorruptible men' and, while this may seem exaggerated, there is no reason to doubt Dale's charitable and benevolent approach to those who found themselves in court.[66] However, benevolence might also have its rewards for all involved – much like the situation in Dale's mills. When three boys appeared before him, Dale took the opportunity to exercise benevolence and restraint, while at the same time recruiting two new apprentices for New Lanark:

> On Saturday last, two boys of the name of McKenzie and McDonald, orphans, and a boy of the name of Skinner, who has been abandoned by his parents, were brought before Mr. Dale, the sitting Magistrate, accused of stealing poultry. Mr. Dale humanely offered to clothe them and to employ them at his cotton works at Lanark and we hear the Procurator Fiscal has, in consequence, applied to the Magistrates for authority to have them apprenticed for a reasonable number of years.[67]

The boys' reaction is not recorded but the *Courier*, at least, was no doubt that the apprenticeship was an act of charity.

The Town's Hospital

Dale's involvement with the pauper children from the Town's Hospital has been discussed in Chapter 6 but as a director, his involvement with this public institution was wide-ranging. As with his involvement with the Chamber of Commerce, it was something of a lifelong commitment. The Town's Hospital was situated in Glasgow's Great Clyde Street, not far from Charlotte Street and the Royal Bank offices in St. Andrew's Square.

It originally opened to receive the city's poor in 1733, largely as a result of pressure from the Kirk on the town council. An Act of the council a few years later legally secured the financial support of important bodies such as the Session and the Merchants' and Trades' Houses and it was considered to be:

> ...to the advancement of religion, virtue and goodness, and the public utility, honour and advantage of the country, that provision be made for the necessities of the Poor indigent Children, old decayed men and women and of others rendered unable to provide for themselves.[68]

In fact, bodies such as the Merchants' House and, in particular, the Trades House (where Dale served as secretary in 1787–1788) and its various incorporations were already significant providers of charitable support for their own members, as were the various churches, including the numerous Secessionist groups. There were also a number of well-endowed charitable mortifications in the city.[69] Overall, there was a substantial network of welfare support across the city, although much depended on the occupation of the male householder.

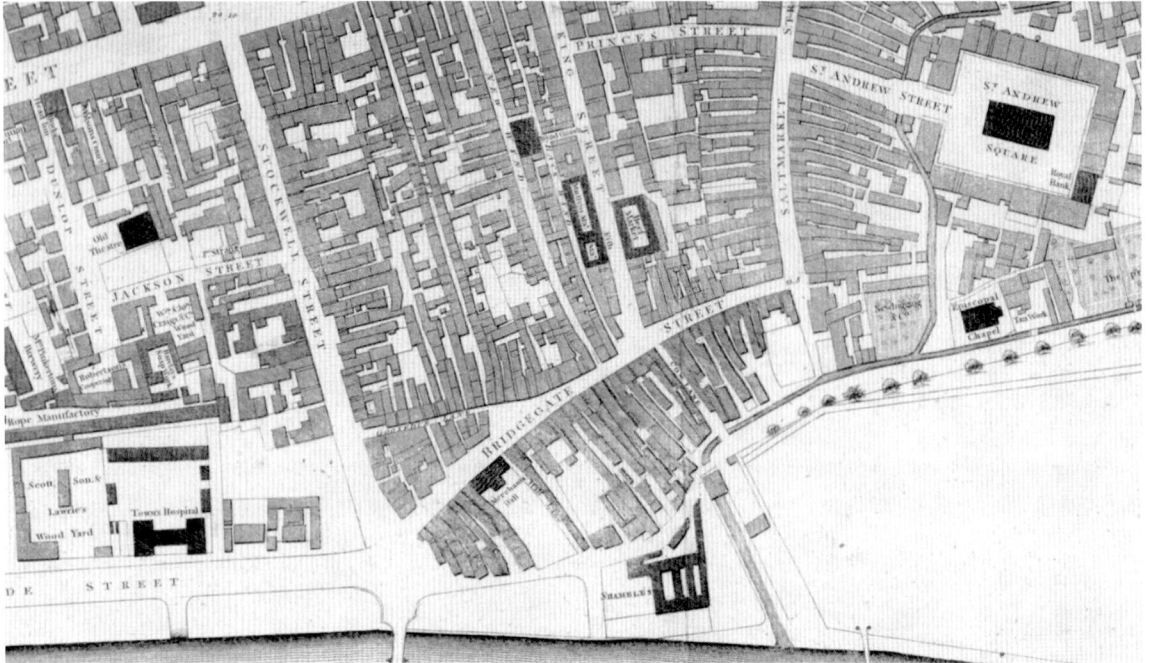

Fleming's Map of Glasgow in 1807. (By permission of University of Glasgow Library, Special Collections.)

As a charity workhouse under the auspices of the council, the Town's Hospital was responsible for feeding, clothing, educating and employing pauper children – or finding others to provide these things. It was also responsible for housing the elderly and the sick, including the mentally ill. To this end, in addition to *a large Hospital and Work house* set in a spacious courtyard, there was *a handsom, well contrived Infirmary* big enough for 36 beds, set *at a small distance from the Hospitall*. All of this was *upon a plot of ground gifted to them by the Magistrates and Town Councill*.[70] By the 1780s, more rooms had been added to the main house and to the infirmary (where *the sick, fatuous persons and the insane* were accommodated), and the buildings formed a square.[71] The courtyard area in the centre was used as an *airing ground* for the paupers.[72]

Town's Hospital, *c.*1812.

All residents had to be fed, clothed and, wherever possible, employed – and all at public expense. William Craig, the Preceptor, and his assistant, Mistress Sinclair, and their staff (usually a clerk, nurses, cooks, a schoolmaster and Dr. Robert Cleghorn, '*physician in ordinary*') were charged, among other things, with keeping an accurate register of the names, ages, length of residence and, where appropriate, time of death for each of the residents.[73] They also had to keep accounts which were inspected by the directors (including Dale) and to arrange the medical inspection of each new inmate. They were not allowed to receive any person who had not been recommended by the directors.

The institution's medical wing or infirmary treated any inmate who required it. This was a relatively advanced provision for its day. There were proper beds, with curtains between them and nurses to tend to the patients. Patients with diseases thought to be curable were housed separately from those thought to be incurable. Medicines were dispensed by an apothecary (who also operated a dispensary for outpatients).[74] The Faculty of Physicians and Surgeons in Glasgow and the University of Glasgow supplied the medical staff, i.e. a physician (Robert Cleghorn) and a surgeon (James Parlane), although their appointment had to be approved each year by the directors.[75] Robert Cleghorn was one of the many prominent physicians (including William Cullen and Joseph Black) who built upon their experience in the Town's Hospital infirmary to establish distinguished careers in medicine. Cleghorn's name appears frequently in the city's public health records. His charity work included the treatment of patients in both the Town's Hospital and the Royal Infirmary and, a few years later, as physician to the newly-opened lunatic asylum. Dale certainly knew him from the Town's Hospital and the Royal Infirmary but also from the Humane Society where Cleghorn served as secretary for three years, one of which (1792) coincided with Dale's period as president.[76]

The residents of the Town's Hospital were generally well looked after but the main point of the institution, as with any charity workhouse, was, perversely perhaps, to ensure that as few people as possible relied upon it and that as many as possible should be in employment. Craig and his staff were primarily responsible for ensuring that those fit enough to work did so.

This was an expensive undertaking which had to be paid for.[77] Most of the money came from assessment and subscriptions from four main sources, each of which elected a number of directors to serve on the board of the Hospital: the town council (thirteen directors); the Merchants' House (twelve); the Trades House (twelve) and the General Session (twelve). Some additional income was provided from the work undertaken by the inmates themselves, both young and old. Those who were fit enough to work and who had no employment elsewhere were involved in:

> ...teazing and spinning of cotton, flax and wool; the old men in picking of oakum, and woolcombing; and the old women such of them as are not fit to be nurses to the children, or to the sick, are employed in Spinning of Linen and woollen yarn.[78]

The account above was penned in the 1740s but little had changed by the 1780s. The work done by the residents had come to include the manufacture of thread lace: some 29 girls were employed at this work in 1784. Profits varied but generally increased each year – £96 in 1787, £116 in 1788, £136 in 1791 and £207 in 1790.[79] By the 1790s some of the younger children in the house were being taught how to set the teeth in woollen and cotton cards. Older children were taught how to work thread lace and tambour muslin '*under the inspection of proper teachers, without interruption to their education*'.[80] Older inmates '*spin, weave, make clothes, shoes, tease oakum etc.*' but most of the profits reported to the house manufacturing committee were generated largely by the production of thread lace.[81] The work was supervised by the 'Overseer of the Manufactures' whose job it was to manage the raw materials and the production process and to give the clerk the completed goods for sale. The overseer reported to the manufacturing committee. Given Dale's commercial experience, it is no surprise to learn that he was a valued member of the manufacturing committee, in addition to his position as a director.

He was first elected to serve as a director of the Town's Hospital on 15th November 1787 and is listed as one of the town council's representatives.[82] Robert Scott Moncrieff, already a serving director elected by the council, was re-elected at the same time.[83] Other notable directors elected (or re-elected) that day included Alex McCall and James Hopkirk from the Merchants' House; William Buchanan from the Trades House and Dr. Porteous and Dr. Taylor (ministers of the Established Church) from the General Session.[84] At a separate meeting on the same day Dale and five others were appointed to serve as members of the manufacturing committee.[85] The brief here was to monitor the work of the hospital's residents and to keep a particular eye on expenditure and profits.

It is worth noting that Dale's involvement with the manufacturing committee, while it might have provided him with some potential employees for his mills, was far more concerned with the house inmates who could not, for whatever reason, be found work. The question of placing paupers and others as bound apprentices was dealt with separately and although Dale was in a prime position to offer employment, he was one of many directors charged with supervising Mr. Craig's management and did not have unlimited access to a labour pool. It is almost certainly the case that Dale was elected to the manufacturing committee in the belief that his experience in the textile industry would enhance the manufacturing processes in the house and raise the small but regular income produced by the residents.

Dale, and many other prominent merchants, councillors and members of the Session, would all have considered their involvement with 'Charity Workhouses' such as the Town's Hospital to be part of their civic responsibilities as well as charitable/philanthropic ventures. Dale served as a director for most of his working life. He represented the town council on the Town's Hospital board from 1787–1795, during which time the council elected him to one of their highest offices – that of 'Bailie'.[86] As a result, Dale's name appears in the Hospital Minutes as 'Bailie Dale' on a number of occasions in 1791, 1794 and 1795.[87] He served on the manufacturing committee (normally comprising six people) between 1787 and 1789 and again in 1792. He seems to have taken a complete break from his involvement with the hospital (and also with his other major public charity, the Royal Infirmary and the Chamber of Commerce) from 1795–1799. The burgh records note that this withdrawal from involvement in the management of the Town's Hospital and the Royal Infirmary in 1795 was due to ill health and, while it is likely that this was indeed the case initially, his duties as a magistrate were proving to be time-consuming and he needed to find more time to develop the mills in New Lanark.[88]

However, after a gap of some four years, Dale's name reappeared in the list of directors of the Towns' Hospital on 21st November 1799, this time as a member of the Merchants' House, alongside people like James Monteith, John McCall, Robert Bogle, Archibald Campbell and James Buchanan. As a representative of the Merchants' House he regularly attended meetings until December 1802.[89] By this time, the manufacturing committee had been replaced by the Industry Committee but the purpose and intentions were exactly the same – to consider how far 'the industry' of residents such as pensioners and children was conducive to the benefit of the house.[90] Dale was not on the industry committee although it would undoubtedly have benefited from his experience and advice. At a time when the cotton industry was in full swing, the best the new committee could come up with was that women in the house should be employed 'in some way or other' and that men might be employed in manufacturing oakum (courtesy of ropes supplied by the Gourock Ropework Company). Equally redolent of an earlier era, and apparently unaware of earlier references to residents working with cotton, was the suggestion that girls should be instructed in spinning linen and woollen yarn and knitting stockings.[91]

References: Chapter 13

1   Richardson, T. (1799) *Guide to Loch Lomond, Loch long, Loch Fine* (sic) *and Inveraray.* 2nd Edition. Glasgow: J. Murdoch. Printed for J. Murdoch, Glasgow. Preface.

2   Ibid., p.157.

3   Wardlaw's obituary notice of March 1806. Quoted in Liddell, A. (1854b) 'Memoir of David Dale', in Chambers, R. (ed), (1855) *A Biographical Dictionary of Eminent Scotsmen.* Glasgow: Blackie, p.176.

4   *The Morning Chronicle & London Advertiser,* 5th July 1788

5   Ibid.

6   *The Times,* 29th February 1796.

7   Ibid.

8   *The Sun,* London, 16th October 1798.

9   *The Caledonian Mercury*, 1st August, 1805.

10 Reid, R. (Senex) (1884) *Glasgow Past and Present*, 3 vols. Glasgow: David Robertson & Co. Vol. III, p.206. See also Cleland, J. (1816) *Annals of Glasgow, Comprising an Account of the Public Buildings, Charities and the Rise and Progress of the City*, 2 vols. Glasgow: James Hedderwick. Vol. 1, p.224.

11 Minutes of the Glasgow Humane Society, 16th August 1790. Glasgow City Archives. DTC 6/262.

12 *The Glasgow Mercury*, 17th August 1790.

13 Minutes of the Glasgow Humane Society, 16th August 1790.

14 Cleland (1816) *Annals*, Vol. 2, p.155.

15 *The Glasgow Mercury*, 17th August, 1790.

16 Excerpt from the Minutes of Council, anent grant to Humane Society. 18th August 1790. Glasgow City Archives. DTC 6/262.

17 Ibid., 19th June 1795.

18 Liddell, A. (1854b) 'Memoir of David Dale', in Chambers, R. (ed) (1855) *A Biographical Dictionary of Eminent Scotsmen*. Glasgow: Blackie, p.176.

19 George Macintosh, Gilbert Hamilton, Henry Glassford and Laurence Craigie were also on the statue committee. See *The Morning Post & Gazeteer*, London, 30th June 1802.

20 Minutes of the Glasgow Chamber of Commerce. 12th April 1791. Glasgow City Archives. TD 161670/1/1-3.

21 *The Glasgow Courier*, 10th December 1791.

22 *London Society*, 8:47, 1865 November, p.468.

23 *The Glasgow Mercury*, 13th March 1783.

24 Statement from James Brown, Camlachie (Meal) Society, dated May, 1791. See Glasgow City Archives: T-mj 36. NB Dale paid another £30 in 1790 but the balance, including £23 interest remained outstanding until May 1791, suggesting that there may have been a dispute over the bill.

25 Sinclair, J. (ed) (1791–99) *The Statistical Account of Scotland, 1791–99*, 21 vols . Vol. VIII, p.371.

26 Ibid., p.371. See also Stewart, G. (1881) *Curiosities of Glasgow Citizenship as Exhibited Chiefly in the Business Career of its Old Commercial Aristocracy*. Glasgow: J. Maclehose, p.79.

27 Liddell, A. (1854b) *Memoir*, p.173.

28 Stewart, G. (1881) *Curiosities*, pp.54–5.

29 Ibid.

30 *The Caledonian Mercury*, 8th December 1800.

31 Liddell, A. (1854b) *Memoir*, p.172.

32 *The Morning Herald*, London, 24th November 1786.

33 *Report of the Committee for procuring information on the subject of establishments for the punishment of crimes and reformation of criminals by means of bridewells and other places of confinement, at hard labour*. Glasgow, 22nd June 1789. Glasgow University Special Collection, Mu26-d.30.

34 Ibid., p.2.

35 Ibid., p.3.

36 Ibid.

37 Note. Examples included Ann Marsh, 18, given five days for 'divers misdemeanours in her Master's service; John Hawkins, fifteen days for a similar offence and John Anderson, 32 yrs, given one month's hard labour for 'refusing to do his work' – making a quantity of hurdles. See *Annex to Report of the Committee for procuring information*, p. 8 (facing)

38 *Report of the Committee for Procuring Information*, p.6.

39 Ibid., p.7.

40 Ibid., pp.7–8.

41 Sinclair, J. (ed) *Statistical Account*, Vol. V, pp.513–4.

42 Cleland, J. (1829) *Annals*, p.174.

43 *The Glasgow Courier*, 22nd December, 1791.

44 Cleland, J. (1829) *Annals*, p.174.

45 Renwick, G. (1913) *Records*, Vol. 8, 1781–95, p. 210 and Vol. IX, 1796–1808, p.162. James Cleland notes that the figure was £200. See Cleland, J. (1829) *Annals*, p.174n.

46 Cleland, *Annals* 1829 edition, p.174n.

47 *The Glasgow Courier*, 31st December 1791.

48 See Cleland (1816) *Annals*, Vol. 1, pp.40, 86.

49 See Faden, W. (1776) *An account of the rise, progress, and present state of the Magdalen Hospital for the reception of penitent prostitutes*. Fifth Edition.

50 Cleland, J. (1816) *Annals*, Vol. 2, p.225.

51 *The Caledonian Mercury*, 18th March 1805.

52 Ibid.

53 Cleland, J. (1816) *Annals*, Vol. 2, p.224.

54 Ibid., Vol. 1, p.100.

55 *The Caledonian Mercury*, 18th March 1805.

56 Cleland, J. (1816) *Annals*, Vol. 2, p.225.

57 Alison, R. (1892) *The Anecdotage of Glasgow, Comprising Anecdotes and Anecdotal Incidents of the City of Glasgow and Glasgow Personages*. Glasgow: Thomas D. Morrison, pp185-6.

58 Ibid.

59 Cleland, J. (1816) *Annals*, Vol. 1, pp.177-8.

60 Sinclair, J. (ed) *Statistical Account*, Vol. V, p.493.

61 Renwick, G. (1913) *Records*, Vol. 8, p. 379.

62 Sinclair, J. (ed) *Statistical Account*, Vol. V, p.534.

63 Ibid.

64 David Dale to Dr. James Currie, Physician in Liverpool, 30th June 1792. Vide infra, Chapter 4.

65 Alison, R. *Anecdotage of Glasgow*, pp.185-6.

66 Owen, R.D. (1874) *Threading My Way: Twenty Seven Years of Autobiography*. New York: Carleton & Co., p.52.

67 *The Glasgow Courier*, 4th February 1792.

68 Copy Act by the Town Council of Glasgow in favour of the Town's Hospital of Glasgow, 3rd January 1744. Glasgow City Archives: DTC 6/528/2: Cited in MacDonald, F.A. (1999) 'The Infirmary of Glasgow Town's Hospital, 1733-1800: A Case for Voluntarism.', *Bulletin of the History of Medicine*, 73.1: 64-105. Baltimore: Johns Hopkins Uni Press, pp.65-8.

69 Sinclair, J. (ed) *Statistical Account* Vol. V, pp.518-22.

70 Copy Act by the Town Council of Glasgow in favour of the Town's Hospital of Glasgow, 3rd January 1744. Glasgow City Archives DTC 6/528/2. Cited in MacDonald, F.A. (1999) *The Infirmary of the Glasgow Town's Hospital*, pp.65-8. See also Renwick. R. (ed) (1913) *Extracts from the Records for the Burgh of Glasgow with Charters and other Documents*. 11 vols. Glasgow. Vol. 6: AD 1739-59, pp.155-160 N.B. Although there was an Infirmary attached to the Hospital throughout the period, the Minutes make only occasional mention of health matters. In particular, there is little mention of the treatment of inmates described as 'lunatics' until c.1803.

71 MacDonald, F.A. (1999) *The Infirmary of the Glasgow Town's Hospital*, p.72, n.104.

72 Ibid., note 105.

73 Craig was in charge for 22 years until his death in 1804. A monument commemorating his 'unremitting zeal and fidelity' was subsequently erected in the committee room of the Hospital. See Cleland (1816) *Annals*, Vol. 1, p.103.

74 MacDonald, F.A. (1999) *The Infirmary of the Glasgow Town's Hospital*, p.78.

75 Ibid., p.81 and Appendix, pp.82-3.

76 See Cleland (1816) *Annals*, Vol. 2, p.155.

77 A contemporary document records the income of the Hospital for the year to June 1796 as £2,359-8s.-½d. see *Income and Expenditure of the Town's Hospital 1796*, Glasgow University Library Special Collections.

78 *A Short Account of the Town's Hospital in Glasgow with the Abstracts of the Expenses for the First Three Years*, 4th Edition, Edinburgh, 1742.

79 *Glasgow Town's Hospital Minutes of Directors' Quarterly Meetings, 1732-1816*. Minutes November, 1788 & 1789, February, 1791. Glasgow City Archives: MLRB 641983. See also Sinclair, J. (ed) *Statistical Account* Vol. V, p.522.

80 *Income & Expenditure of the Towns Hospital*, 1796.

81 Cleland, J. (1829) *Annals of Glasgow, Comprising an Account of the Public Buildings, Charities and the Rise and Progress of the City*. Glasgow: J. Smith, p.202.

82 Glasgow Towns Hospital Minutes, 15th November 1787.

83 He had been a Director since at least 1787. See Glasgow Towns Hospital Minutes, 16th March 1787.

84 Ibid., November, 1787. There were several other ministers but his group also included a brushmaker, a cooper and a barber.

85 Ibid.

86 The Council comprised the Lord Provost; 3 Baillies; Dean of Guild; Deacon Convener; Treasurer; Master of Works; 13 Merchant and 12 Trades Councillors. See Sinclair, J. (ed) *Statistical Account* Vol. V, p. 495.

87 Glasgow Town's Hospital Minutes, 17th November 1791; 20th November 1794; 22nd February 1794; 20th August 1795.

88 Renwick, R. (1913) *Extracts from the Records*. Vol, 8. 1781-95, p.624.

89 Glasgow Town's Hospital Minutes, 2nd December 1802. This was his last recorded meeting.

90 Ibid., 31st March 1801

91 Ibid.

Chapter 14:
Anderson's University, the Royal Infirmary and the Bible Society.

Dale's involvement with the nascent Anderson's University came about because John Anderson (1726-1796) specifically named Dale as one of the trustees he wished to appoint to establish and manage this new city institution. Interestingly, Anderson also named 'David Dale Jnr' as trustee.

Anderson, a son of the manse (both father and grandfather were Presbyterian ministers) was a distinguished professor of natural philosophy at Glasgow University (or 'College'). Brilliant though he was, he was also a disputatious and litigious character, prone to choleric outbursts at perceived injustice or corruption in the university and not above holding a grudge when he felt like it. Known to his students as 'Jolly Jack Phosphorous', he raged against what he saw (with some justification) as serious mismanagement of the university's finances, the poor behaviour of many of the professors and the less than utilitarian nature of the curriculum.[1] There was to be none of this in his new institution:

> *...the almost constant intrigues which prevail in the Faculty of Glasgow College about their revenue and the Nomination of Professors, or their Acts of vanity, or Power, inflamed by a Collegiate life, will be kept out of Anderson's University.*[2]

Anderson was perpetually in dispute with his employers and frequently took legal action against them, eventually becoming in the process something of a figurehead in the fight for university reform. Unsurprisingly, the university suspended him in 1784. Although he was reinstated in 1792, he was in poor health by that time and did not attend very often. He had spent the period of his suspension developing his considerable expertise in ballistics and mechanics and inventing new cannons and small arms. His attempts to sell the designs to the British Government met with limited success but he had no difficulties convincing the French and was made an honorary citizen of the French Republic by the National Convention.[3] Naively, perhaps, he believed that improved artillery would, in the long run, produce fewer casualties. When John Paul Jones, the American admiral began to show an interest, Anderson wrote to George Washington offering to take charge of a Federal arsenal and provide training for all involved. Washington, however, did not reply.[4] The painting on the left shows Anderson surrounded by some of his inventions and apparently in the process of designing even more.

As for David Dale, it might be argued that, although he would have known of Anderson, he might not have entirely approved of him, at least not during Anderson's

Left: Professor John Anderson (1793). (University of Strathclyde Library. Department of Archives & Special Collections.)

lifetime. For example, while Dale was happy to sell French Cambrics, he refused to stock French wines in his ample wine cellar and it is doubtful if he would have approved of Anderson's involvement with the National Convention in Paris – the very heart of revolutionary (and post-revolutionary) fervour.[5]

Similarly, trade with the United States was desirable but arming the U.S. navy was quite another matter. Anderson's constant public battle with the university also carried with it the whiff of rabble-rousing. Taken in the round, none of this was really in tune with Dale's view of the world. His nephew, however, would have been more sympathetic to some of the issues around John Anderson.

Anderson drew up his will in May 1795, some eight months before his death, with the express intention of establishing an eponymous new institution '*for the good of mankind and the improvement of science*'.[6] Unlike Glasgow University, Anderson's institution was to be run largely by lay people rather than academics – principally by 81 trustees, grouped into nine 'classes' (e.g. tradesmen, lawyers, merchants) of nine members each.[7] Anderson named the individuals he wanted in each class. Thus in 'Class 4 – Manufactures or Merchants', 'Mr. David Dale Senr.' is first on his list, followed by 'David Dale Jnr.' Among the others were well-known figures such as George Macintosh, Dale's friend and business partner in Dalmarnock and Spinningdale, and William Gillespie, mill owner also involved in bleaching, dyeing and calico printing.[8]

The trustees were to meet four times per year (March, June, September and December) and each class was to elect one '*Ordinary Manager*' to meet monthly. Trustees who missed six general meetings were to be disqualified but could stand again.[9] Most importantly, the intention was that the university would eventually become '*a seminary of sound religion; useful knowledge and Liberality of Sentiment*'.[10] Dale accepted the position as a trustee and, as such, and as an 'Enlightened' man, would have presumably have agreed with John Anderson's general intentions. Dale might well have been particularly attracted to the requirement in Anderson's will that, in addition to four '*Colleges*', there should be '*a School or an Academy*', also run by the trustees, '*in order to carry on the early part of the Education of the Youth*'.[11] For reasons unknown, this was never actually built but the thinking behind it at the time would certainly tie in with the 'Academy' movement in Scottish education and the increasing emphasis on science and technology in the curriculum – including the new sciences associated with mechanical engineering in the new factories and the bleaching and dyeing of cotton cloth – again, issues not unrelated to the Enlightenment and one which Dale would have supported.

However, Anderson's '*liberality of sentiment*' was in rather short supply in his own will where he made it clear that a principal aim of the new university was to challenge bad practice at Glasgow University. Further, he decreed that no-one who had any connection with Glasgow University should be employed in Anderson's University and that '*the irregularities and neglect of duty in the Professors of Glasgow College*' would naturally '*and in some degree, be corrected by a rival school of Education*'.[12] Again, it is likely that David Dale would have been uncomfortable with the spirit of this. A few years later, in 1798, when money was being raised all over the country to support the army and local militias, Dale, gave the handsome sum of £300 to the College of Glasgow '*for the defence of the country*'.[13]

This kind of dispute and the public (and often strong) sentiments it aroused were much more in tune with David Dale Junior's democratic sentiments than those of his more conservative uncle. Dale Senior would have been much more comfortable with the sentiment expressed at an early meeting of the managers where it was stated that one of the principal aims of the University was to afford young gentlemen '*intended for the Arts, Manufactures or Commerce, an opportunity of acquiring a portion of useful knowledge as will qualify them for the society to which their fortunes insure* (sic) *them admission*'.[14]

As the principal merchant named by Anderson in 'Class 4' and as an experienced businessman and banker, it was no surprise that Dale Senior was asked by his fellow trustees to lead a small group in drawing up plans for raising funds for the new institution. This he did and the proposals, '*signed by Mr. Dale and other gentlemen*' were discussed at a meeting on 17th May, 1796. The plans were approved and sent to the other trustees and to '*the principal citizens agreeable to a list made out*'.[15] At the first ever full quarterly meeting of the trustees the following month, Dale Senior and Junior were both present. The chairman indicated that the list of subscribers was already producing some income, '*to which a large addition was made by the Gentleman now present*'.[16]

As a prominent businessman and as trustee with responsibility for fundraising, Dale would probably have made a significant financial contribution. At the same meeting, it was agreed that the Royal Bank should hold all the funds, again indicating the trustees' recognition of and faith in the elder David Dale. After the meeting, both Dales attended a celebratory dinner of the trustees in the Star Inn in John Street.[17] In fact, this meeting in June 1796 was the only meeting which David Dale Senior attended in person. From that point on, he disappears from the picture, to be replaced by David Dale Junior (referred to as 'Manufacturer in Glasgow') who became a very regular attender at trustees' meetings until the end of 1799.[18]

Under the rules, Dale Senior stood to be disqualified for non-attendance, which he duly was in June 1797, being one of 'twenty seven gentlemen' disqualified, although they were eligible to be re-elected.[19] Dale appears to have allowed his name to go forward for re-election because at the January 1798 meeting, it is recorded that the trustees of the 4th class re-elected 'David Dale Esq.' – a decision ratified at the next quarterly meeting in March of that year. Dale Senior is always referred to in the minutes as 'David Dale Esq.', or 'David Dale Senr.', so there is no doubt which member of the family is being referred to.[20]

It is interesting to speculate as to why Dale's involvement in an institution designed for the public good was so minimal. Almost certainly, he would have given a respectable donation to the cause but as a man with such a commitment to education and social wellbeing and with an established reputation for benevolence and philanthropy, he might have been expected to play a greater part. The lack of involvement may simply have been because of recurring illness during 1797–1799. This is borne out to some extent by his non-attendance at chamber of commerce and Royal Infirmary meetings during this period. Ill-health was certainly cited as the reason for non-attendance at meetings of the Royal Infirmary managers from December 1795 onwards.[21]

However, there may well be other reasons for Dale's lack of involvement. There was certainly much about the new university which Dale would have approved of, such as the focus on useful learning for the good of society and of John Anderson's philanthropy in this respect. Dale would also have approved of Anderson's religious views and the latter's support for Secessionist churches. It seems likely also that Dale would have been impressed by Thomas Garnett and George Birkbeck's attempts not only to broaden the curriculum by including bleaching, dyeing, mechanics and commerce but also to widen access to such a curriculum by offering it to working tradesmen and others 'whose occupations have not allowed leisure for investigating these subjects'.[23] He would have surely approved of the plans for a school/academy and as a banker, he would have been very happy to have the University's money in the Royal Bank's Glasgow office.

However, the school or academy idea was never developed by Anderson and disappeared from view.[24] In any event, a school or academy for sons of the new middle classes was some way away from factory schooling for pauper apprentices. Similarly Dale was unlikely to have been impressed by Anderson's disapproval of the treatment of Thomas Paine and Thomas Muir.[25]

Dale was an ardent royalist, as were the vast majority of the Glasgow entrepreneurs. Events in Revolutionary France had been well reported in the press and had provoked a reaction throughout the country. These were tense and nervous times for all in positions of power and there were many public expressions of support for the king and parliament. In January 1793 Dale attended a meeting in Hamilton of the 'Noblemen, Gentlemen, Freeholders, Justices of the Peace, Commissioners of Supply and heritors of the County of Lanark'. The members expressed loyalty to the king and pledged to 'stand by his Majesty with our personal fortunes and our lives'.[26] They also pledged loyalty to 'the Constitution'. Any attempt to subvert it would lead to anarchy and chaos. Dale was one of the signatories, along with other well-known business people – Robert Bogle, John Dunlop, Gilbert Hamilton, Andrew Buchanan, Henry Glassford and James Monteith. A few days later, a very similar meeting took place in Ayr. Heritors, businessmen and others declared their public support for 'the Constitution' and expressed their 'astonishment and horror' at any attempt to undermine it. Mindful of France, they were understandably fearful of the idea of reform and resolved that :

> ...in the momentous and alarming progress of a neighbouring nation, the avowed enemy of all Monarchy, any discussion of the kind could only tend to embarrass the Government at a time when all hearts and all hands ought to unite in its support.[27]

Dale's colleague and friend, George Dempster wrote to Sir Adam Fergusson on a number of occasions expressing shock at what he called *'the horrors in France'*, which he said had sickened him of the human race and noting that *'a just reference for the laws and a lively sense of religion'* were required to ensure the happiness of the people and the quiet of the community. He described Thomas Paine as *'the most despicable of all political writers'*.[28]

David Dale Senior was very much part of that kind of thinking. Any suggestion of dissatisfaction with the established order and, in particular, any suggestion of supporting any government which had executed its king would have met with Dale's disapproval. The activities of the protest group known as 'The Friends of the People', innocent enough by today's standards, would have met with a similarly hostile response from Dale at the time. He would have agreed with Lockhart's view, expressed in the *Statistical Account* that such groups were supported by hotheads who *'either from ignorance or from violence of temper, will not listen to the cool voice of reason, who chime in with the ravings of* The Friends of the People, *as they call themselves'*.[29] Others (and this would include Dale and most of the business establishment) drew a sharp lesson from *'a neighbouring kingdom'*:

> *...where Anarchy sits triumphant upon the guillotine, with Murder at her back, trampling upon law, liberty and religion and treading the rights of mankind under her feet.*[30]

Dale obviously felt strongly that the country, its constitution (unwritten as it may have been) and its institutions needed to be stoutly maintained and defended. Issues of reform or even of constitutional debate, however, were strongly supported by David Dale Junior and this in itself may have been a reason for Dale Senior's lack of involvement. His nephew was something of an irritation to the older man, particularly the former's public support for The Friends of the People.[31] Dale Senior was frequently annoyed by newspaper reports of meetings in the city, particularly of this group, which erroneously reported that *'David Dale'* rather than *'David Dale Junior'* had attended. It is difficult to imagine, however, that anyone who knew Dale Senior could possibly imagine that he would attend such a meeting. Dale Junior, although a supporter of the Friends of the People, could hardly be described as a radical, having been set up in business in the city's Ingram Street (Messrs. Dale, Campbell, Reid & Dale, suppliers of cotton cloth for printing) by his uncle but relations between them could be extremely strained at times.

There could be no clearer example of the differences between the two Dales than in their various public appearances in 1793. While Dale Senior was busy making public his support for the King and the constitution, his nephew was appearing at the High Court of Justiciary in Edinburgh in the now infamous trial of Thomas Muir, the former advocate, who at the end of August that year was facing numerous charges of sedition. The trial merits some closer examination because there are features of it which further explain Dale senior's reluctance to associate himself with his nephew in any cause which the latter chose to support.

Muir's alleged crimes fell into two main categories – being a fugitive from justice and *'wickedly and feloniously'* encouraging the people to rebel against the king and government. He had previously been charged and had left the country to visit France (arguing that his intention was to persuade the revolutionaries to spare the life of the French king). On his return, he was seized at Portpatrick as a fugitive and found to have in his possession passports (visas) allowing him to visit three Departments in France and a receipt for a passage to New York. He was also in possession of a copy of [Thomas] *'Paines Works'* and various pamphlets associated with an organisation known as *'...the Friends of the People ... or some such name'*.[32] These were very serious matters and a raft of charges was drawn up against Muir, all accusing him of recommending people to buy and/or read seditious literature. A particular crime was to encourage people to support, or even to read the ideas contained in Paine's *Rights of Man* – *'a most wicked and seditious publication'* and one which was *'calculated to vilify the constitution of this country , to produce a spirit of insurrection among the people and to stir them up to acts of outrage & opposition to the established government'*.[33] The transcript of the trial contains page after page of similar charges.[34] Muir conducted his own defence in what he referred to (quite correctly) as a *'wretched mockery'* of a trial. He admitted to being a member of the Friends of the People but argued at some length that the members of this organisation and others like it were good citizens who supported the king, abhorred revolutionary ideas and were committed only to constitutional reforms.[35]

The Crown case was led by H.M. Advocate Robert Dundas, a nephew of Henry Dundas, Home Secretary and former Lord Advocate, with whom Dale Senior was acquainted and who was later to visit New Lanark.[36] The Lord Justice Clerk led the Lords on the bench. In this case, the Lord Justice Clerk was Robert McQueen, Lord Braxfield, the landowner who had sold Dale the land on which New Lanark was built and a man described by Robert Owen as 'very friendly to Mr. Dale' and one who had given Dale 'great encouragement to establish his works near to him' and who was 'to his death an excellent neighbour'.[37] McQueen was also strongly connected to the Royal Bank of Scotland in Edinburgh and served as a director from 1778–1799. Interestingly, the Royal Bank connection does not end there. Robert Dundas, the H.M. Advocate prosecuting, had also been a director of the Royal Bank between 1787 and 1789.[38] The chancellor (foreman) of the jury was 'the great millionaire', Gilbert Innes of Stow, who at the time of the trial was a director of the Royal Bank and became deputy governor a few months later. He was, effectively, Dale Senior's employer.[39] Also on the jury was Sir Archibald Hope, a director of the Royal Bank from 1778 to 1794. The links, direct or otherwise, between the members of the Royal Bank establishment at the trial and David Dale, manager of the bank's most successful agency, are clear enough.

Muir called a significant number of witnesses 'in exculpation', i.e. in his case for the defence. David Dale Junior gave evidence, stating that he had seen Muir at meetings of the Friends of the People in the Star Inn in Glasgow where a motion had been made that political books be recommended to the society. Dale Junior stated that Muir had publicly opposed the motion, advising 'general reading' instead.[40] Further, Muir had advised people to consider both sides of the question; 'to seek reform by measures calm and constitutional' and that this should only be done by petitioning parliament. Muir had, according to this evidence, advised the Friends of the People to expel any member who might behave 'seditiously or disorderly' and had told the meeting that he (Muir) would absent himself if unconstitutional measures were adopted.[41] Dale Junior told the court that he had never heard Muir say anything which had a tendency to excite sedition and that he had no knowledge of Muir ever distributing books or recommending Paine's works.[42]

From his evidence, the young Dale showed he had his own views on the British constitution which his uncle supported so strongly. When asked by Muir if he had ever heard Muir speak against the constitution, the following exchange occurred:

Dale Junior:	Will you be pleased, Mr. Muir, to explain what you mean by the constitution and then I shall be able to answer the question?
Mr. Muir:	Did you ever hear me say any thing against the King, the Lords and Commons?
Dale Junior:	I never did.[43]

Under cross-examination, Dundas pressed the young man on the precise date of Muir's apprehension and there was a sharp exchange between the two when the witness seemed unable or unwilling to remember details:

| Lord Advocate: | You have a very short memory, Mr. Dale. |
| Dale Junior: | I have a very short memory, my Lord.[44] |

What Dale Senior would have made of his nephew confronting the established order and supporting what he would have seen as dangerous political hotheads in this way can only be imagined. Inevitably, the jury, led by the Royal Bank's Gilbert Innes, returned a unanimous verdict. Muir was found guilty and McQueen's comments at sentencing underlined the strength of Establishment opposition to 'wicked persons' calling themselves 'most falsely and insidiously ... the Friends of the People and of Reform, although they deserve the very opposite denomination'.[45] McQueen had been particularly irritated by the public applause in court for Muir, referring to it as 'indecent'. It had convinced him that the spirit of discontent still lurked in the minds of the people and that it would be dangerous to allow Muir to remain in the country.[46] Despite McQueen's reputation as a 'Hanging Judge', he sentenced Muir to transportation for a period of fourteen years – a harsh sentence but one which accurately reflected the Establishment's fear of social upheaval.

The events of August 1793 were still very much part of the political landscape when John Anderson's will was published in 1795. Given their opposing positions on matters of reform and given Dale Junior's very public profile at the trial, it is understandable that relations between uncle and nephew were strained and might well explain why the older man, having dutifully responded to Anderson's initial 'call', was thereafter unwilling to ally himself publicly with his nephew.

Glasgow Royal Infirmary

Dale's involvement in the Town's Hospital may have provided him with a small number of apprentice children for the New Lanark Mills but his intentions were also charitable. The same is true – perhaps even more so – of his involvement with the Glasgow Royal Infirmary. The town council received a letter in December 1786 informing them that funds were being raised by public subscription for 'an Infirmary for the reception of indigent persons under bodily distress in the west of Scotland and for establishing a fund towards its permanent support'.[47] Further, because this 'charitable scheme' was of such importance to this part of the country, particularly the city of Glasgow, the council and magistrates were asked to take it under their care and protection, which, being 'duly convinced of the utility of the plan', the council agreed to in March 1787, donating £500 towards the building costs in the process.[48] Three months later, the subscribers met together for the first time. They were an eclectic mix of people. The Lord Provost & Dean of Guild were there, ex-officio. Dale was there as a member of the council but also, presumably, as a well-known businessman and banker in the city, along with twenty others, including doctors, weavers, printers and members of the Grand Antiquity Society.[49] As with all organisations of this type, the focus had to be on raising funds, finding land and drawing up plans for building. A sub-committee was formed and Dale was elected to chair the first meeting of the new eleven-man group (which included Scott Moncrieff) in January 1788. For Dale, this marked the beginning of a lengthy period of involvement with the Royal Infirmary. He was particularly active in the crucial early years between 1787, when the idea was first mooted, and 1795 when the building finally opened. The minute books show that he attended at least twenty meetings of the sub-committee and the main committee during this period.[50]

Dale and his committee managed to find a suitable plot of land next to the Archbishop's Castle[51] and engaged the services of architect Robert Adam who provided an estimate of £7,768 for design and construction.[52] There was a minor crisis in early 1792 when Robert Adam died and his brother James withdrew from the construction part of the project. However, the committee, having already agreed terms, paid for Robert Adam's architectural plans and awarded the construction project to a different builder.[53]

While all this was going on, Dale, Moncrieff and several others were engaged in the ongoing business of drafting a constitution which was to form part of a submission to the king for the granting of a royal charter. A draft of the constitution and of the wording of a proposed charter appeared in the minutes of 4th August, 1791 and the royal charter was granted in December that year.[54] The charter contains all the necessary business information about internal structures and government. The Infirmary was to be run by 25 managers or directors. Certain office-bearers were designated as 'Perpetual Managers' and were ex-officio members, e.g. the provost, the M.P. and various professors of medicine and anatomy. The remaining eighteen had to be elected annually and included the usual representatives from each of the major city authorities, including the town council, the Merchants' and Trades' Houses and the Established Church, along with representatives from the Faculty of Physicians and Surgeons. Subscribers could also become managers, at least in name, if they subscribed ten pounds as a one-off payment or two guineas annually.[55]

Most importantly, several individuals were named specifically in the charter and were given a major role:

> ...George Oswald of Scotstown Esq, David Dale, Robert Scott-Moncrieff, Archibald Grahame, William Craig, merchants in Glasgow, Thomas Reid, D.D. ... shall take upon themselves the management and direction of the whole affairs of the said corporation...[56]

Their period of office ran from January 1792 until February 1793, during which time the foundation stone was laid amid much public pomp and circumstance in the city. The grand ceremony was perhaps ironic given that the Latin wording on the stone in translation notes that the building was for healing the diseases of the poor, to be erected with money 'voluntarily *contributed by the inhabitants of this city and other benevolent people in Scotland*.[57] A year later, Dale was reappointed as a manager for another twelve month period, representing the magistrates and town council.[58] This meeting was an important one as it identified the number of patients a subscriber could recommend for treatment (Table 13) – something which Dale was to take full advantage of when the Infirmary opened.

Table 13: Financial Contributions / Patient Allocation

Contribution	No. of patients per annum
Individual:	
£10 or more or 1 guinea annually	1
£20 or more or 2 guineas annually	2
£50 or more or 3 guineas annually	4
£100 or more or 5 guineas annually	6
Corporate:	
£50 or more or 3 guineas annually	2
£100 or more or 5 guineas annually	4

Any combination of the above was possible, i.e. someone like Dale could (and Dale did) donate more than £100 as an individual and there was an additional £100 (almost certainly Dale's own money) from a 'Society' in New Lanark which would allow him to recommend ten patients for treatment. However, the main priority at this stage was to complete building work and arrange the formal opening. Dale was re-elected in January 1793 and again in January 1794 and by the end of that year, construction was almost complete. The managers were able to meet in the new building but the Infirmary itself, although it was admitting patients, was not fully operational until 1795.[59] Dale was again elected as manager in January 1795 and the Infirmary opened officially in December that year.

The new facility, designed in the shape of a triple cross, provided 136 beds in a four-storey building. Each floor had a ward, four small rooms and two W.C.s. One floor had a room for managers and physicians and one had an octagonal operating room 40 feet in diameter and about the same height, lighted by thirteen skylights from the dome. The octagonal room is reminiscent of Dale's study in his Charlotte Street house (also designed by Robert Adam and also used at a later date as an operating theatre). The dome itself was supported by twelve columns, on a circle of 28 feet diameter, behind which there was a seated area for students, *'and the area within for the operators'*.[60]

The *Abstract* from the *Annual Report* for 1795 (opposite) shows Dale as one of the managers and notes that some 3,000 patients were seen (either as in or outpatients) by the physicians during 1795.[61] Perhaps a more accurate picture of events emerges from the figures minuted for admissions during 1795. Appendix 11 indicates that there were 186 men and 90 women admitted. Of those 276 patients, 145 were medical and 131 were surgical. Most were cured, relieved or dismissed but eighteen patients died and 50 remained in the wards for treatment.[62] The appendix also provides a snapshot of the illnesses prevalent at the time – or, at least, the illnesses suffered by patients fortunate enough to be referred to the Infirmary. The illnesses generally reflected the general public health issues of the day.

Dale's own health – probably gout or dropsy – was causing him problems and, having seen the Infirmary project through to completion, he *'declined to officiate any longer upon account of his health'* in December 1795.[63] Although he did not attend any more meetings of the managers, he supported the project financially until his death.

A REPORT

OF THE ROYAL INFIRMARY OF GLASGOW, FROM ITS FIRST ESTABLISH-
MENT 8th. DECEMBER 1794, TILL 1ft. JANUARY 1796,

FOR THE YEAR 1795.

ROYAL Infirmary GLASGOW.

LIST OF MANAGERS, 1795.

John Dunlop, Efq. Lord Provoft,
William McDowall, Efq. M. P.
John Laurie, Efq. Dean of Guild,
William Auchinclofs, Efq. Deacon Convener,
Dr. Tho. Charles Hope, Profeffor of Medicine,
Dr. James Jeffray, Profeffor of Anatomy and
    Botany,
Dr. Cleghorn, in place of the Prefident of the
    Faculty of Phyficians and Surgeons,
Dr. Wright,
Dr. Taylor,
Meffrs. David Dale,
    Robert Waddel,
    Archibald Grahame,

Meffrs. John Stirling,
    Henry Riddel,
    John Buchanan,
    John Alfton,
    Gilbert Hamilton,
    Walter Ewing McLae,
    William Wardlaw,
    William Couper,
    John Swanfton,
    James Monteith,
    Archibald Smith,
    John Gordon.
    Profeffor Jardine,

Abstract from the *Glasgow Royal Infirmary, Annual Report, December 1794–January 1796.* (NHS Greater Glasgow & Clyde Archives)

His initial contribution in 1795 was £200 and he is named in the same year as an annual subscriber of two guineas. He raised this to five guineas in 1797 and continued to contribute this sum until his death. The sum of £200 was a great deal of money in those days. It was the largest donation given by any individual (with the exception of one or two members of the aristocracy) and was only surpassed by institutional contributions, e.g. the Merchants' House (£400), the Trades House (£400) and the town council (£500). Dale's sometime partners, Claud Alexander and George Macintosh gave £50 each; Scott Moncrieff contributed ten guineas and all became annual subscribers.[64] There were some 285 individual annual subscribers in 1795 and numbers were growing all the time. By 1801 this figure had increased to 420.

Glasgow Royal Infirmary, c.1812.

Also in 1795 a donation of £50 was received from '*the Work people at the Cotton mills near Lanark, under the name of the Benevolent Society there*'.[65] In a letter to the Earl of Galloway some years later, James Currie mentions a savings scheme in New Lanark and this is possibly the source of the contribution although Dale may simply have donated £50 of his own money and requested that it be entered under the name of the Benevolent Society.[66] Whatever the case, a total of £250 came from Dale and New Lanark in 1795.

From 1797 until 1801, 'David Dale Junior' contributed one guinea annually. Robert Owen's name appears for the first time in 1797 as a subscriber (three guineas annually) and he remained a subscriber until at least 1811.[67] In addition to his annual contribution, Owen became one of the 'Visitors' (i.e. monitors on behalf of the managers and directors) in 1802 and 1803. A year later he is shown as a director.

David Dale's contributions remained at five guineas annually throughout, up to and including 1806, the year of his death but he did actually contribute more than this. Between 1804 and 1806 there was an additional annual sum of eight guineas subscribed by David Dale '*for four ladies*' and in 1807, the year after his death, their identities were revealed – '*Miss Dale; Miss Mary Dale; Miss Margaret Dale and Miss Julia Dale*' – a contribution of two guineas is recorded against each of their names.[68]

Dale was well known as a supporter of good causes and the Infirmary certainly marketed itself as such. Managers, for example, were described as '*stewards for the diseased and miserable*'.[69] As a '*humane institution*', it depended on '*the united and continued exertions of those who are not ashamed of being friends to the poor and the afflicted*'.[70] Similarly, when seeking contributions, it described itself as '*a noble monument of Brotherly Love and Christian Charity*'.[71] There was little return for Dale personally because the Infirmary was designed as a charity for those who did not have the means to pay for medical care. His contributions, however, entitled and enabled him to recommend a significant number of deserving causes to the Infirmary for treatment and he took full advantage of this.

Appendix 12 contains a list of all the patients recommended by Dale Senior, Dale Junior, Robert Owen and also the Benevolent Society at New Lanark.[72] Between January 1795 and September 1803, some 64 patients were recommended by Dale Senior for treatment. Most of these were personal recommendations but some came from his Benevolent Society in New Lanark. The list of illnesses makes relatively little mention of the two biggest killers, i.e. smallpox and typhus. There had been an epidemic of smallpox between 1783 and 1792, when it accounted for nearly one third of all deaths under the age of ten.[73] Inoculation was still in its infancy and was more commonly the preserve of the middle classes. Dale wrote to Claud Alexander in 1789 and expressed his satisfaction that Alexander's son had been inoculated.[74] In another letter to Alexander Campbell in 1791, Dale wrote:

I came from Lanark on Tuesday morning and left Mrs. Campbell & Miss Campbell, Miss Jane Campbell and my children well. I was happy to learn that your children have got happily through the smallpox.[75]

These were the lucky ones. Between 1793 and 1802, when the epidemic had supposedly passed, mortality rates barely improved at all. The *Statistical Account* for the Barony Parish in Glasgow, originally penned in 1794, confirms the fact that smallpox was *'very frequent'* among the children and that *'vast numbers'* had died.[76] This may account for the relatively few adults admitted to Glasgow Royal Infirmary who had smallpox.

The range of illnesses and the number of patients treated expanded as the number of subscribers increased but, as already noted, neither Dale nor members of his family would have been likely to avail themselves of the services of the Infirmary. He donated a great deal of time and money to the Infirmary for very little, if any, material return. Andrew Brown's observations in 1797 regarding the Royal Infirmary might well have been written about Dale:

Here we see the influence and effects of benevolence, silently pouring in from all ranks of the truly good, upon the distressed poor.[77]

British & Foreign Bible Society

Given Dale's evangelical religious views, his personal fortune and his commitment to good causes, it is no surprise to find him involved in two charitable organisations dedicated to translating the Bible into various languages and spreading the Word across the world. Dale was first involved with the Baptist Missionary Society, who were in the process of circulating Bibles to what was described as *'our eastern empire'*.[78] Andrew Fuller, a Baptist fundraiser, visited Dale and was kindly received, probably around 1803–1804. Liddell reports that Dale made large contributions to the cause.[79] The second organisation was the British & Foreign Bible Society, formed in London in March 1804 and dedicated to distributing Bibles throughout the U.K. and internationally. Dale supported the organisation wholeheartedly and, more importantly, financially, from the outset and was impressed by the simplicity of the system and the grandeur of the scale.[80] Precisely how much money he subscribed at this stage is not clear but it was described as *'worthy of his usual benevolence'*.[81] From July, 1804 he began collection donations from local churches and sending the money to British & Foreign Bible Society headquarters in London.[82]

Dale was evidently passionate about British & Foreign Bible Society and its work and wanted to set up an auxiliary branch in Glasgow. In 1805, he recruited one or two fellow sympathisers and persuaded the London office to establish a Glasgow branch with its own treasurer, secretary and committee of management. Dale was happy to act as treasurer and general agent for Glasgow and the west of Scotland.[83] During the year ending May 1805 he received contributions amounting to £384. 18s. 1d. – most of it (£321. 12s. 1d.) coming from his own Independent Meeting House in Greyfriars Wynd and two other independent churches in the area.[84] To this figure, Dale added a personal contribution of £50. Figures for May 1806 show that donations had increased to £668. 4s. – drawn from churches across Glasgow, Dumbarton and Ayrshire.[85] For example, in October 1805, the Rev. Mr. Stephen in Kilwinning sent Dale £33. 10s. 6d., raised from a special collection in aid of the British & Foreign Bible Society. In the same month, the Rev. Mr. Smith of the Relief Congregation in Old Kilpatrick sent him £17. 1s. and in November the Parish of Dalry sent £30. 6s. 3d., *'being the collections at the front door'*.[86] These must have been among the last few donations Dale was able to forward to the British & Foreign Bible Society, given that he had only months to live. His charitable, fund-raising efforts on behalf of the British & Foreign Bible Society, however, represented a fraction of his commitment to Christian values.

References: Chapter 14

1   See Butt, J. (1996) *John Anderson's Legacy. The University of Strathclyde and its Antecedents, 1796–1996*. East Linton: Tuckwell Press, Chapter 1 for more information on John Anderson.

2   Last Will of Professor John Anderson. 7th May 1795, p.19. *Anderson's University Minute Book. Vol. 1, 1796–1799.* University of Strathclyde Archives, OB/1/1/1.

3   Butt, J. (1996) *John Anderson's Legacy*, p.9.

4   Ibid., p.10.

5   Malloch, D.M. (1913) *The Book of Glasgow Anecdote*. NewYork: Scribners, p.25.

6   *Last Will of Professor John Anderson*, p.3.

7   The nine Classes were: Tradesmen; Agriculturalists; Artists; Manufactures/Merchants; Mediciners; Lawyers; Divines, Clergymen & Ministers of the Gospel; Natural Philosophers; Kinsmen.

8   *Last will of Professor John Anderson*, pp.4–7. The others were: Patrick Colquhoun, former tobacco merchant, Lord Provost and leading citizen; Alex Oswald of Shieldhall, former tobacco merchant and now involved in sugar & cotton; John Pattinson, Kelvingrove, mill owner and George Rutherford, cotton merchant/manufacturer in the city and a Baillie.

9   Ibid., pp.9–10, 13–17.

10 Ibid., p.17.

11 Ibid., p.11–13.

12 Ibid., p.19.

13 *The Star*, London, 15th March 1798.

14 Minute of 24th October 1796. *Anderson's University Minute Book*. Vol. 1, 1796–1799, p.91.

15 Minute of 17th May 1796. *Anderson's University Minute Book*. Vol. 1, p.67.

16 Minute of 21st June 1796. *Anderson's University Minute Book*. Vol. 1, p.71.

17 Ibid., pp.73–4.

18 There is a possible entry in December 1800. See *Anderson's University Minute Book*, Vol. 2, p.20 but the Minutes are very poorly recorded from late 1799.

19 Minute of 21st June 1797. *Anderson's University Minute Book*. Vol. 1, pp.137–8.

20 Minute of 4th January 1798 and 1st March 1798. *Anderson's University Minute Book*. Vol. 1, pp.162, 167. N.B. there is no doubt that it is Dale Senior who is referred to here. His nephew is always referred to as David Dale Junior.

21 Renwick. R. (ed) (1913) *Extracts from the Records for the Burgh of Glasgow with Charters and other Documents*, 11 vols. Glasgow. Vol. 8, 1781–95, p.624. Chamber of Commerce records show he did not attend between October 1796 and December 1799.

22 Anderson's will stipulates that professors be appointed in the Burgher, Anti-Burgher and relief systems; Gaelic Language and Sacred Music.

23 Minute of 2nd September 1796. *Anderson's University Minute Book*, pp.91–2.

24 Anderson's Will refers to a Codicil which is to contain further information on the operation of the school. However, there is no such information in the Codicil.

25 See Butt, J. *John Anderson's Legacy*, p.11. Butt argues that Anderson was not a supporter *per se* of Paine or of Muir. Anderson believed that poor treatment of them would make them more popular.

26 *The Star*, London, 15th February 1793.

27 *The London Chronicle*, 15th January 1793.

28 George Dempster to Sir Adam Fergusson, 15th May and 9th September 1792, in Fergusson, J. (ed) (1934) *Letters of George Dempster to Sir Adam Fergusson, 1756–1813*. MacMillan: London., pp.216 & 222.

29 Sinclair, J. (ed) (1791–99) *The Statistical Account of Scotland, 1791–99*, 21 vols. Vol. XV, p.42.

30 Ibid.

31 Liddell, A. (1854b) 'Memoir of David Dale', in Chambers, R. (ed) (1855) *A Biographical Dictionary of Eminent Scotsmen*. Glasgow: Blackie, p.11.

32 Howell, T. (1817) *A Complete Collection of State Trials & Proceedings for High Treason and other Crimes & Misdemeanors from the Earliest period to the Year 1783, with Notes & Illustrations: Compiled by T.B. Howell Esq. FRS, FSA and Continued from the Year 1783 to the present time by Thomas Jones Howell, Esq. Vol XXIII (being Vol. II of the Continuation). 33 & 34 George III. A.D. 1793 & 1795*, London, Longman, Hurst et al., p.124.

33 Ibid., p.119.

34 Ibid., pp.117–129.

35 Ibid., p.191. See also pp.186–228 for Muir's summing up.

36 *The London Chronicle*, 10th–12th March, 1789.

37 Owen, R. (1857) *The Life of Robert Owen Written by Himself*, 2 vols. Vol. 1. London: Effingham Wilson. New impression (1967) London: Frank Cass & Co., p.99.

38 Munro, N. (1928) *The History of the Royal Bank of Scotland, 1727–1927*. Edinburgh: Clark Ltd., pp.400, 403, 406.

39 Ibid., pp.398–401. See also Malloch, D.M. (1913) *The Book of Glasgow Anecdote*. NewYork: Scribners, p.24. If anecdotal evidence is correct, Innes was present at the Dales' famous dinner party in Charlotte Street in 1795 when the river burst its banks and flooded the cellars.

40 Muir called 54 witnesses in total. Significantly, there were almost no merchants or public figures called as witnesses, with the exception of John Tennant, brewer in the city, James Craig, manufacturer in Paisley and Col. Wm. Dalrymple of Fordell, who was an unusual choice, given that he had, with Dale Senior, sworn allegiance to the King and the Constitution at the Lanark meeting in January of that year. See *The Star*, London 15th February 1793.

41 Howell, T. (1817) *A Complete Collection of State Trials*, p.174.

42 Ibid.

43 Ibid.

44 Ibid., p.175.

45 Ibid., p.234.

46 Ibid., p.236.

47 Renwick. R. (ed) (1913) *Extracts*, Vol. VIII, 1781–1795, p.210.

48 Ibid., pp.210, 222.

49 Minute of 5th June 1787. *Glasgow Royal Infirmary Minute Book*. Vol. 1, 1787–1802. Greater Glasgow Health Board Archives: HB/14/1/1.

50 Ibid., Vol. 1. 1787–1802, HB/14/1/1 and Vol. 2, 1803–1812, HB/14/1/2.

51 Ibid, Vol. 1. Minutes of 6th February 1788; 23rd January 1789; 24th June 1791; 7th July 1791.

52 Ibid., 10th November 1791; 13th December 1791; 12th January 1792; 19th January 1792; 1st February 1792.

53 Ibid., 16th February 1792; 18th April 1792.

54 Ibid., 4th August 1791.

55 *Copy of the Charter of the Glasgow Royal Infirmary. Granted December 21st 1791. Printed at the Courier Office by Wm Reid & Co. Glasgow. 1792.* pp.5–6. University of Glasgow Special Collections: Mu26-d.30.

56 Ibid., p.7.

57 *Glasgow Royal Infirmary Minute Book*. Vol. 1. 7th June 1792. See also Cleland, J. (1816) *Annals of Glasgow, Comprising an Account of the Public Buildings, Charities and the Rise and Progress of the City*, 2 vols. Glasgow: James Hedderwick. Vol. 1, pp.77–78.

58 Renwick. R. (ed) (1913) *Extracts*. Vol. VIII, p.495. Also *G.R.I. Minute Book*, Vol. 1, 7th January 1793.

59 *G.R.I. Minute Book*, 8th December 1794.

60 Brown, A. (1795–7) *History of Glasgow and of Paisley, Greenock, and Port-Glagow, comprehending the ecclesiastical and civil history of these places, from the earliest accounts to the present time: and including an account of their population, commerce, manufactures, arts, and agriculture*, 2 vols. (1795, 1797) Glasgow: W. Paton. Vol. 2, p.65.

61 *Glasgow Royal Infirmary Annual Report*, 8th December 1794–1st January 1796. Greater Glasgow Health Board Archives. HB 14/2/1.

62 *G.R.I. Minute Book*. Meeting of General Court, 4th January 1796.

63 Renwick. R. (ed) (1913) *Extracts*. Vol. VIII, p.624.

64 *G.R.I. Annual Report*, 8th December 1794–1st January 1796. Moncrieff subscribed between one and three guineas annually until 1805.

65 Ibid.

66 James Currie to the Earl of Galloway, December 1802. I am indebted to Prof. E. Royle of York University for providing me with a copy of this letter.

67 *G.R.I. Annual Reports*, December 1794–January 1811. Owen may well have continued beyond 1811 but the *Annual Reports* from 1811–1822 are missing.

68 Ibid. These contributions continued until at least 1811. Presumably the first name was Carolina but there is no mention of Jean Maxwell Dale, born 1785. Dale's half-brother James is shown as a contributor (one guinea) from 1806.

69 *G.R.I. Annual Report*, 8th December 1794–1st January 1796.

70 Ibid.

71 *G.R.I. Annual Report*, 1st January 1799–1st January 1800.

72 Compiled from *G.R.I. Admissions Registers* 1794–1800 and 1800–1803. Greater Glasgow Health Board Archives: HB14/67/56/1A and HB14/67/56/1B.

73 Glaister, J. (1886) *Epidemic History of Glasgow 1783–1883*. Glasgow.

74 David Dale to Claud Alexander, 26th August 1789. *Dale–Alexander Correspondence, 1787–1797*. Glasgow City Archives, MS 63/7.

75 David Dale to Alexander Campbell of Barcaldine, 18th August 1791. National Archives of Scotland. GD.170/1743/13, in Johnston, W.T. (ed) (2000) *David Dale & Robert Owen Studies*. Livingston: Officina Educational Publications.

76 Sinclair, J. *Statistical Account*, Vol. XII, Barony of Glasgow, p.110.

77 Brown, A. *History of Glasgow*. Vol. 2, p.6.

78 Liddell, A. (1854b) *Memoir*, p.173.

79 Ibid.

80 Cleland, J. (1816) *Annals*. Vol. 1, pp.236–7.

81 Liddell, A. (1854b) *Memoir*, p.173.

82 Cleland, J. (1816) *Annals*. Vol. 1, pp.236–7.

83 Liddell, A. (1854b) *Memoir*, p.173. N.B. it was not officially known as the Glasgow Auxiliary Bible Society until 1812.

84 Cleland, J. (1816) *Annals*. Vol. 1, pp.238.

85 Ibid.

86 *The Caledonian Mercury*, 19th October, 30th October and 23rd November 1805. N.B. At the same time as their donation to the Bible Society, Dalry sent £50, *'being an additional contribution to a former £50'* to Glasgow Royal Infirmary, in order to double the number of patients they might recommend and to encourage *'that humane and truly valuable institution'*.

Part 6

Christian Evangelism

Chapter 15: Behold Dale's Works

Dale can be presented, with some justification, as a very successful businessman who, although motivated by the desire for a profit, provided educational and social conditions far in advance of anything available at the time and contributed large amounts to charitable organisations. Although it can be argued that he benefited directly and indirectly from such philanthropy and benevolence, there is considerable evidence to suggest that he was a person driven, in equal measure, by a desire for profit and for philanthropic work. While this may well be true, there is a third element in all of this, the absence of which makes any account of Dale's life quite incomplete. Dale's life revolved around his religious beliefs. These influenced Dale before he was a rich man, were maintained during his extensive business career, continued after his retirement until his death in 1806 and were an enormously powerful directing force in his life.

A contemporary poem about Dale neatly sums up this combination of industry, benevolence and pious zeal:

BEHOLD DALE'S WORKS

Come here ye sons of indolence! and know
What genius and industry can bestow.
Behold DALE'S Works! and think how ye've abus'd
The talent heaven but lent you to be us'd.
These prove the active and persevering man,
Through every part of this extensive plan.
And tacitly reprove each little mind,
Whose aims are to its little self confin'd.
Admitting that his int'rest led him on,
Still the benevolent actions he has done
Form the true test by which the man is prov'd;
And which is priz'd wherever worth is lov'd.
Nor question ye his steady pious zeal,
It ne'er ran counter to the public weal;
And though he differ'd in religious forms,
His conduct gave his principles their charms.
In spite of that detraction which obtains,
His character for honest worth remains;
And to the world the name of DALE is dear,
And will outlive his earthly labours here.[1]

Dale believed that it was his duty to spread the Gospel as widely as possible and to practise what he preached. His Christianity was not something aesthetic and part-time, but a firm set of convictions upon which to base his life and, as such, it played a crucial role in his success. According to Liddell's *Memoir*, Dale's association with the Established, Presbyterian church began during his apprenticeship in Paisley. He sought the company of religious people and '*attached himself to the evangelical party in the Established Church*' and to the fellowship meetings being held during the evening in a private house.[2] When Dale came to Glasgow in 1763, this religious consciousness and commitment was continued in his association with the College Church under Dr. Gillies and it was during this period that the question of patronage came to the fore and heralded the beginning of a series of disputes which eventually led to the secession of large numbers of the Established Church congregations. 'Patronage' generally meant that the local landowners, town councils, universities and other wealthy and influential people presented or selected a minister. Although this practice had been abolished in 1690 as being opposed to the Presbyterian notion of a 'call' to a charge (where a congregation invited and selected their own minister), the principle of patronage had been restored by Westminster in 1712.[3]

Blackfriars/College Church, *c*.1800.

Until 1764 the General Session had exercised the right to appoint all the ministers in the parish churches. In Glasgow, the Session, comprising the elders and ministers from the eight parishes within the city, appointed the ministers as they saw fit. However, by 1764, this right was challenged by the town council and the magistrates. The case was taken to the Court of Session and in 1766, '*by a decree of the court, the council and the magistrates prevailed and were declared patrons.*'[4]

The first vacancy was at Dale's church in the College Wynd. The council lost no time in exercising their new power, promptly installing a minister of their own choosing. '*Thus a clergyman was thrust into the Wynd Church against the will of the congregation*'.[5] According to Liddell, the appointment of a minister considered to be '*obnoxious to the orthodox party*' of the Wynd Church caused great offence, not only to the parishioners but to all who valued their religious privileges.[6]

One of the members of this 'orthodox party' was David Dale. Another was Archibald Paterson, the candlemaker who had entered into partnership with Dale in the High Street. Dale, Paterson, Matthew Alexander and four others felt unable to continue under the new arrangements and opened a subscription in an attempt to break away from the Wynd Church.[7] They managed to raise enough money to build a new meeting house in North Albion Street.[8] This building was named 'The Chapel of the Scotch Presbyterian Society' but was later changed to 'The Chapel of Ease'. Dale was a subscriber and voted for the first minister, a Mr. Cruden.[9] Shortly thereafter, John Barclay, assistant minister in Fettercairn (and later leader of the dissenting sect known as the Bereans), visited Glasgow '*for the purpose of being introduced to Mr. Dale, with whom he subsequently had many meetings*'.[10] Barclay was sympathetic to their cause and persuaded Dale and the others that Congregational principles of church government, rooted in notions of Christian brotherhood and brotherly love were the only truly Christian route to salvation. These ideas were '*incompatible with the systems they had hitherto been attached to*'.[11] While this debate was ongoing, Cruden left for a post in London and this split the congregation.[12] It had the effect:

> ...*of leading those individuals to a more thorough searching of the Scriptures for light and guidance, which ended in their gradually embracing Congregational principles in church government.*[13]

Dale, Paterson and the others were similarly minded and left the Chapel of Ease in 1768. They began to assemble every Sunday in a private house until the end of that year, when the numbers reached 25 and a new meeting house was erected in Greyfriars Wynd.[14] The group, calling themselves 'The Scotch Independents', now had their first church building.[15] It could seat 500 (although it was unlikely to fill quite so many pews) and was financed entirely, it seems, at Archibald Paterson's expense. Paterson has been described as a modest, unassuming man, '*of primitive manners and of great piety*'. It became known as the "Caunnel Kirk" because of Paterson's original association with candle making. He apparently charged the congregation only £20 in rent – a sum which barely paid for the running repairs.[16] Two other groups, equally disaffected by the patronage issue, split from the Wynd Church at the same time to establish their own congregations.[17]

Although the question of patronage brought the issue to a head, the concept of religious groups believing their many and various interpretations of faith and church government to be incompatible with those of the Established Church (or other dissenting churches) was far from new and far from unusual. The period was characterised for many years by the secession of various religious groups and the rise of independent churches, often small in terms of their membership and often based along Congregationalist lines. Prior to the Disruption in 1843, the Established Church endured at least two secessions, both of which were primarily caused by the issue of patronage. However, the Secessionist groups themselves were later subject to subdivision and factionalism, often caused by such issues as the role of song in the service or the place of the 'Amen', rather than matters related to church government. The first Secession Church (or Associate Presbytery) had been established as early as 1733 but by 1774 had subdivided into two factions, the Burghers and Anti-Burghers, depending on whether the members agreed to take the Burgess Oath, which acknowledged the '*true religion presently professed*', implying acknowledgement of the Established Church. Appendix 13 contains the full text of the oaths for Protestants and for Catholics, who were allowed to enroll from 1793.

By 1800 each of the factions had further subdivided into either 'New Lichts' or 'Auld Lichts', depending on their acceptance or otherwise of new, more evangelical views and other matters relating to church government.[18] In parallel with all of this, the Relief Church (or Presbytery) had been formed in 1761. A more liberal group in terms of its offer of communion, it had stronger leanings towards complete independence from the Established Church.

In the wealthier, middle-class burghs, the Burghers and Relief Churches developed as the largest dissenting churches. In the poorer and/or more rural areas, the Anti-Burghers were more numerous. In the cities, the situation was often even more complicated – as it was in Glasgow where the composition of the population was changing rapidly. On the one hand, the influence of the Secession was clear enough. Burghers, Anti-Burghers, Relief Churches, Chapels of Ease, Baptists and so on could be found everywhere. Professor C.G. Brown may have had Dale in mind when he noted that:

> New textile manufacturers, their servants and their workers formed small sects called the Glasites, the Scotch Baptists, the Old Scotch Independents and the Bereans – many of which had originated amongst fishermen, weavers and spinners in East Fife, Dundee and Perth.[19]

This is certainly the case with Dale and the Scotch Independents. John Glas had published his views on the necessary separation of the church from any civil authority in 1726 and, despite his inevitable suspension by the General Assembly, set up his own meeting houses. His ideas about an independent church based on Congregationalist principles lived on after his death and found favour with two ministers in Fife, James Smith of Newburn Parish and Robert Ferrier of the neighbouring Largo Parish. Inspired by Glas's views, Smith began writing his own tracts on independent churches. Ferrier had also read Glas's works and became acquainted with Smith. They both resigned from the Established Church on 17th August 1768 and began holding meetings in local farm buildings, eventually managing to establish a meeting house at Balchristie in Fife where they presided as 'elders' – a term which is more accurately translated as 'preacher' or 'pastor'.[20] They publicised their views on the non-intervention of civil powers in church affairs and the congregation's power of censure and discipline in a pamphlet entitled *The case of James Smith and Robert Ferrier truly represented and Defended*. It was this pamphlet which brought them to the attention of Dale's Glasgow congregation.

Liddell notes that there was a correspondence between the two seceding groups which resulted in their union but the general register of the Old Scotch Independents Church indicates that some members actually went to Fife to persuade Ferrier to come to Glasgow, which he did in 1769 'and was set apart as their Elder, Mr. Dale being unanimously chosen as another and both set apart with fasting and prayer'.[21] The extract below from the general register confirms these appointments but it seems that Ferrier's 'Glassite' views were not sufficiently satisfied.[22] According to one source, Glassites (or Glasites) advocated the washing of each other's feet and 'the abstinence from the use of things strangled and of blood'.[23] Another source suggests that Ferrier was unhappy with practices such as standing while singing and praying and the audible repetition of the 'Amen'.[24] In the late 18th century, these matters were taken very seriously indeed and were the cause of numerous schisms and factions. Whatever the reasons, the date of Ferrier's departure is not given.

Dale remained and served as an elder from 1769 until his death in 1806 – 'a long and faithful ministry', as the general register recorded.[25] A separate list indicates that Archibald Paterson, Matthew Alexander and John Forsyth were appointed in the same year as deacons, important office-bearers in the church.[26] Also noteworthy here is the appointment of Dale's manager, William Kelly, as an elder in 1800, after his departure from New Lanark.

33

List of Elders in the Church at Glasgow from 1768 ~~till 1800~~.

	appointed	
Robert Ferrier	1769	Left the Church from Glassite views
David Dale	1769	Died 17 Mar 1806, after a long & faithful ministry.
Robert Moncrieff	1774	Left the Church from Baptist views
William Cleland	1778	died 16 Dec 1801, after a long & faithful ministry.
William Kelly, ~~...~~	1800	died 15 June 1839 at Row near Helensburg.
David Hill	1801	Resigned the office 1810. went to Edin' 1811.

List of Elders from the General Register of the Old Scotch Independents. (Glasgow City Council: Archives)

Other dissenting sects were busy establishing their own meeting houses in Glasgow at the time – the Bereans (named after the Biblical town of Berea), Anabaptists, Glassites, Baptists and others. The Baptists, in particular, drew many away from the Old Scotch Independents' congregation. Even Dale's wife, 'with blamable contumacy ... took up the side of the argument in opposition to him whom she should have been the first to honour' and joined the Baptists.[27] She remained a member until her death in 1791. However:

> Nothing daunted, Mr. Dale stuck to his colours, and though the church was reduced to a mere skeleton, yet by renewed exertions it soon recovered its wonted strength and numbers.[28]

Many of these dissenting sects were in decline by the 1780s and the townspeople were being drawn in large numbers to the Burgher, Anti Burgher and Relief Churches and by the prospect of 'New Licht' evangelism. The groups eventually came together in 1820 in the United Secession Church. However, although the Scotch Independents did suffer a decline in numbers during the 1780s, it is simply not the case that the church 'fell off' after Dale's death, as Robert Dale Owen suggested in his autobiography.[29] In fact, their numbers recovered significantly. In 1786 they had 45 members, but this number increased to

139 in 1804 and 189 in 1812.[30] James Brown, writing in 1860, reported that the Old Scotch Independents remained in excellent health. Although the congregations in Edinburgh, Kirkcaldy and Balchristie had disappeared, there were healthy numbers in Dundee, Arbroath, Perth, Hamilton, Lesmahagow, Paisley and New Lanark. The church had united with the Inghamites in England in 1814 and the Independents were to be found across the U.K. – in *Kendal and other towns in England and many parts of the Canadas, and one body in the United States*. In Glasgow, the congregation had kept up a *firm and uniform interest* – even more so since their removal in 1836 to their new and comfortable chapel in Oswald Street.[31]

Nevertheless, to begin with, members – and particularly elders or preachers of the dissenting sects – were not well received by members of the Established Church in the city. The fact that Dale and others were not trained, licensed preachers aroused anger and opposition amongst many Glasgow citizens in the early days of the dissenting movement – *no denomination endured more reproach and ridicule than Mr. Dale and his friends*.[32] Dale is reported to have been booed and jostled in the streets and sometimes had to take refuge in a sympathiser's house.[33] He was *denounced as a Nadab or Abihu; he was hooted and pelted on his way to his Sunday labours and his little chapel was attacked by the crowd*.[34] Stones and missiles were hurled at the Meeting House until the windows, roof and other parts of the building were badly damaged.[35] When the protesters were threatened with legal action, they changed tactics and *packed the meeting with a rabble ... for mischief and merriment*.[36] Even Ferrier, who was licensed to preach, was subjected to shouts and insults, but more personal respect was shown to him than to Dale.[37]

Exactly how long this went on is not clear. Certainly Dale put up with it for some time but eventually *he lived down the scathe and the scorn*.[38]

> The good man, Mr. Dale, struggled on, comforted and strengthened by the grand old Apostolic philosophy upon which he preached his first sermon – '*I am debtor both to the wise and the unwise, so, as much as in me is, I am ready to preach the Gospel to you; for I am not ashamed of the Gospel of Christ, for it is the power of God unto salvation to everyone that believe it.*[39]

The tide turned and eventually *a sympathy was created in his favour*.[40] One source describes him as the first man in Glasgow to break down the opposition to unlicensed preachers once and for all.[41] The congregation increased and *men of influence were added to them*.[42] Liddell reports that Dale was a popular preacher whose sermons attracted an audience from far and wide.[43] By 1791 the mob which had once abused him now cheered him on his walk through the streets as a magistrate of the city. This support for Dale represented a very public sea-change in the attitude, not only of the of the crowd but also in that of the civic authorities.

At civic functions, it was the custom in the city for magistrates to process through the streets to and from the Established Church building, dressed in their full robes and chains of office and accompanied by the city officers dressed in their own livery of scarlet coast, cocked hats and ceremonial silver axes. As a dissenter, Dale could not agree to attend the Established Church. Nor would he have been particularly welcome, despite the fact that, after initial hostility and suspicion, relationships between the church and the Secessionist groups within Presbyterianism were eventually characterised by tolerance and some understanding. Rather than embarrass Dale, the authorities arranged to have the city officers escort him to his own church – a clear sign that he had become a respected public figure.

Theoretically, members of the Scotch Independents recognised no authority, civil or ecclesiastical, other than the Bible. Civil authorities such as town councils or magistrates (and even the Crown) had no right to appoint ministers on the congregation's behalf. Anyone could receive the call of God and could preach if he fitted the Apostolic conditions in Scripture. Indeed, such individuals were duty-bound to do so. This required not only a strong belief in God but a willingness to become actively involved in the work of preaching the Word and saving souls. The Scotch Independents, led by Dale, had a plurality of elders who believed they had been 'called' and would preach if required, while continuing to follow their normal occupations.

It should be emphasised, however, that the Independents were not a group of messianic radicals out to reorganise the social structure. Far from it. They were a conservative, pro-Establishment sect. According to Brown's *Religious Denominations of Glasgow*, they retained a strong bias for the doctrines of the Established Church, believing that they were clarifying and purifying these doctrines – '*they agreed to build on the same foundation but differed on the mode of building*'.[44] Further:

> *Degeneracy from original principles, which has overtaken many, has not yet overtaken the Old Scotch Independents. They may not have progressed according to their advantages, but they have not retrograded*.[45]

Despite their religious differences the Secessionist churches and the Established Church all tolerated each other's existence with reasonably good grace. For example, when the Rev. William Menzies arrived in Lanark as a new minister in 1793, having been found '*agreeable to all in the parish*', there was no suggestion of hostility between Menzies and the other preachers in the town.[46] Menzies certainly knew of Dale's small Scotch Independent Church in New Lanark. He knew also of Dale's involvement as a preacher in Glasgow and across the country but the two men were no real threat to each other and got on well.[47] Similarly, Dale made use of the parish church on occasion and was happy to rent pews for any of his employees who wanted to attend or to send some of the children to Sunday school there. There were several dissenting churches in the area and the *Statistical Account* notes that relations between them were harmonious and that there was '*no sense at all of trouble or disputes*'.[48]

Dale had the reputation of being a tolerant man in matters of religious faith – if not always in business. According to one source, Dale was '*destitute of bigotry*' and supported every Christian cause.[49] This view of Dale is reinforced by Stewart in his *Curiosities of Glasgow Citizenship*, although he notes that Dale was '*scarcely free from the prevailing prejudices of the times*'.[50] His cordial relations with other faiths might have been tested (or perhaps reinforced) by his wife's decision, only three years after their marriage, to join a number of others and leave the Independents for the Baptist Church. If this caused any marital friction, it is not recorded anywhere.

As a preacher concerned with saving Christian souls, Dale was always interested in people who had been brought to see the Light. He was particularly intrigued by the apparent conversion from Judaism to Christianity of one Rabbi Moses Levi. Levi, a German, had changed his name to John Joseph Heideck after his conversion. He was forced to flee to France when his enraged father hired three assassins to kill him. He left France for Dublin where he became professor of oriental languages and preached in some of the dissenting churches. When the university insisted on his signing the 39 Articles of the Church of England, he left the country and came to Glasgow, by which time he had become something of a celebrity. At this point, according to one newspaper, Dale sought him out and invited him to stay in Charlotte Street for a few days.[51] During his stay, Dale invited a number of ministers from the Established and Secessionist churches to dinner and arrangements were made for Heideck/Levi to preach at Dr. Gillies' church (the College Church) on the Sabbath afternoon and a different church in the evening, followed by a week preaching in churches across the city. Heideck duly obliged and the churches were crowded, although the *Public Advertiser*'s observation that '*thousands could not get admittance*' seems somewhat exaggerated. He left for London shortly theratter, with the intention of publishing a book in Hebrew. Dale reveals his thoughts on the situation in a letter to his brother-in-law:

> *I have had a very extraordinary Man for my guest for some days past. his name is John Joseph Heideck formerly Moses Levi a Jewish Priest & Rabbi brought to confess Christ about 3 years ago ... he speaks 9 different languages, & has I suppose a greater knowledge of the Hebrew & the other oriental languages than any Christian in Europe...*
>
> *I am perswaded he is a real Christian though in some things he needs to be taught the way of God more perfectly. had you been in your house in Edin[bu]r[gh] I should have recommended him to you f[or] a lodger for a few days his views of several passages of the [Old] Testament are very striking. he is just now Preachi[ng] [in] one of the Meeting houses & Mr. Moncrieff & Mr. Walker [with] him. he is rather confused in some things & I am afraid has got a manner of speaking from the Methodists as it is quite inconsistent with his principles & his conversation in private*
>
> *I think that he should be gently treated, in talking with him on religious subjects. He does not seem to perceive any thing of the order of Christs House but carries the spirituality of his Kingdom to any extreme but not like the Quakers he had formerly such a carnal view of the Kingdom of God that he is afraid of any thing which he calls the Utter. Mr. S M gives him a letter to Doctor Erskine. I will probably give him one to you.*[52]

Dale gave Heideck the benefit of the doubt and became convinced of the man's sincerity. Writing some years later, Robert Reid, who knew Dale and had worked for him for a time, was convinced that Dale and other *Dissenting gentlemen* (Dr. Balfour of the Established Church, William Wardlaw and Archibald Paterson) had all been taken in by a *'pretended convert'*, whose credentials were untenable.[53] Heideck/Levi had not asked for money, but Reid suggests that the visitor did ask for donations before he left, under the pretence that they were for religious undertakings. According to Reid, Heideck 'neither was, nor ever had been a Christian' and was instead *'an arrant imposter and a needy adventurer'*.[54]

Dale, an accomplished preacher himself, would preach at least twice on Sundays, often in the Glasgow Meeting House but also in other places, including the Bridewell and New Lanark and is reported to have learned some Hebrew and Greek to enable him to better understand Biblical texts.[55]

The rest of the week was spent actively carrying out these principles. If talents had to be used, then what better way to do it than by using one's own talents to develop successful businesses and to provide educational and moral training for young children. First among the skills taught in any Scottish school would be reading – to enable personal access to Scripture.

Entrepreneurial business schemes were important in this religious context. Personal election to Grace could be achieved only if the individual lived by the Bible and used any wealth, power or influence to do good in the world. This had its origins in Calvinism and emphasises the utilitarian deployment of wealth created by individual entrepreneurial skills. These were talents to be fostered and Dale had undeniable talents which he used to the full. Combined with his philanthropic and charitable work, his membership of the 'Elect' would seem to have been assured.

These strong religious beliefs provided the moral compass for Dale's professional and personal life, notwithstanding the (very) occasional lapse in his treatment of one or two of his business partners. A sermon given by Dale on 8th January 1792 on the Biblical text Luke X, 42 (on *'choosing the right thing'*) illustrates how he interpreted the Scriptures for everyday living. He noted that the Lord was always to be found doing good and that this was a duty for all:

> *Our minds should be convinced that every thing we do is present duty and in discharge of it we should aim at glorifying God and doing good to ourselves and others.*[56]

Further:

> *Diligence in business matters is a duty; but in this and in all things, we should be 'fervent in spirit, serving the Lord', which cannot be the case if this duty is attended to at the expense of another more important.*[57]

The Gospel demands our utmost attention and ready obedience, making salvation known to us. From his own experience of the Gospel:

> *I hesitate not to say that nothing is capable of giving the mind real happiness but the glorious gospel of God.*[58]

He talks of the folly of three *'objects of pursuit'*, namely, riches, pleasure and honour. As far as riches are concerned, his message is clear – as are the implications and inferences to be drawn regarding his own life as a wealthy businessman:

> *Riches are one great object. These frequently take to themselves wings and flyaway; and though they should not, yet they profit not in the day of wrath. And if these are obtained by oppressing the poor, or withholding from the needy what his wants demand from us, the consequence is awful ... your riches are corrupted.*[59]

Human pleasures, if they were not 'enjoyed under the influence of the word of God', produced *'thorns which more than overbalance all the enjoyment they afforded'*. Honour was a transient, ephemeral thing if it came from man rather than God. 'Those whom God honours shall shine forth as the sun in the kingdom of their father'.[60]

Salvation was the ultimate aim and was one of Dale's greatest concerns from the very earliest days. Dale's youngest daughter, Katherine, aged six months, died in May 1783 from 'chincough' or whooping cough. This was the second daughter the family had lost to illness. Katherine's older sister, Arabella, had died, ostensibly of 'teething' in 1780, aged eight months.[61] Dale wrote to his father on 26th May, nine days after Katherine's death.

In this letter, Dale attempts to comfort his father on the death of another grandchild. He sees it as the will of the Lord and writes at great length on the issue of salvation and how this is a perennial, assured to all believers. He exhorts his father to search the Scriptures where he will find that we are all *self-destroyed sinners* who can find help only in God. Intended as a letter of *'filial love'* to his father, with the wish that the Lord would give them both *'understanding in all things'*, it becomes something of a sermon on salvation:

> *...when we think of the great importance of this salvation we have reason to be astonished at our own indifference about it. In a little time the triffles (sic) that now engage our attention will vanish like a dream the earth over it and all that is therein shall be burnt up. But the will of the Lord endureth forever.*[62]

Letter from Dale to his father, 26th May 1783. (Glasgow City Council: Archives)

In an age when many children died in infancy, a sure and certain faith in an enduring Christ and the certainty of salvation for those who repented their sins would have been a considerable comfort. Dale's faith in these twin pillars of Christianity never wavered throughout his life. It was also part of his nature to support those of similar beliefs and it is therefore no surprise to find him doing so in his declining years in Rosebank. A Secessionist group in Cambuslang calling themselves 'Brethren' had been formed in 1799 and, *'dissatisfied with the unevangelical preaching then prevalent'*, they built a small chapel (known variously as the Congregational Church or 'the Tabernacle') on the Rosebank estate in 1801. Dale, who had recently bought the estate, contributed financially to the building work and attended some of the services.[63]

Dale's own life certainly seemed to be a combination of entrepreneurialism, philanthropy and education – all driven by a strong religious evangelism. He was no saint, however, and would not have pretended to be so. In his *Memoir*, Liddell makes an interesting (if not entirely convincing) case that Dale's pursuit of profit and new business was not always in line with

Christian moderation. Liddell appears to approve of Dale's business flair when it was successful and when, as a result, many were employed by him. However, Liddell notes that when there were crises (and Dale is quoted here as referring to three such unnamed and undated occasions when bankruptcy loomed and he was '*thrown back on the world*'), then people, including Dale's family, would suffer.[64] According to this line of thought, Dale's behaviour brought discredit to his Christian character.[65] However, Dale, it seems, '*with all his shortcomings*' was a great and good man who did essential service to the country when it required the impetus of such a mind.[66]

Other commentators, particularly of a religious background, simply accepted Dale's human frailties without any great debate. His successes were seen as a sign of God's blessings:

> *A zealous promoter of the general industry and manufactures of his country, his schemes of business were extensive and liberal; conducted with simple prudence and perseverance; and, by the blessing of God, were crowned with such abundant success as served to advance his rank in society, and to furnish him with the means of that diffusive benevolence which rendered his life a public blessing, and shed a lustre on his character rarely exemplified in any age of the world.*[67]

All were agreed, however, that a strong religious faith was an enormously powerful driving force throughout Dale's life and one which lay behind all his commercial successes and his charitable works.

References: Chapter 15

1   From *A Walk from the Town of Lanark* (Anonymous). No date but presumed to be *c*.1800. Quoted in Donnachie, I. and Hewitt, G. (1993) *Historic New Lanark*. Edinburgh: E.U.P., pp.55–6.

2   Liddell, A. (1854b) 'Memoir of David Dale', in Chambers, R. (ed.) (1855) *A Biographical Dictionary of Eminent Scotsmen*. Glasgow: Blackie, p.167.

3   Brown, C.G. (2004) 'Religion & Social Change', in Devine, T.M. & Mitchison, R. (eds) *People & Society in Scotland*, Vol. 1, 1760–1830. Edinburgh: J. Donald, p.146.

4   'The Rise of the Congregational or Independent Churches in Scotland' in *General Register of the Old Scotch Independent Church*, Glasgow City Archives, TD 420/1, p.27.

5   Ibid.

6   Liddell, A. (1854b) *Memoir*, p.168.

7   The others were: Paterson's wife; Mrs. Orr; John Forsyth and Mr. James Allan.

8   Mechie, S. (1960) *The Church and Scottish Social Development 1780–1870*. Oxford: OUP, p.11. N.B. There is some debate as to the location of this church. Stewart argues that it was in Shuttle Street. See Stewart, G. (1881) *Curiosities of Glasgow Citizenship as Exhibited Chiefly in the Business Career of its Old Commercial Aristocracy*. Glasgow: J. Maclehose, p.116. Cleland favours Canon Street. See Cleland, J. (1816) *Annals of Glasgow, Comprising an Account of the Public Buildings, Charities and the Rise and Progress of the City*, 2 vols. Glasgow: James Hedderwick. Vol. 1, p.136.

9   Liddell, A. (1854b) *Memoir*, p.168.

10 Ibid.

11 *The Rise of the Congregational or Independent Churches*, p.27.

12 Stewart, G. (1881) *Curiosities*, p.116n. There is some doubt about the date. Cleland notes that Cruden did not leave until 1774. See Cleland, J. (1816) *Annals*, Vol. 1, p.136.

13 Liddell, A. (1854b) *Memoir*, p.169.

14 *The Rise of the Congregational or Independent Churches*, p.28.

15 The 'Old' came many years later, to distinguish it from the more modern independent sects set up by people like Haldane and Ewing and the Inghamites in England, with whom the Old Scotch Independents joined forces in 1814. See Liddell, *Memoir*, p.169.

16 Reid, R. (Senex) (1884) *Glasgow Past and Present*, 3 vols. Glasgow: David Robertson & Co., Vol. III, p.180n. This source notes that the church was in the Grammar School Wynd.

17 Note also that many Dissenting Presbyterian groups referred to themselves as Presbyteries or Synods rather than Churches. See Brown, C.G. (2004) *Religion*, p.145.

18 Brown, C.G. (2004) *Religion*, pp.150–151.

19 Ibid.

20 Murray, D.B. (1976) *The Social and Religious Origins of Scottish Non-Presbyterian Dissent from 1730–1800*. St Andrew's university: Unpublished Ph.D thesis, Chapter 2.

21 Liddell, A. (1854b) *Memoir*, p.169 and *Rise of the Congregational or Independent Churches*, p.29.

22 *Rise of the Congregational or Independent Churches*, p.33.

23 Stewart, G. (1881) *Curiosities*, p.57.

24 McGavin, J. (1814) *Historical Sketches of the rise of the Scots Old Independent Church & the Inghamite Churches*. Colne, p.vi.

25 *Rise of the Congregational or Independent Churches*, p.33. The Robert Moncrieff mentioned who joined the OSI in 1774 and who later became a Baptist is most likely to have been a local apothecary.

26 *Rise of the Congregational or Independent Churches*, p.36.

27 Stewart, G. (1881) *Curiosities*, p.60.

28 Brown, J. (1860) *Religious Denominations of Glasgow*. 2 vols. Glasgow, Vol. I, p.24.

29 Owen, R.D. (1874) *Threading My Way: Twenty Seven Years of Autobiography*. New York: Carleton & Co., p.37.

30 *Rise of the Congregational or Independent Churches*, p.30.

31 Brown, J. (1860) *Religious Denominations*. Vol. 1, p.27.

32 McGavin, J. (1814) *Historical Sketches*, p.vi.

33 Brown, J. (1860) *Religious Denominations*. Vol. 1, p.23.

34 Mitchell, J.O. 'David Dale – A Model Old Glasgow Worthy', in *The Glasgow Herald*, 27th August 1886.

35 Liddell, A. (1854b) *Memoir*, pp.169–70.

36 Ibid.

37 Ibid.

38 Mitchell, J.O. *David Dale*.

39 Stewart, G. (1881) *Curiosities*, pp.60–61.

40 Brown, J. (1860) *Religious Denominations*. Vol. 1, p.23.

41 Ibid.

42 Ibid.

43 Liddell, A. (1854b) *Memoir*, p.175.

44 Brown, J. (1860) *Religious Denominations*. Vol. 1, p.26.

45 Ibid., p.28.

46 Sinclair, J. (ed) (1791–99) *The Statistical Account of Scotland*, 1791–99, 21 vols. Vol. XV, p.41.

47 The same could not be said of the relationship between Menzies and Robert Owen. Vide supra Chapter 17.

48 See Sinclair, J. (ed) *The Statistical Account*, Vol. XII, pp.109, 120–121. Also Vol. V, pp.517–8, 523. Dissenting groups included the Burghers, Anti-Burghers, Baptists, Bereans, Glassites, Reformed Presbytery/Cameronians, Quakers, Methodists, Relief churches, Anabaptists.

49 Malloch, D.M. (1913) *The Book of Glasgow Anecdote*. NewYork: Scribners, p.38.

50 Stewart, G. (1881) *Curiosities*, p.60.

51 *The Public Advertiser*, London, 8th August 1785.

52 David Dale to John Campbell, 4th July 1785. In Johnston, W.T. (ed) (2000) David Dale & Robert Owen Studies. Livingston: Officina Educational Publications.

53 Reid, R. (Senex) (1884) Glasgow Past and Present, Vol. II, pp.96–7.

54 Ibid.

55 Liddell, A. (1854b) Memoir, p.175. This story various according to source. An obituary in *The Lancaster Gazette & General Advertiser* on 5th April 1806 noted that Dale had learned Greek and Latin, while A.D. Robertson avoids controversy by referring simply to Dale's knowledge of 'ancient tongues'. See Robertson, A.D. (1975) *Lanark: the Burgh and its Councils, 1469–1880*, p.255.

56 Substance of a Discourse by David Dale, 8th January 1792. Glasgow University Library Special Collections: Mu22-a.12, pp.4–5.

57 Ibid.

58 Ibid.

59 Ibid., p.6.

60 Ibid., p.9.

61 National Records of Scotland: Old Parish Records. OPR Deaths 644/01 0590 0066 Glasgow. Vide infra, Chapter 1.

62 Dale to William Dale, 26th May 1783. Glasgow City Archives. MS 63.

63 Wilson, J.A. (1929) *A History of Cambuslang*. A Clydesdale Parish. Glasgow: Jackson Wylie & Co., p.122.

64 Liddell, A. (1854b) Memoir, pp.175–176.

65 Ibid.

66 Ibid.

67 *Glasgow Herald*, 21st March 1806. Obituary Notice written by Ralph Wardlaw.

Part 7

The End of the Beginning

Chapter 16: Dale and Owen, 1798–1806.

Sale of New Lanark and Marriage of Anne Caroline

Robert Owen's first recorded visit to New Lanark was on 9th March 1798 and coincided with the period when Dale's health was at its most unpredictable (just prior to a fairly acute stage between 1801–1803), well-documented in Moncrieff's Royal Bank letters of the time. We know that Dale's health had been an issue since at least 1795 and that this had affected his involvement with the Chamber of Commerce and the Royal Infirmary. It is also possible that, as his health began to cause concern, Dale became increasingly conscious of the absence of a male heir and began to look around for a suitable successor. This seems a much more plausible explanation for the sale of the mills than that offered by Owen, i.e. that Dale felt that the mills were not as successful as they should have been because William Kelly and James Dale were poor managers. In fact, Kelly had nothing to prove and Dale had every confidence in him. Similarly, Dale was more than capable of dealing with any initial doubts he might have had about James Dale. The fact that he did not choose to do so suggests that mismanagement of the mills was not the reason for their sale.

Dale's letter to Dr. Currie in July of 1798 makes it perfectly clear why the mills were on the market and also the conditions attached to the sale. Dale was concerned about his health and wanted to retire. Any new owner would have to manage the mills in such a way as to ensure that the children, particularly the pauper apprentices, were well cared for:

> I have been rather indifferent in my health for some time past, and I wish much to retire from business but I am afraid that I shall not get the works easily disposed of. I would not wish to dispose of them to any person that would not follow out the plan I have laid down for preserving the health and morals of the children.[1]

It is likely that Currie would not have been particularly surprised to hear that Dale considered the welfare of the children to be paramount. He had been aware of Dale's views for some time. Dale had written to him in 1795, reflecting on the difficult and stormy financial situation the New Lanark community had weathered in 1790 and indicating that his greatest concern, apart from paying wages to those who were owed them, had been 'keeping together the people and particularly the children'.[2]

Given the commercial success of New Lanark, there were many suitable candidates and several potential buyers – many of whom had visited New Lanark, but none, it seems, were quite so persistent in their efforts as Robert Owen, on behalf of the Chorlton Twist Company. However, Dale's letter to Currie of July 1798 makes no mention of Owen's visit to New Lanark in March of that year. It is possible that Dale, while he may have been aware of Owen's existence, simply did not consider this young Welsh employee of a Manchester firm to be a serious contender. Equally likely is the fact that they did not meet at all at this early stage. Dale was frequently in Glasgow and would have left the business in the hands of William Kelly and James Dale. Owen himself rather confirms this view when he notes that his first visit to the village was to meet James Dale, not David Dale.[3]

This visit marked the beginning of one of the most important ventures in the history of both cotton spinning and communitarianism, one which was to have worldwide impact within a few years. At this stage, however, Dale was the major figure – something which Owen clearly recognised. He considered Dale to be one of the most extraordinary men in the commercial world of Scotland – a major figure in the manufacturing world, a cotton spinner, merchant, banker and preacher and a man who was universally trusted and respected.[4] This view is likely to have been shared by Messrs Atkinson, Barton, Heatly and Price, Owen's bosses, who had sent him north in the first place. Their company was a relatively new one which relied to a significant extent on the demands of the manufacturers in Manchester and Glasgow. Owen's job was to buy cotton, have it made into yarns and then sell it and he claims to have had many customers in the Glasgow area.[5]

It was at this point that the personal and professional relationship between Dale and Owen began to establish itself. Owen had met Dale's eldest daughter, Anne Caroline, then aged 19, through a Miss Spear, sister of his friend and fellow Manchester broker, Robert Spear. Miss Spear was a close friend of Caroline's and a frequent visitor to the house in Charlotte Street. After some initial conversation, Caroline asked Owen to visit New Lanark to meet her uncle James. This may or may not have been the visit recorded in the visitors' book on 9th March 1798. Owen cannot fail to have been impressed with the scale of the operation but his memoir, written when he was a very old man, undervalues and underestimates the business and the community at that time. He considered New Lanark to be '*a primitive manufacturing Scotch village*' with '*four mills for manufacturing cotton*'.[6]

Caroline's mother had died seven years earlier and the young girl now had the responsibility of looking after the rest of the family. Owen began to meet her on a regular basis for walks in Glasgow, often chaperoned by Miss Spears without Dale's knowledge in the initial stages. Given that Caroline's sisters also began to act as chaperones, the situation could not be kept from Dale for very long and the two men met for the first time on the pretext (and pretence, according to Owen) that Owen and his Manchester partners were interested in buying New Lanark. Owen noted in his autobiography years later that Dale was cold and suspicious at this first meeting.[7] They met again but things did not improve. By now, Dale had had time to think about the suggestion that Owen would be involved in taking over and managing the business. Caroline had told her father about the courtship but Dale was less than impressed by this news. Owen's recollection is that Dale was hostile to the suggestion of a wedding and to any notion of a business partnership. According to Owen, Dale accused him of being a '*landlouper*' – an opportunist on the lookout for a wealthy bride and Dale refused to countenance any idea of marriage between Owen and his daughter and of any business partnership or takeover. On both counts he indicated that he would prefer '*a Scotchman*' – one he knew something about and could trust.

Whether Owen's account of events is accurate or not is open to question. Given that Dale kept a close eye on his competitors north and south of the Border, it seems highly unlikely that he had never heard of the young businessman who was carving out such a successful career for himself. Liddell is clear that Dale did know Owen '*as having, by his talent and persevering industry, raised himself from humble circumstances to be manager of an extensive spinning-mill at Chorlton*'.[8] Nevertheless, if Owen is correct, Dale appears to have been opposed to the idea of Owen becoming a son-in-law and the new manager and part-owner of New Lanark.

Caroline, however, although she would never have married without her father's consent, stuck to her guns and the old man's views began to moderate. Over a period of almost two years, his resistance was gradually worn down, helped in part by Scott Moncrieff and his wife who lent their support to the young couple and persuaded Dale that the match was a good idea.

Before any wealthy businessman could be married, certain financial arrangements had to be made. It is likely that these were brokered in summer 1799. According to Owen, Scott Moncrieff played a significant role in arranging these.[9] Owen had capital of his own amounting to £3,000 and Dale offered the same sum as a dowry, provided Owen settled £300 per annum on Caroline and any children in the event of the latter's death.[10] This dowry was separate from any money, property, shares etc. which Caroline might inherit on her father's death.

While all this was going on, separate discussions were in progress regarding the mills – Dale having apparently changed his mind about Owen's involvement. According to Owen, when he asked Dale about a selling price, Dale had great difficulty in coming up with a figure. Owen attributes this to the fact that Dale spent most of his time in Glasgow and was seldom in the village.[11] This seems an incredible account of events. With one or two exceptions such as Spinningdale, which was more of a charitable venture than anything else, and his later involvement in Stanley Mills, Dale's businesses were profitable. Further, there is considerable evidence throughout his career that he kept a very close eye on prices, profit margins and market conditions affecting not just his own businesses but those of his competitors. He would know exactly what New Lanark was producing, how much profit was being generated and how much the business was worth. If Dale agreed, as he did, to a selling price of £60,000 payable over 20 years at 5% interest then we can be sure that these figures were not arrived at randomly.[12] Similarly, if these terms are relatively generous, then, given that Dale could take a firm line with people like Monteith and drive a hard bargain when necessary, we can assume that Dale meant them to be generous – perhaps because of the new family connection with Owen and/or because he believed that Owen and the Manchester partners could not only maintain the business but also expand it. As far as the family is concerned, it is worth noting that Dale's terms extended well beyond the likely date of his death. His family, therefore, would be the main beneficiaries in the longer term – the funds being handled by a group of trustees which now included Robert Owen. Finally, given Dale's concerns about the welfare of the children in his mills, it is also reasonable to argue that he was happy with the new owners' plans for the child employees, pauper or otherwise.

These agreements are likely to have been largely in place by the time of Caroline's wedding in September 1799 because the wedding plans also included a three month honeymoon away from the business from October until the end of December. In fact, although the Manchester firm were not to assume full control until 1st January, 1800, Owen began to take over some of the management of New Lanark before his wedding, basing himself in the Clydesdale Inn when the Dale sisters were in New Lanark.[13]

Clearly, Owen was not going to be the sole owner of New Lanark – a fact which is sometimes overlooked in some potted histories of the community. He was to have a ninth share in the business and a salary of £1,000 per annum.[14]

The wedding itself took place in the family house in Charlotte Street with Dale's friend, Rev. Mr. Balfour, officiating. Balfour was minister of the Outer High Church, part of the Established Church. Although Dale was a pastor and preacher himself, he and other Secessionist ministers were not licensed and therefore legally unable to perform wedding ceremonies. Owen was apparently surprised at the brevity of the ceremony. Balfour explained that it was normally a longer process where he would explain to the couple their duties in a marriage. However, Balfour felt that he could not presume to do this 'with Mr. Dale's children while he lived and was present', knowing that Dale would have already given the couple 'such advice as he deemed necessary and sufficient'.[15] After the honeymoon in Manchester, the couple returned to Glasgow at the end of December 1799. The portrait of Owen below (by Mary Ann Knight, c.1800) is the earliest known representation of him and is one of the very few to show him as a young man.

Robert Owen 1771–1854. Pioneer Socialist. (undated)
Mary Ann Knight. (Scottish National Portrait Gallery)

Retirement

From the beginning of 1800, therefore, Dale was officially relieved of the huge responsibilities associated with New Lanark. However, it is important to note that, although the period 1800–1806 saw a decline in Dale's public and professional profile, often because of ill-health, the decline was a fairly controlled affair, managed jointly by Dale and his new son-in-law, who seems to have won Dale's confidence fairly quickly after such an unpromising start just a few years earlier. From 1800 Dale took little to do with the day-to-day running of New Lanark and before long Owen installed his own manager, Robert Humphreys, in place of William Kelly and James Dale. Owen knew Humphreys from their time (1791–1994) at Peter Drinkwater's Bank Top Mills in Manchester where Owen had been the manager. In his autobiography, Owen gives a number of reasons for the dismissal of Kelly and Dale – some more plausible than others. He claims that there was 'little cordiality' between the two men and that they had not been keeping up with new developments, particularly in relation to factory machinery.[16] Kelly and James Dale may or may not have been friends but the charge of failing to keep up with developments in technology is a strange one to level at Kelly, who was something of an expert in matters mechanical. Much more likely is Owen's assertion that the mills were simply not being managed the way he wanted them to be managed and that Kelly and James Dale 'had old notions and habits directly opposed' to Owen's and were therefore 'incompetent to comprehend' his views or to assist him in his plans.[17]

David Dale did not interfere with Owen's plans for New Lanark and it seems that he began to trust Owen's judgement in matters of business. Dale, with one eye firmly on retirement, was concerned to reduce his business partnerships. Owen refers to Dale's 'anxiety' about the matter.[18] The process began fairly quickly, in 1801 with the Catrine mill – Dale's other great success story, in partnership with Claud Alexander, which was sold to the powerful Finlay family.[19] This was followed by the disposal of the mills in Newton Douglas and in Spinningdale. The date of withdrawal from the Newton Douglas mill is not known but, as far as Spinningdale is concerned, Owen's memory of events is that Dale asked him to travel to Sutherland to look at the business, which Owen duly did in 1802, in the company of Dale's friend and business partner, George Macintosh.[20] Owen found the place unsuitable as a permanent site, largely because of the location, and there seems little doubt that he advised Dale to sell up, but Dale and Macintosh continued to support the venture (largely as a charitable concern) until 1804. Owen's view of events was that the disposal of the mills in Sutherland, Newton Douglas and Catrine allowed Dale 'to pass the remainder of his life more quietly and much more to his satisfaction'.[21]

Owen's account conveniently ignores the long-running saga of the Stanley Mills in Perthshire which began in 1801 and which, according to Liddell, caused Dale 'much uneasiness during the latter years of his life' – as well it might.[22] In this case, rather than refraining from any financial involvement with cotton mills, Dale began to contribute large sums of money to support his friend, James Craig, in the latter's involvement at Stanley. Owen's role in all of this is not entirely clear. His memory is that he advised Dale against any such involvement.[23] This may well have been true but is not a view shared by Liddell who noted that 'unaccountably, through the influence of Mr. Owen', Dale began to contribute large amounts of money (totalling £24,270 according to one source) to help Craig keep the mills afloat – a situation which continued until Dale's death in 1806.[24] His money continued to provide significant support for the Stanley mills well after his death and there is some evidence to suggest that Owen approved the transfer of funds for this purpose.

However, the decision to plough good money after bad into Stanley between 1801 and 1806 was, at the end of the day, Dale's own. Dale may have been old and in poor health but he was still entirely capable of making decisions. He decided, for example, that, in addition to his house in Charlotte Street, which became his base during the winter months, a country estate would help him relax in the summer, away from the bustle of city life and which might, 'when his advancing years required repose', improve his health.[25] In April 1801, only a year or so after the sale of New Lanark, he bought Rosebank, a small landed property and dwelling house in Cambuslang, about four miles east of the city, on the banks of 'the yet unpolluted and beautiful Clyde'.[26] He bought the property from John Dunlop of Carmyle, a wealthy Glasgow merchant councillor who had been Provost in 1794–1795 and whose family had interests in tobacco, coal, tanning and textiles.

Dale's grandson, Robert Dale Owen, born in 1801, recalls visiting Rosebank as a young child, describing it as a '*veritable fairy land*':

> *...the quaint, old fashioned mansion, with its honeysuckle-shaded porch, its pointed gables ... its unexpected nooks and corners and its perfume of mignonette from boxes set in window sills ... the marvellous garden in front with its succession of terraces, its gigantic evergreen hedges, its enigmatical sun-dial, its wonderful bowling green, and its wilderness of roses with a thousand unknown flowers beside ... an abode of bliss apart from the real world.*[27]

Idyllic as Rosebank apparently was, it was also where Dale 'practised a handsome hospitality'.[28] Scott Moncrieff could certainly attest to that. Moncrieff thoroughly enjoyed his visits to Rosebank. While these visits were ostensibly a mix of Royal Bank business and pleasure, Moncrieff was greatly taken by Dale's new, modern 'Rumford' kitchen and the abundant produce that came from the estate, notably the oats and potatoes. It was a great delight for him to sample the great 'boiling, roasting and baking' on offer to dinner guests and he took full advantage of it, although his letters show that he was constantly aware (and concerned about) Dale's frequent bouts of ill-health, which Moncrieff put down to gout.[29] Ever the banker, Moncrieff wrote in 1803 to William Simpson, the chief cashier, that, despite Dale's jest that Rosebank had cost him 'ten thousand', Dale could, if he wished, make a considerable profit, given that the price of the land in the neighbourhood was 'going beyond all sense and reason'.[30] It is unlikely that Dale bought it as an investment for himself as Rosebank was where he could relax, particularly when he was ill.

Nevertheless, he did try to continue his Royal Bank work in Glasgow when his health permitted and the journeys to and from Rosebank became quite difficult at times. Dale attempted to reduce his commitment to the bank and by 1803, when Moncrieff was ready to retire, had largely achieved this. He offered to act as an adviser to John More, who had taken over but this did not happen. John More, although on very friendly terms with Dale, never asked for any advice and Dale effectively retired from the banking business at the end of December 1803 at the same time as Moncrieff.

It would be a mistake to think that Dale had retired from the financial world altogether. He continued to invest (and speculate) in the world of finance, despite his fluctuating health and, two months before he retired from the Royal Bank, turned his attention to the insurance business, The Glasgow Fire Insurance Society included Dale as one of their founding directors and was a viable business during the remaining years of Dale's life. The intention was not only to provide business insurance but also to lend money – hence the involvement in 1805 of John More from the Royal Bank.[31]

Similarly, Dale had built up a considerable property portfolio during his life and he continued to "trade" in property, sometimes on his own, sometimes as part of Campbell, Dale & Co. and sometimes in partnership with other individuals, well after he sold New Lanark. In 1803, for example, he was involved in the purchase of land and property in Glassford Street and in a very extensive land deal in the Shettleston area. Between 1804 and 1805 he bought additional land in Charlotte Street and sold land and property in Ingram Street. There is no indication that Robert Owen was directly involved in any of this although it is interesting to speculate as to who was directing Dale's financial affairs in 1806. It seems likely that Dale's lawyers were looking after property matters in January of that year when eight acres of land in Barrowfield were purchased in his name. The Sasines also show an entry on 15th March, 1806 – after Dale's death – indicating a purchase of land and tenements, listed as 'David Dale in trust and behoof of David Dale & Co.' in Clyde Street and Parson's Haugh.[32] Even allowing for the fact that there was always a gap between the date of purchase and the entry into the register, there is no doubt that these transactions were carried out in the last few weeks, or even the last few days of Dale's life. Clearly, he could not hope to gain anything personally. Assuming he was aware of these and consented to them, he (or someone representing him) may have been increasing the value of his estate up to the very last.

As this biography has been at pains to point out, Dale had an extensive public profile of philanthropic activities and although his property portfolio remained active, the charitable activities which demanded attendance at committee meetings and public functions were curtailed somewhat in the final few years of his life. Again, Robert Owen's involvement is quite noticeable. Presumably this involvement was because of his relationship with Dale and his desire (and his duty) to offer assistance to his father-in-law but there is also at least some evidence that Owen became personally involved in some of these causes, albeit briefly.

At the beginning of December 1800, for example, Owen accompanied Dale to a meeting of the great and good ('noblemen, gentlemen, freeholders, Justices of the Peace, Commissioners of Supply, Clergy and Heritors of the County of Lanark') in Hamilton. Chaired by the Duke of Hamilton, the group were trying to do something about the high price of grain and meal which was having an adverse effect on the local population and wanted to supply the local markets at a much reduced price, recognising that this might require 'voluntary subscription or otherwise'.[33] A few months later, in February 1801, Owen joined a committee in Glasgow, convened by Dale, of 'The Manufacturers & Cotton Spinners in Glasgow and its Vicinity' which was opposing plans to introduce a tax on printed cotton (calico) goods. Given that other members of the committee included the likes of James Monteith, Kirkman Finlay and John McIlwham, it would have done the newcomer no harm at all to make himself known to these men. Also, if Dale were to become indisposed, Owen could continue at least some of his work.

Much the same is true of Dale's work with the Chamber of Commerce, an extensive contribution made over a number of years. His last recorded appearance was in January 1805 when he was re-elected as a director. Even at this stage, he was still involved in a number of committees – one looking at government legislation which would adversely affect the price of corn and the other looking at government proposals to establish a paper stamp office in Edinburgh,[34] but this belies the fact that he had attended very few meetings in the previous three years because of his health.

What is less well-known is that Owen must also have been elected as director sometime in 1805 because in December that year when the secretary wrote to all the directors regarding the annual elections, both Dale and Owen appear in the 'List of the Twenty Three Gentleman who continue in the Direction of the Chamber of Commerce and Manufactures in the City of Glasgow for the Year 1806'.[35] Given that Dale must have been very ill by this time, his work in the chamber during 1805 and 1806 appears to have been covered by Owen, who served as a director until December 1806, attending the four quarterly meetings (and receiving a Burgess Ticket in the June of that year).[36]

Chamber of Commerce and Manufactures.
Glasgow, 26th December, 1805.

Sir,

You are desired to attend a General Meeting of the Chamber of Commerce and Manufactures in this City, on Wednesday the 1st. day of January next, at one o'clock afternoon, in order to give your voice for the election of six new Directors, in the room of six who are disqualified in terms of the Royal Charter; and one in room of Alexander Gordon, Esq. who has resigned.

In order to enable you to make your choice, I annex a list of the Twenty-three Gentlemen who continue in the Direction, of those who are disqualified, and of the other Members of the Society.

I am, Sir,

Your most obedient Servant,

Secretary.

Glasgow Chamber of Commerce Election Notice, December 1805. (Glasgow City Council: Archives)

LIST of the TWENTY-THREE GENTLEMEN who continue in the Direction of the Chamber of Commerce and Manu
tures in the City of Glasgow, for the year 1806.

Messrs. John Gordon	Messrs. Hugh Crofs	Messrs. Robert Owen
Arch. Graham	John Swanston	John Stirling
Robert M'Nair	Robert Carrick	David Dale
Will. M'Neill	Willm. Wardlaw	Henry Glassford
David Mutrie	Kirkman Finlay	James Black
Gilbert Hamilton	W. Ewing M'Lea	Robert Bogle, jun.
Dugald Bannatine	Arch. Smith	Colin M'Lachlan
Alexander Crum	Henry Monteith	

LIST of SIX GENTLEMEN who go out of the Direction.

Messrs. John Alston	Messrs. Robert Dunlop	Messrs. Will. Orr, Paisley
John Campbell, sen.	John Hamilton	Will. Shortridge

LIST OF THE MEMBERS.

Messrs. Claud Alexander	Messrs. Alex. Gordon	Messrs. John Perston
Alexander Allan	Arch. Hamilton, jun.	Matt. Perston
John Austin	James Hopkirk	W. Robertson
John Buchanan	John Laurie	John Semple
Patrick Colquhoun	John Leitch	James Smith
Cunningham Corbett	John Mair	Thos. Stewart
Robert Cowan	John M'Caul	Andrew Stirling
James Crum	W. M'Dowall, Garthland	James Stirling
James Denniston	Geo. Mackintosh	George Thomson
William Finlay	James Mackenzie	David Todd
James Fyffe	John Monteith	Archd. Wallace
Will. Gillespie		

IN PAISLEY.

Messrs. Herb. Buchanan	Messrs. Claud Neilson	
Will. Carlile	William Orr	
Robert Fulton	John Pollock	
James Kibble		
William King		

IN GREENOCK.

Messrs. John Hamilton
Walter Ritchie

Dale's involvement with charitable institutions was also supported by Owen. At its lowest level, this took the form of matching Dale's donations to charities such as the Magdalen Society, to which they both contributed £5 in 1804.[37] Much more significantly, there is a strong sense that, as Dale's contribution and attendance at meetings of major institutions declined, Owen was on hand to take over if necessary, or at least to represent the Dale family. For example, the Merchants House elected Owen as their director on the board of the Town's Hospital in November 1806, – a role he was happy to take on, albeit briefly, presumably out of respect for his father-in-law's work there.[38]

Owen's role in the affairs of the Royal Infirmary, another of Dale's philanthropic ventures, was a more enduring one. Having seen the Infirmary project through to completion in 1795, Dale declined to officiate any longer because of his health. Although he stepped down as a manager and attended no further meetings, he did continue to contribute financially for the rest of his life, ensuring that a significant number of the workforce at New Lanark would be eligible for treatment. What is interesting is that

Robert Owen's name also appears as a subscriber to Glasgow Royal Infirmary in 1797. (Dale was still listed as one of the 'Visitors' at that time.) This was some months before Owen's first recorded visit to New Lanark and some considerable time before he met Dale himself. It is possible that Owen was allying himself with Dale's charitable causes from the earliest opportunity. Owen was a regular and faithful subscriber from 1797 until at least 1811 and took on the role of visitor in 1802–1803 and director (manager) in 1804–1805.[39] While Dale had made full use of his position as subscriber to refer patients to the Infirmary, Owen appears to have referred only one patient, but he did support the institution and the family name by continuing to pay subscriptions for Dale's other daughters, 'the Misses Dale', for a long time after Dale's death.[40] As Owen's autobiography indicates, Caroline's sisters played a significant part in Owen's family life after Dale died and Owen was at pains to look after their welfare.

Things had clearly come a long way from the frosty and suspicious atmosphere between Dale and Owen in early meetings. Relations between them and between family members in general appear to have been very good, which is just as well, given that they all inhabited the same space on many occasions. The Owens stayed at various times at Charlotte Street (usually the winter months) and at New Lanark or Rosebank. Fortunately, Owen describes Dale as being 'much attached to family'.[41] Owen's autobiography is the main source of evidence here and although Owen's recollections are often inaccurate in terms of dates, business arrangements etc. throughout his long life, there is little reason to doubt much of what he says regarding domestic arrangements at this stage. There was a 'sincere friendship and strong affection' between the two men, based on mutual respect.[42] When Robert Dale Owen was born, Scott Moncrieff was on duty in the Royal Bank when 'in comes Mr. Dale and Mr. Owen' in great excitement, to announce the new arrival.[43] Dale and his son-in-law clearly got on well and Owen says that his affection for Dale increased daily.[44] Owen frequently refers to Dale's amenable and benevolent nature – he was 'affectionately kind' and 'one of the most liberal, conscientious, benevolent, kind-hearted men' he had ever met and there was never an unkind word exchanged between them.[45] This kindness and benevolence is echoed, as might be expected, by the young Robert Dale Owen who paints an affectionate portrait of his grandfather:

> …his gold-headed cane; his portly form filling the large easy chair; then the hand on my head and the face lighted up with kindness – the nicest face, I thought, in the world – that always welcomed me when I was brought to see him and talk to with him in the parlour after dinner.[46]

Owen senior describes Dale as 'a genuinely good and religious' man, which is praise indeed, given his own open hostility to organised religion and those who practised it,[47] but one wonders how accurate Owen's reflection is when he argues that he never fell out with Dale over religious matters because Dale 'admitted the truth' of many of Owen's 'ideas and facts' on religion. Discussions on religious matters were held 'with full charity for each of their opinions'.[48] Dale was indeed a kind and benevolent gentleman for the most part but in matters of business and religion, he had strong principles and was not known for giving way easily – or, on occasion, for giving way at all.

Similarly, Owen's claim that he enjoyed Dale's 'full confidence in all his affairs' and that Dale accepted his advice on all matters from 1800 is probably true for the most part but Owen himself goes on to cite an incident where this clearly was not the case.[49] In March 1804 Dale established a trust (registered in the Books of Council & Session in Edinburgh) and in November of that year he was in the process of finalising the details of his will.[50] He asked Owen for his advice on how much money ought to be left to the Misses Campbell, his late wife's sisters. Dale intended to leave them nothing at all but Owen advised the sum of £100 per annum for each and drew up a codicil to that effect. Dale refused to sign it, despite Owen's advice. Not for the first time in his life, Dale simply refused to budge. According to Owen, Dale left the matter hanging: 'I leave it to my son-in-law to act after my death as he may decide'.[51] Around this time, Dale wrote to Campbell of Jura asking him to transfer his money (some £20,000, according to Owen) to the New Lanark Twist Company, explaining that Owen would continue to send accounts and provide cash as required.[52]

Death of David Dale

Inevitably, a combination of old age and poor health took their toll. Dale had first declared his health to be a matter of concern as far back as the mid 1790s and from Scott Moncrieff's correspondence with the Royal Bank head office it would appear that he was suffering from gout. This caused him particular difficulties from 1801 onwards, although his symptoms may have been more closely linked to the condition which was eventually recorded on the death certificate as the cause of death – 'dropsy'.[53] The swelling and pain caused by dropsy might well have been diagnosed as gout, although the latter has more to do with joint pain. Whatever the cause, Dale had been subject to frequent and painful bouts of illness and considered himself to be seriously ill on several occasions, such as between December 1803 and January 1804 when he had confined himself to his bed.[54] Although he recovered, these episodes continued to recur.

Liddell, writing some years after the event, states that Dale was confined to bed in Charlotte Street from the beginning of March 1806. This time the illness did not subside and Dale died peacefully there on 17th March.[55] Another account, also written some years later, has a slightly different version of events, noting that Dale was able to walk about in comparatively good health until a short time before his death.[56] This version includes a poignant and somewhat melodramatic death-bed scene, where Dale summond leading members of his church to his bedside and exhorted them:

> ...to remain steadfast in their Christian profession and gave them the dying testimony of his faith in the Gospel – asked them for forgiveness if on any occasion he had given them offence and prayed for a blessing on them, after which, as the elders of Ephesus did to Paul, they all fell upon his neck and kissed him, sorrowing most of all for the words that he spake, that they should see his face no more.[57]

After this, 'exhausted by the parting scene, he rapidly sank' and on the following day, 'he departed in the sixty-eighth year of his age, deeply regretted by all parties':

> ...by the church, who loved and revered him as their faithful partner; by the poor who largely participated in his liberal charities and by the general community who esteemed him both as a man and as a Christian.[58]

Events took their normal course and the funeral took place in the city on 21st March. As might be expected, given Dale's high profile, it was a large and very public affair, a fitting tribute for a man who was so well-known and well-liked. Mourners included the magistrates and ministers of all denominations and between 200 and 300 'respectable inhabitants'.[59] Other reports echo these figures.[60] In addition, The Times noted that what it called 'the concourse of spectators', i.e. those who were not officially attending the funeral, was 'immense'. Owen acknowledged the great public loss of a man universally loved and respected by all who knew him and added that, on a more personal level, he felt a heavy loss.[61] For the young Robert Dale Owen, not yet five years old, and walking with his father behind the hearse, the funeral was a profound experience – the new black suit straight from the tailor's shop, 'the stream of visitors; the stir in the house; the show of carriages; the interminable procession ... the crowds in every street as we passed on'.[62]

Dale's body was interred beside the other deceased members of his family in the lair he had purchased 26 years earlier, in 1780, when his daughter Arabella had died. The resting place in the Ramshorn Kirkyard was marked, not by any sculptured marble but by a plain 'hewn stone' built into the east boundary wall with a simple inscription which merely notes 'This Burying Ground is the property of David Dale, Merchant, Glasgow'.[63] The date below the inscription is 1780, the year he had purchased the lair. It is still visible today.

The 'greatest cotton magnate of his time in Scotland' was finally at peace.[64] The ceremony was concluded by one final act of kindness which reflected the way in which Dale had lived his life. Small sums of money were distributed to 'several hundreds of the poor' after the interment.[65] Dale would certainly have approved.

The newspapers of the day were not slow to report the demise of such a prominent and popular figure. Obituaries and fulsome tributes appeared in newspapers and magazines across Britain within a few days.[66] Appendix 14 contains a selection of these. It is perhaps an indication of Dale's national standing not only that an obituary appeared in The Times but that the paper considered him to be 'a truly great gentleman'. All the notices cover, to a greater or lesser extent, the main aspects of his life and work and see these as inseparable. Hence the great success in business, for example, is always set against a backdrop of civic duty, Christian charity, benevolence and evangelism and an engaging and personable nature. In Glasgow, the notices in *The Courier* and *The Herald* were particularly warm, which seems appropriate, given that he had done so much for the city. In Montrose, 'Plorator' was clearly moved on a personal level to respond to a perceived loss and here too, the full range of Dale's attributes was recognised.

The great man had been laid to rest, the tributes had been paid and the family mourned their loss. In most cases, that would have been largely the end of the matter. Wills would be read, monies distributed and businesses already signed over would continue. The deceased's great success and charitable deeds, having been publicly recorded, would be an important part of his legacy for future generations.

In David Dale's case, however, it was not quite so straightforward.

References: Chapter 16

1   Extract from letter of David Dale to James Currie, 9th July 1798, in Currie, W.W. (1831) *Memoir of the Life, Writings and Correspondence of James Currie*, 2 vols. London: Longman, Rees, Orme, Brown & Green. Vol. I, p.162

2   David Dale to James Currie, 8th August 1795 in Johnston, W.T. (ed) (2000) *David Dale & Robert Owen Studies*. Livingston: Officina Educational Publications.

3   Owen, R. (1857) *Life*, pp.42–44.

4   Ibid., pp. 45, 53.

5   Ibid., pp.42–44.

6   Ibid., p.46. He makes a similar comment later in reference to the population's alleged ignorance of gold coinage –'I wondered if I had come into a very primitive district'. Ibid., p.52.

7   Ibid., pp.50–51.

8   Liddell, A. (1854b) 'Memoir of David Dale', in Chambers, R. (ed), (1855) *A Biographical Dictionary of Eminent Scotsmen*. Glasgow: Blackie, p.164.

9   Owen, R. (1857) *Life*, p.54.

10 Butt, J. (1971) 'Robert Owen as a Businessman', in Butt, J. (ed) *Robert Owen. Prince of Cotton Spinners*. Newton Abbot: David & Charles, p.171.

11 Owen, R. (1857) *Life*, p.53.

12 Butt, J. (1971) *Owen as Businessman*, pp.171–2.

13 Podmore, F. (1906) *Robert Owen – A Biography*. London: Hutchinson & Co., p.53.

14 Butt, J. (1971) *Owen as Businessman*, pp.172.

15 Owen, R. (1857) *Life*, p.55.

16 Owen, R. (1857) *Life*, pp.56, 59.

17 Ibid., pp.56, 59, 71–78.

18 Ibid., p.78.

19 Vide infra. Chapter 9.

20 Owen, R. (1857) *Life*, pp.72–75.

21 Ibid., p.78.

22 Vide infra. Chapter 9. See also Liddell, A. (1854b) *Memoir*, p.167.

23 Owen, R. (1857) *Life*, pp.59, 71–5.

24 Liddell, A. (1854b) *Memoir*, p.167. Also Cooke, A.J. (1977) 'The Early Development of Stanley', in *Stanley: its History and Development*. University of Dundee Extra-Mural Dept. pp.11–18 and Cooke, A. (2010) *The Rise and Fall of the Scottish Cotton Industry*, pp.52–3.

25 Liddell, A. (1854b) *Memoir*, p.167.

26 Stewart, G. (1881) *Curiosities of Glasgow Citizenship as Exhibited Chiefly in the Business Career of its Old Commercial Aristocracy*. Glasgow: J. Maclehose, p.61.

27 Owen, R.D. (1874) *Threading My Way: Twenty Seven Years of Autobiography*. New York: Carleton & Co., p.40.

28 Eyre-Todd, G. (1934) *A History of Glasgow*, 3 vols. Glasgow: Jackson, Wylie & Co. Vol. III, p.318.

29 Moncrieff to Simpson, 6th April 1802. R.B.S. Archives: RB /837/152. Vide infra, Chapter 10.

30 Moncrieff to Simpson, 20th August 1803. R.B.S. Archives: RB/837/1262.

31 Vide infra, Chapter 11.

32 Vide infra, Chapter 11.

33 *The Caledonian Mercury*, 8th December 1800.

34 Glasgow Chamber of Commerce. *Minutes*, 2nd & 22nd January 1805. Glasgow City Archives: TD 1670/1/3.

35 Chamber of Commerce Minutes. TD 1670/4/104cc1805.

36 Entry is dated 2nd June 1806. Burgess ticket. R. Owen, merchant. B&G.B. as mar. Anne Caroline, dau. to David Dale, merchant. B&G.B. 2nd June 1806. See Anderson, J.R. (ed) (1935) *The Burgesses and Guild Brethren of Glasgow, 1757–1846*. Edinburgh. J. Skinner & Co., p.240.

37 *The Caledonian Mercury*, 18th March 1805.

38 *Glasgow Towns Hospital Minutes of Directors Quarterly meetings, 1732–1816*. Minute of November, 1806. Glasgow City Archives. Rare Bk No. 641983.

39 Vide infra, Chapter 14. Owen may well have continued beyond 1811 but the Annual reports from 1811–1822 are missing.

40 Ibid.

41 Owen, R. (1857) *Life*, p.71.

42 Ibid., p.81.

43 Moncrieff to William Simpson, 7th November 1801. R.B.S. Archives: RB/837/443.

44 Owen, R. (1857) *Life*, p.72.

45 Ibid., p.71.

46 Owen, R.D. (1874) *Threading My Way*, p.40.

47 Owen, R. (1857) *Life*, p.82.

48 Ibid., p.72.

49 Ibid., pp.82–3.

50 The Trust was dated 10th March 1804 and was registered in Edinburgh on 29th March that year. His will was dated 10th November 1804. See Butt, J. (1971) *Owen as Businessman*, pp.172n, 203.

51 Owen, R. (1857) *Life*, pp.82-3.

52 Ibid., p.86. Also Butt, J. (1971) *Owen as Businessman*, p.173.

53 National Records of Scotland. OPR. Deaths. 21st March, 1806. 644/0106000362 Glasgow.

54 Atholl MSS. Letter Book of Robert Owen. R. Owen to J. Craig, 19th December, 1803, 25th January & 17th May, 1804. Cited in Donnachie, I. (2000) *Robert Owen of New Lanark and New Harmony*. East Linton: Tuckwell Press, p.91.

55 Liddell, A. (1854b) *Memoir*, p.174.

56 Stewart, G. (1881) *Curiosities*, p.62.

57 Ibid.

58 Ibid.

59 *The Times*, Obituary. 28th March, 1806, p.3.

60 Liddell notes ' a numerous assemblage of private friends, amounting to several hundreds'. Liddell, A. (1854b) *Memoir*, p.174.

61 Owen, R. (1857) *Life*, p.83.

62 Owen, R.D. (1874) *Threading My Way*, p.40.

63 Liddell refers to The Ramshorn Kirkyard as 'St. David's Churchyard' See Liddell, A. (1854b) *Memoir*, p.174. It is in the street currently marked Ingram St. in Glasgow.

64 Devine, T.M. (1999) *The Scottish Nation 1700–2000*. London: Penguin, p.115.

65 *The Times*, Obituary. 28th March, 1806, p.3.

66 For example: *The Bury & Norwich Post*, 2nd April, 1806; *The Lancaster Gazette & General Advertiser*, 5th April, 1805; *The Aberdeen Gazette*, 26th March, 1806.

Chapter 17: Legacy and Reputation

David Dale.
(Provenance unknown. Robert Owen Museum, Newtown.)

In September 1806, *The Scots Magazine* noted that David Dale had left '*at least £100,000 to his family, after having appropriated in his lifetime more than twice that sum to purposes of purest benevolence*'.[1] This reappeared, verbatim, in *The Gentleman's Magazine* of that year and again some years later in the *New Statistical Account* for the Parish of Stewarton.[2] However, in reality, neither *The Scots Magazine* nor anyone else had the remotest idea in 1806 what Dale was actually worth and it is doubtful even now if an accurate figure can be arrived at with any certainty. Similarly, *The Preston Chronicle* confidently reported some 30 years after Dale's death that Owen came into his wife's fortune of £30,000 when Dale died but there is little evidence of this.[3]

When Dale established the trust in 1804, he had appointed a number of trustees to look after his estate. Most of the names are familiar figures – family members or men whom Dale, rightly or wrongly, believed to be trustworthy: Archibald Campbell of Jura; John Campbell, W.S. and Brigadier General Colin Campbell, his two brothers-in-law; Claud Alexander of Ballochmyle; Robert Owen; John More from the Royal Bank (who kept the books of the trustees and the ledger of accounts between Campbell of Jura and Robert Owen). Two other less well-known figures were also appointed by Dale – Walter Ewing Maclae of Cathkin – an accountant from a Glasgow merchant family with interests in the West Indies and Robert Gray, who is simply referred to as '*jeweller in Glasgow*'. His firm produced some of the most prestigious gold and silverware to be found anywhere in Britain. Presumably Dale knew him because of this but nothing is known about their relationship or why Dale would have appointed him as a trustee.[4]

The trustees were directed to pay each of Dale's two younger daughters, Jean Maxwell and Julia Johnston, £3,000 each, two years after their father's death, thus equalising the amount given to Caroline on her marriage. Each of the five daughters was to receive £2,000 three years after Dale's death and the residue of the estate was to be held in liferent for his daughters.[5] Robert Owen was to receive a sum of £2,000.[6] However, there were some problems with the estate from the very beginning. Dale, in common with most of his late 18th century business colleagues, formed multiple partnerships on a very regular basis and disentangling these was inevitably going to be a time-consuming business. Liddell was correct when he observed that the nature of Dale's contracts and joint partnerships made it impossible to free the estate from responsibility until some years after his death.[7]

Just a few days before he died, Dale wrote a memorandum – effectively a codicil – which was discovered in his personal papers shortly after his death. In this, he was concerned to look after some other members of his family and some old family friends in Stewarton whom he had apparently been supporting for some time:

> It is Mr. Dale's desire that the pensions which he has hitherto given to some of the inhabitants of Stewarton, paid to them by Mr. Blackwood, should be continued as long as the said inhabitants shall live – That Mrs. Dale, wife of his late brother Hugh, should receive £50 annually and retain the occupation of the house in which she now resides as long as her son James shall live with her and after her death that £30 per annum should be given to board James in some respectable family in the country. That £20 should be paid to each of his sisters in law, namely Arabella, Christy, Mrs. Yuill and Jane as long as they shall live. That £15 per annum should be paid to Betty Grierson as long as she shall live. £30 to Robert Walker and £20 to Andrew Gerrard during their natural lives. That the £800 due to Mr. Dale by his brother James shall not be considered as a debt but as now given to him. That one year's salary be given to Alexander Louden. And that Charles, Mr. Dale's present house servant, have £10 for his attention during Mr. Dale's illness. That his nephew David Dale should be exonerated from debt due by him to Mr. Dale and if he should by indisposition be prevented from gaining a livelihood then he should have £25 a year during such indisposition.[8]

Dale's inventory on 7th August 1806 consisted of only two items – 25 shares (each worth £230) in the Forth & Clyde Navigation Company and the sum of £5,683, being his share of the capital stock of the Royal Bank.[9] John More signed an affidavit to the effect that these sums were all that could be traced at the time but he promised to investigate further and once he had identified '*with precision*' the other elements of the estate (which at that point he estimated to be worth £10,000–£12,000), he would make the necessary financial arrangements.[10]

Much the same was true of the heritable property. Dale owned Charlotte Street and Rosebank but both properties were used by the family (a situation which continued until 1823 when Charlotte Street was sold to Moses McCulloch for £2,200 – considerably less than it cost to build.)[11] However, as far as other properties were concerned, the situation was much more complicated because of Dale's partnerships in numerous land and property deals throughout the city and the role of the trustees here is unclear. There was a period following Dale's death when some of these investments were disposed of. In June 1806 – '27 Falls of land' held by Dale and others in the Wellshot area were sold off, with the consent of the other partners. The following month, the land and properties in Clyde Street which had been bought only a few months earlier were also sold. In 1807, George Macintosh '*surviving partner of Dale and Macintosh*' sold the dyeworks in Dalmarnock. In June 1809, the land and properties in the Shettleston area, bought in partnership with others for £20,000 in 1803, were sold to a group of businessmen. Some land in Cambuslang was sold in 1812 and the inkle factory in Shuttle Street was sold in 1819.[12] These disposals must have raised a great deal of money but its whereabouts and the role of the trustees in the process remain shrouded in mystery. Perhaps some of it did go to the Dale sisters because they bought land and properties in the Bridgeton/Barrowfield area and were in a position to help Robert Owen financially but there appear to be no records indicating that they received very much at all. It seems that a great deal of Dale's money never reached its intended recipients:

> That Dale was a very rich man is beyond question. It is, however, doubtful whether it reached his daughters in the ample way his friends expected.[13]

This point was echoed by Liddell who, while acknowledging that things were complicated and that land and property fluctuated in value, is forced to conclude that '*a comparatively small part came ultimately to his family*'.[14]

There was a further, more detailed, inventory of Dale's estate in 1811, by which time it might have been expected the picture would have been much clearer. However, this inventory revealed a number of surprising and potentially disturbing matters regarding the management of his estate. Far from clarifying matters, the inventory opened up new issues.

The estate was now valued at £64,684 (approximately £6m in current terms) but much of this was still tied up in one way or another with various cotton mills. For example, despite the fact that the Newton Stewart mill had been sold off years before, it appeared that Sir William Douglas still owed the Dale estate £6,378. Dale's joint partnership in Catrine with Claud Alexander was valued at £6,666, Dale's share being one half of that sum.

The 1811 inventory also indicated that Alexander owed Dale a considerable sum of money – some £8,199 in this case.[15] The private papers of the Hagart-Alexander family, however, indicate quite a different situation. The *Inventory of the Personal Estate of the late Claud Alexander of Ballochmyle, given up in December 1811* notes that the Dale estate actually owed Claud Alexander a similar sum of money:

> The sum due by the heirs of David Dale Esq. for which a Decreet Arbitral has now been pronounced by Mr. Archibald Smith has not been confirmed – about £8,000.[16]

There is one figure in Dale's inventory which stands out ahead of all the other sums of money and which caused considerable controversy at the time. This appears as 'Stock in company with James Craig, Spinner at Stanley Mill – £10,000'. The equivalent figure nowadays would be somewhere approaching £1m. Six years after Dale's death, it appeared that his trustees had continued to invest a fortune in an enterprise which was spectacularly unprofitable and which suffered from very poor management. John More at the Royal Bank had sanctioned these payments to Craig but it seems that Robert Owen had also approved these transfers without the knowledge of the other trustees. The matter only surfaced because John More had been embezzling large sums from the Royal Bank to finance an extravagant lifestyle. When the bank finally began to investigate all of this in 1816–1817, the earlier payments to Craig and the others came to light. The figure of £10,000 may in fact be an underestimate of the actual sums involved between 1801 and 1811. Research by Butt indicates that in January 1817, a total of £33,186 (plus interest of £8,096 in bills) was missing from the accounts of the Dale estate and had been paid, without the knowledge or approval of the other trustees, to James Craig, Robert Owen (who had personally signed many of the bills involved) and Stewart Douglas, all of whom had been involved in managing (or supervising the management of) the Stanley Mills between 1806 and 1813.[17]

Significantly, not all of the money involved in Stanley was actually Dale's. A great deal of it belonged to Archibald Campbell of Jura, described by Cooke, in a fine example of ironic understatement, as 'an unwitting investor in Stanley'.[18]

Campbell had agreed to Dale's 1806 request to transfer his considerable funds to the New Lanark Twist Company. Dale knew that his own life was coming to a close and the situation with Campbell which had previously pertained (i.e. where Campbell had banked with Dale personally) had to change. Campbell must have been reassured by Dale's promise that Owen would continue to send accounts and provide cash as required. However, Owen did not transfer the money to the company account. He kept it in his own partnership account, although he did send annual statements. For the next 17 years, Owen's finances seemed to lurch from one crisis to the next, usually as a result of the frequent changes to the business partnerships involved with New Lanark. At the same time, he was pursued by Campbell for the return of his money. In 1810, Owen still owed nine instalments on the New Lanark purchase deal and a further £13,000 (plus interest) to Campbell. The trustees themselves owed Campbell £10,000. By 1812, Owen's debt to Campbell had increased to £25,000, by which time Campbell, concerned about Owen's possible bankruptcy, had started proceedings against him.[19] Having paid some of the money back, Owen was lucky to avoid sequestration in 1813 thanks to the Dale sisters who put up all their property as security. Jean Maxwell Dale wrote to one of Owen's partners in July of that year:

> That you may be able to judge the sufficiency of the security offered, I beg to inform you that a sum considerably above the amount of Jura's debt is in the hands of our father's trustees belonging to us, which, if you wish, will be certified by them.[20]

Ironically, no one did actually check the health of the Dale estate at that point. Had they done so, they would have discovered some of the problems which were to surface three years later. The Dale sisters believed they had more than enough to bail Owen out, however, and they further agreed to pay Campbell five annual instalments of £4,000, should it be necessary.[21]

Things quietened down until 1816 when the John More story became public and the question of missing funds came to the fore. Once again, Owen was in trouble and, once again, Dale's daughters were in the firing line. The Royal Bank disposed of Stanley Mills, demanded its money from the trustees and threatened to stop all payments to the Misses Dale until Owen repaid Campbell of Jura. Finally, Owen managed to retrieve the situation by offering the New Lanark Company as additional security. Dale's daughters did not lose their property but it was a close-run thing.[22] The debt was eventually settled but not until 1822, some sixteen years after Dale's death. Owen's role in the management of his father-in-law's estate has, understandably, been called into question What Dale would have thought about his daughter's inheritance being put in jeopardy can only be guessed at. Mary Dale's husband, James Haldane Stewart, accused both Owen and More of misappropriation of funds.[23]

Mary Dale & James Haldane Stewart. (George Patten, A.R.A., 1839. Private collection. Courtesy of David & Sebatian Blackie.)

More recently, Robertson's close examination of the finances involved led him to conclude that the affair reflected little credit on Owen. According to Robertson, Owen seemed to have been guilty of something very closely akin to 'fraudulent conversion' and was lucky to escape the ruin of his career through bankruptcy.[24] In the same piece, however, Robertson throws Owen's reputation a fairly generous lifeline, in which it is suggested that Owen was constantly having to worry about new partnerships and this, along with the sheer scale of the business at New Lanark, meant that he had to take more financial risks than he might otherwise have done, particularly if finance and investment was hard to come by.[25] Whatever the case, there can be no doubt that Owen's management of the Dale estate left much to be desired.

It is also arguable that Owen was largely responsible for mismanaging the other part of Dale's legacy – his reputation. This caused a great deal of upset at the time, not least, it must be assumed, amongst Dale's daughters, including Owen's wife. While there is no suggestion that Owen deliberately set out to denigrate the achievements of his father-in law, many of his comments from 1812 onwards, designed to advertise his own emerging 'New View' of society, were clearly intended to emphasise how far the village had progressed under his inspired and visionary management. In so doing, however, he overplayed the contrast between New Lanark under Dale and under himself. The result was that he upset a lot of people who had known Dale personally or who had worked with him or who had sung the praises of the village under Dale's ownership. Many of them felt obliged to spring to the defence of the late proprietor. Was it possible that all the visitors who had written in such glowing terms of their visits to New Lanark over a period of some fifteen years had got it all wrong? Were the obituary notices all wrong? This would seem to be highly unlikely and yet Owen, never one to underplay his own achievements or the erroneous thinking of those opposed to his views, called it all into question – probably unwittingly.

At various points throughout Robert Owen's life (although not during Dale's lifetime) he made a number of less than flattering comments about the New Lanark community during the period of Dale's ownership. Owen's negative description of the village and its people were sometimes seized upon and exaggerated by Owen's acolytes and this in turn produced an equally robust and exaggerated response from Dale's supporters. The reality of life in Dale's New Lanark, of course, lay somewhere in between.

Dale's Reputation

The problem really began in 1812, at the height of the Campbell of Jura affair, when Owen was involved in a rather frantic search for new business partners for the mills in an attempt to stave off imminent bankruptcy. His *Statement Regarding the New Lanark Establishment* of 1812 therefore needs to be seen in this context and has been accurately described as more of a refined company prospectus, intended to outline his plans for the community, than anything else.[26] Nevertheless, Owen sowed the seeds of a controversy which lasted for many years. He began by acknowledging, as he was subsequently to do on many occasions, that his father-in-law had been well-known for his benevolence and philanthropy. However, later in the *Statement*, he described Dale's villagers thus:

> ...a collection of the most ignorant and destitute from all parts of Scotland, possessing the usual characteristics of poverty and ignorance. They were generally indolent and much addicted to theft, drunkenness and falsehood, with all their concomitant vices, and strongly experiencing the misery which these ever produce.[27]

According to Owen, these people had now been transformed after a period of twelve years under his direction. Their vices had disappeared and a form of *tabula rasa* had been created, on which a new script, not necessarily determined by the people themselves, could be written:

> ...they are now become conspicuously honest, industrious, sober and orderly; so that an idle individual, one in liquor, or a thief, is scarcely to be seen ... and they are become almost a new people, and quite ready to receive any fixed character which may be deemed the most advantageous for them to possess.[28]

This was a theme which Owen returned to at various points in the years which followed. He always recognised Dale's personal benevolence and philanthropy but argued that the mills had been poorly managed during Dale's ownership. Owen's intention was not to denigrate Dale personally but to demonstrate how transformational his own management and directorship had been and how powerful his 'new view' actually was. He always sought extensive publicity for his own achievements at New Lanark – a point noted by many commentators down the years. Nevertheless, even if his comments were sometimes ill-considered, they were extremely powerful.

He did something very similar in the second essay of *A New View of Society* and in his evidence to the Parliamentary Select Committee looking into factory conditions in 1816. In *A New View of Society*, the acknowledgement of Dale's benevolence was delayed for a few lines to allow Owen a vivid and dramatic description of the village during Dale's time – or perhaps, more accurately, the village before the arrival of Robert Owen.

> ...a very wretched society ... every man did that which was right in his own eyes, and vice and immorality prevailed to a monstrous extent. The population lived in idleness, in poverty, in almost every kind of crime; consequently, in debt, out of health, and in misery ... the whole was under a strong sectarian influence, which gave a marked and decided preference to one set of religious opinions over all others, and the professors of the favoured opinions were the privileged of the community.[29]

Dale is subsequently praised as a benevolent proprietor who spared no expense in providing high quality food, comfortable accommodation and clothing for his pauper children. Owen went on to applaud Dale's employment of a surgeon and '*the best instructors in the country*' who were employed to teach in the schools. Continuing the theme of Dale's benevolence, he noted that '*kind and well-disposed persons*' were appointed as supervisors.[30]

However, at the same time, Owen argued that it was impossible for children to work, as they did in most cotton factories from 6 a.m. until 7 p.m. and then be fit for school in the evening. Warming to his theme, he noted that many of them 'became dwarfs in body and mind and some of them were deformed'.[31] Many ran away and fell prey to all sorts of temptations in Glasgow and Edinburgh:

> Thus Mr. Dale's arrangements, and his kind solicitude for the comfort and happiness of these children, were rendered in their ultimate effect almost nugatory.[32]

Owen's evidence to parliament in 1816 made exactly the same points about the village prior to his involvement.[33]

In May 1813 *The Belfast Monthly Magazine*, ostensibly reporting on an extract from *The Philanthropist* regarding Owen's *New View*, provided an even more extreme version of New Lanark, pre-Owen. In this emotive and occasionally histrionic piece, which takes Owen's *New View* as its starting point, Dale's village begins to sound like something from Dante's *Inferno*. The 'sickly, feeble and decrepid' children lived amongst and were corrupted by a 'vicious' population of the 'least reputable classes'.[34] Family life consisted of 'wretched moral discipline', intoxication, poverty, nakedness, hunger and filth. Lying and thieving prevailed; women were corrupted; mothers were ignorant of housekeeping and everywhere was dirt and confusion. On closer inspection, the article indicates that this was the magazine's general view of all cotton mills at the time but that 'these productive causes of depraved and noxious character in the manufacturing population were attended with several aggravating circumstances in the case of New Lanark mills'.[35] Dale's irregular attendance is cited as the principal (and only) cause of the people living 'pretty nearly as they pleased'. As a result, 'all the vices ... and all the misery which usually characterise a manufacturing population raged among them with more than usual violence' and Dale was forced to sell up because of his age and because of his 'disgust with the scene'.[36] The article ends with a straight 'lift' from Owen's *New View of Society*:

> Theft and the receipt of stolen goods was their trade, idleness and drunkenness their habit, falsehood and deception their garb, dissensions, civil and religious, their daily practice; they united only in a zealous systematic opposition to their employers.[37]

Interestingly, this piece is also at pains not to blame Dale personally for the problems. He is seen once again as a good man who simply was not in control of events. The implication in both pieces is that Dale's managers were to blame for failing to create (and monitor) the correct conditions for moral improvement. In this view, the subsequent success of the schools, the mills and the community must be attributable to better, more enlightened, visionary, 'hands on' management under Owen's direction.

This kind of thinking was revisited by Owen in his autobiography many years later. He argues that, despite Dale's best intentions, New Lanark had been populated by idle, intemperate, dishonest, drunken characters living in 'evil' conditions under a 'wretchedly bad' system prior to the change of ownership.[38] But the key to this is the word 'system'. Owen did not blame Dale explicitly for all the perceived problems of the community – although, given the nature and tone of some of his comments, there is more than a degree of naivety, irresponsibility or culpability if he thought that other people would see it that way. The New Lanark system, 'kindly intended', had been 'constructed and managed by ordinary minds, accustomed only to very primitive proceedings', and was itself only a reflection of a wider social system, based on erroneous, traditional views of society, employment and human relations – a system which Owen believed was entirely responsible for all the evils in society and which required to be swept away and replaced with his own 'New Social System'.[39]

Owen's comments and those of *The Belfast Magazine* (and other commentators who based their views on Owen's public statements) seem strikingly at odds with the huge number of positive descriptions of the community under Dale. Many of the positive comments emphasize Dale's personal benevolence and kindness and, as such, there is no contrast with Owen's views. Every view of Dale notes his kindly disposition, his sense of humour, benevolent rule, his piety and evangelism. He is a 'father to the indigent', 'a true patriot' and 'a bright luminary to Scotland'. *The Caledonian Mercury* observed:

> Never was the phrase applied with greater propriety than to say of Mr. Dale, 'he deserves well of his country'.[40]

Where the contrast occurs more obviously is in the description of events and conditions in the village. There are two points to consider here – firstly the general view of New Lanark under David Dale and secondly, the reaction to some of Owen's critical remarks about the community.

Many of these positive views of the community have already been aired in earlier chapters but there are additional examples which emphasise the point. Liddell notes that the morals of the villagers were good and the *Statistical Account* is very clear that Dale and his managers paid great attention to morals. The people were decent, orderly and '*generally industrious*' and there was a lower crime rate than in any parish of similar population.[41] Garnett in his visit noted that the people were happy and comfortable, living in '*neat, substantial houses*' in '*a charming village*', the crime rate was enviably low and that the community was healthy and well regulated, in striking contrast to other mill communities which could only be regarded as '*seminaries of wickedness and disease*'.[42] The pauper children were better treated in New Lanark than anywhere else in Britain, amply demonstrated in Dale's detailed response to Bailey's letter in 1796, and the system was considered to be a model of good practice at the time. Indeed, as Davidson has pointed out, when The Health and Morals of Apprentices Act was passed in 1802, it sought to impose conditions which were already in place in New Lanark. These included maximum working hours of twelve per day (bearing in mind that Owen increased these hours for a time); the provision of at least two suits of clothes and a requirement for education and religious instruction.[43] *The Caledonian Mercury*, reporting the sale of New Lanark in 1799, was very clear about the public view of the community and its response to the news that the business had been sold was typical of newspaper reports all over the country at that time:

> These works have long attracted the notice and admiration of the public. In point of extent, they are unequalled in this country and the gratitude of thousands will ever attend Mr. Dale who erected them and gave employment to an incredible number of people.[44]

The paper also raised another issue which was often mentioned in relation to New Lanark – its social function in providing employment and education for children who might otherwise have become '*burthensome to society*' or have fallen victims to '*every species of vice*'.[45] New Lanark is seen as rescuing the children from the latter fate.

McNayr's Guide refes to '*elegant and lofty*' houses and streets which were '*broad, regular and clean*'.[46] In his *Tour* of 1801, John Bristed describes Dale as a man committed not only to the health of the community but to their morals – as one might expect of such an evangelical Christian and Secessionist pastor.[47] Like Garnett, Bristed describes, not the '*wretched society*' of Owen's *New View of Society*, but '*neat, well-built houses, forming broad, regular and cleanly (sic) streets*'.[48] The children who lived with their parents did so in '*comfortable and neat habitations*' while the pauper children were well cared for at Dale's expense. All the children were pictures of '*health and happiness*'. Their healthy bodies and minds:

> ...are such as do honour to the goodness and discernment of Mr. Dale and present a striking contrast to the generality of large manufactories in this kingdom, which are the schools of vice and of profligacy, the very hotbeds of disease and of contagion.[49]

And so it could go on, with countless examples of reports and comments praising New Lanark. The contrast with Owen's description of a 'wretched society' is stark. He could not have been surprised (although one wonders) that his comments provoked an outcry from individuals and organisations who had known Dale or who had come into contact with New Lanark. Chief among these was the Church of Scotland.

It might be seen as surprising that the Established Church should leap to the defence of Dale, given that he had left the Church of Scotland and had suffered for some time because of this. However, after a very shaky start, Dale had enjoyed good relations with the Established Church in Glasgow and in Lanark, where the redoubtable William Menzies was the parish minister. However, it is no exaggeration to say that Menzies and Robert Owen loathed each other and the disagreements between them became increasingly personal after Dale's death. When Owen's views of the New Lanark community were published, Menzies, entirely opposed to what he saw as Owen's anti-religious views, began to voice that opposition and to draw the Presbytery into his battle. Menzies was outraged at Owen's comments about Dale and New Lanark but it is also true that this provided a useful platform from which he could attack Robert Owen's anti-religious sentiments and the battle became personal.

Menzies, ordained in Lanark in December 1793, was a strong-minded man, not afraid of challenging established views wherever he found them, including his own church.[50] Despite Dale's position in the Scotch Independents, Menzies had had no difficulties with him because of Dale's Christian witness and the fact that he sent many of his apprentice children to the parish church and supported the new Sunday school there. Menzies approved of the inclusion of the Catechism in the New Lanark schools. Similarly, the Presbytery, who had the right to inspect parish schools, had never felt the need to concern themselves with the schools in the village. Menzies considered Dale to be '*benevolent and pious*' and was aware of '*much good*' being done at New Lanark.[51]

After Dale died, Menzies became increasingly concerned and irritated by Owen's refusal to include the Catechism in the curriculum and by the '*falseness and anti-scriptural character*' of his system.[52] Menzies took his concerns to the Presbytery, who (probably unlawfully) claimed jurisdiction over all the schools in the parish, including the private or 'adventure' schools. The Presbytery were, predictably, less than impressed by Owen's new system of schooling and were incensed by Owen's claims that the community had been a disaster under Dale but was now entirely reformed. This point in particular became a bone of contention between Owen and a number of others.

For his part, Owen claimed that he was '*checked and obstructed*' in his '*straightforward honest progress by religion*', which, in Lanarkshire, meant William Menzies and the Presbytery.[53] Owen accused Menzies of opposing him at every turn, knowing that Menzies considered him nothing less than a traitor to church and state.[54] He claimed that Menzies had been parish minister in Lanark for twenty years and that there had been no improvement in the morals of the parishioners, whereas, in a short period of time, the morals and behaviour of the New Lanark people had been transformed. According to Owen, theft and vice of every kind had disappeared – preparatory steps along the way to a gradual transformation of the entire world.

All of this was too much for Owen's critics. By 1823, *The Morning Chronicle* was describing the situation as '*serious warfare*' between the Presbytery of Lanark (including Menzies) and Robert Owen.[55] This was ostensibly about the Presbytery's objections to the Catechism being removed from the New Lanark curriculum (which Owen denied) and Owen's refusal to allow the Presbytery to inspect his schools but, in reality, the Presbytery were particularly annoyed about Owen's claims that he had transformed the morals and the behaviour of the community. The Presbytery countered by noting that, despite the presence of many good Christians in the village, '*illicit intercourse between the sexes*' had increased since Dale's time. Indeed, the moral state of the villagers had not improved at all since the death of '*the late, excellent Mr. David Dale*'.[56] *The Christian Remembrancer* picked up the story later the same month and accused Owen of '*much deception and much delusion*'.[57] They too were incensed at what they saw as an attack on the memory of David Dale. Owen, they argued, had '*unceremoniously vilified the management of that pious and benevolent man, his late father-in-law*'.[58]

Owen found himself under attack from William McGavin, a merchant in Glasgow who took strong exception to what he saw as Owen's overblown claims about the improvements he had made to New Lanark. McGavin was concerned about the damaging effects of Owen's comments on the clergy and on David Dale's reputation.[59] He wrote a series of fifteen letters to *The Glasgow Chronicle* between 20th October 1823 and 24th January 1824 in which he took Owen to task, accusing him of failing to understand (among many other things) human nature, encouraging anarchy and insubordination: being the author of '*visionary, insane projects*' and insulting the common sense of mankind.[60] According to McGavin, the state of morals in New Lanark was equal to that of any other village in the kingdom. That situation, however, was not because of Owen's principles, but in spite of them. Good principles he told Owen, '*were inculcated there by your predecessor*'. These principles, combined with Dale's insistence that the people should read the Bible, had been responsible for the good moral behaviour of the villagers, '*not ... your new views and principles*'.[61] He warmed to his theme the following month:

> I cannot believe that it [New Lanark] *was pandemonium before you came to it, or that it is a paradise now. I had the honour of being personally acquainted with Mr. Dale, to whom you pay a becoming tribute of respect; and knowing that he was just such a man as you say, I think it was impossible that, with his benevolent heart and ample means, his workers could have been in such a state of wretchedness and degradation as that which you describe. Besides, I have long been in habits of close intimacy with persons who were connected with the establishment while it belonged to Mr. Dale, who have assured me, that then the utmost attention was paid to the education of the young and the comfort of all classes of the work people.*[62]

McGavin argued that Dale represented Christianity in action – a committed Christian living a virtuous life, working to better the lives of others. He was *'an eminent example of industry, probity, benevolence and almost unequalled munificence'*.[63]

Owen came under attack again later in 1824 when the Rev. William Aiton of Hamilton published *A Plain Statement of Facts*, refuting Owen's views.[64] Almost inevitably, this accused Owen of being *'an infidel of no ordinary cast'*, bent on destroying Christianity and fomenting anarchy. Nevertheless, in the process, Aiton made some relevant points about Dale, who had *'laid the foundation stone of everything truly useful'* in New Lanark.[65] Owen was accused of 'calumny' against Dale and of grossly libelling *'one of the most enterprising, benevolent, sound-headed men of his age'*.[66] The population under Dale *'were as happy, as well managed and as well conducted in all respects as they are at this hour'*, largely because Dale had provided jobs, housing, schools, etc.[67] Aiton strongly supported the Presbytery's view that, contrary to Owen's claims, the moral state of the community had not improved from the time of the *'late, excellent Mr. Dale'*.[68] New Lanark under Owen was far from being *'an Elysium of superlative happiness, unequalled or unattainable in Old Society'*.[69] Aiton may have had a point. In November 1823, Jean Kay a resident in New Lanark, wrote to her sister and it is clear that all was not well in the village at the time (Appendix 15). Jean indicates some of the problems with the Village Society – problems which were to re-surface a year later.

> I received till now 15 shillings per month from the Village Society which was all but Mr Owen declared it bankrupt nearly 200 in debt...[70]

Kay blames *'sadly imposed reform by the Mannagers of this place'* (and the increasing numbers of infirm people *'receiving from the box'*) for this situation. She notes that most of the local ministers are *'up in arms'* against Owen and see him as *'the great apostel of Infidility... a declared infidel'*. Significantly, she adds that the villagers, *'...cannot, to our sad experience, deny what they say'*. She mentions in passing that one of Owen's partners at the time, *'the great William Allen of London'*, had done all in his powers to end the slave trade, perhaps suggesting that the villagers were themselves enslaved and required to be rescued. The situation was fast becoming intolerable and the villagers decided to act, despite concerns about their employment:

> *'...we are in danger to say a word for the mannagers of the place are tools in his hand but I hope the prayers of so many good men have had access to the throne of grace ... things are beginning to go against him even as a population of more than 25 hundred have held a meeting chused a committee wrote out a few of our grievances and sent them up to the company in London it was out of the power of the manager to suppress it but numbers of the people are afraid of losing their imployment for this...'*[71]

The letter concludes by referring to one of Owen's most unpopular proposals – that of communal living and the seperation of children from their parents. None of this actually happened in New Lanark but plans were clearly being discussed. Jean Kay talks of plans to accommodate about 50 families in a communal space – *'so that we will never have the pleasure of lighting a candle in our own houses'*. According to Kay, Owen and his managers planned:

> *'...to bring us all into one house prepared for that purpose to mix together like so many swine we will get our meat & clothing and our children taken from us to be brought up as he pleases this likewise he calls ... a blessing ... these are only a few of the blessings we are about to receive from this great man but we hope god will change these blessings for others.'*[72]

The following year, there was an outbreak of typhoid in the village and a great deal of bad feeling was aroused when Owen intervened in the financial affairs of the Friendly Society and dismissed seven workers who had opposed his intervention.[73]

There is a danger in all of this that extreme views polarise the debate. In the same way that *The Belfast Monthly Magazine*, for example, had exaggerated and misrepresented Owen's version of events, *The Preston Chronicle* did likewise for the Dale case some years later, albeit more briefly. According to the *Chronicle*, the New Lanark people were noted, *'even amongst the Scottish population for their zeal in the cause of religion and morality'*.[74] Managers were men *'of tried moral worth and religious principles'*. Similarly, *'the most beautiful morality, order, peace and harmony prevailed for many years at New Lanark'*. Thefts were unheard of and doors were merely latched, not bolted.

On his death, David Dale was 'almost canonised' by the people.[75] Predictably, the villain of the piece is Robert Owen who becomes something of a Satanic figure – at least in comparison with the saintly David Dale:

> If David Dale could see to what uses his wealth has been applied, he would curse the day upon which his misled bounty conceded to this most pernicious of charlatans the means of setting the world in a flame, to minister to his depraved appetite for distinction.[76]

References: Chapter 17

1   *The Scots Magazine*, September, 1806, p.654.
2   *The Gentlemen's Magazine*, 1806, p.771. See also *The New Statistical Account of Scotland (1834–40)*. 15 vols. Edinburgh: Blackwood. Vol. V, p.729.
3   *The Preston Chronicle*, 21st March 1840.
4   Regality Club (1889–1912) *Transactions of the Regality Club*, 4 vols., Glasgow: James Maclehose & Sons, p.114.
5   Ibid., pp.114-5.
6   Butt, J. (ed) (1971) Robert Owen as Businessman', in Butt, J. (ed) *Robert Owen, Prince of Cotton Spinners*. Newton Abbot: David & Charles, p.172.
7   Liddell, A. (1854a) *Memoir of David Dale*, Glasgow: Blackie, p.167.
8   I am indebted to the Stewarton & District Historical Society for this information.
9   Regality Club, *Transactions*, p.115.
10 Ibid.
11 Ibid., p.116.
12 Register of Sasines, Barony & Regality of Glasgow. Glasgow City Archives, T-SA 5/1/1-2.
13 Regality Club, *Transactions*, p.115.
14 Liddell, A. (1854a) *Memoir*, p.175.
15 National Archives of Scotland. Sheriff Court, Glasgow: SC36/48/1. Will of David Dale, 4th August 1806 and SC 36/48/3 fol.412, Additional Inventory of Estate of Dale, 9th January 1811. Cited in Cooke, A. (2010) *The Rise and Fall of the Scottish Cotton Industry, 1778–1914: The Secret Spring*. Manchester: M.U.P., pp.177–8.
16 I am indebted to Lady Hagart-Alexander of Ballochmyle House for access to these papers and for her permission to use the information therein.
17 Butt, J. (ed) (1971) *Robert Owen as a Businessman*, p.180.
18 Cooke, A. (2010) *The Rise and Fall of the Scottish Cotton Industry, 1778–1914: The Secret Spring*. Manchester: M.U.P., p.178. See also Cooke, A.J. (1979) 'Robert Owen and the Stanley Mills, 1802–1811', *Business History*, XXI, (1), 107–11 and Robertson, A.J. (1969) 'Robert Owen and the Campbell Debt, 1810–1822', *Business History*, XI, (1) 23–30.
19 Butt, J. (ed) (1971) *Robert Owen as a Businessman*, p.174.
20 Jean Maxwel Dale to Colin Campbell, 5th July 1813. See Robertson, A.J. (1969) 'Robert Owen and the Campbell Debt, 1810–1822', *Business History*, XI, (1), 23–30, p.28.
21 Butt, J. (ed) (1971) *Robert Owen as a Businessman*, pp.175–9.
22 Ibid., pp.180-81.
23 Ibid., p.182.
24 Robertson, A.J. (1969) 'Robert Owen and the Campbell Debt, 1810-1822', *Business History*, XI, (1), 23-30, p.30.
25 Ibid.
26 Owen, R. (1812) *A Statement Regarding the New Lanark Establishment*. Glasgow: J. Moir. Facsimile edition, Molendinar Press, 1973. See Introduction by John Butt.
27 Ibid., p.5.
28 Ibid.
29 Owen, R. (1813-16) 'A New View of Society; or Essays on the Principle of the Formation of Human Character and the Application of the Principle to Practice', Second Essay, in G. Claeys (ed) (1991) *Robert Owen: A New View of Society and Other Writings*. London: Penguin, p.24.
30 Ibid., p.25.
31 Ibid.
32 Ibid.
33 'Report of the Minutes of Evidence taken before the Select Committee on the State of Children Employed in the Manufactories of the United Kingdom, 1816', (397) III, pp.20-21. Cited in Donnachie, I. and Hewitt, G. (1993) *Historic New Lanark*. Edinburgh: E.U.P., pp.47, 49.

34 'An Account of an Important Reformation effected in the Moral Habits of the Workmen at the Lanark Cotton Mills', *The Belfast Monthly Magazine*, Vol. 10, No. 58, May 1813. pp.364–5.

35 Ibid., p.366.

36 Ibid.

37 Ibid., p.368.

38 Owen, R. (1857) *The Life of Robert Owen Written by Himself*. Vol. 1. London: Effingham Wilson. New impression (1967) London: Frank Cass & Co., p.57.

39 Ibid., p.60.

40 Bristed toured in 1801. See Bristed, J. (1803) *A Pedestrian Tour Through Parts of the Highlands of Scotland*. 2 vols. London: J. Wallis. Vol. 2. p.668. Also Sinclair, J. (ed) (1791–99) *The Statistical Account of Scotland, 1791–99*, 21 Vols. Vol. XX, pp.88–9: *The Caledonian Mercury*, 10 August, 1799.

41 Liddell, A. (1854a) *Memoir*, p.116. Sinclair, J. (ed) *Statistical Account*, Vol. XV, pp.38–42.

42 Garnett, T. (1811) *Observations on a Tour through the Highlands and Part of the Western Isles of Scotland. A New Edition in Two Volumes*. London: John Stockdale., pp.228, 232, 233, 236.

43 Davidson, L. 'The New Lanark Pauper Apprentices.' Unpublished Conference paper, 'The Legacy of David Dale – Industry, philanthropy and Heritage', 4th November 2006. Glasgow Caledonian University, p.5.

44 *The Caledonian Mercury*, 10th August 1799.

45 Ibid.

46 McNayr, J. (1797) *A Guide from Glasgow to some of the most Remarkable Scenes in the Highlands and to the Falls of Clyde*. Glasgow: Courier Office, p.231.

47 See Bristed, J. (1803) *A Pedestrian Tour Through Parts of the Highlands of Scotland*. 2 vols. London: J. Wallis. Vol. 2. p.668.

48 Ibid., p.670.

49 Ibid., p.671.

50 Robertson, A.D. (1975) *Lanark: the Burgh and its Councils, 1469–188*. Lanark Town Council, p.304. He challenged the Presbytery on practices at Communion, and Orders of Service. He also challenged the council on his stipend.

51 Davidson, H. (1910) *Lanark: A Series of Papers by the late Hugh Davidson, Writer*. Edinburgh, pp.216–7.

52 Ibid., p.220.

53 Owen, R. (1857) *Life*, p.103.

54 Ibid., p.118.

55 *The Morning Chronicle*, 10th September 1823.

56 Ibid.

57 *The Christian Remembrancer*, 5:57 (1823, September), p.575.

58 Ibid.

59 McGavin was also an Anti-Burgher preacher and the author of a book entitled *The Protestant*.

60 McGavin, W. (1824) 'The Fundamental Principles of the New Lanark System Exposed in a Series of Letters to Robert Owen Esq.' Glasgow: Andrew Young, in *British Labour Struggles: Contemporary Pamphlets 1727–1850. Robert Owen at New Lanark. Two Booklets and One Pamphlet 1824–1838*. New York: Arno Press 1972, p.23, 12th November 1823 and p.96, 24th January 1824.

61 Ibid., p.24, 12th November 1823.

62 Ibid., p.51. 8th December 1823.

63 Ibid., pp.68–69. 3rd January 1824.

64 Aiton, J. (1824) *Mr. Owen's Objections to Christianity and New View of Society and Education. Refuted by A Plain Statement of Facts with a Hint to Archibald Hamilton Esq. of Dalziel*. Edinburgh: James Robertson & Co..

65 Ibid., p.14.

66 Ibid., p.26.

67 Ibid., pp.15–20.

68 Ibid., p.22.

69 Ibid., pp.37–38.

70 Jean Kay (Mrs. Sutherland), New Lanark, to Betty Kay, Auldearn, 8th November 1823. Richard Stenlake Collection.

71 Ibid.

72 Ibid.

73 Donnachie, I. (2000) *Robert Owen of New Lanark and New Harmony*. East Linton: Tuckwell Press, pp.198–99.

74 *The Preston Chronicle*, 12 March, 1840. The article is attributed to *The London Magazine* (n.d.).

75 Ibid.

76 Ibid.

Chapter 18: This Singular Man

David Dale Esq. (*Imperial Magazine*, 1822)

It is unhelpful when strongly-held views are pushed to the extreme. What then was the truth of the matter? Owen was always clear that he did not blame Dale personally for the allegedly poor conditions in New Lanark prior to the change of ownership. Dale was simply a representative of a system which Owen believed to be wrong and which required to be completely renewed. On many occasions he recognised his father-in-law's achievements. Unfortunately, Owen himself was prone to hyperbole and rhetoric, not to mention contradiction and inconsistency – none of which negates his enormous achievements in New Lanark over a period of 25 years. However, no matter how often Owen claimed that it was the '*system*' which produced the problems of Dale's period, he obscured the message by dwelling at length on the alleged '*wretchedness*' of the place. Inevitably, because Owen's New Social System was not yet understood (or accepted) by large numbers of people at this time, his comments were seen as an attack on Dale's achievements. Equally inevitable was the counter-attack which followed, where Dale's New Lanark was presented as something akin to an earthly paradise, presided over by a benign and saintly David Dale.

The reality of Dale's New Lanark lies, of course, somewhere in between these extreme views. By far the overwhelming body of evidence is to the effect that Dale's community was as advanced and enlightened as the late 18th century would allow. It was not paradise but it was a place worthy of great credit to its founder and very far from the dreadful, evil place alluded to by Owen. In the same way, Owen's New Lanark was a truly unique social experiment of monumental historic importance, but far from the idyllic community he wrote about in his many papers.

To get a more accurate picture of life in New Lanark, it is worth looking at some of the more realistic descriptions of Dale and of the community he founded. Smout argues that Dale and others like him approached the problem of management 'in a thoroughly eighteenth–century spirit of benevolent absolutism':

> They worked their labour long hours, they kept a tight rein over behaviour on the factory floor and in the village and they emphasised above all else the virtues of obedience, industriousness and cleanliness, but they also generally provided reasonable houses, paid for a schoolmaster who at least taught the children to read, and tried to keep a paternal and friendly element in labour relations. They were much more like improving lairds than tycoons.[1]

Smout goes on to describe Robert Owen as 'the great paternalist' whose theories of co-operative socialism 'were strictly for extra mural use'.[2]

In Dale's case, paternalism and 'benevolent absolutism' had been part of his formative years. As a young man in Stewarton, Hamilton and Cambuslang, he would have been well aware of the division of labour on the farms, the runrig system and the often precarious position of farm workers. He would have known about the traditionally powerful but often paternalistic landowners who necessarily charged their tenants rent and who expected much but who also realised their responsibility to their workers when times were hard and who were prepared to subsidise sales of grain during such times. He also knew that many of the landowners were willing to support the poor of the parish, even the able-bodied poor. Such 'paternalistic regulation' of the social conditions lasted well into the 19th century.[3]

It is not entirely surprising then that, as a factory owner, Dale continued this paternalistic tradition, providing flexibility and security for his workers. New Lanark under Dale was certainly an enlightened and progressive community for its time but it was a large factory community, increasingly forging its own dynamic in a new industrial age. As such, it was a community which, however 'benevolent' the conditions, was always going to be subject to the vagaries of human behaviour. Lockhart was careful to note in the *Statistical Account* that the people were 'generally industrious', that crimes were 'seldomer', (rather than never) committed in the village.[4] There was undoubtedly some drunkenness – also alluded to by Lockhart – although it is highly unlikely that it reached the devastating proportions described by Owen.

In a letter to Andrew Mitchell in Glasgow, Robert Lyon, the much-respected teacher who worked under both Dale and Owen, noted that the people first employed by Dale were 'remarkable for sobriety, virtuous dispositions and propriety of conduct'.[5] As the village became more populous, Lyon took the view that some characters 'not quite so correct' got in amongst them. However, his conclusion regarding the morals of the population could not be clearer: 'the morals of the whole village were certainly equal to those of other villages of the same population'.[6] Owen's claim to have effected some kind of moral transformation are firmly rejected. Lyon, while acknowledging that the people were 'rather improved in cleanliness' during Owen's time, and that the houses and streets were kept cleaner, was clear that their 'circumstances, comforts and applause' were much the same as they had been under Dale. Further, 'their morals are certainly not improved'. As an instance of this, Lyon writes that there were 'very few' illegitimate children born in the village while it belonged to Dale – perhaps one child in seven years – but that, during Lyon's last few years under Owen, there were 'from ten to fourteen' illegitimate births in the village.[7]

This tends to support some of the points made by Aiton, McGavin and even the Presbytery – sources whose criticisms of Owen have sometimes been dismissed as biased or bigoted because of their opposition to Owen's anti-religious views. In fact, one of Owen's biographers, Frank Podmore, described Aiton as 'on the whole, a fair-minded witness'.[8] Referring to Owen, Aiton always claimed that, in some respects, he admired '*the benevolent practice of this well-meaning but deluded man*'.[9] McGavin also claimed to admire Owen's benevolence and zeal. Even the Presbytery, opposed to Owen in most things, did try to end the public row between Owen and Menzies. Aiton and McGavin both agreed that Owen had made certain '*improvements*'. In December 1823, McGavin wrote :

> *...I do not deny that you have made some improvements in the condition of your labourers. With such means and the concurrence of such benevolent men as your partners, it would have been inexcusable if you had not. The suppression of tippling houses, for instance, was a good work, although I suspect it must have been a measure of coercion ... you did right to remove the temptation to vice as far out of the reach of your workers as you could.*[10]

Neither Aiton nor McGavin denied that there had been at least some illegitimate births, some drunkenness and some petty offending during Dale's time.[11] What they could not accept was Owen's claim that all the problems had been swept away by his new system. Aiton claimed that, far from taking a stand against the consumption of alcohol, Owen had allowed three public houses in the village and had charged £20–£40 per annum in rent from each of the three landlords.[12] He continued in similar vein, accusing Owen of lengthening the working day, halving the time allowed from breakfast from 30 to fifteen minutes and paying employees monthly rather than weekly – all of which were true.[13] Far from achieving a crime-free, harmonious society which stood in stark contrast to Dale's New Lanark, Aiton reminded Owen that his employees were still prone to petty crime. Men with lanterns had been stationed at the mill gates to prevent the theft of cotton and there had been attempts to break into the store and the Counting House.[14] Many employees were dissatisfied with Owen's management style; there were disputes, complaints and threats of rebellion.[15] According to Aiton, '*there were no such feuds under Mr. Dale's administration, nor have there been any at Catrine*'.[16]

Dale's lifelong concern had been the social, educational and personal welfare of his employees, particularly the children. Owen's comments about them being '*dwarfs in mind and body*', '*deformed*' and too exhausted to profit from evening schooling are often quoted. While it is generally accepted that Owen was prone to exaggeration, these claims do have some validity in relation to children employed in any cotton mills up to 1816 (and well beyond, in many cases). Three examples will serve to illustrate the point. In the medical report presented to the Factory Commissioners in 1833, the cases of William Stewart, Archibald Turner and Mary Bell are discussed. William Stewart began work in New Lanark in 1795 and the other two were apprenticed c.1802. It is not clear exactly how many employees were affected in this way but there is no reason to believe their ailments were atypical:

> *WILLIAM STEWART, an orphan from poor's house at Edinburgh. Does not know his own age. Has been here about thirty-eight years. Thinks he was about seven years of age when he entered this factory. Felt pain in his knees in the year 1800 for the first time, and went to the infirmary in Edinburgh to be cured, when Dr Munro said that the bones were wholly out of their place, and too long gone to do any thing for them. State at present – Both knees much bent inwards; condoyles of both femora much enlarged; right patella nearly absorbed. Stands on the outside of both feet, which are smaller than natural, and turned inwards and upwards. Cannot extend either leg, nor raise himself higher than four feet nine inches. Was at first a piecer, then a card-feeder. Was sent out of the poor's house because he was "full-size". Was poorly when he first came to Lanark.*[17]

> *ARCHIBALD TURNER, aged thirty-eight. Now a labourer. Has worked twenty-seven years in this factory. Both knees are now bent inwards. Height five feet eight inches and a half. States that his knees became crooked between sixteen and eighteen; suffered no pain then. There is no enlargement of the bones. Walks straight upon his feet. Was an orphan from Glasgow. Knows nothing of his own early life before entering the mill.*[18]

> *MARY BELL, an orphan from the poor's house at Edinburgh. Does not know her own age. Has been here about thirty years; might be six or seven years of age when she came here. Thinks that she was not quite straight when she first came. Is now four feet two inches high. Legs distorted and bent as if from rickets. Has enjoyed good health as long as she can recollect. Thinks that her legs have become more bent since she has been at these works. Arms, head, and trunk, though under size, are naturally formed. She picks cotton. Cannot sign her name.*[19]

Clearly, working conditions were often appalling, particularly for very young children. Despite the fact that Owen lengthened the working hours for a number of years, there is no doubt that his efforts were enormously influential in bringing about major reforms. The point here, however, is that during Dale's period in New Lanark, these conditions were accepted as being part of the job. Indeed, as the factory system established itself, the employment of children was considered as essential, even charitable, and was supported by all the authorities and most of the families concerned – as all the reports about Dale's pauper children indicate. Thus, it is important to recognise that conditions were poor by modern standards but that they were acceptable in the late 18th century. Dale went well beyond any other employer in Great Britain in his attempts to provide the best possible working and living conditions for all his employees but particularly for the pauper apprentices. Fundamental to this was the provision of schooling. Owen was correct to point out that many children would be too exhausted after hours of work to learn very much. The fact that Mary Bell could not sign her name, however, does not indicate that the schooling system was failing large numbers of pupils.[20] Arithmetic and writing were taught separately, even in the parish school, where there was an additional charge for the latter. It was not at all uncommon for girls to spend more time on 'domestic' lessons such as sewing, than on writing and arithmetic.

Similarly, Hugh Dick's letter to the West Kirk Charity Workhouse notes that all except four children could read '*with considerable propriety*'.[21] This should not be taken to mean that the four others could not read at all or that strenuous efforts were not employed to help them to read. Also, the fact that nineteen boys were learning to write, some with '*considerable proficiency*' and that a few of the boys were learning figures while some of the girls were working on needlework are indicators of a relatively successful school in the era of the 18th century parish school, which is the context of the time.[22]

Undoubtedly, Owen's educational revolution which followed came to overshadow the achievements of Dale's schools but Owen's schools were for a different purpose altogether and inspired by a different view of children – particularly infants – and a 'new view' of society (although even in Owen's classrooms the factory system necessitated a great deal of rote learning and monitorial teaching for the older children). By the 1820s, the entire nature of Scottish schooling was being transformed, as much by demographics as anything else. Dale's pupils were the very first to experience life in uncharted territory – a large factory community with schools which drew on the traditions of the parish school but which began to adapt these in response to a new environment and the need to prepare children for a working life in the industrial age.

To his credit, Owen phased out the employment of pauper children altogether as their indentures ran out and eventually no one under ten was employed in the mills as the Factory Reform movement began to have some influence. However, Dale also deserves credit for what he was able to achieve in the 1780s and 90s. His lifelong concern was for the welfare of his work people, particularly his child employees and the many positive accounts of life in New Lanark under his regime, while they cannot mask the fact that conditions were harsh by modern standards, do have considerable validity.

James Currie, writing in 1792, was in no doubt about David Dale's achievements. For Currie, these were exemplified by the creation of the highly successful factory community of New Lanark, Dale's most obvious success at that time. But, significant as New Lanark was, Currie realised that it went beyond bricks and mortar and that the community represented a successful combination of potentially conflicting issues – some of which were to be found in Dale's own personality:

> *Whoever wishes to see a combination of the wonders of nature and art, of beauty and sublimity, of magnitude and order, of patriotism and private interest, of power and benevolence, let him repair to the falls of Clyde and do homage to this singular man.*[23]

It is entirely appropriate that Dale is remembered for his achievements at New Lanark in his own time and for laying the very considerable foundation stones upon which Robert Owen was to build. Owen himself recognised this on several occasions, perhaps most obviously on New Year's Day, 1816 when he addressed the community at the opening of the New Institution for the Formation of Character. He told the audience, the vast majority of whom would have lived in the village when Dale was alive, that Dale could not have known at the time of New Lanark's construction, that he was commencing a work '*from whence not only the amelioration of his suffering countrymen should proceed, but the means of happiness be developed to every nation in the world*'.[24]

Many commentators have written about Owen's great triumph in the New Institution but until relatively recently, very few had devoted much space to Dale's part in it all. This neglect may have begun with Owen's attempts to focus on his own achievements from 1816. Despite occasional reminders from periodicals such as *The Imperial Magazine* in 1822 that Dale's '*virtues deserve more publicity than they have otherwise attained*', and Liddell's *Memoir* of Dale in the 1850s, the role of the '*honest man*', the '*bright luminary to Scotland*' in the success of New Lanark has been undersold.

Owen was correct about one thing. Dale could certainly not have imagined that his factory community would become an internationally renowned centre for infant and child education or the '*think tank*' for a proposed new social system – a '*new moral world*'. These were Owen's achievements, based on Dale's community. Dale's achievements were different. He had no intention of creating a new world order based on utopian, communitarian living. Such ideas would have been entirely alien to him, as they would to many of the Glasgow merchants, traders, brokers and churchmen of his generation. Dale's success at New Lanark was to create, from an unlikely piece of rocky ground, a profitable business operating within a successful community and one where living and working conditions were as enlightened as the times would allow. Indeed, he created conditions for many of his child employees which could not be found elsewhere in Britain, ensuring that the vast majority of the children were able to take advantage of a proper, structured curriculum, taught by qualified teachers. There were some difficulties and not everything matched the picture of perfection portrayed by some of the visitors but, for its time, it was a model, progressive community and one for which Dale deserves more credit.

However, as this book has tried to demonstrate, there was much more to Dale than New Lanark, significant as that was. This short, rather stout, amiable and benevolent family man, a good host and fond of a Scotch song, was no fool. Benevolent magistrate, Christian pastor and evangelist he may have been but he was an astute businessman. His commercial dealings were focused and, on occasion, unsentimental to the point of ruthlessness. This ruthlessness applied even to members of his own extended family, such as James Dale, if their poor performance was giving the business a bad reputation. Partners who failed to meet his standards were simply removed from the business without delay. Banking and matters of finance were delegated, as necessary, to those with more expertise, but the business of credit rating and the decision-making associated with that remained in the hands of the man who knew the city and its businessmen better than most. Multiple business partnerships were the order of the day and Dale took full advantage of this in his dealings with other, smaller mills. His property portfolio became extensive across the city.

As a result, he became a very wealthy man. Just how wealthy will never really be known, largely because his estate was grossly mismanaged to the extent that Haldane and some others were convinced that criminal behaviour had taken place. It is also unclear just how much Dale gave away to charitable causes, but if all the reports are accurate this amounted to the modern equivalent of hundreds of thousands of pounds. The private charity work was certainly extensive and always aimed at improving the social and moral condition of the recipients. Some of the more public partnerships (e.g. Spinningdale) were in reality charitable donations – business ventures, knowingly operated at a considerable loss to enable local people to improve their lot. Civic duties and charitable work were often combined, as in his support for and involvement in the affairs of the Town's Hospital and the Royal Infirmary, the Humane Society and the Chamber of Commerce and the Bridewell.

Like many of his contemporaries, he was motivated by a Christian desire to do good in the world while at the same time making sure that any business ventures made a profit – indeed, they were interdependent. Unlike some of his contemporaries, Dale was hugely successful on both counts and it is no surprise that he became a well-known public figure in Glasgow. Over the years, however, his importance has not always been fully recognised. In recent years, the Royal Bank reminded the public of Dale's important role in their history when in 1966 they issued a new full-colour banknote depicting Dale, in a portrait taken from the 1797 Tassie medallion. Another tribute followed a year later when the Royal Bank became the first public bank in the U.K. to introduce savings stamps, the design of which incorporated Dale's portrait. Such stamps were intended to help those on low incomes to gain access to banking. Stamp vending machines were placed in schools, workplaces and other locations where savers could buy stamps and collect them in a savings book. The value of the stamps could then be paid into a Royal Bank savings account. It seems likely that Dale would have approved of such a scheme!

The city of Glasgow has done its best to commemorate Dale by naming a street and a further education college (now defunct) after him, although his house in Charlotte Street was demolished in the 1950s to make way for an extension to a local secondary school. The site is currently occupied by the WISE Group who kindly gave permission for the Friends of New Lanark to erect a plaque there. The life and work of David Dale is commemorated in a permanent display in the foyer of the company's offices in Charlotte Street.

Royal Bank of Scotland Commemorative Banknote (1966) and Savings Stamp (1967).
(Reproduced by kind permission of the Royal Bank of Scotland Group plc © 2015)

A similar plaque, also erected by the Friends of New Lanark, marks the spot in Glasgow's High Street where Dale established his first business. His name does feature in some of the brief potted histories of the city – most recently in the Calton Trail literature but outwith the city (and possibly still within the city), relatively few people have heard about Dale. The hundreds of thousands of visitors who visit New Lanark each year will, quite properly, marvel at the achievements of Robert Owen but it would also be fitting if some were to echo Dr. Currie's sentiments and 'repair to the Falls of Clyde and do homage', not just to Robert Owen but to David Dale.

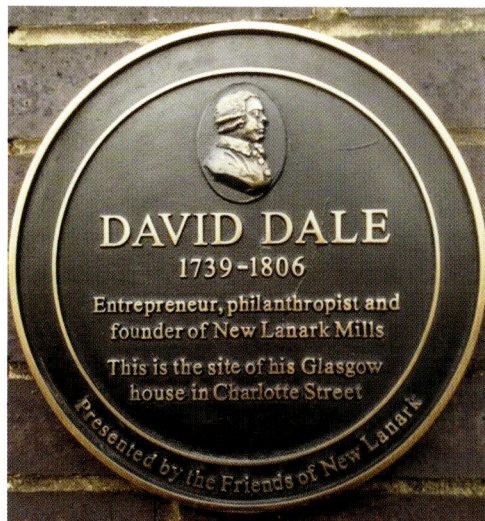

Commemorative Plaque, Charlotte Street. (David McLaren Collection)

References: Chapter 18

1   Smout, T.C. (1998) *A History of the Scottish People 1560–1830*. London: Fontana, p.383.

2   Ibid., p.384.

3   Devine, T.M. (1999) *The Scottish Nation 1700–2000*. London: Penguin, p.218.

4   Sinclair, J. (ed) (1791–99) *The Statistical Account of Scotland, 1791–99*, 21 vols. Vol. XV, p.42.

5   Letter from Robert Lyon, Edinburgh to Andrew Mitchell, 16th April 1816. *Glasgow Association of Master Cotton Spinners. Sederunt Book, 1816.* Glasgow City Archives. T-MJ100.

6   Ibid.

7   Ibid. N.B. Lyon left New Lanark in September, 1814.

8   Podmore, F. (1906) *Robert Owen – A Biography*. London: Hutchinson & Co., p.82n.

9   Aiton, J. (1824) *Mr. Owen's Objections to Christianity and New View of Society and Education. Refuted by A Plain Statement of Facts with a Hint to Archibald Hamilton Esq. of Dalziel*. Edinburgh: James Robertson & Co., p.26.

10 McGavin, W. (1824) 'The Fundamental Principles of the New Lanark System Exposed in a Series of Letters to Robert Owen Esq.' Glasgow: Andrew Young, in *British Labour Struggles: Contemporary Pamphlets 1727–1850. Robert Owen at New Lanark. Two Booklets and One Pamphlet 1824–1838.* New York: Arno Press 1972, p.52, 8th December 1823.

11 Aiton, J. (1824) *Mr. Owen's Objections*, pp.24–5.

12 Ibid., pp.21–22.

13 Ibid., p.21.

14 Ibid., p.35.

15 Ibid., pp.37–38.

16 Ibid.

17 In Davidson, L. 'The New Lanark Pauper Apprentices.' Unpublished Conference paper, 'The Legacy of David Dale – Industry, philanthropy and Heritage', 4th November 2006. Glasgow Caledonian University, pp.7–8.

18 Ibid.

19 Ibid.

20 Mary's problem may have been much more widespread than previously thought . See Houston, R.A. (1985) *Scottish Literacy and the Scottish Identity: Illiteracy and Society in Scotland and Northern England, 1600–1800*. Cambridge: Cambridge University Press.

21 Hugh Dick to J. Linsay, Treasurer, West Kirk Charity Workhouse. Monthly Meeting, 6th October 1795. West Kirk Charity Workhouse Minutes. Edinburgh City Archives, SL222/1/7.

22 Ibid.

23 James Currie to Mrs. Greg & Miss Kennedy in Manchester. Written from Liverpool, 27th May 1792. Quoted in Currie, W.W. (1831) *Memoir of the Life, Writings and Correspondence of James Currie*, 2 vols. London: Longman, Rees, Orme, Brown & Green, Vol. 1, p.161.

24 Owen, R. (1816), 'Address to the Inhabitants of New Lanark on Opening the New Institution for the Formation of Character. I January, 1816', in Claeys, G. (ed) (1991) *Robert Owen: A New View of Society and Other Writings*. London: Penguin, p.108.

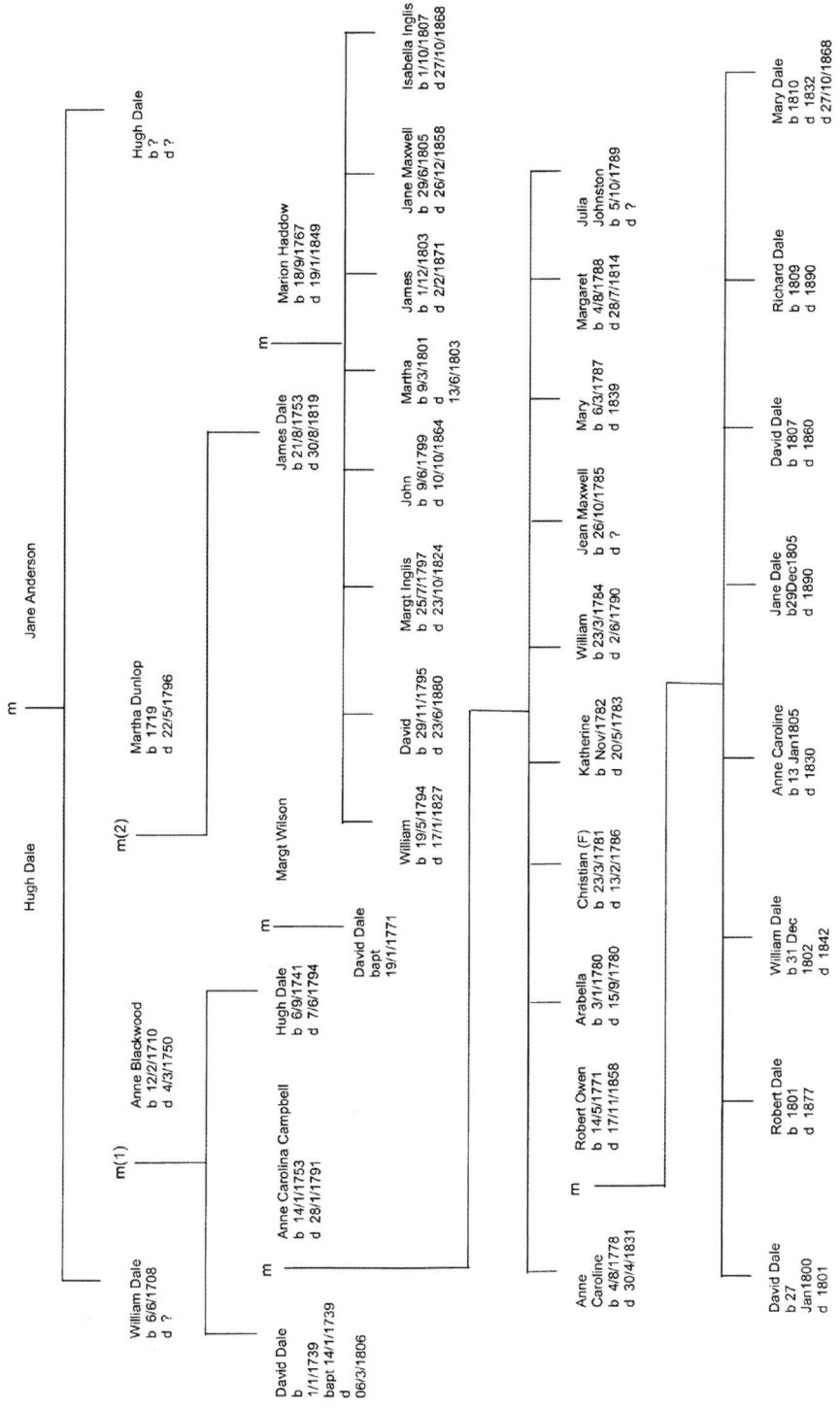

Family Tree

Hugh Dale — m — Jane Anderson

William Dale
b 6/6/1708
d ?

David Dale
b 1/1/1739
bapt 14/1/1739
d 06/3/1806

m(1) Anne Blackwood
b 12/2/1710
d 4/3/1750

m(2)

Anne Carolina Campbell
b 14/1/1753
d 28/1/1791

Hugh Dale
b 6/9/1741
d 7/6/1794

Martha Dunlop
b 1719
d 22/5/1796

Hugh Dale
b ?
d ?

James Dale
b 21/8/1753
d 30/8/1819
m
Marion Haddow
b 18/9/1767
d 19/1/1849

David Dale
bapt 19/1/1771
m
Margt Wilson

Anne Caroline
b 4/8/1778
d 30/4/1831
m
Robert Owen
b 14/5/1771
d 17/11/1858

Arabella
b 3/1/1780
d 15/9/1780

Christian (F)
b 23/3/1781
d 13/2/1786

Katherine
b Nov/1782
d 20/5/1783

William
b 23/3/1784
d 2/6/1790

Jean Maxwell
b 26/10/1785
d ?

Mary
b 6/3/1787
d 1839

Margaret
b 4/8/1788
d 28/7/1814

Julia Johnston
b 5/10/1789
d ?

William
b 19/5/1794
d 17/1/1827

David
b 29/11/1795
d 23/6/1880

Margt Inglis
b 25/7/1797
d 23/10/1824

John
b 9/6/1799
d 10/10/1864

Martha
b 9/3/1801
d 13/6/1803

James
b 1/12/1803
d 2/2/1871

Jane Maxwell
b 29/6/1805
d 26/12/1858

Isabella Inglis
b 1/10/1807
d 27/10/1868

David Dale
b 27 Jan1800
d 1801

Robert Dale
b 1801
d 1877

William Dale
b 31 Dec 1802
d 1842

Anne Caroline
b 13 Jan1805
d 1830

Jane Dale
b29Dec1805
d 1890

David Dale
b 1807
d 1860

Richard Dale
b 1809
d 1890

Mary Dale
b 1810
d 1832
d 27/10/1868

Appendix 2: Glasgow Chamber of Commerce Committee Membership – David Dale.

(Extracted from the Minutes of the Glasgow Chamber of Commerce, Vols 1–3. Glasgow City Council Archives, Mitchell Library TD 161670/1/1–3)

17 Dec 1783	D. Dale and six others to form a committee. Purpose – to consider a 'memorial' from Incorporation of Weavers regarding variation in counts/twists in linen & cotton yarn.
25 May 1784	D. Dale and four others to form a committee. Purpose – to consider a memorial from silk & linen manufacturers on quality and prices.
12 July 1785	D. Dale and five others to form a committee. Purpose – to consider a memorial from Perth on the examination of yarn spun in that city (to quality, length, twist etc.).
27 Dec 1785	D. Dale and nine others (incl. J. Stirling, W. Stirling, R. Finlay) to form a committee. Purpose – to consider where Chamber of Commerce might allocate funds disbursed by Govt.
10 Jan 1786	**David Dale elected Deputy Chairman for 1786**
	D. Dale and four others to form a committee. Purpose – to consider Lawn & Cambric manufacture.
	D. Dale and seven others to form a committee. Purpose – to consider 'a junction' with the London Chamber of Commerce.
7 Mar 1786	D. Dale & W. Carlisle to visit Board of Trustees for Fisheries, Manufactures & Improvements in Edinburgh to lobby their support for the Thread Bill.
13 Dec 1786	D. Dale and nine others to form a committee. Purpose – to consider a report from the Trustees on the Thread Bill.
9 Jan 1787	**David Dale elected Deputy Chairman for 1787**
25 Apr 1787	D. Dale and five others to form a committee. Purpose – to consider issues should the Govt. decide to impose a duty on banknotes.
21 Feb 1788	D. Dale and four others to form a committee. Purpose – to consider a memorial from cotton & muslin manufacturers.
29 Feb 1788	D. Dale and four others (Arch'd. Grahame; John Gordon; Jas. Grahame and the secretary, Gilbert Hamilton) to form a committee. Purpose – to consider a letter from a 'Committee at London and a number of papers relative to the slave trade'.
	D. Dale and four others to form a committee. Purpose – to consider issues re a petition to Parliament on bleaching.
4 Mar 1788	D. Dale and four others to form a committee. Purpose – to consider a memorial from linen manufacturers on export duties.
19 Jan 1791	D. Dale and four others to form a committee. Purpose – to consider the viability of a weaving machine invented by Arch'd. Shuttleston of Bridgeton. Machine described on 22nd Feb as 'exceedingly inginious' (sic).
12 Apr 1791	D. Dale and two others to form a committee. Purpose – to consider the viability of a new road from Lanarkshire to England – minutes note that this 'appears to be of considerable importance'
20 Feb 1792	D. Dale and others to form a committee. Purpose – to consider the East India Company's involvement in importing manufactured goods from' the Parts East of the Cape of Good Hope'.
3 July 1792	D. Dale and five others to form a committee. Purpose – to consider the viability of a Canal between Loch Gilp & Loch Crinan (i.e. Crinan Canal)
26 July 1792	D. Dale and six others to form a committee. D. Dale specified as convener. Purpose – to consider issues re the count and short-reeling of thread.
11 Feb 1801	D. Dale, R. Dunlop, Wm. Wardlaw, Wm. Craig and others (number unclear) to form a committee. Purpose – to consider Mill-spun linen yarn & taxes on it.
31 Dec 1801	D. Dale, Kirkman Finlay, Wm. Wardlaw and six others to form a committee. Purpose – to look at uniformity of wages for weavers.
22 Jan 1805	D. Dale, Robt. Carrick, H. Glassford and two others to form a committee. Purpose – to consider issues re establishment of an office Edinburgh for purpose of stamping paper. Last meeting at which David Dale is recorded as being present.

From Glasgow Chamber of Commerce Minutes. Glasgow City Council Archives.

Appendix 3:
Men & Boys Sent to Cromford, 13th March, 1785

Men	Boys
Robert Allan	William Brown
Archibald Davidson	William Barr
David Gillespie	Thomas Cassels
James Martin	William Gavin
John Winn	John Gavin
Joseph Kirkwood	William McMillan
Robert Allin	John Allan
Robert Young	James Ritchie
Charles Dunlop	Daniel Tod
John Murray	Robert Main
Henry Dougls	John Thomson
	James Young
	James Dobbie
	John Hamilton
	Stephen Bertram

Appendix 4:
New Lanark Population, November 1793

	Male	Female
Married persons	181	184
Widows and widowers	4	34
Unmarried persons above 21 years of age	15	22
Between 21 and 22	1	3
20 and 21	2	3
19 and 20	14	21
18 and 19	10	11
17 and 18	15	18
16 and 17	17	27
15 and 16	30	29
14 and 15	32	36
13 and 14	27	36
12 and 13	29	30
11 and 12	51	47
10 and 11	31	31
9 and 10	42	54
8 and 9	34	40
7 and 8	40	37
6 and 7	39	32
5 and 6	20	16
4 and 5	12	18
3 and 4	17	10
2 and 3	9	22
1 and 2	12	14
Between ½ year old and 1	11	12
Under ½ year old	19	18
Total	**714**	**805**

Total number of souls   1519

Among these are: 54 Jenny Spinners; seven Clockmakers; 45 Labourers; five Weavers; three Schoolmasters; eleven Smiths; ten Wrights; eight Taylors; seven Masons; three Shoemakers; three Turners; and two Merchants.

From: *The Statistical Account of Scotland*, Sir John Sinclair (ed) Vol XV, 1795, pp38-9.

Appendix 5: Overseas Visitors by Address/Date

Europe

Norway: M. Andielus + four merchants, 3rd October 1795.

Dusseldorf: Mr. Jacobs, 22nd March 1796.

'Spain': Unnamed couple, 8th August 1796.

'Siena': Lewis Morelli, 7th September 1796.

Lisbon: Mr. Matta, 15th September 1796.

Lisbon: Dr. Constance & Mr. Matta 7th June 1797.

Geneva: John Peschier M.D., 10th July 1797.

Lisbon: Alex Wilson, 8th September 1797.

Naples: sixteen visitors, 16th August 1798

'Leipsic': G. Rosentrater, 26th January 1799.

Hamburg: E. J. Martin (?), 25th February 1799.

North America

New York: John Aspinwall, 6th October 1795.

New York: John MacGregor, 5th March 1796.

Charleston, S.C.: C. Fuller & E. Thomas, 17th June 1796.

Kentucky: James Spiel, 25th August 1796.

Virginia: John Watson, 25th August 1796.

Nova Scotia: Wm. Jack, 19th May 1797.

Boston, Mass.: Mr. Tudor, 27th June 1797.

New York: Mr. Hopkins, 27th June 1797.

New York: Wm. Little, 8th November 1797.

New York: Mr. McGrigor, 29th June 1798.

N. Caroline: T. & G. Pollok, 8th August 1798.

Savannah, Ga.: Thos. Gardner, 19th June 1799.

West Indies

Barbados: Dominik Lynch, 22nd August 1795.

Dominica: Mr. & Mrs. Pajan, 26th September 1795.

Jamaica: John Carlyle & Robt. Long, 6th October 1795.

'West Indies': Charles Hogart, 7th October 1795.

Jamaica: James Inglis, 29th October 1795.

Jamaica: Mr. Smith, 2nd August 1796.

Jamaica: Mr. Balfour, 7th January 1797.

Antigua: Thos. Coull, M.D., 16th September 1797.

Grenada: John Horne, 2nd May 1798.

Tortola: Robt. Dougan, 16th October 1798.

Jamaica: James Dickson, 3rd July 1799.

'West Indies': J. Lewis, 2nd September 1799.

Africa/India

Sierra Leone: Zachary Macaulay Esq., 19th October 1795.

Bengal: Mr. R. Tulloch, 2nd July 1798.

Calcutta: R. Stewart, 16th October 1798.

Extracted from New Lanark Visitors' Book 1795-1799. University of Glasgow Archives Services, New Lanark Mills Collection.

Appendix 6: Selected U.K. Visitors by Date: 1795–99.

Date	Name	Address
8th Aug 1795	Robert French	Glasgow
19th Aug 1795	John Bogle	Glasgow
2nd Sept 1795	Thos. Graham	Glasgow
10th Sept 1795	Lord Advocate of Scotland	–
19th Sept 1795	James Dunlop	Linwood
19th Sept 1795	Robt. Tennent	Glasgow
19th Sept 1795	Mr. Dinwoodie (sic – Dinwiddie)	Glasgow
26th Sept 1795	Hugh Auld	Glasgow
6th May 1796	Wm. Ballantyne	Glasgow
12th May 1796	James Gillespie	Douglas Mill
13th May 1796	James McNair	Greenfield
21st May 1796	Mr. & Mrs. Speirs	Glasgow
13th June 1796	Adam Bogle	Glasgow
15th June 1796	Provost Harvie	Rutherglen
20th June 1796	Mr. Watt	Birmingham
20th June 1796	Robt. Fleming	Glasgow
19th July 1796	Adam, John & James Dunlop	Stewarton
2nd Aug 1796	John McIlwham	Glasgow
11th Aug 1796	Robt. & Wm. Dunlop	Stewarton
22nd Aug 1796	Mr. Henry, a friend of Thos. B. Bailey	Manchester
26th Aug 1796	Mr. Burnside	Glasgow
29th Aug 1796	James Finlay	Glasgow
6th Sept 1796	Henry Brougham	Edinburgh
7th Sept 1796	George Bogle	Glasgow
24th Sept 1796	J. H. Oswald	Glasgow
24th Sept 1796	Wm. Brown	Glasgow
24th Sept 1796	Walter Graham	Glasgow
5th Oct 1796	Dr. Porteous Snr. & Mrs. Porteous	Glasgow
5th Oct 1796	Mr. Alexander of Ballochmyle	Ballochmyle
8th Oct 1796	John Dale	Glasgow?
13th Oct 1796	Mr. Scott Moncrieff Jnr. & Daughter	n.a.
19th May 1797	Chas. Macintosh	Glasgow
10th June 1797	Jas. Graham	Glasgow
21st July 1797	R. Scott Moncrieff	n.a.
22nd July 1797	Thos. & Jas. Buchanan, David Graham & John Leckie	Glasgow
27th July 1797	Adam Monteith	Glasgow
28th July 1797	Walter, Ralph & Robert Wardlaw	Glasgow
28th July 1797	Robt. Reid & Archibald Patterson	Glasgow
24th Aug 1797	Mr. McGuffog	n.a.
1st Sept 1797	Allan Bogle	Glasgow
4th Sept 1797	David Dale Jun.	Glasgow

Date	Name	Address
8th Sept 1797	Wm. Dick & John Dick	Glasgow
2nd Oct 1797	C., G. & J. Dunlop	n.a.
2nd Nov 1797	Mr. Douglas	Newton Douglas
8th Nov 1797	James Gillespie	Anderston
13th Nov 1797	Mr. Douglas	Douglas Mill
13th Nov 1797	William Dale	Glasgow
5th Feb 1798	Mr. Robinson	Johnstone Mill
9th March 1798	Robert Owen	Manchester
9th March 1798	Mr. Finlay	n.a.
9th Apr 1798	Robert Graeme	n.a.
10th May 1798	James Dennistoun	n.a.
16th May 1798	John Barton	Manchester
16th May 1798	Mr. Heatly	Manchester
16th May 1798	Mr. Owen	Manchester
16th May 1798	Dr. Brice	Glasgow
15th Jun 1798	Mr. Owen	Manchester
29th Jun 1798	Wm. Dunlop	n.a.
27th Jul 1798	Mr. Finlay	n.a.
28th Jul 1798	Archd. Campbell	Glasgow
30th Jul 1798	John James & Wm. McCall	Glasgow
4th Aug 1798	David Dale Jun.	Glasgow
14th Aug 1798	John Orr	Paisley
16th Aug 1798	Dr. Garnet, Mrs. Garnet & a Gentleman	n.a.
4th Sept 1798	Henry Brougham	n.a.
12th Sept 1798	Miss Gillespie	Douglas Mill
14th Sept 1798	Mr. Bialey (sic)	Manchester
14th Sept 1798	Richard Ainsworth	Bolton
18th Sept 1798	Mr. Dundas of Dundas	n.a.
21st Sept 1798	Arthur Spear & Miss Spear	Manchester
4th Oct 1798	James Gillespie & Miss Gillespie	Douglas Mill
9th Oct 1798	Mr. Snodgrass & another Gentleman	n.a.
26th Jan 1799	Andrew Reid	Glasgow
29th May 1799	Mr. Kennedy & Mr. Pollard	Manchester
24th Jun 1799	James Craig	Paisley
15th Jul 1799	Mr. & Miss Macintosh	Glasgow
29th Jul 1799	Mr. Atkison (sic), Mr. J. Barton & Mr. Owen	Manchester
14th Aug 1799	Mrs. R. Tennent & Patrick Tennent	n.a.
14th Aug 1799	George Dempster Jun.	n.a.
2nd Sept 1799	Mr. Barton	Manchester
25th Sept 1799	John Stodart	n.a.
25th Sept 1799	Robt. Dunlop & James Black	n.a.

Extracted from New Lanark Visitors' Book 1795–1799. University of Glasgow Archives Services, New Lanark Mills Collection.

Appendix 7: Dale's Letter to T. B. Bayley, 1796

The questions and Dale's response appeared in many of publications and periodicals of the time, although often in an abbreviated or truncated form.

The full letter below is drawn from two sources:

1   Maltby, S.E. (1918) *Manchester and the Movement for National Elementary Education, 1800–1870*. Manchester. M.U.P. pp.124–5 which contains the opening paragraph (below) not found in the second source:

"I AM quite satisfied in my own mind, that cotton mills, under proper management, are as favourable to health as any other employment. Indeed it is observed by the parents of the children who work at my mills for wages, and are fed and lodged by their parents in their own houses, that the part of their family which works at the mills, is more healthy than the part that is at home, and with regard to their morals, I have no hesitation in saying, that they are, at least, as correct as will be found among an equal number in any manufacturing business; and when it is considered, that the greater part of the children who are in the boarding-house, consists of destitute orphans, children abandoned by their parents, some of whose parents are transported as felons, many who know not who were their parents, and who brought with them a weakly constitution, transmitted to them by diseased parents, it gives me pleasure to say, that by proper management, and attention, much good, instead of evil, may be done at cotton-mills. For I am warranted in affirming, that many now have stout, healthy bodies, and are of decent behaviour, who in all probability would have been languishing with disease, and pests to society had they not been employed at Lanark cotton-mills."

2   Brown, A. (1795–1797) *History of Glasgow and of Paisley, Greenock, and Port-Glagow, comprehending the ecclesiastical and civil history of these places, from the earliest accounts to the present time: and including an account of their population, commerce, manufactures, arts, and agriculture*, 2 vols. (1795, 1797) Glasgow: W. Paton, Vol. 2, 1797, pp.231–239., which contains a full version of the remainder of the letter, as follows:

Queries submitted to Mr. Dale of Glasgow by Mr. Bayley of Manchester

1   The dimensions of spinning rooms, especially the height
2   Number of spindles in a room?
3   Modes of ventilation and purification?
4   Number of boys and girls in one room ?
5   Hours of labour, of rest and for meals?
6   Rules for cleanliness and for health?
7   Time and manner of teaching the children to read , and of religious instruction?
8   Mode and time of hiring?
9   Whence the mills are supplied with labourers?
10 Means employed to prevent or correct the typhus fever?
11 Mode of lodging and feeding the children?
12 What are they fit for when too big for the spindles?
13 Are they commonly strong for labour?

Mr. Dale's answer to the same

1   The spinning, and all the other rooms, are of the whole extent of the buildings, without any subdivisions, and are from 120 to 150 feet long; from 26 to 30 feet wide, and all of them in height ten feet from floor to floor, or nine feet clear of the beams.

2   The spinning rooms contain each about 2000 spindles.

3   Ventilation is greatly promoted by the rapid motion of many parts of the machinery. Fresh air is introduced by regularly opening the windows at top, on both sides of the house. To increase the circulation still more, air holes, six inches square, on a level with the floor, are opened below every other window through the walls, at the distance of fourteen feet from each other; but these are only of advantage in summer, as the cold in winter precludes the use of them. The means of purification in use, are, washing the walls and ceilings of the rooms at least once a year with new slacked (sic) lime, weekly washings of the floors and machinery with scalding water, and frequent and constant brushings of the walls, ceilings and floor.

4   The greatest number of persons in one room is 75, in some there are only 50.

5   The hours of labour are eleven and a half each day, viz. from six o'clock in the morning till seven o'clock at night, with half an hour of intermission at nine o'clock for breakfast, and a whole hour at two for dinner.

6   The only rules for cleanliness and health, are such as enjoin the practices above mentioned, in answer to the third query.

7   Seven is the hour for supper; in half an hour after at most, and as much sooner as possible, the teaching commences and continues till nine o'clock. The schools at present are attended by five hundred and seven scholars, in instructing whom sixteen teachers are employed; thirteen in teaching to read, two to write, and one to figure, besides a person who teaches sewing, and another who occasionally teaches church music. The mode of teaching is as follows. The course is divided into eight classes according to the progress of the scholars; to each of these classes one or more teachers are assigned, as the numbers in that stage of advancement may require. To the teachers is specified in writing, how far they are respectively to carry forward their scholars; which, so soon as they have accomplished, the scholars are transferred to the next highest class and the teacher receives a premium for everyone so qualified.* In their respective classes, the teachers promote emulation in the usual way, by making the top of the class the post of honour, which is still farther kept up by the distribution of rewards every half year to such as, from an account taken once a fortnight, appear to have been most frequently uppermost. On Sundays, that part of the children who cannot go to church for want of accommodation are kept busy at school; and in the evenings, after public worship, the usual teachers spend regularly three hours in giving religious instruction, by causing the scriptures to be read, catechising etc. As there is accommodation at church for only 150 children, they all go to it in rotation. Besides the night schools, there are two day schools for children to young for work, which, as well as the night ones (except the providing of their own books), are entirely free of expence to the scholars.

*The following is a statement of the number in each class at present, which affords an accurate view of the general state of their education:

In the first or latter class there are	65 scholars
second	85
third	76
fourth	65
fifth	44
sixth	44
seventh	51
eighth	80

The eighth or highest class are all good readers and employ half their time each night in writing. Such as stand in no need of farther instruction in reading, of whom there are about twelve boys and twelve girls, employ the remainder of their time, after writing, in learning arithmetic and sewing, except on occasional nights appointed for reviving their reading.

8   The time of hiring differs with the different descriptions of children. Those who agree for a stipulated weekly wage, and who are generally such as live with their parents, are commonly engaged for four years; while such as are received from the workhouse in Edinburgh, or who are otherwise without friends to take charge of them, and who, in lieu of wages are maintained and educated, are bound four, five, six or seven years, according to their age, or generally till they have completed their fifteenth year. The mode of hiring is generally by contract of the parents or curators of the children in their behalf.

9   The supply of workers for the mills comes either from the native inhabitants of the place; from families who have been collected about the works from the neighbouring parishes and more distant parts of the country; or lastly from Edinburgh or Glasgow, by the number of destitute children these places constantly afford.

10 When fevers, or any epidemical distempers appear in the boarding house where that description of workers who do not receive their wages are accommodated, the means used to prevent the spreading of infection are, the immediate removal of the sick to a detached part of the house, and frequent sprinkling and fumigating of the bed rooms with vinegar. Typhous fevers have not appeared there for years, but have, during that time, been in the village, though never general; yet in no case, so far as circumstances afforded the means of judging, did it appear to originate in the mills, or even to be communicated by the intercourse the workers have there with each other.*

*The following statement of the number of children in the boarding house at different periods, and the annual deaths there, best evinces their general state of health.

In 1792	272 boarders	2 deaths
1793	288 ditto	1
1794	306 ditto	0
1795	384 ditto	6
		9 deaths

11 The greatest part of the workers are lodged in their parents houses in the village, in the immediate neighbourhood of the mills, or in the town of Lanark, one mile distant. The principal part of their food, as is usual, in the country, consists of oatmeal. Those who get their maintenance in lieu of wages are lodged all together in one house. They consist, at present, of 396 boys and girls. There are six sleeping apartments for them and three children are allowed to each bed. The ceilings and walls of the apartments are white-washed twice a year with hot lime, and the floors washed with scalding water and sand. The children sleep on wooden bottomed beds, on bed-ticks filled with straw, which is in general changed once a month. A sheet covers the bed-ticks, and above that are one or two pair of blankets, and a bed cover, as the season requires. day. Of late, cast iron beds have been introduced in place of wooden ones.

The upper body clothing in use in summer, both for boys and girls, is entirely of cotton, which, as they have spare suits to change with , are washed once a fortnight. In winter, the boys are dressed in woollen cloth, and they, as well as the girls, have complete dress suits for Sundays. Their linens are changed once a week. For a few months in summer, both boys and girls go without shoes and stockings. The provisions are dressed in cast iron boilers and consist of oatmeal porridge for breakfast and supper, and milk with it in its season. In winter its substitute is a composition of molasses, fermented with some new beer, which is called swats . For dinner, the whole of them have every day, in all seasons, barley broth made from fresh beef. The beef itself is divided among one half of the children, in quantities of about seven ounces English to each.; the other half is served with cheese in quantities of about five ounces English each; so that they have alternately beef and cheese for dinner, excepting now and then a dinner of herrings in winter, and fresh butter in summer. To the beef and cheese is added a plentiful allowance of potatoes or barley bread, of which last they have also an allowance every morning before going to work.

12 & 13   As far as observation, with regard to these two queries has extended, the workers, when too big for spinning, are as stout and robust as others. The male part of them are fit for any trade. A great many, since the commencement of the war, have gone into the army and navy, and others are occasionally going away as apprentices to smiths and joiners etc. but especially to weavers; for which last trade, from the expertness they acquire in handling yarn, they are particularly well fitted, and of course are taken as apprentices on better terms. The females generally leave the mills, and go into private family service when about 16 years of age. Were they disposed to continue at the mills, these afford abundant employment for them at reeling, picking etc. as well as to many more young men that ever remain at them.

Appendix 8

Ballamyl 15th May 1801

My Dear Boyd,

I have never yet thanked you for your letter in March enclosing McLeans check acct. discharged, the fact is I rec'd it in Edin. where I was only in for six days having sold the Mills to Kirkman Finlay & Co I was hurried back to deliver them over to the new Comp's which was done on the 13th of last month that is to say they began spinning on their own account on that day but all my trouble began from that period & I have scarcely written to any person since then excepting to Mrs A & to my friend David Dale – However as it is the last year's trouble I shall have with the Mills I do not begrudge it.

I rec'd the Books which you was so good as send & have now to trouble you with another Commssion – I am much in want of a coat & have written the enclosed to Douglas & Lambeth ordering one & if you could bring it down with you so much the better or if Enterkin could bring it if not you can order it to be sent by the Waggon to Glasgow to the care of Mr. Dale if I receive it a couple of months hence it is time enough.

I must also trouble you to pay them as well for this coat as the coat Sandy Porterfields check bespoke for me in the year 1799 but which left town without paying – I have settled your account with the ingrams so that we can set the one against the other when we meet you can also let me know what you paid for the Tax Tables Pamphlets etc.

You must not forget to get from Tom Brown or his Partner Cales Whitefoord the Volm. of the Transactions of the Society for encouraging Arts Commerce & Agriculture fot the year 1800 as a perpetual subscriber I am entitled to a book annually – I am glad to hear that Browns Nephew is Commercial President at Patna – you say many of my friends are making enquiries for me and express their surprise at my so seldom making my appearance in London, but those friends know not what I have all to do, else their surprise would cease, However, every year after this I shall have less to do & then

I long very much to see the Gazette Accounts of the Battles in Egypt with the list of the killed and wounded, the Gazette acct of the battle of 13th March I expect to see this night I hope Napier of Blackstones son has escaped I think it looks by the Newspapers as if Buonaparte intended an invasion of this Kingdom. Is it certain that he made such an extravagant demand as is mentioned in the Newspapers before he would treat about peace, if so the Ministry should make it known Is Will'm Dundas's marriage with Lady Landown still talked of in London?

I hope you will get your Business well settled for the Town of Greenock. I see that McDowall has brought in a similar bill for Port Glasgow.

I am ever yours Affectly
Claud Alexander
PS Do not forget the East India Kallendar? for 1801

Appendix 9: Location & Number of Boarders 1801–1802.

Location		No.	
Spinning Room	Old Mill	31	including 4 boys
No. 2	Old Mill	27	" 5 boys
No. 3	Old Mill	29	" 18 boys
Spinning Room	2nd Mill	35	" 12 boys
No. 2	New Mill	22	" 12 boys
No. 3	New Mill	29	" 11 boys
No. 4	New Mill	15	" 8 boys
No. 5	New Mill	17	" 8 boys
No. 6	New Mill	18	" 3 boys
No. 1	Jenny House	5	" 1 boy
No. 2	Jenny House	13	" 4 boys
No. 3	Jenny House	17	" 3 boys
No. 4	Jenny House	5	" 4 boys
No. 5	Jenny House	3	" 1 boy

Appendix 10: Glasgow Fire Insurance Company. Initial Shareholdings, May 1803.

Name	No. of £250 Shares	Value
David Dale*	6	£1,500
George Oswald	6	£1,500
Alex Oswald*	6	£1,500
John McIlwham*	6	£1,500
Kirkman Finlay	6	£1,500
Adam Crooks	6	£1,500
Arch'd Grahame*	6	£1,500
James Hill	6	£1,500
Robert Graham	6	£1,500
John Hamilton	6	£1,500
Walter Ritchie	6	£1,500
John Campbell Snr.	4	£1,000
Gilbert Hamilton*	4	£1,000
John Stirling*	4	£1,000
Arch'd Smith*	4	£1,000
Walter Ewing McLae*	4	£1,000
James Buchanan	4	£1,000
Charles Hagart	4	£1,000
John Smith	4	£1,000
Robert Dunlop	4	£1,000
David Denny	4	£1,000
John Scott	4	£1,000
William Craig	2	£500
Alexander Dunlop	2	£500
John Monteith**	–	–
Dugald Bannatine**	–	–

* First directors of the company.
** Monteith and Bannatine are named but no further information is supplied.

From Glasgow Fire Insurance Records. University of Glasgow Archives Services.

Appendix 11:
Patient Illness on Admission to Glasgow Royal Infirmary: 8th Dec 1794–1st Jan 1796

(Original terms, spellings retained throughout)

Total 276 patients (186 men, 90 women). Medical (145); Surgical (131).

Cured	142	Relieved	28	Dismissed	34
Irregular	4	Dead	18	Remaining	50

Fractures	13	Pox & Gonnorhea	20
Cancers	14	Sibbens	6
Herpetic eruptions	5	Sore throat	1
Fever	18	Difficulty swallowing	1
Hysteria	8	Abscess of Breast	1
Consumption & Pulmonic Affection	14	Measles	9
Dropsy	13	Small Pox	4
Hydrocele	3	Double hair lip	1
Palsy	11	Schirries	1
Disorders of the Eye	9	Diabetes	1
Looseness	2	Diseased Liver	1
Rheumatism	11	Palpitations	1
Ague	1	Stone	1
Swelling of the knee	3	Paraphyniosis	1
Retention of menses	2	Aneurism	2
Fist: Lachrym	3	Epilepsy	3
Fist: in ano.	2	Bite of mad dog	1
Fist: in pennae.	2	Abscess of tongue	1
Ulcers	68	Imperforated nostrils	1
White swelling	6	Polypi in ears	1
Anomalies	4		

Operations

Breast; ear; hair lip; polyps; various cancers (8); amputations (8); trepanning (2). **32**

From *Glasgow Royal Infirmary Minute Book 1787–1802*. GCHB Archive HB14/1/1/ Meeting og General Court 4th Jan 1796. p175.

Appendix 12: Admissions Registers, Glasgow Royal Infirmary 1795–1803. (Extracts)

Patients Admitted by David Dale Senior:

Date	Name	Occupation/Locality	Dismissed	Illness	Comment
30th Jan 1795	James Horn	Nailer, Glasgow	23rd Mar	Fracture & Ulcer	–
16th Feb 1795	James Munro	Gardener	2nd Mar	Intermittent Fever	Cured
6th Feb 1795	Mary White	Glasgow	22nd Mar	Palsy	–
12th Feb 1795	James Bland	Cotton Spinner, Sorn	8th Sept	Sibbens,[1] leg amput.	Cured
25th May 1795	Wm. Walkinshaw	Cotton Spinner, Lanark	28th Aug	Blindness (?)	–
6th Jun 1795	John Campbell	Soldier	16th Jun	Dropsy[2]	–
4th Sept 1795	Christian Martin	–	16th Oct	White swelling of knee	Cured
15th Apr 1796	Eliz. Morris	–	25th May	Burning	Cured
15th Apr 1796	Eliz. McAllum	Medical	25th Jul	Pox	Cured
25th Sept 1796	Wm. Knox	Paisley	12th Oct	Marasmus[3]	Cured
14th Oct 1796	Mary Macintyre	Highlands	31st Oct	Cornea...	–
16th Dec 1796	Anne Ritchie	Glasgow	17th Dec	Catarrh & Hunger	Dead
9th Mar 1797	John Stalker	Campbeltown	19th Apr	Hydrocele[4]	Cured
28th Apr 1797	Agnes Macallum	Argyleshire	17th June	Sibbens	Cured
9th May 1797	Isobel Hay	–	5th Jul	Opthalmia	Cured
24th Jun 1797	Colin Campbell	Greenock	21st Jul	Ulcers	Dead
12th Aug 1797	Catherine Anderson	Agyleshire	14th Dec	Sibbens	Relieved
13th Feb 1798	Mary Lamont	Rutherglen	11th Apr	Wounded trachea	Relieved
14th Mar 1798	Matthew Williamson	Bothwell	23rd Apr	Cencerous lip	Relieved
21st May 1798	John Turner	Glasgow	10th Jul	Fever	Cured
10th Jun 1798	Mary Macintyre	Highlands	20th Nov	Ulcer hand	Cured
27th Jun 1798	David Millar	Glasgow	20th Jul	Consumption	Dead
17th Jul 1798	Anabella Campbell	Glasgow	26th Jul	Headach	Dead
1st Sept 1798	Alex Maclean	Isla	12th Feb	Sivvens	Dead
4th Oct 1798	Margaret Campbell	Inverness-shire	16th Nov	Eruption	Cured
15th Jan 1799	Jean Fulton	Glasgow	27th Feb	Abscess neck	Relieved
22nd Mar 1799	John Ferguson	Glasgow	27th Apr	Fever	Cured
22nd Sept 1799	Cecilia Pollock	Glasgow	31st Oct	Fever	Cured
6th Dec 1799	Janet Campbell	Glasgow	3rd Feb	Sibbens	Cured
24th Feb 1800	Duncan Brown	Islay	21st Apr	Dysentery	–
6th May 1800	Wm. Perry	Ireland	16th Aug	Ulcer Leg	–
24th May 1800	George Robertson	Carnwath	10th Jul	Diseased ankle	Cured
24th May 1800	Alexander Maxwell	Glasgow	18th Jul	Cough etc.	Cured
7th Jun 1800	James Kelso	Glasgow	18th Aug	Ulcer nose	Relieved
3rd Oct 1800	Kate Russel	Glasgow	22nd Oct	Dysentery	Cured

Date	Name	Occupation/Locality	Dismissed	Illness	Comment
19th Nov 1800	Isobel Johnston	Glasgow	26th Dec	Fever	Cured
? Jan 1801	Mary Patrick	Glasgow	1st Feb	Fever	Cured
? Jan 1801	John Buchanan	Barony	21st Feb	Amaurosis[5]	Relieved
26th May 1801	Matthew Dale	–	5th June	Amaurosis	–
25th Jul 1801	John McNab	–	19th Aug	Rheum & Diarrh.	Relieved
17th Nov 1801	Margt. McLean	–	1st Dec	Hydrocele	Cured
5th Jan 1802	Margt. Wilson	–	1st Feb	Rheumatism	Cured
27th Apr 1802	John Purdie	–	19th May	Typhus (?)	Cured
27th July 1802	Robert...	–	21st Aug	Asthenia[6]	Relieved
24th Sep 1802	George Levoch	–	–	–	–
3rd Dec 1802	Alexander Watt	–	–	–	–
6th Jan 1803	Christian Mayne	–	11th Apr	Hemiplegia[7]	–
11th Jan 1803	Janet Limeburn	–	21st Jan	Rheumatism	Cured
22nd Jan 1803	Peter Mclean	–	29th Jan	Gonorrhea	Cured
27th Feb 1803	Matthew Murphy	–	23rd Apr	Rheumatism	Cured
21st Mar 1803	John Henry	–	21st May	Hepatitis	Cured
26th Mar 1803	Mary Kennedy	–	9th Apr	Opthalmia	Cured
2nd Apr 1803	Ann Bremner	–	1st May	Scrophula[8]	–
14th Apr 1803	John White	–	14th May	Opthalmia	Cured
20th Apr 1803	Rebecca Templeton	–	28th Jul	–	–
21st Sep 1803	Ebeneezer Findlayton	–	–	–	–
28th Sep 1803	Ann ...	–	9th Nov	Ulcers	Cured

Patients Admitted by 'The Benevolent Society at Lanark'.

Date	Name	Occupation/Locality	Dismissed	Illness	Comment
11th Aug 1795	Eliz. Gun	New Lanark	28th Oct	Rheumatism	–
19th Nov 1795	Francis Brown	Lanark	3rd Jan	Epilepsy	Cured
6th Jul 1796	Martha Simpson	Lanark	31st Jul	Ensephalus	Relieved
15th Jul 1800	Peter Taylor	Lanark	17th Jul	White Swelling	–
24th Sep 1800	George Burns	Lanark	1st Oct	Ulcer Leg	–
3rd April 1801	James Jack	Lanark	21st Apr	Hypochondriasis	Relieved
26th May 1801	William McBeth	Lanark	4th Aug	Rheumatism	Cured

Patients Admitted by David Dale Junior.

Date	Name	Occupation/Locality	Dismissed	Illness	Comment
20th Feb 1795	Jeremiah Ryding	Soldier	10th May	–	–
1st Aug 1796	David Hall	Glasgow	–	Ulcer hand	Cured
14th Apr 1798	Philip Rodger	Ireland	25th May	Pleurisy	Cured
10th Nov 1799	Wm. Jeffray	Anderston	27th Nov	Ulcerated leg	cured
22nd Dec 1799	John Nisbet	Glasgow	23rd Jan	Dropsy	–
12th Dec 1800	Margt. Thomas	Glasgow	29th Dec	Fever	Cured
26th Aug 1801	Nathan Mitchell	–	14th Sept	Intermittent Fever	Cured

Patients Admitted by Robert Owen.

Date	Name	Occupation/Locality	Dismissed	Illness	Comment
17th Jan 1803	Mary Harvey	–	–	–	–

N.B. Original spellings etc. have been retained throughout.

1   Contagious infection. Throat & nose ulcer & skin eruptions.
2   Swelling caused by fluid retention
3   Malnutrition
4   Fluid in the scrotum
5   Eye disease causing blindness
6   Weakness, general debility
7   Palsy, partial paralysis
8   TB affecting lymph nodes

From Glasgow Royal Infirmary Admissions Registers 1794–1800 and 1800–1803. Greater Glasgow Health Board Archives: HB14/67/56/1A and HB14/67/56/1B.

Appendix 13: Oaths required for issue of a Glasgow Burgess Ticket

An oath for the faithful discharge of duty (*the oath de fidele*) is administered:

Oath for a Burgess Ticket (Protestant)

Here I protest, before God, that I confess and allow with my heart the true religion, presently professed within this realm, and authorised by the laws thereof. I shall abide thereat, and defend the same, to my life's end, renouncing the Roman religion, called Papistry. I shall be leal and true to our Sovereign Lord the King's Majesty, and to the Provost and Bailies of this Burgh. I shall obey the officers thereof, fortify, maintain, and defend them in the execution of their office with my body and goods. I shall not colour Unfreemens' goods under colour of my own. In all taxations, watchings, and wardings, to be laid upon this Burgh, I shall willingly bear my part thereof, as I am commanded thereto by the Magistrates; I shall not purchase nor use exemptions to be free thereof, renouncing the benefit of the same for ever. I shall do nothing hurtful to the liberties and common-well of this Burgh. I shall not brew nor cause brew any malt but such as is grinded at the Town's Mills, and shall grind no other corns, except wheat, pease, rye, and beans, but at the same allenarly. And how oft as I shall happen to break any part of this my oath, I oblige me to pay, to the common affairs of this Burgh, the sum of one hundred pounds, Scots money, and shall remain in ward while the same be paid. So help me God.

I shall give the best counsel I can, and conceal the counsel shown to me. I shall not consent to dispone the common goods of this Burgh, but for ane common cause, and ane common profit, I shall make concord, where discord is, to the utmost of my power. In all lienations and neighbourhoods, I shall give my leal and true judgement, but price, prayer, or reward. So help me God.

Oath for a Burgess Ticket (Roman Catholic)

From 1793 an Act of Parliament was passed, authorising Magistrates of Royal Burghs to admit Roman Catholics to Burgesses and Guild Brethren of their respective Burghs. In Glasgow, the first applications under this Act were made in 1801. The oath for Catholics took a different form:

I do hereby declare that I do profess the Roman Catholic religion. I do sincerely promise and swear that I will be faithful, and bear true allegiance to His Majesty, King George III. and him will defend to the utmost of my power, against all conspiracies and attempts whatever, that shall be made against his person, crown, or dignity, and I will do my utmost endeavour to disclose and make known to His Majesty, his Heirs and Successors, all treasons and traitorous conspiracies, which may be formed against him or them. And I do faithfully promise to maintain, support, and defend, to the utmost of my power, the succession of the Crown, which succession, by an act, (entitled, an Act for the further limitation of the Crown, and better securing the rights and liberties of the Subject,) is, and stands limited to the Princess Sophia, Electress and Dutchess Dowager of Hanover, and the Heirs of her body being Protestants, hereby utterly renouncing and abjuring any obedience or allegiance unto any other person, claiming or pretending a right to the Crown of these realms. And I do swear that I do reject and detest, as an unchristian and impious position, that it is lawful to murder or destroy any person or persons whatsoever, for, or under pretence of their being heretics or infidels, and also that unchristian and impious principle, that faith is not to be kept with heretics or infidels. And I further declare, that it is not an article of my faith, and that I do renounce, reject, and abjure the opinion, that Princes, excommunicated by the Pope and Council, or any authority of the See of Rome, or by any other authority whatsoever, may be deposed or murdered by their subjects, or any person whatsoever. And I do promise that I will not hold, maintain, or abet, any such opinion, or any other opinion, contrary to what is expressed in this declaration. And I do declare, that I do not believe that the Pope of Rome, or any other foreign Prince, Prelate, State, or Potentate, hath, or ought to have, any temporal or civil jurisdiction, power, superiority, or pre-eminence, directly or indirectly, within this realm. And I do solemnly, in the presence of God, profess, testify, and declare, that I do make this declaration, and every part thereof, in the plain and ordinary sense of the words of this oath, without any evasion, equivocation, or mental reservation whatever, and without any dispensation already granted by the Pope or any authority of the See of Rome, or any person whatever, and without thinking that I am or can be acquitted before God or man, or absolved of this declaration, or any part thereof, although the Pope or any other person or authority whatsoever, shall dispense with, or annul the same, and declare that it was null or void. So help me God.

Adapted from Cleland, J. (1816) *Annals of Glasgow*. 2 vols. Vol II. pp 304–5

Appendix 14: Obituary Notices and Memoirs

Glasgow Courier, 20th March 1806.

Died here, on the 17th current, in the 67th year of his age, DAVID DALE, Esq. formerly proprietor of the Lanark Cotton Mills, and one of the Magistrates of Glasgow – generally known and admired for a noble spirit of philanthropy – in whose character were strikingly combined, successful commercial enterprise with piety, active benevolence and public spirit. Here, if ever, a tribute of respect and admiration is due to departed worth. Originally in a lowly station of life, by prosperous adventures in trade, he was raised to a state of affluence, which he directed, on a grand scale, to the encouragement of industry and relief of the distressed. In a romantic den, on the banks of the Clyde, the lofty Mills of Lanark arose, under his eye and fostering hand; surprised and delighted the traveller, as with a scene of enchantment, and exhibited a pleasing picture of industry walking hand in hand with instruction and comfort. Thither were transplanted, and trained to virtuous habits, numerous orphans and outcasts of our streets who had been a prey to vice and misery. And there many "hapless sons of Caledonia," who were emigrating to a foreign land, found a comfortable asylum. As a Magistrate, he tempered justice with mercy; and, on trying occasions, he displayed a spirit of resolution, scarcely expected by those who were familiar with his unassuming manners in private life. Though warmly attached to a particular religious sect, he was free from bigotry, and extended his friendship and charity to many others of different religious principles. Hence the poor blessed him, and the eminent vied with each other in swelling his fame. In private life he was very affectionate to his relatives and intimate friends; sometimes in a musing contemplative frame, and sometimes endearing by a peculiar vein of cheerful pleasantry. Hence they bewail the loss of a kind father, friend and faithful monitor. The poor will feel the want of a bountiful benefactor. Glasgow is deprived of an illustrious citizen. Public institutions, have lost him who was looked up to, as the general patron of every generous and laudable undertaking. Humanity has lost a warm and steady friend.

Glasgow Herald, 21st March 1806.

MR. DALE.–Died, at Glasgow, on the 17th current, in the 68th year of his age, David Dale, Esq. of Rosebank, late one of the Magistrates of this city. The character of this good man comprehends in it so many points of distinguished excellence, that nothing more than an imperfect outline of it can here be inserted. He had not, in the outset of life, enjoyed the advantage of a polished or liberal education; but the want of this was greatly compensated by a large share of natural sagacity and good sense; an extensive and discriminating knowledge of human character; and by a modest, gentle, dignified simplicity of manner, peculiar to himself, and which secured to him the respect and attention of every company, and of men in every walk of life. A zealous promoter of the general industry and manufactures of his country, his schemes of business were extensive and liberal; conducted with simple prudence and perseverance; and, by the blessing of God, were crowned with such abundant success as served to advance his rank in society, and to furnish him with the means of that diffusive benevolence which rendered his life a public blessing, and shed a lustre on his character rarely exemplified in any age of the world. Impelled by the all-powerful influence of that truth, which he firmly believed and publicly taught; constrained by the love, and animated by the example of his blessed Master, his ear was never shut to the cry of distress; his private charities were boundless; and every public institution which had for its object the alleviation or prevention of human misery, in this world or in the world to come, received from him the most liberal support and encouragement. For, while the leading object of his Heaven-born soul was the diffusion of the light of truth in the earth, he gladly embraced every opportunity of becoming, like the Patriarch of old, "Eyes to the blind, feet to the lame, and to cause the Widow's heart to sing for joy." In private life, his conduct, actuated by the same principles, was equally exemplary – for he was a kind parent, a genuine friend, a wise and faithful counsellor. "A lover of hospitality, a lover of good men, sober, just, holy, temperate." And now, having "thus occupied with his talents," he hath "entered into the joy of his Lord." "Mark the perfect, and behold the upright, for the latter end of that man is Peace."

The Evening Star, 22nd March 1806. Cited in Liddell, A. (1854b) *Memoir of David Dale*, pp.176–7

In "The Evening Star," a London paper, of March 22, 1806, appeared a similar eulogium, written by the editor, Dr. Alexander Tilloch, a native of Glasgow, and author of various publications – literary, scientific, and religious. "His life (said this writer) was a life of benevolence and extensive charity, without ostentation, without pride. Indeed, his constant aim was to hide from the eye of man his numberless acts of mercy; even the individuals who were saved from wretchedness and want by his liberality, were often ignorant of the instrument which Providence had raised up for their deliverance. Agreeably to the injunction of the Master whom he served, his alms were done in secret, but they could not be entirely hid. Mr. Dale was the first who erected cotton-mills in Scotland on the plan of Sir Richard Arkwright. His motives for doing so was highly praiseworthy; it was to extend the means of employment for the labouring poor, to introduce habits of industry among the lower orders, and render them useful to their families and the community. Nor was his attention merely confined to the object of finding them bread; he erected and maintained schools, at his own expense, for the education of all the young people employed, and every means which he could devise was used to have them instructed in religious knowledge.

"Mr. Dale was a Dissenter, and for many years one of the pastors of an Independent congregation in Glasgow. In this character he possessed the esteem, the love, and affection of not only the flock over which he presided, but of the clergy and people of every other denomination. In his conversation and uniform practice, he gave a meritorious example of the powerful influence of the Christian precepts, when men live under their influence, in leading them not only to attend with diligence to all the relative duties, making them good husbands, fathers, and neighbours, but loyal and dutiful subjects. Modest and unassuming in his manners, he endeavoured to hide himself from public notice; but 'a city set on a hill cannot be hid.' His fellow-citizens, hailing him as a father, and anxious to extend his sphere of useful action, showed their high esteem of this charitable Dissenter – charitable in the true sense of the word – by calling him into the council of the city, and making him one of its magistrates, an office which he discharged with singular diligence and paternal solicitude.

"During many years of the latter period of his life, he was consulted on all important measures, not only in matters relating to the public welfare of the city, but the private concerns of its citizens; nor did he ever refuse his services, for he considered not his life as his own, but as devoted to the welfare of his fellow creatures."

The Scots Magazine, March 1806, pp.239–240.

17 [March 1806]. At Glasgow, in the 67th year of his age, David Dale, Esq. formerly proprietor of the Lanark Cotton Mills, and one of the Magistrates of Glasgow – generally known and admired for a noble spirit of philanthropy – in whose character were strikingly combined, successful commercial enterprize with piety, active benevolence, and public spirit. Here, if ever, a tribute of respect and admiration is due to departed worth. Originally in a low station of life, by prosperous adventures in trade, he was raised to a state of affluence, which he directed, on a grand scale, to the encouragement of industry and relief of the distressed. In a romantic den on the banks of the Clyde, the lofty Mills of Lanark arose, under his eye and fostering hand; surprised and delighted the traveller, as with a scene of enchantment; and exhibited a pleasing picture of industry walking hand in hand with instruction and comfort. Thither were transplanted, and trained to virtuous habits, numerous orphans and outcasts of the streets who had been a prey to vice and misery. And there many "hapless sons of Caledonia," who were emigrating to a foreign land, found a comfortable asylum. For many years he discharged, with distinguished reputation, the office of Pastor to the Independent Congregation in Glasgow, for which he was peculiarly fitted, by a thorough knowledge of the Hebrew and Greek languages. His discourses bespoke a cultivated understanding, and liberality of sentiment. A steady friend to civil and religious liberty, he embraced men of every persuasion. Possessed of a disposition, kind, hospitable and benevolent, of a heart generous, sincere, and truly philanthropic, his charities, public and private, were probably not surpassed by any individual in Scotland. As a Magistrate, he tempered justice with mercy; and, on trying occasions, he displayed a spirit of resolution, scarcely expected by those who were familiar with his unassuming manners in private society. In private life he was very affectionate to his relatives and intimate friends; sometimes in a musing contemplative frame, and sometimes

endearing by a peculiar vein of cheerful pleasantry. Hence they bewail the loss of a kind father, friend and faithful monitor. The poor will feel the want of a bountiful benefactor. Glasgow is deprived of an illustrious citizen. Public institutions have lost him who was looked up to, as the general patron of every generous and laudable undertaking. Humanity has lost a warm and steady friend.

Air Advertiser (sic), 27th March 1806. Courtesy of Stewarton Historical Society.

This gentleman contributed materially to the commercial prosperity of his country, considerably enlarged the sum of human happiness and effectually promoted the Public weal. Born in the shades of human poverty and obscurity, by assiduous application, uniform regularity of conduct, and perseverance in the paths of Virtue, he rose to distinction, independence and esteem. The Cotton Mills and New Town of Lanark, which he erected, are noble monuments to his memory. As the patron of many unfortunate and deserted beings employed at those factories, he considered it incumbent on him to provide for them instruction, religious and moral. Ever unaffected and unassuming, he appeared the friend of merit, humble and unadorned, exciting among his artificers a lively interest in their respective duties.

From a general intercourse with mankind he acquired a quick perception of the human character. With strong natural conception, a discerning judgement, a judicious application of the most respectable talents to business, he surmounted every barrier that opposed his success; and, as the merit by which he attained made him worthy of his fortunes, so the benevolent purposes he applied it to endeared him to the world.

In the public situations he held, his integrity and ardent zeal for the interests of the community were eminently displayed. For many years, he discharged with distinguished reputation the office of Pastor to the Independent Congregation in Glasgow, for which he was peculiarly fitted, by a thorough knowledge of the Hebrew and Greek languages. His discourses bespoke a cultivated understanding and liberality of sentiment.

A steady friend to civil and religious liberty, he embraced men of every persuasion. Possessed of a disposition kind, hospitable, and benevolent, of a heart generous, sincere and truly philanthropic, his Charities, public and private, were not surpassed by any individual in Scotland. As a magistrate he tempered justice with mercy and on trying occasions, he displayed a spirit of resolution fiercely expected by those who were familiar with his unassuming manners in private life.

The Times, 28th March 1806.

At Glasgow, on the 17th instant, in the 68th year of his age David Dale, Esq. of Rosebank, late one of the Magistrates of that City. The character of this good man comprehend in it so many points of distinguished excellence, that nothing more than an imperfect outline of it can here be inserted. He had nor, in the outset of life, enjoyed the advantage of a polished or liberal education; but the want of this was greatly compensated by a large share of natural sagacity and good sense; an extensive and discriminating knowledge of human character; and by a modest, gentle, dignified simplicity of manner, peculiar to himself, and which secured to him the respect and attention of every company, and men in every rank of life. A zealous promoter of the general industry and manufactures of his country, his schemes of business were extensive and liberal; conducted with singular prudence and perseverance; and, by the Blessing of God, were crowned with such abundant success, as served to advance his rank in society, and to furnish him with the means of that diffusive benevolence which rendered his life a public blessing, and shed a lustre on his character, rarely exemplified in any age of the world. Impelled by the all-powerful influence of that truth, which be firmly believed, an publicly taught; constrained by the love, and animated by the example of his blessed Master, his ear was never shut to the cry of distress; his private charities were boundless; and every public institution which had for its object the alleviation pr prevention of human misery in this world, or in the world to come; received from him the most liberal support and encouragement. For, while the leading object of his Heaven-born soul was the diffusion of the light of truth in the earth, he gladly embraced every opportunity of becoming, like the Patriarch of old, "Eyes to the blind, feet to the lame, and to cause the Widow's heart to sing for joy." In private life, his conduct, actuated by the same principles, was equality exemplary; for he was a kind parent, a generous friend, a wise and faithful counsellor, "a lover of hospitality, a lover of good men, sober, just, holy, temperate." And now, having "thus occupied with his talents," he hath "entered into the joy of his Lord," "Mark the perfect and behold the upright, for the latter end of that man is peace". The remains of this truly great man were interred on the 21st instant. The funeral was attended by the Magistrates and Ministers of all denominations, and between two and three hundred of respectable inhabitants. The concourse of spectators was immense. Several hundreds of poor received a small gratuity in money after the interment. He honoured God while he lived. He was honoured by all descriptions of people in his life, and at his death; and will, though dead, live in the affectionate remembrance of thousands.

The Caledonian Mercury, 21st March 1806.

ON THE DEATH
OF
THE MUCH-LAMENTED
DAVID DALE, Esq. of GLASGOW

Non sibi sed toti genitum se credere mundo. LUCAN

SAD Caledonia mourns *the Virtues* fled,
Laments her *honour'd friend*, her *Patriot dead*,
With deepest anguish, see her bosom toss'd,
Her weeping sons proclaim what she has lost;
His worth transcendent reach'd to distant climes,
His fair example speaks to future times;
He needs no tablet to record his fame,
No monument to eternize his name;
His god-like deeds are stamp'd on mem'ry's page;
Fathers shall tell their sons from age to age,
"That DALE, *the good*, to bless mankind was giv'n."
O precious gift of all-indulgent Heaven !
Life's humble shade, and Scotia's favoured coast,
Gave birth to him who might be empire's boast:
What energies of mind did he disclose !
From his great plans what benefits arose !
Public with private good how did they blend !
How *wise* their *origin*, how *good* their *end*!
His schemes embraced men's morals, wants and health,
A nation's industry, a nation's wealth:
He taught the young to live by Wisdom's rule
And train'd them up in labour's useful school;
His for the friendless to procure employ,
And *his* to fill the aching heart with joy.
Ye offspring fair, of an all-honour'd Sire,
How did his worth exceed your proud desire !

You saw the Saint in every action shine,
And all the charities of life combine;
Bless'd with a father, with a pattern rare,
Ye saw *mankind* enjoy his *feeling* care.
In every deed, philanthropy we trace,
His generous heart beat for the human race:
Heav'n crown'd with blest success his ev'ry plan'
And smiled benign on this angelic man:
In acts of charity he pass'd his hours,
POPE's *Man of Ross*, with more extensive pow'rs.
 O! Hapless widow, youth and helpless age,
Who shall your wants supply, your cares assuage;
When shall again another DALE arise,
As great, as humble, pious, good and wise.
Should distant times, enamour'd with his name,
Enquire "When liv'd this prodigy of fame?"
Blush not, Britannia's sons, to tell the age,
The proudest period of her glorious page,
"He grac'd the aera, his lov'd country serv'd,
"When NELSON conquer'd and when PITT preserv'd."

PLORATOR
Montrose, April 14, 1806.

The Scots Magazine, September 1806, pp.653–654.

Biographical Account of Mr. DAVID DALE

Mr. Dale, whose death we have recorded, was born January 6, 1739, in the town of Stewarton in Ayrshire, where his father was a shop-keeper, who dealt in groceries, yarn, &c. His remote ancestors, however, had been farmers, according to a family tradition, importing, that, till about 100 years before his time, a particular farm in the neighbourhood of Stewarton had been in their possession for 300 years. He received that education which is usually given in the small towns of Scotland; and his first employment was the herding of cattle; after which he was sent to Paisley, to serve his apprenticeship to the weaving business. Perhaps owing to the roving nature of his former employment, he was not very fond of that sedentary occupation, and even, on one occasion, left it abruptly. From Paisley he went to the neighbourhood of Hamilton, in the capacity of a journeyman weaver. Afterwards he removed to Glasgow, and was a clerk for some years to a silk mercer. With the assistance of some friends, he began, and carried on business for many years, in the linen yarn branch. in this situation, he imported French yarn from Flanders, and sold it with great advantage to the manufacturers. This laid the foundation of his fortune. Sir Richard Arkwright having successfully put in practice his great improvement of cotton spinning machinery, an agreement was made between him and Mr. Dale to erect works adapted to it on the Clyde; and mechanics were sent to England, and there instructed in the business. Thus originated the well-known Lanark Mills. But Sir Richard having lost the monopoly of that business, the connection was dissolved; and Mr. Dale erected and carried on the business of the Mills entirely on his own account. The first mill was accidentally burnt soon after it was built; but he heard the intelligence with the greatest composure, and persevered in his design, till, mill after mill arising, a cluster of these wonders of Art adorned a most romantic situation, greatly improving the country around, and giving employment to thousands. In consequence of the success of these works, and to their obvious advantage to the landed property, many land-holders applied to Mr. Dale to erect such works on their estates; and some were accordingly erected. Of these, the most successful were those established in the valley of Catrine, on the banks of the river of Air, upon the estate of Claud Alexander, Esq. of Ballamyle [Ballochmyle]. Besides these cotton spinning concerns, Mr. Dale manufactured large quantities of cotton cloth – in concert with another gentleman, he established the first works in Scotland for dyeing cotton Turkey Red – was a partner also in a manufactory of incles or tapes (which still has in its possession the original loom that was brought from Holland) and imported cotton wool from abroad. By these means, with great natural sagacity, and an enlarged benevolent mind, the little herd-boy came in course of time to ride in his own carriage, was visited by the great, and extolled by the learned. At the mills which Mr. Dale had erected on the banks of the Clyde, great numbers of destitute children were engaged for certain terms of years, for their board, cloathing, and lodging; besides which, by employing a number of teachers, he carefully attended to their education and religious instruction. In viewing the mills no particular was more pleasing to a stranger than the excellent order in which the boarders were kept. A vessel, freighted with Highland families from the Hebrides, emigrating to America, being driven by foul weather into Greenock, Mr. Dale sent agents there, and engaged the most of them to settle at his Mills; where they were comfortably provided for. And he built a great number of houses, to accommodate such Highland families as could not find employment in their own country. His exertions in behalf of the Highlanders were not confined to the sphere of the Lanark Mills – for he made various attempts to introduce the cotton manufacture in the Highlands – particularly, in concert with some other patriotic gentlemen, by erecting a mill at Spinningdale, on the Firth of Dornoch, in Sutherlandshire. At an early period of life, he was religiously disposed, attended prayer-meetings, and went to Cambuslang, at the time of the striking revival of religion there. Dissatisfied with the Established Church, a few friends united with him in founding a Church on the Independent plan; and he became one of the preachers. In this capacity he continued to officiate stately till his last illness. With no fluency of eloquence, he was a plain, serious, and very scriptural preacher. To enable him the better to expound the Bible, he received some instructions in the Hebrew and Greek languages. In his own temper and conduct, appeared much of the humble, meek, and forgiving spirit of Christianity. When only a journeyman weaver, it has been said, that he appropriated a part of his earning to the poor. When his resources were greater, during a time of scarcity, he imported a large quantity of meal, and sold it to the poor at a low rate. That he was the general patron of generous and laudable undertakings, the Glasgow Infirmary, and Missionary and Bible Societies, among many other public institutions, can thankfully bear testimony. We have much pleasure in adding, that Mr. Dale has left at least 100,000/. to his family, after having appropriated, in his life-time, more than twice that sum to purposes of the purest benevolence.

New Lanark 8 Novr 1823

Dear Sister

This comes to let you know that we are all in good
Health at present thanks be to god for it hoping these will find you
all in the same. We received your kind letter on the 2nd and also
Mr Barcleys on the 3d. We sent down to glasgow on the 4 and received
Back word on the 6 with their reciept signed. They wish the money
to come this way as she intends to come up 2 or 3 days. Junir
Samuel is
gone up to the highlands for this winter as he was out of Imployment
You will give the reciepts to Mr Barcley and he will put the money
Into the comercial Bank of Nairn (If the reciept is there) and he
will give you the check and we will receive the money from the
Commercial. Bank of Lanark this is the Safest way that we
know off. Dr Sister Alex has got an addition to his family a fine lovly boy
My husband is still alive and takes his retutes as well as ever very frachrus
and ill to mannage he destroys about 14 or 16 hundred weight of coals
every month working with the fire I received till now 15 shillings
pr month for him from the village society. Which was all but Mr Owen
at the end of last month declared it bankrupe nearly 200 in debt
this society has existed for nearly 24 years but sadly Imposed upon by the
Mannagers of the place who Imploy a great number of Infirm people
who in the course of 6 months throd themselves upon the society rather as worse
and some of them has ben on for 12 = 14 Six years / who are up and down working and
receiving from the box too

I think it would be needless to give you the news of the place as we are become as a comen proverb among the nations, you will see from the public papers a way of news the most of the ministers in the nibourhood are up in arms against Mr Owen and we cannot to ours sad experience deny what they say not only in the public papers but books in abundance are in sirculating the Reverand Mr Thomson in Edinburgh heath just now Sent out one calling him the great apostle of Infedelity and 2 of the chool masters he compairs to the scape goat in the wildernefs he likewise Menehors hes partners for giving hem the superintendance of so many hundred children who is a declareed Infedale One of the partners is the great Mr Allan of London who heas for nearly 20 years done all in his power to abolish the slave trade. Mr Owen is but a man and his Brieth is in hes nostderals - we are in danger to say a word for the mannagers of the place are tools in his hand but I hope the prayers of so many good men have had accefs to the throne of grace for things are beginning to go against him even us a population of more then 25 hundred souls have held a meeting chused a comittee wrote out a few of ours greveinces and sent them up to the company in london it was out of the power of the mannagers to Suprefs it but numbers of the people are afraid of losing their Imployment for this; he is proposing to do a great dale of good for us yet, that is to make one fire serve for about 50 familys by puting a stove at the end of a building and bending pipes through all the different departments so that we will never have the pleasure of lighting a candle in ours own houses this he stiles hapyynefs and likewise to bring us all into one house prepared for that purpose to mifs together like so many swine we will get ours meat and clothing and ours children taken from us to be brought up as he pleases this likewise he culls a prevelege and a blefsing these are only a few of the blefsings we are about to Receive from this great meen but we hope god will change these blefsings for others

When you write besure to direct as follows

to Mrs Sutherland care of Alexr Milne No 41 or it will

go to the Mannager of the Mills give over best love to all

Inquiring friends

address

Enclose Sophia's

Mr Donald Macarthur

Glasgow

N. B. The money was sent them in Post Office Orders

New Lanark 8 Nov 1823

Dear Sister

This comes to let you know that we are all in good Health at present thanks be to god for it hoping this will find you all in the same. We received your kind letters on the 2nd and also Mr Barclays on the 3rd. We sent down to glasgow on the 4 and received Back word on the 6 with their receipt signed, they wish the money to come this way as she??? intends to come up 2 or 3 days, danniel junior is gone up to the highlands for this winter as he was out of employment. You will give the receipts to Mr. Barclay and he will put the money into the commercial bank of nairn if the (merchant is there) and he will give you the check and we will receive the money from the Commercial Bank of Lanark this is the safest way that we know off.

Dr Sister Alexr has got an addition to his family a fine lovly boy my husband is still alive and takes his ?????? as well as ever very ??????? and ill to manage he destroys about 14 or 16 hundred weight of coals every month working with fire I received till now 15 shillings pr. month for him from the village society. Which was all, but Mr. Owen at the end of last month declared it bankrupt nearly 200 in debt this society has existed for nearly 24 years but sadly imposed upon by the mannagers of the place who employd a great number of infirm people who in the course of 6 months thro. themselves upon the society rather as work and some of them ????

????? on for 12=14 age years/who are up and down working and receiving from the ??? too. I think it would be needless to give you the news of the place as we are become as a common proverb among the nations, you will see from the public papers a ????? of news the most of the ministers in the neighbourhood are up in arms against Mr owen and we cannot ?? our sad experience deny what they say not only in the public papers but books in abundance are in circulating the Reverend Mr Thomson in Edinburgh ?????? ??????? now sent out one calling him the great apostel of infidelity and 2 of the school masters he compairs to the scape goat in the wilderness he likewise ??????? his patrons for giving him the superintendence of so many hundred children who is a declared infidel one of the partners is the great Mr Allan of London who has for nearly 20 years done all in his power to abolish the slave trade Mr Owen is but a man and his breath is in his nosetrails - we are in danger to say a word for the mannagers of the place are tools in his hands but I hope the prayers of so many good men have had access to the throne of grace for things are beginning to go against him even us a population of more than 25 hundred souls have held a meeting ?????? a committee wrote out a few of our grievances and sent them up to the company in London it was out of the power of the mannagers to suppress it but numbers of the people are afraid of losing their employment for this; he is proposing to do a great deal of good for us yet, that is to make our fire serve for about 50 familys by putting a stove at the end of a building and sending pipes through all the different departments so that we will never have the pleasure of lighting a candle in our own house, this he stiles happiness and likewise to bring us all into one house prepared for that purpose to mix together like so many swine we will get our meat and clothing and our children taken from us to be brought up as he pleases this likewise he calls a privilege and a blessing These are only a few of the blessings we are to receive from this great man, but we hope god will change these blessings in others.

When you write be sure to send as follows

Mr Sutherland care of Alexr Milne No 41 or it will go to the Mannagers of the Mills give our best love to all Inquiring friends

address
Enclose Sophia
Mr Donald Macarthur
Glasgow

NB the money was ent them in Post Office orders

Bibliography

Manuscripts

Anderson's University Minutes Book, Vol. 1, 1796–1799. University of Strathclyde Archives: OB/1/1/1.

Anderson's University Minutes Book, Vol. 2, 1799–1810. University of Strathclyde Archives: OB/1/1/2.

Contract of Marriage between Mr. David Dale, Merchant in Glasgow and Miss Anne Carolina Campbell, second daughter of the deceased John Campbell, Esq, First Cashier of the Royal Bank of Scotland. Royal Bank of Scotland Archives: R.B.S. 1480/17.

Copy of the Minutes of the First meeting of the Glasgow Humane Society, 16th August 1790. Glasgow City Council Archives: DTC 6/262.

Dale–Alexander Correspondence, 1787–1797. Glasgow City Council Archives: Mitchell Library: MS 63.

Dempster, G.S. *The Papers of George Soper Dempster*, 19 vols. University of Toronto, Thos. Fisher Rare Book Library, MS 126 Also catalogued as *The Dempster Papers. A Collection of Letters & Papers relating to George Dempster of Dunnichen*, 19 vols. MS 126.

Dickson, W. *Diary of a Visit to Scotland 5th Jan–19th March 1792 on behalf of the Committee for the Abolition of the Slave Trade.* London: Friends Library: MSS 10/14.

Excerpt from Minutes of Council anent grant to Humane Society. At Glasgow the eighteenth day of August Seventeen hundred and ninety years. Glasgow City Archives: DTC 6/262.

General Register of the Old Scotch Independent Church. Glasgow City Council Archives: TD 420/1.

Glasgow Association of Master Cotton Spinners Sederunt Book, 1816. Glasgow City Council Archives: T-MJ100.

Glasgow Chamber of Commerce Minutes. Glasgow City Council Archives: TD 1670/1/1–3.

Glasgow Humane Society Minutes. Glasgow City Council Archives: DTC 6/262.

Glasgow Royal Infirmary Admissions Register 1794–1800. Greater Glasgow Health Board Archives: HB14/67/56/1A.

Glasgow Royal Infirmary Admissions Register 1800–1803. Greater Glasgow Health Board Archives: HB14/67/56/1B.

Glasgow Royal Infirmary Annual Reports, December 1794–January 1811. Greater Glasgow Health Board Archives: HB 14/2/1.

Glasgow Royal Infirmary. Copy of the Charter Granted December 21, 1791. Printed at the Courier Office by Wm Reid & Co. Glasgow. 1792. University of Glasgow Special Collections: Mu26-d.30.

Glasgow Royal Infirmary Minute Book. Vol. 1, 1787–1802. Greater Glasgow Health Board Archives: HB/14/1/1.

Glasgow Royal Infirmary Minute Book. Vol. 2, 1803–1812. Greater Glasgow Health Board Archives. HB/14/1/2.

Glasgow Town's Hospital. Minutes of Directors' Quarterly Meetings, 1732–1816. Glasgow City Council Archives: Rare Book No. 641983.

Marshall, J. (1803) *Tour Book for Scotland and Ireland.* University of Leeds: Brotherton Collection: MS 200/62.1800-1803.

New Lanark Monthly Report Book and Wage Book including Boarders, 1801–02. University of Glasgow Archives Services, New Lanark Mill Collection: GB 0248 UGD 42/7/10.

New Lanark Report Book: Monthly. 1803–1808. University of Glasgow Archives Services, New Lanark Mill Collection: GB 0248 UGD 42/7/11.

New Lanark Visitors Book 1795–99. University of Glasgow Archives Services, New Lanark Mill Collection: GB 0248 UGD 42/7/1/1.

New Lanark Visitors Book 1821–24. University of Glasgow Archives Services, New Lanark Mill Collection: GB 0248 UGD 42/7/1/2.

Plymley, K. *Diaries, 1791–92.* Shropshire County Council Archives: MS 1066/4.

Register of Sasines, Burgh of Glasgow. Glasgow City Council Archives: B10/2.

Register of Sasines, Barony & Regality of Glasgow. Glasgow City Council Archives: T-SA 5/1/1-2.

Report of the Committee for procuring information on the subject of establishments for the punishment of crimes and reformation of criminals by means of bridewells and other places of confinement, at hard labour. 22nd June 1789. University of Glasgow Library Special Collections: Mu26-d.30.

Scott Moncrieff Letters. Royal Bank of Scotland Archives: RB/837.

Substance of a Discourse by David Dale, 8 January 1792. University of Glasgow Library: Special Collections: Mu22-a.12.

West Kirk Charity Workhouse Minute Book. Edinburgh City Archives: SL222.

Newspapers & Periodicals

London Society
The Annual Register
The Belfast Monthly Magazine
The British Evening Post
The British Gazette & Sunday Monitor
The Christian Remembrancer
The Derby Mercury
The Edinburgh Magazine or Literary Miscellany
The English Chronicle or Universal Evening Post
The Gazeteer and New Daily Advertiser
The General Evening Post
The Gentlemans Magazine
The Glasgow Courier
The Glasgow Herald
The Glasgow Journal
The Glasgow Mercury
The House of Commons Journal
The Imperial Magazine
The Lancaster Gazette & General Advertiser
The London Chronicle
The Manchester Mercury
The Monthly Magazine & British Register
The Morning Chronicle
The Morning Herald
The Morning Post & Gazeteer
The New Quarterly Review or Home, Foreign & Colonial Journal
The Nottingham Journal
The Preston Chronicle
The Public Advertiser
The Scots Magazine
The Star
The Sun
The Times
The Whitehall Evening Post

Print Sources (incl journal articles) pre 1900

Aiken, A. (ed) (1805) 'Reports of the Society for Bettering the Condition of the Poor'. Vol. IV: 323–5 in *The Annual Review & History of Literature for 1804*, Vol. III, London: Longman, Hurst, Rees & Orme.

Aird, A. (1894) *Glimpses of Old Glasgow*. Glasgow: Aird & Coghill.

Aiton, J. (1824) *Mr. Owen's Objections to Christianity and New View of Society and Education. Refuted by A Plain Statement of Facts with a Hint to Archibald Hamilton Esq. of Dalziel*. Edinburgh: James Robertson & Co.

Alison, R. (1892) *The Anecdotage of Glasgow, Comprising Anecdotes and Anecdotal Incidents of the City of Glasgow and Glasgow Personages*. Glasgow: Thomas D. Morrison.

Baines, E. (1835) *History of the Cotton Manufacture in Great Britain*. London: Fisher.

Bernard, T. (1800) *Reports of the Society for Bettering the Conditions of the Poor*, 2 Vols. London: Bulmer & Co.

Bremner, D. (1869) *The Industries of Scotland. Their Rise, Progress and present Condition*. London: Black. Reprint (1969), Newton Abbot: David & Charles.

Bristed, J. (1803) *A Pedestrian Tour Through Parts of the Highlands of Scotland*, 2 vols. London: J. Wallis.

Brown, A. (1795–1797) *History of Glasgow and of Paisley, Greenock, and Port-Glasgow, comprehending the ecclesiastical and civil history of these places, from the earliest accounts to the present time: and including an account of their population, commerce, manufactures, arts, and agriculture*, 2 vols. (1795, 1797) Glasgow: W. Paton.

Brown, J. (1860) *Religious Denominations of Glasgow*, 2 vols. Glasgow.

Chapman, R. (1812) *The Picture of Glasgow or a Stranger's Guide*. (2nd ed.). Glasgow.

Clarkson, T. (1808) *The History of the Rise and Progress of the African Slave Trade by the British Parliament*, 2 vols. London: Longman, Hurst, Rees & Orme. New impression, (1968) London: Frank Cass.

Cleland, J. (1816) *Annals of Glasgow, Comprising an Account of the Public Buildings, Charities and the Rise and Progress of the City*, 2 vols. Glasgow: James Hedderwick.

Cleland, J. (1829) *Annals of Glasgow, Comprising an Account of the Public Buildings, Charities and the Rise and Progress of the City*. Glasgow: J. Smith.

Corry, J. (1807) *Observations Upon the Windward Coast of Africa*. London: G. & W. Nicol.

Cowan, W.A. (1867) *History of Lanark and a Guide to the Surrounding Scenery*. Lanark: Robert Wood.

Currie, J. (1797) *Medical reports on the Effects of Water, Cold and Warm as a Remedy in Febrile Diseases*. Liverpool: J. McReery.

Currie, W.W. (1831) *Memoir of the Life, Writings and Correspondence of James Currie*, 2 vols. London: Longman, Rees, Orme, Brown & Green.

Dalrymple, D. (Lord Hailes) (1826) *Decisions of the Lords of Council and Session from 1766–91*, 2 vols. Edinburgh: Wm. Tait.

Davidson, W. (1828) *A History of Lanark & Guide to the Scenery with a list of Roads to the Provincial Towns*. Lanark: Shepherd & Robertson.

Dickson, W. (1803) *Hints to the People of the United Kingdom in General and North Britain in particular on the Present Important Crisis and some interesting collateral subjects*. Edinburgh: Oliver & Co.

Dodd, W. (1776) *An Account of the Rise, Progress, and Present State of the Magdalen Hospital for the Reception of Penitent Prostitutes*. London: W. Faden.

Elmes, J. (1854) *Thomas Clarkson: A Monograph, Being a Contribution towards the History of the Abolition of the Slave Trade and Slavery*. London: Blackader & Co.

Garnett, T. (1800) *Observations on a Tour through the Highlands and Part of the Western Isles of Scotland*. London: Cadell & Davies.

Garnett, T. (1811) *Observations on a Tour through the Highlands and Part of the Western Isles of Scotland. A New Edition in Two Volumes*. London: John Stockdale.

Glaister, J. (1886) *Epidemic History of Glasgow 1783–1883*. Glasgow.

Howell, T. (1817) *A Complete Collection of State Trials & Proceedings for High Treason and other Crimes & Misdemeanours from the Earliest period to the Year 1783, with Notes & Illustrations: AD 1793 & 1795*. London: Longman, Hurst et al.

Ingham, F.G. (1894) *Sierra Leone after a Hundred Years*. London. New impression (1968) London: Cass.

Jones's Directory or Useful Pocket Companion Containing an Alphabetical List of the Names and Places of Abode of the Merchants, Manufacturers, Traders and Shopkeepers in and about the City of Glasgow Compiled as Accurately as the Time Allowed Would Admit. Published by John Mennons Editor of *The Glasgow Advertiser*, (1787) Glasgow: J. Mennons.

Kydd, S. ('Alfred') (1857) *The History of the Factory Movement From the Year 1802 to the Enactment of the Ten Hours Bill in 1847*, 2 vols. London: Simpkin, Marshall & Co.

Liddell, A. (1854a) *Memoir of David Dale*, Glasgow: Blackie.

Lloyd Jones, M. (1889) *The Life, Times & Labours of Robert Owen*. London: Swann, Sonnenshein & Co.

McGavin, W. (1824) 'The Fundamental Principles of the New Lanark System Exposed in a Series of Letters to Robert Owen Esq., Glasgow', Young. A., in *British Labour Struggles: Contemporary Pamphlets 1727–1850. Robert Owen at New Lanark. Two Booklets and One Pamphlet 1824–1838*. New York: Arno Press 1972.

McNayr, J. (1797) *A Guide from Glasgow to some of the most Remarkable Scenes in the Highlands and to the Falls of Clyde*. Glasgow: Courier Office.

Memoirs & Portraits of 100 Glasgow Men (1886), 2 vols. Glasgow: James MacLehose & Sons.

Montgomery, J. (1840) *A Practical detail of the Cotton Manufacture of the USA, and the State of the Cotton Manufacture of that Country Contrasted and Compared with that of Great Britain*. Glasgow: J. Niven.

New Statistical Account of Scotland (1834–40). 15 vols. Edinburgh: Blackwood.

Owen, R. (1812) *A Statement Regarding the New Lanark Establishment*. Glasgow: J. Moir.

Owen, R. (1813–1816) 'A New View of Society; or Essays on the Principle of the Formation of Human Character and the Application of the Principle to Practice. Second Essay', in G. Claeys (ed) (1991) *Robert Owen: A New View of Society and Other Writings*. London: Penguin.

Owen, R. (1857) *The Life of Robert Owen Written by Himself*. Vol 1. London: Effingham Wilson. New impression (1967) London: Frank Cass & Co.

Owen, R. (1858) *A Supplementary Index to the First Volume of the Life of Robert Owen*. Vol. 1A. London: Effingham Wilson. New impression (1967) London: Frank Cass & Co.

Owen, R.D. (1874) *Threading My Way: Twenty Seven Years of Autobiography*. New York: Carleton & Co.

Parliamentary Paper. 1816 (397) III. *Report of the Minutes of Evidence taken before the Select Committee on the State of Children Employed in the Manufactories of the United Kingdom*.

Regulations of the Town's Hospital with the Original Constitution of the House, Glasgow, 1844.

Reid, R. (Senex) (1884) *Glasgow Past and Present*, 3 vols. Glasgow: David Robertson & Co.

Richardson, T. (1799) *Guide to Loch Lomond, Loch long, Loch Fine* (sic) *and Inveraray*. 2nd ed. Glasgow: J. Murdoch. Printed for J. Murdoch, Glasgow.

Royal Highland Society. (1802) *Report of the Committee on Emigration. Sederund Book*, Vol. III, January.

Short Account of the Town's Hospital in Glasgow with the Abstracts of the Expenses for the First Three Years, 4th ed., Edinburgh, 1742.

Sinclair, J. (ed) (1791–99) *The Statistical Account of Scotland, 1791–99*, 21 vols. Edinburgh.

Sinclair, J. (1825) *An Analysis of the Statistical Account of Scotland*, 2 vols. Edinburgh: Constable & Co.

Sinclair, J. (1831) *The Correspondence of the Rt. Hon Sir John Sinclair, Bart.*, 2 vols. London: Colburn & Bentley.

Smith, J., Mitchell, J.O. and Buchanan, J. (eds.) (1878) *Old Country Houses of the Old Glasgow Gentry* (2nd ed.). Glasgow: Maclehose.

Stewart, G. (1881) *Curiosities of Glasgow Citizenship as Exhibited Chiefly in the Business Career of its Old Commercial Aristocracy*. Glasgow: J. Maclehose.

Stuart, R. (1848) *Views and Notices of Glasgow in Former Times*. Glasgow: Allan & Ferguson.

Subscriptions of the Matriculated Members of the Merchants House, Glasgow, from 3rd Oct 1768. Glasgow 1853.

Tait, J. (1784) *Directory for the City of Glasgow from 15 May 1783 to 15 May 1784*. Glasgow.

Ure, A. (1835) *The Philosophy of Manufactures*, London: C. Knight.

Wadstrom, C.B. (1794) *An Essay on Colonization, Particularly Applied to the Western Coast of Africa, with some free thoughts on Cultivation and Commerce. Also Brief Descriptions of the Colonies already Formed or Attempted in Africa, including those of Sierra Leona and Balama*. 2 parts. London: Darton & Harvey.

Print Sources (incl journal articles) post 1900

Allen, H.C. (1964) *The United States of America*. London: Benn Ltd.

Annan, T. (1871) *Old Maps of Glasgow*. Glasgow: Maclehose.

Anderson, J.R. (ed) (1925) *Burgesses and Guild Brethren of Glasgow*, 2 vols. Edinburgh: Scottish Records Society.

Anderson, J.R. (ed) (1935) *The Burgesses and Guild Brethren of Glasgow, 1757–1846*. Edinburgh. J. Skinner & Co.

Ansley, R. (1975) *The Atlantic Slave Trade and British Abolition, 1760–1810*. London: Macmillan.

Black, W.G. (1912) 'David Dale's House in Charlotte Street', in *Transactions of the Regality Club (1889–1912)*, 4 vols. Vol. 4 (1912): 93-121. Glasgow: James Maclehose & Sons.

Bold, A. (1983) *Modern Scottish Literature*. London: Longman.

Bold, A. (ed) (1993) *Rhymer Rab: an Anthology of Poems & Prose by Robert Burns*. London: Black Swan.

Brion Davis, D. (1975) *The Problem of Slavery in the Age of Revolution, 1770–1823*. Ithaca: Cornell University Press.

Brion Davis, D. (2006) *Inhuman Bondage. The Rise and Fall of Slavery in the New World*. Oxford: O.U.P.

Brogan, H. (1985) *History of the U.S.A.* London: Guild Publishing.

Burton, A. (1984) *The Rise and Fall of King Cotton*. London: BBC/Deutsch Ltd.

Butt, J. (1967) *The Industrial Archaeology of Scotland*. Newton Abbot: David & Charles.

Butt, J. (ed) (1971) *Robert Owen. Prince of Cotton Spinners*. Newton Abbot: David & Charles.

Butt, J. (1977) 'The Scottish Cotton Industry during the Industrial Revolution, 1780-1840', in Cullen, L.M. and Smout, T.C. (eds.) *Comparative Aspects of Scottish and Irish Economic and Social History, 1600–1900*. Edinburgh: John Donald.

Butt, J. (1996) John Anderson's Legacy. *The University of Strathclyde and its Antecedents, 1796–1996*. East Linton: Tuckwell Press.

Butt, J., Donnachie, I., and Hume, J.R., (1968) *Industrial History in Pictures: Scotland*. Newton Abbot: David & Charles.

Calder, S.B. (1974) *The Industrial Archaeology of Scotland*. University of Strathclyde: Unpublished M.Litt thesis.

Campbell, R.H. (1977) 'The Scottish Improvers and the Course of Agrarian Change in the 18th Century', in Cullen, L.M. and Smout, T.C. (eds.) *Comparative Aspects of Scottish and Irish Economic and Social History, 1600–1900*. Edinburgh: John Donald.

Checkland, S.G. (1975) *Scottish Banking: A History, 1695–1973*, Glasgow: Collins.

Claeys, G. (ed) (1991) *Robert Owen: A New View of Society and Other Writings*. London: Penguin.

Cohn, D.L. (1973) *The Life and Times of King Cotton*. Connecticut: Greenwood Press.

Cooke, A.J. (1977) *Stanley: its History and Development*. University of Dundee Extra-Mural Dept.

Cooke, A.J. (1979) 'Robert Owen and the Stanley Mills, 1802–1811', *Business History*, XXI, (1), 107–11.

Cooke, A.J. (ed) (1979) 'Richard Arkwright and the Scottish Cotton Industry', *Textile History*, X: 196–202.

Cooke, A.J. (1995) 'Cotton and the Scottish Highland Clearances – Spinningdale, 1791–1806', *Textile History*, XXVI: 89–94.

Cooke, A.J. (2009) 'The Scottish Cotton Masters', *Textile History*, 40(1): 29–50.

Cooke, A. (2010) *The Rise and Fall of the Scottish Cotton Industry, 1778–1914: The Secret Spring*. Manchester: M.U.P.

Cooke, A. (2012) 'An Elite Revisited: Glasgow West-India merchants 1783–1877', *Journal of Scottish Historical Studies*, 32.2, November: 127–165.

Cowper, A.S. (2000) 'Corstorphine history: an eighteenth century vignette. William Finlay, David Ramage, John Geddes, and others not named, pauper children sent to the New Lanark Mills' in W.T. Johnston (ed), *David Dale & Robert Owen Studies*. Livingston: Officina Educational Publications.

Cullen, A. (1910) *Adventures in Socialism*. Glasgow: John Smith.

Cullen, L.M. and Smout, T.C. (eds.) (1977) *Comparative Aspects of Scottish and Irish Economic and Social History, 1600–1900*. Edinburgh: John Donald.

Daniels, G.W. (1916) 'American Cotton Trade with Liverpool under the Embargo and Non-Intercourse Acts', *American Historical Review*, 2, January: 276–287.

'David Dale, Scots Banker, Benefactor & Industrialist, 1739–1806', *Three Banks Review*, June 1952, XIV: 38–44 author unknown.

Davidson, H. (1910) *Lanark: A Series of Papers by the late Hugh Davidson, Writer*. Edinburgh.

Davidson, L. 'The New Lanark Pauper Apprentices.' Unpublished Conference paper, 'The Legacy of David Dale – Industry, philanthropy and Heritage', 4th November 2006. Glasgow Caledonian University.

Davis, R. and O'Hagan, F. (2010) *Robert Owen*. Continuum: London.

Devine, T.M. (1975) *The Tobacco Lords. A Study of the Tobacco Merchants of Glasgow and their Trading Activities, 1740–90*. Edinburgh: John Donald.

Devine, T.M. (1977) 'Colonial commerce and the Scottish economy c.1730–1815', in Cullen, L.M. and Smout, T.C. (eds.) *Comparative Aspects of Scottish and Irish Economic and Social History, 1600–1900*. Edinburgh: John Donald.

Devine, T.M. (1978) 'An 18th Century Business Elite: Glasgow-West India Merchants, c.1750–1815' in *Scottish Historical Review*, Vol. 57. pp.40–67.

Devine, T.M. (1983) 'Highland Migration to Lowland Scotland, 1760–1860', *Scottish Historical Review*, LXII, 2, October: 137–149.

Devine, T.M. (1999) *The Scottish Nation 1700–2000*. London: Penguin.

Devine, T.M. (2004) *Scotland's Empire 1600–1815*. London: Penguin.

Devine, T.M. and Jackson, G. (eds.) (1995) *Glasgow, Volume I: Beginnings to 1830*. Manchester. M.U.P.

Devine, T.M. & Mitchison, R. (eds.) (2004) *People & Society in Scotland, Vol. 1, 1760–1830*. Edinburgh: J. Donald.

Donnachie, I. (1994) 'A Tour of the Works': Early Scottish Industry Observed, 1790–1825, in A.J.C. Cummings and T.M. Devine (eds) *Industry, Business and Society in Scotland since 1700. Essays Presented to John Butt*. Edinburgh: John Donald.

Donnachie, I. (2000) *Robert Owen of New Lanark and New Harmony*. East Linton: Tuckwell Press.

Donnachie, I. (2004) 'Historic Tourism to New Lanark and the Falls of Clyde, 1795–1830. The Evidence of Contemporary Visiting Books and related Journals', *Journal of Tourism and Cultural Change*, 2(3): 145–162.

Donnachie, I. and Hewitt, G. (1993) *Historic New Lanark*. Edinburgh: E.U.P.

Drake, T.E. (1965) *Quakers and Slavery in America*. Gloucester, Mass: Peter Smith.

Durie, A.J. (1977) 'The Scottish Linen Industry in the 18th Century; some Aspects of Expansion', in Cullen, L.M. and Smout, T.C. (eds.) *Comparative Aspects of Scottish and Irish Economic and Social History, 1600–1900*. Edinburgh: John Donald.

Edwards, O.D. and Shepperson, G. (eds.) (1976) *Scotland, Europe and the American Revolution*. Edinburgh: EUSPB.

Eyre-Todd, G. (1934) *A History of Glasgow*, 3 vols. Glasgow: Jackson, Wylie & Co.

Fergusson, J. (ed) (1934) *Letters of George Dempster to Sir Adam Fergusson, 1756–1813*. MacMillan: London.

Fitton, R.S. (1989) *The Arkwrights: Spinners of Fortune*. Manchester: M.U.P.

Fitton, R.S. and Wadsworth, A.P. (1958) *The Srutts and the Arkwrights 1758–1830. A Study of the Early Factory System*. Manchester: M.U.P.

Fraser, H., Maver, I., Devine, T.M., and Jackson, G. (1995) *Glasgow, 1830–1912*, 2 vols. Manchester: M.U.P.

Hankins, N.P. and Strawhorn, J. (eds.) (1998) *The Private Papers of James Boswell*. New Haven: Yale.

Herford, C.H. (ed) (1929) *Journal of a Tour in Scotland in 1819*. Southey, R. (1829) London: John Murray.

Hills, R.L. (1979) 'Hargreaves, Arkwright and Crompton. Why Three Inventors?', *Textile History*, Vol. 10: 114–122.

Houston, R.A. (1985) *Scottish Literacy and the Scottish Identity: Illiteracy and Society in Scotland and Northern England, 1600–1800*. Cambridge: Cambridge University Press.

Jackson, G. (1995) 'New Horizons in Trade' in Fraser, H., Maver, I., Devine, T.M., and Jackson, G. (1995) *Glasgow, 1830–1912*, 2 vols. Vol. 2. Manchester: M.U.P.

James Finlay & Co. Manufacturers & East India Merchants 1750–1950 (1951), Glasgow: Jackson & Son.

Knight, W. (ed) (1904) *Journals of Dorothy Wordsworth*, 2 Vols. London: MacMillan

Kyros-Walker, C. (2002) *Breaking Away. Coleridge in Scotland*. New Haven & London: Yale University Press.

Lang, A.M. (1998) *A Life of George Dempster, Scottish M.P. of Dunnichen (1732–1818)*. Lampeter: Edwin Mellen Press.

MacDonald, F.A. (1999) 'The Infirmary of Glasgow Town's Hospital, 1733–1800: A Case for Voluntarism?', *Bulletin of the History of Medicine*, 73.1: 64–105. Baltimore: Johns Hopkins University Press, pp.64–105.

Macintosh, H. (1902) *The Origin and History of Glasgow Streets*. Glasgow: James Hedderwick & Sons.

MacNair, P. (1914) 'Argyllshire and Buteshire', *Cambridge County Geographics*. Cambridge: C.U.P.

Maltby, S.E. (1918) *Manchester and the Movement for National Elementary Education, 1800–1870*. Manchester: M.U.P.

Malloch, D.M. (1913) *The Book of Glasgow Anecdote*. New York: Scribners.

McLaren, D.J. (1983) *David Dale of New Lanark*. Glasgow: Heatherbank Press.

McLaren, D.J. (1996) 'Robert Owen, William Maclure and New Harmony'. *History of Education* Vol. 25, No 3.

McLaren, D.J. (1999) *David Dale of New Lanark*. (2nd Eedition) Glasgow: Caring Books.

McLaren, D.J.(2000) 'Education for Citizenship & the New Moral World of Robert Owen'. *Scottish Educational Review* Vol. 32, No.2. Nov 2000.

McLaren, D.J. (2003) 'Parish, Town & Factory Community: The Place of the New Lanark Schools in the Scottish Educational Tradition.' *Robert Owen Memorial Lecture*. New Lanark. Unpublished paper.

McLaren, D.J. (2012) 'David Dale, Scott Moncrieff and the Royal Bank of Scotland, 1783–1806' in *Scottish Business and Industrial History*. Vol 27, Series 2, July 2012. pp48–79

Mechie, S. (1960) *The Church and Scottish Social Development 1780–1870*. Oxford: OUP.

Murray, D.B. (1976) *Social & Religious Origins of Scottish Non-Presbyterian Dissent from 1730–1800*. St. Andrews: Unpublished PhD thesis.

Murray, N. (1978) *Scottish Handloom Weavers, 1790–1850. A Social History*. Edinburgh: John Donald.

Munro, N. (1928) *The History of the Royal Bank of Scotland, 1727–1927*. Edinburgh: Clark Ltd.

Nicolson, M. and Donnachie, I. 'The New Lanark Highlanders: Migration, Community & Language 1785–c.1850', *Family & Community History*, 6/1, May 2003: 19–31.

Nisbet, S.M. (2008) *The Rise of the Cotton Factory in Eighteenth-Century Renfrewshire*. British Archaeology Report, Series 464. Oxford: Alden Press.

Nisbet, S.M. (2004) 'Early Cotton Spinning in the West of Scotland, 1778–1799: Rothesay Cotton Mill', *Transactions, Buteshire Natural History Society*, XXVI: 39–47.

Nisbet, S.M. (2009) 'The Making of Scotland's first Industrial Region. The Early Cotton Industry in Renfrewshire', *The Journal of Scottish Historical Studies*, 29.1:1-28.

Nisbet, S.M. (2009) 'The Making of Scotland's First Industrial region: The Early Cotton Industry in Renfrewshire', *The Journal of Scottish Historical Studies*, 29.1: 1–28. Edinburgh: E.U.P.

Perry, L. and Fellman, M. (eds) (1979) *Antislavery Reconsidered. New Perspectives on the Abolitionists*. Baton Rouge: Louisiana State University.

Podmore, F. (1906) *Robert Owen – A Biography*. London: Hutchinson & Co.

Raistrick, A. (ed) (1967) *The Hatchett Diary – A tour through the counties of England & Scotland in 1796, visiting their Mines and Manufactories*. Truro: Bradford Barton.

Reed, R. (2006) 'David Dale and the Royal Bank of Scotland's Glasgow Agency'. Unpublished conference ('The Legacy of David Dale') paper. Glasgow.

Regality Club. *Transactions of the Regality Club* (1889–1912), 4 vols. Glasgow: James Maclehose & Sons.

Renwick. R. (ed) (1913) *Extracts from the Records for the Burgh of Glasgow with Charters and other Documents*, 11 vols. Glasgow.

Renwick, R. and Lindsay, J. (1921) *History of Glasgow*, 4 vols. Glasgow: Maclehose, Jackson & Co.
Rice, C.D. (1975) *The Rise and Fall of Black Slavery*. London: Macmillan.

Rice, C.D. (1976) 'Scottish Enlightenment, American Revolution and Atlantic Reform', in Edwards, O.D. and Shepperson, G. (eds.), *Scotland, Europe and the American Revolution*. Edinburgh: EUSPB.

Rice, C.D. (1979) 'Controversies over Slaves in 18th and 19th Century Scotland', in Perry, L. & Fellman, M. (eds.), *Antislavery Reconsidered. New Perspectives on the Abolitionists.* Baton Rouge: Louisiana State University.

Rice, C.D. (1983) 'Archibald Dalzel, the Scottish Intelligentsia and the Problem of Slavery', *Scottish Historical Review*, LXII,2, 174, October: 121–136.

Robertson, A.D. (1975) *Lanark: the Burgh and its Councils, 1469–1880.* Lanark Town Council.

Robertson, A.J. (1969) 'Robert Owen and the Campbell Debt, 1810–1822', *Business History*, XI, (123–30).

Rose, M.B. (2000) *Firms, networks and Business Values: the British and American Cotton industries since 1750.* Cambridge: C.U.P.

Scarfe, N. (1995) *Innocent Espionage. The La Rochefoucauld Brother's Tour of England in 1785.* Woodbridge: Boydel Press. pp.62, 65.

Simon, B. (ed) (1968) *Education in Leicestershire 1540–1940. A Regional Study.* Leicester University Press.

Smout, T.C. (1977) 'Famine and Famine Relief in Scotland', in Cullen, L.M. and Smout, T.C. (eds.) *Comparative Aspects of Scottish and Irish Economic and Social History, 1600–1900.* Edinburgh: John Donald.

Smout, T.C. (1998) *A History of the Scottish People 1560–1830.* London: Fontana.

Southey, R. (1972) *Journal of a Tour in Scotland in 1819.* (Facsimile). Edinburgh: J. Thin

Stenlake, R. (2011) *A Lot o Genuine Folks and a Wheen o Rogues.* Catrine: Stenlake Publishing.

Thistlethwaite, F. (1961) *The Great Experiment. An Introduction to the History of the American People.* Cambridge: C.U.P.

The Three Banks Review. No. 14. June 1952; No. 40. March, 1960.

Tindal, G.B. and Shi, D. (1984) *America: A Narrative History.* 3rd Edition. New York: Norton & Co.

Walker, C.K. (2002) *Breaking Away. Coleridge in Scotland*, New Haven & London: Yale University Press.

Whyte, I. (2006) *Scotland and the Abolition of Black Slavery.* Edinburgh: E.U.P.

Wilson, J.A. (1929) *A History of Cambuslang. A Clydesdale Parish.* Glasgow: Jackson Wylie & Co.

Wrigley, W. (2011) "Cromford Mills, Lea Mills and the Lumsdale Valley", *The Historian*, Autumn 2011, pp.26–31.

Electronic/AV Sources

Basker, J. (2006) *Johnson, Boswell and the Abolition of Slavery.* Online at http://untoldlondon.org.uk/articles/read/johnson_boswell_and_the_abolition_of_slavery

Boswell, J. (1791) *No Abolition of Slavery or the Universal Empire of Love: A Poem by James Boswell Esq.* Online at http://www.gutenberg.org/files/20360/20360-h/20360-h.htm

Douglas Archives. A collection of Historical and Genealogical Records. Online at http://douglashistory.co.uk/history/william_douglas8.htm

Johnson, S. (1758) *The Idler.* No. 11, 24th June. Online at www.samueljohnson.com/slavery.html

Johnson, S. (1775) *Taxation No Tyranny.*
Online at http://www.samueljohnson.com/tnt.html

Johnston, W.T. (ed) (2000) *David Dale & Robert Owen Studies.* Livingston: Officina Educational Publications.

Laurie, A.E. and Young, N. (2009, 2013) *New Lanark's People. A Collection of Transcribed Archive material from over 70 Different Sources.* 2 Vols. Private CD Publication. New Lanark Conservation.

National Records of Scotland/National Archives of Scotland. *Old Parish Records.* Online at http://www.scotlandspeople.gov.uk

Picture Acknowledgements

Covers & introductory pages

Spinningdale Mill – David McLaren photograph.

David Dale portrait by Hugh Williams. © CSG CIC Glasgow Museums & Libraries Collections.

New Lanark – Richard Stenlake photograph.

Part 1
Chapter 1

Dale from 'The Morning Walk'. Stuart, R. (1848) *Views and Notices of Glasgow in Former Times*. Glasgow: Allan & Ferguson, p.117.

Portrait: *Mrs David Dale, nee Campbell and her only son, William*. W. Stavely, 1790. Private collection. Courtesy of David and Sebastian Blackie.

Chapter 2

Merkdailly Lands. Plan of the Low Green of Glasgow and its Environs, 1760. Reid, R. (Senex) (1884) *Glasgow Past and Present*, 3 vols. Glasgow: David Robertson & Co. Vol. III, frontispiece.

McArthur's Map of Glasgow, 1778. Reid, R. (1884). *Glasgow Past & Prersent*. 3 Vols. Glasgow. D. Robertson & Co. Vol. 1, p.584

Flemings Map of Glasgow, 1807. By Permission of the University of Glasgow Library Special Collections. Mu24.y.21.

House Plans & Elevations. New Lanark Trust.

Picture of David Dale's House in Charlotte Street. New Lanark Trust.

Fireplace Corner Detail. *Transactions of the Regality Club*, p.96.

Plan of David Dale's House in Glasgow. Black, W.G. (1912) 'David Dale's House in Charlotte Street', *Transactions of the Regality Club (1889–1912)*, 4 vols. Glasgow: James Maclehose & Sons, Vol. 4.

Charlotte Street, c.1845. Small, D. (1887) *Sketches of Quaint bits of Old Glasgow still standing in the year 1885*. Glasgow: D. Bryce & Sons. Plate XXII.

David Dale's List. Stewart, G. (1881) *Curiosities of Glasgow Citizenship*. Glasgow: J. Maclehose, p.246.

Town Hall & Tontine Buildings. Chapman, R. (1812) *The Picture of Glasgow or a Stranger's Guide*. (2nd Ed.) Glasgow, p.114.

Chapter 3

Portrait of Richard Arkwright. Baines, E. (1835) *History of the Cotton Manufacture in Great Britain*. London: Fisher, preface.

Arkwright's Spinning Jenny. Baines, E. (1835) *History of the Cotton Manufacture in Great Britain*. London: Fisher, facing p.155.

Hargreaves' Spinning Jenny. Baines, E. (1835) *History of the Cotton Manufacture in Great Britain*. London: Fisher, facing p.158.

George Dempster of Dunnichen & Skibo (1732–1818). George Willison (1786). Oil on canvas. Dundee City Council (Dundee's Art Galleries and Museums.)

Part 2
Chapter 4

New Lanark, *c*.1818. John Winning. J.R. Hume/New Lanark Trust.

David Dale's House in New Lanark. New Lanark Trust.

New Buildings pre restoration. (1961) RCHAMS. New Lanark Trust.

View of New Lanark. *The Edinburgh Magazine or Literary Miscellany*. Vol. II, London: Laurie & Symington, 1793. Frontispiece.

Drawings & Elevations of Caithness Row. © Dr. Peter Robinson. New Lanark Trust.

Caithness Row. David McLaren, private collection.

New Lanark, Braxfield Row and the Village Store. Richard Stenlake, private collection.

Letter from Dale to Claud Alexander, 9th November 1789. Glasgow City Council: Archives. MS 63/8.

Value of Scottish Cotton Mills by Partnership Groupings, *c*.1795. Extracted from S. M. Nisbet. (2009) 'The Making of Scotland's First Industrial Region: The Early Cotton Industry in Renfrewshire'. *Journal of Scottish Historical Studies* 29.1, 1–28. Page 25.

Chapter 5

New Lanark aerial photograph. New Lanark Trust.

New Lanark Visitors' Book, 1795–1799. University of Glasgow Archives Services, New Lanark Mills Collection. GB 0248. UGD 42/7/1/1.

Chapter 6

Blank Indenture Form, *c*.1790–1800. Robert Owen Museum, Newtown.

Part 3
Chapter 8

Blantyre Mill. Richard Stenlake, private collection.

Birthplace of David Livingstone. Richard Stenlake, private collection.

Chapter 9

Claud Alexander and his brother, Boyd. Sotheby's.

Plan of Catrine Village. *Statistical Account of Scotland*, Vol. XX, pp.184–5.

Catrine Mill, Mill Street & St. Germain Street. Richard Stenlake, private collection.

Spinningdale Mill. Photographs by Richard Stenlake & David McLaren.

Stanley Mills. David McLaren, private collection.

Chapter 10

John Campbell by William Mosman (1759). Reproduced by kind permission of The Royal Bank of Scotland plc © [2015].

Robert Scott Moncrieff, Treasurer of the Orphan Hospital (1772–1781), Henry Raeburn, oil on canvas. (McManus Galleries, Dundee. On loan from the Dean and Cauvin Trust; City Art Centre, Edinburgh Museums and Galleries.)

Royal Bank of Scotland, Queen Street, Glasgow. Chapman, R. (1812) *The Picture of Glasgow or a Stranger's Guide*. (2nd Ed.) Glasgow, p.114.

Margaritta MacDonald, Mrs. Scott Moncrieff (d.1824). Oil on canvas. Henry Raeburn (c.1814). National Galleries of Scotland. NG302.

Chapter 11

Glasgow Fire Insurance Society Notice. *The Caledonian Mercury*, 31st March 1804.

Part 4
Chapter 12

Bance Island. Corry, J. (1807) *Observations Upon the Windward Coast of Africa*. London: G. & W. Nicol, facing p.33.

John Glassford & Family by Archibald McLauchlan, 1767. © CSG CIC Glasgow Museums & Libraries Collections.

Anti-slavery image, based on Josiah Wedgewood's medallion of 1778. (Library of Congress LC–USZC4–5321)

Stowage of Slaves. (c.1789) *Stowage of the British Slave ship Brooks under the Regulated Trade Act of 1788*.

William Dickson. Friends Library, London. © Religious Society of Friends in Britain.

Part 5
Chapter 13

Fleming's Map of Glasgow in 1807. By permission of University of Glasgow Library, Special Collecctions. Mu24-y.21.

Town's Hospital. Chapman, R. (1812) *The Picture of Glasgow or a Stranger's Guide*. (2nd Ed.) Glasgow, facing p.101.

Chapter 14

Professor John Anderson (1793). University of Strathclyde Library. Department of Archives & Special Collections. OP 4/1/3.

Glasgow Royal Infirmary, Annual Report, 8th December 1794–1st January 1796. NHS Greater Glasgow & Clyde Archives. HB 14/2/1.

Glasgow Royal Infirmary. Chapman, R. (1812) *The Picture of Glasgow or a Stranger's Guide*. (2nd Ed.) Glasgow, facing p.105.

Part 6
Chapter 15

Blackfriars/College Church. Stuart, R. (1848) *Views and Notices of Glasgow in Former Times*. Glasgow: Allan & Ferguson, facing p.67.

List of Elders/General Register of the Old Scotch Independents. Glasgow City Council: Archives. TD 420/1, p.33.

Dale's letter to his father, 26th May 1783. Glasgow City Council: Archives.

Part 7
Chapter 16

Robert Owen. 1771–1858. Pioneer Socialist. Watercolour on paper by Mary Ann Knight. (Undated.) Scottish National Portrait Gallery. PG 1606.

Rosebank. Wilson, J. A. (1929) A *History of Cambuslang. A Clydesdale Parish.* Glasgow: Jackson Wylie & Co., facing p.156.

Rosebank. Smith, J., Mitchell, J. O. and Buchanan, J. (eds.) (1878) *Old Country Houses of the Old Glasgow Gentry* (2nd ed.). Glasgow: Maclehose, p.217.

Glasgow Chamber of Commerce Election Notice, December 1805. Glasgow City Council: Archives. TD 1670/4cc1805.

Chapter 17

Portrait of David Dale. Provenance unknown. Robert Owen Museum, Newtown.

Mary Dale and James Haldane Stewart by Gearge Patten, A.R.A. (1839) Private collection. Courtesy of David and Sebastian Blackie.

Chapter 18

David Dale Esq. *Imperial Magazine*, 4/46. November, 1822, facing p.1068.

R.B.S. Banknote (1966) and Savings Stamp (1967). Reproduced by kind permission of The Royal Bank of Scotland Group plc © 2015.

Commemorative Plaque, Charlotte Street. David McLaren, private collection.

Index